SYDENHAM, M. J. The First French Republic, 1792–1804. California, 1974. 360p il map tab bibl 73-85796. 13.00. ISBN 0-520-02577-6

Sequel to the author's *French Revolution* (CHOICE, Dec. 1966), which took the story to 1794. The present work begins with the king's overthrow in 1792, but the first chapter is a mere summary of the war and terror already covered in the earlier work. Similarly, the concluding chapter, "Empire and Republic, 1802–04," is summary, since the Republic effectively died in 1802, although Sydenham believes it "remained a reality after Napolean's *coup d'état* in 1799." Readily admitting his debt to Georges Lefebvre's *French Revolution, v.2: From 1793 to 1799* (CHOICE, Mar. 1965) and *Napoleon, v.1: From 18 Brumaire to Tilsit* (CHOICE, May 1969), Sydenham replaces Lefebvre's specialist interpretation with one that attributes more importance "to ideas and ideals, to political factors, and to the part played by particular personalities and by accident alone" (p.308). Since, unlike Lefebvre, Sydenham does not presume the reader's familiarity with the period, his book is excellent for all undergraduates. The story is well written, exciting even, and there are numerous excellent illustrations, maps, an index, and critical bibliographical essay.

The First French Republic, 1792-1804

The First French Republic

1792-1804

M. J. SYDENHAM

UNIVERSITY OF CALIFORNIA PRESS
Berkeley and Los Angeles 1973

University of California Press
Berkeley and Los Angeles, California

ISBN 0-520-02577-6
Library of Congress Catalog Card Number: 73-85796
First published 1974
Copyright © M. J. Sydenham, 1974

Printed in Great Britain

Contents

Illustrations

Permission to reproduce these illustrations is gratefully acknowledged to the organizations mentioned in brackets.

Maps

Maps

Preface

For some time past, histories of the French Revolution have ended more or less abruptly in 1794 or 1795. This is, no doubt, in part a consequence of the fact that historians are now expected to deal with one subject at a time and to do so within the confines of a single volume; for any attempt to write an adequate account of the tremendous events that occurred in France between 1789 and either 1794 or 1795 must impose a severe strain upon an author's space, to say nothing of his readers' patience.

Weightier issues, however, are also involved. As all good historical writing is in some degree interpretative as well as descriptive, almost all histories of the Revolution suggest that the revolutionaries had certain fundamental objectives, whether for good or ill, and that the Revolution itself began and ended with the story of their endeavour to achieve those goals. Thus the selection of a terminal date is in reality indicative of a particular interpretation of the Revolution, and the present practice of concluding the tale in 1794 or 1795 reflects the prevailing conviction that the Revolution was essentially one for the attainment of social democracy. When Robespierre was generally regarded as the principal champion of the common people, his death in July 1794 seemed to many historians to mark the final failure of the most progressive movement of the period; and now that the *sans-culottes* are seen as providing both the real radicalism and the effective physical force of the Revolution, the repression of the people in 1795 similarly seems to end everything of any significance. Babeuf's 'Conspiracy for Equality' in 1797 is, indeed, inconveniently belated; but it can either be dismissed as an isolated episode or treated primarily as a portent of the future.

However illuminating these views may be, the concentration of scholarship upon the most egalitarian phase of the Revolution, that from the fall of the monarchy in 1792 until either 1794 or 1795, may well be thought to have serious disadvantages. For one thing, it tends to diminish the importance of the years 1789 to 1792. These are now often represented as comparatively insignificant except insofar as developments in them presaged the more popular revolution which was to follow; but it might equally well be supposed that the earlier phase of the Revolution is the more indicative of its real character, and of that of the society in which it occurred. Similarly, the years after 1795 are commonly consigned to oblivion. Although several important studies of particular aspects of this later period have been published recently, it still stands generally condemned as a time of unmitigated social and political reaction. So damning a description is unlikely to be wholly true; but even if it were, fuller knowledge of a period in which men abandoned free institutions in favour of dictatorship would seem sufficiently appropriate to our own uncertain age.

It is, at least, a remarkable fact that almost the only books easily available in English about the period 1794–9, a period practically as long as that between 1789 and 1794, are the translations by Robert Baldick of the two volumes by Georges Lefebvre, *Les Thermidoriens* and *Le Directoire*; and for the story of the Consulate, from 1799 to 1804, one must again look initially to Lefebvre's great biography of Napoleon. No reader of the present book will remain long unaware that I have relied heavily upon Lefebvre's scholarship and authority, and that I am obviously deeply indebted to him. This, however, is not to say that his work, which often presupposes familiarity with the period, is necessarily ideal reading for those uninitiated in its mysteries; nor, indeed, is it satisfactory that only one interpretation of the time should present itself to interested readers.

In this situation, this book should be seen primarily as a challenge. Although some research lies behind it, it does not purport to be an account of original investigation and new discoveries; nor has it been written simply as a textbook, whatever that may mean. What I have tried to do is to make the whole period of the First Republic more interesting and intelligible, so that others, as I hope, may be encouraged to look more closely at its unresolved problems. In doing this, I have not hesitated to suggest a personal interpretation of the period, avowedly founded upon what are nowadays more or less derisively described as 'value-judgements'; but I am well aware that a great deal more investigation in detail must be done before this interpretation, or indeed any other, can be properly substantiated. I should also warn the reader that as I have emphasised the significance of political events and political attitudes, I have not dealt at length with social and economic developments or with diplomatic and military matters; and the question of religion, which was so central to the time, is here sadly neglected. The book, like its predecessor *The French Revolution*—to which the reader is referred for a fuller account of the years 1792-4—is nevertheless dedi-cated to the propositions that events happen simultaneously, not in neat categories, and that what is now the past was once the future.

It is a matter of considerable regret to me that some recent books, notably G. D. Homan's biography of Reubell, R. B. Rose's work on Babeuf and Professor Richard Cobb's *Reactions to the French Revolution* (Oxford, 1972), were not available to me before this book was sent to press. I am nonetheless happy to be able to recommend my own readers to move forward to these exciting studies, the appearance of which is in itself a confirmation of the opportunities still offered to historians in this field.

As always, my most grateful thanks are due to many people who have, in various ways, helped me to complete this volume. More particularly, I am deeply indebted to Miss F. S. Montgomery and her brother for their assistance with the index and I should acknowledge the generous aid of The Canada Council, which alone made it possible for me in three successive summers to work in Europe. I should also like to record my appreciation of the kindly encouragement offered to me by my publishers and by my colleagues at Carleton University, for these have all allowed me a great deal more latitude than I could reasonably have requested.

M.J.S.

June 1973

'*The French government is now concerned with a problem of interest to all nations. How does one come out of a regime of violence after having once been in it? How to get back on the road of justice and moderation once it has been left?*'

The Count of Montlosier, *London, 1796*

(*R. R. Palmer, The Age of the Democratic Revolution, Princeton, 1964, Vol. II, p. 210*)

Part One
The Revolutionary Republic, 1792-1795

*'But I tell you, who are pure and perceptive men, that
there does exist this magnanimous ambition to establish
on earth the first Republic in the world, this
selflessness of incorruptible men who find spiritual
satisfaction in the calm of an untroubled conscience and
in the entrancing spectacle of public well-being. You feel
this passion burning at this hour in your souls; I feel it
also in my own.'*

Robespierre, *26 July 1794*

1. War and Terror, September 1792-July 1794

In the month of September 1792 some 700 men assembled in Paris to take their places as deputies in the newly-elected National Convention of France. Predominantly professional men, educated, 'enlightened', and experienced in the law courts and in local administration, they believed their mission to be the completion of the work which the National Constituent Assembly had begun in 1789, the First Year of Liberty. That assembly had struck down absolutism and aristocracy; but the constitutional monarchy so painstakingly constructed between 1789 and 1791 had proved unequal to the strains imposed upon it by internal dissension and war against Austria and Prussia. As recently as 10 August 1792 the royal palace of the Tuileries, which the men of the Revolution regarded as the fountain-head of foreign intrigue and counter-revolutionary conspiracy, had been stormed; the King, Louis XVI, had been made a prisoner; and the first constitutional parliament of France, the Legislative Assembly (1791-2), had been compelled to refer the whole question of the future government of the nation to a new constituent assembly, the National Convention.[1]

Since many of those who were elected to this new body had previously sat either in the Legislative Assembly or in the National Assembly, they were already deeply divided by the suspicions and hatreds born of rapid revolutionary change. Many of the newcomers, too, knew well where their own loyalties would lie: Louis Antoine Saint-Just, a young man of statuesque beauty and icy fanaticism, had long admired and even idolised Maximilien Robespierre, the first deputy of Paris and the principal champion of the people; but the dashing young Barbaroux of Marseille was almost immediately to denounce Robespierre to the Convention as

---

[1] For the general history of the earlier part of the French Revolution, reference may be made to the present writer's *The French Revolution* (London, Batsford, 1965 and Methuen, University Paperback, 1969) pp. 13-113; for the fuller consideration of the period between September 1793 and July 1794, with which this chapter is concerned, see in the same work pp. 114-228.

a conspirator and would-be dictator.[1] There nevertheless remained in the new assembly a solid core of uncommitted and comparatively obscure moderates, men who would soon be derisively referred to as 'the croakers of the Marshland'.[2] Typical of these at this time was one whose name will recur in these pages, Antoine Claire Thibaudeau, one of the deputies for the Department of Vienne. Aged 27 in 1792, he had risen to the position of *procureur* in Poitiers whilst his father, as a deputy in the National Constituent Assembly, had had his share in the destruction of the old order, and now he came to Paris in his turn to help to provide France with a revised system of government and an enduring body of constitutional law. Although well aware that the hour was critical—for until the battle of Valmy took place on 20 September the armies of Austria and Prussia were advancing steadily upon Paris—he had no doubt that his work would be done and that he would be back again in Poitiers within six months.[3]

Thibaudeau was in fact to remain a deputy throughout the next four years. Striving always for the achievement of his original purpose, he was to stand in many turbulent scenes as one of the staunchest supporters of moderate republicanism. Coming eventually to believe that the Republic was 'by no means incompatible with the existence of a head of the state',[4] he was also for a time to be closely associated with Napoleon as a trusted Councillor of State. In 1792, however, his initial optimism illustrates the confidence with which men confronted the hopes and fears of the day, which were in modified forms to remain those of the next decade.

In 1792 the great majority of Frenchmen wanted to see the completion and consolidation of the Revolution which had been begun in 1789.[5] As their hope was still for the security of person and property in an independent and 'regenerated' France, their worst fear was of the restoration of the *ancien régime* by some combination of internal conspiracy and foreign conquest. More specifically, in place of the chaos of local jurisdictions and corporate rights characteristic of the old France, they hoped to see the country rationally and progressively governed as one nation,

[1] In 1792 both Saint-Just and Barbaroux were 25 years of age, and Robespierre was 38; all three were to be guillotined in 1794.

[2] *'les crapauds de la marais'*.

[3] A. C. Thibaudeau, *Mémoires sur la Convention et le Directoire* (Paris, 1824), Vol. I, pp. 1–11. *Biog. Notes:* THIBAUDEAU.

[4] A. C. Thibaudeau, *Mémoires sur le Consulat* (Paris, 1827), trans. and edited by G. K. Fortescue as *Bonaparte and the Consulate* (London, 1908), p. 216.

[5] I.e., the revolution of the Third Estate, as distinct from the 'revolt of the nobility' in 1788.

in which a law common to all Frenchmen would be applied through a uniform system of administration. In place of the arbitrary government which had once ultimately depended upon 'the king's good pleasure', local and national affairs would be ordered by elected assemblies, and all officials, high or low, would be answerable to the electors for their actions. Further, instead of 'aristocratic' privileges and venality, there would be equality in citizenship: the fundamental freedoms being guaranteed by an established law and an independent judiciary, the law would be the same for all, and all would be eligible for office according to their abilities. In this self-governing community, too, men would be united not by force but by fraternity, not as the subjects of a single ruler but as free men bound together by their strong sense of common citizenship, each being concerned with the welfare of all.

To such an astonishing extent had these high aspirations been realised by the Revolution of 1789 that in 1792 it seemed to many to be more necessary to defend the new France than to initiate further changes. The speed and violence with which the old order of things had been destroyed had in fact raised up a host of enemies for the revolutionaries. From 1789 onwards, each important stage in the development of the Revolution had had as its corollary a wave of emigration, the exodus in 1789 of the 'pure' royalists (who opposed any concession whatever to the Third Estate) being followed in time by that of many lesser nobles and the great majority of the officers of the royal army. Imitating the evil example of the King's youngest brother, the Count of Artois,[1] many of these exiles in Italy and in the Rhineland became ever more intransigent, and their plots and parades eventually provided the *casus belli* for the conflict which began between France and Austria in April 1792. By then, too, the reduction of the Church to a department of state and the imposition of an oath of loyalty upon its priests had completed the alienation of the King from the Revolution and turned at least half the clergy of France into potential counter-revolutionaries and traitors. As effective central government had disappeared altogether since 1789, men had good reason to fear that without strong leadership a divided nation would fall an easy victim to reaction and retribution.

On the other hand, the very successes of the Revolution had inevitably opened new possibilities of social and political conflict. While the more prosperous townsmen were staunchly liberal vis-à-vis the absolutism and exclusiveness of the old order, they were also firmly attached to the relatively new doctrines of economic liberalism, as indeed were the great majority of educated men. Freedom, to them, included the ab-

---

[1] *Biog. Notes:* ARTOIS.

solute sanctity of property-right and the abolition of all restrictions upon internal trade, including any form of interference by the state, and they generally regarded equality as no more or less than equality of opportunity and the abolition of privileges before the law. Their ideal state was therefore one in which political rights were limited by some form of property-qualification; and, despite the Declaration of the Rights of Man, this distinction had been firmly written into the Constitution of 1791. Even before that constitution was completed, however, popular resentment of the new discrimination had led to both agitation and repression, perpetually symbolised by the 'massacre' on the Champ de Mars in July 1791.[1] In their growing fear of an anarchical democracy, many of these well-to-do bourgeois gave their support to the group of liberal nobles known as the Feuillants, men who hoped to strengthen— or, later, to re-establish—the monarchy and to consolidate the position of the proprietors by a conservative revision of the Constitution of 1791.

For very different reasons, the peasantry of France were also well on the way to becoming the conservative force they were to remain throughout the next century. Since these countrymen comprised some 20 millions of the national population of about 26 millions, and since their number included the innumerable grades of wealth and status separating the substantial proprietor and farmer from the cottager and casual labourer, generalisation about them is clearly dangerous. By 1792, however, the countryside might be described as turbulent but not revolutionary. On the one hand, local and traditional antagonisms were acute, relationships being acerbated both by the encroachment of proprietors upon ancient communal rights and by the power and prosperity some men had somehow acquired during the upheaval of 1789. The schism in the Church, anxiety about local shortages of food, resentment of the ever-increasing interference of townsmen in the countryside—all these were to make rural rioting commonplace for years to come. On the other hand the peasantry had gained a good deal by the Revolution, and in September 1792 the Austrian and Prussian armies found them vigorous defenders of the new order. By their risings in 1789 and by their systematic evasion of the law thereafter, they had almost freed themselves from

[1] Although the Declaration of Rights of 1789 had proclaimed that 'All men are born and remain free and equal in rights', the constitutional legislation which followed distinguished between 'active' and 'passive' citizens, the latter being disenfranchised by a property qualification. Resentment of this was strongly reflected in the republican agitation in Paris in 1791, after the King's flight to Varennes; and when on 17 July 1791 the National Guard fired on a crowd in the Champ de Mars, this 'massacre' and the ensuing repression undoubtedly had very strong social implications.

the multiplicity of taxes, tithes and dues characteristic of the *ancien régime*, and in 1793 the Convention was to abandon the protracted official effort to make redemption payments compulsory. Moreover, many of the more prosperous peasants were acquiring some share in the *biens nationaux*, the estates which the revolutionaries had confiscated from the Church and were continuing to confiscate from the *émigrés*. On balance it would seem that except in the remoter districts of western France, where the general traditional attachment to royal government and the Catholic faith was particularly strong, the men of rural France were prepared to accept any régime which seemed capable of guaranteeing their gains.

In the towns, however, powerful minorities rejected all this conservatism. The urban poor, far more politically conscious than the peasants, were also even more vulnerable than they to any sudden shortage of food supplies or rapid increases in the cost of living. Since trade in 1792 was perpetually disrupted by the disorders and insecurity endemic to revolutionary France, and since inflation was beginning to follow the increasing issues of the *assignat*[1] as paper currency, the great majority of townsmen had the strongest personal interest in the restoration of the control of the corn trade which had once been maintained by the monarchy. To the more militant townsmen known as the *sans-culottes* the question of the supply and price of bread and other essential commodities was therefore one of constant concern, and in this their attitude differed sharply from that of those cultured and comfortable people who could afford to extol economic freedom. Moreover, to the *sans-culottes* democracy had come to mean not only the universal manhood suffrage denied them by the Constitution of 1791, but also the very real and personal control of affairs by the people of each district in their own general assemblies. To them, all officials were delegates, whose authority was revokable at will, and laws were only binding while they were sanctioned by the consent of the people themselves. In their eyes, too, equality had the very literal sense that no one should presume, whether by conduct, speech, dress or manner, to assert any superiority over another; and although in the pre-industrial society of the time the majority of the *sans-culottes* were themselves the owners of small shops or workshops, they believed that property-right should be limited to the

---

[1] The *assignats* were initially interest-bearing bonds issued upon the security of the lands confiscated from the Church. By September 1790 they had become simply a form of paper money, the value of which declined as its quantity was increased. By October 1792 *assignats* to the nominal value of 2,400 million livres were in circulation, although the first issue had been restricted to 400 millions.

reasonable necessities of life, and that the state should help the poor materially by the provision of poor-relief and education. To these men the Revolution in 1792 was very far from being complete: rather did the fall of the monarchy herald 'the reign of holy equality'.

The rapid course of the Revolution had in fact encouraged belief in the eighteenth-century faith that there was no limit to what could be accomplished by good government, and this belief was perhaps particularly characteristic of the Jacobins, the most powerful political organisation in France. Educated men generally drawn from the lower middle classes, the Jacobins were members of political societies which had sprung up throughout France in 1789 and gradually affiliated themselves to the parent club in Paris. By correspondence and the exchange of delegates, by the use and abuse of electoral procedures and the right of petition, the Jacobins had largely infiltrated local government and enabled the original society in the rue Saint-Honoré in Paris to become a successful rival to the national parliament in the Tuileries nearby.

Although in practice they always tended to assume that their own increasingly exclusive societies were alone in truly representing enlightened public opinion, the Jacobins believed in theory that democracy must be based on universal manhood suffrage. If they shared the prevailing belief in economic individualism, they also shared the sans-culottes' dislike of extreme difference of wealth; regarding riches as evidence of a lack of patriotism, and poverty as indicative of immorality, the more radical of them were inclined to share the belief of their principal spokesman, Robespierre, that property-right ought at least to be limited by some sense of responsibility for the general welfare. Strongly anti-clerical and rationalist in outlook, they had nevertheless made enthusiasm for the Revolution an intensely emotional patriotic religion, and many of them anticipated the advent of a free society in which the common welfare would be the first concern of regenerated men. An active minority whose power in 1792 was already out of all proportion to their numbers, they undoubtedly desired further power, both to promote the defence of the Revolution and to consummate it by creating the Republic of their dreams.

The Revolution of 10 August 1792, which occurred because the King was generally believed to be acting in collusion with the enemies of France and of the Revolution, naturally intensified all these various fears and hopes. On the one hand, the advance of the Austro–Prussian armies, who came with the émigrés in their wake, made the dangers of reaction manifest. As their commander, the Duke of Brunswick, had announced in a notorious manifesto, they came 'to terminate anarchy in France' and to enable the King 'to exercise the legitimate authority which is his due'; Paris was therefore to submit at once, under pain of 'exemplary and ever-memorable vengeance'. On the other hand, the Jacobins and the *sans-culottes*, the men who had overthrown the monarchy, had promptly made it plain that the sovereign people had little respect for the authority of the existing national parliament. The last weeks in the life of the Legislative Assembly were marked by the assumption of power by a new popular municipality in Paris, the 'Commune of the Insurrection', and by the savage murders of priests and supposed royalists in the prisons of the city. Thus from both sides moderate men were menaced by violence, the use of which was justified by the assertion of one form or another of sovereign authority.

This situation gave the convocation of the new National Convention quite exceptional significance. Paradoxical though it may seem, the first, the most general and the most enduring desire of the men of the Revolution was to end arbitrary government and to establish the rule of law.[1] It was for this reason that the Third Estate in 1789 had transformed the Estates General into the National Constituent Assembly, and it was to produce the Constitution of 1791 that these first deputies had laboured and debated for more than two years. Moreover, despite the fact that the Constitution had excluded the poor from the franchise and had left a hostile King with the power to veto essential legislation at a time of grave national danger, it had long commanded respect amounting almost to reverence. The Jacobins themselves were properly *The Society of the Friends of the Constitution*,[2] and Robespierre, himself the author in 1792 of the journal *Le Défenseur de la Constitution*, had only come in extremity to the conclusion that 'the safety of the state is more important than the Constitution'.[3] On the eve of the rising of 10 August, the Jacobins and the *sans-culottes* had looked no further into the future than to demand the immediate convocation of the electoral assemblies to elect a new constituent assembly, and when on 10 August itself the Legislative Assembly enacted in the presence of the people a decree to suspend the

---

[1] The reader should recognise here that this is an opinion, and that much of this book is an expression of it. It is not, of course, new, but it has been largely lost sight of in modern writing about the Revolution, in which other aspects of the time, particularly the economic and social interests of the various classes, predominate.

[2] After 10 August 1792, the *Friends of Liberty and Equality*.

[3] *Défenseur*, No. 11.

King, the first clause of that act was one inviting the French people to form a national convention.

The fact that Pierre Vergniaud,[1] the deputy from the Gironde who proposed this decree, subsequently paid for it with his life illustrates the deepest and most enduring difficulty the revolutionaries experienced. In order to limit the traditional sovereign authority of the monarchy, the men of 1789 had had to assert as a higher principle the democratic view that law is ultimately the expression of the general will, and that only power exercised in conformity with this could be legitimate. Although for most men the 'general will' was not a philosophical abstraction, but quite simply the will of the majority, the determination of it on any specific occasion inevitably presented serious problems. If to the deputies it was the will of the people as represented in parliament, to the Jacobins it was of necessity the will of enlightened people like themselves, tried and tested in public debate in the clubs; and to the *sans-culottes* it could never be anything but the present will of the people themselves in their primary assemblies. Thus Vergniaud, in referring the final decision on the King's fate to the country as a whole, seemed to the Jacobins and to the *sans-culottes* to be deliberately flouting the will that the people of Paris and their allies from the provinces had already expressed by the fact of their insurrection—which was, at the least, aimed at the deposition of the King.

Moreover, as the very use of the word *will* suggests, the revolutionaries had quite naturally adopted the habits of thought and the terminology traditional to the autocratic state in which they had lived before 1789, and in seeking to limit the sovereign authority of the King they had asserted as a new source of law the still greater sovereignty of the people. The problem of identifying 'the people' was therefore but one aspect of the more fundamental difficulty of subordinating democratic right and popular power to an established constitutional law which had itself originated from the people. This the Constitution of 1791 had failed to do: at the first opportunity, the *sans-culottes* had reasserted popular sovereignty, the Jacobins had blessed their endeavours, and the Constitution had been repudiated along with the monarchy and the restricted franchise. After the insurrection, therefore, men looked to the Convention to establish enduring legality. Far from being a mere parliament, it was an assembly which, being elected by universal suffrage, embodied the full constituent power of the sovereign people, and did so far more effectively than the artificially created National Assembly of

---

[1] *Biog. Notes:* VERGNIAUD.

1789 had ever been able to do.[1] Its first function, that of deciding whether France was to remain a monarchy or to become a republic, was but a part of its greater mission of providing the nation with a new constitution which would really reconcile general freedom with the permanent rule of law.

As it happened, however, the immediate emergency of September 1792 was so great, and proved in one form or another so protracted, that the Convention became a form of government, and as such its name became in time synonymous with both the use and the abuse of authority. Nevertheless, the deputies' recognition of their principal purpose is apparent in their initial unanimous declaration on 21 September: the constitution they were to draft would be submitted to the people for approval, and in the meanwhile life and property stood under the protection of the nation. They also established the Republic, although rather more hesitantly: while there was enthusiastic and unanimous support for the decision to abolish royalty in France, the word *Republic* only occurred as it were incidentally, in a later regulation that 'in future the acts of the assembly shall be dated "The First Year of the French Republic" '. Only on 25 September did the Convention accept the momentous decree declaring the French Republic to be 'one and indivisible', and not until a year had elapsed did it reveal 'its detachment from every opinion not sanctioned by reason and philosophy' by naming 22 September 1792 as the beginning of the French era.[2]

Being thus informally established, the first French Republic has seemed to some an essentially transitory régime which was foisted on France by a fanatical minority. Certainly the complex process of indirect election which produced the National Convention robbed universal suffrage of much of its meaning. The votes of the great rural majority of the population and those of the poorer townsmen were absorbed between the primary and the secondary electoral assemblies, so that the Convention was composed of the same sort of more or less prosperous legal and literary people as had sat in the two previous assemblies. It

[1] This point may be disputed, since both assemblies were elected by indirect processes, and fewer people actually voted in 1792 than in 1789; but the theoretical right of the Convention would still seem to be the greater.

[2] Adopted by the decree of 5 October 1793, the Republican Calendar had retrospective effect from 22 September 1792 for the numbering of the years, and from the first anniversary of that date for the identification of days and months. Thus 22 September 1793 became the first day of Vendémiaire (the 'month of vintage') in Year II of the Republic. It was officially abandoned as from 1 January 1806. Generally it will not be used here save for those dates which became historic. See also *Chronology*, p. 310.

was also, of course, wholly composed of men who had made some reputation for themselves as 'patriots' and revolutionaries—deeply as men divided about the definition of such terms. In Paris, at least, known or suspected royalists were struck off the electoral rolls as people who had forfeited their rights of citizenship, and the general domination of the elections by the Jacobins is reflected in the fact that even those deputies who, like Vergniaud, were soon to be condemned as moderates, were men who were prominent in their own towns as Jacobins.[1] Moreover, it was soon recognised that the republican Convention could never risk an attempt to resolve differences by a direct appeal to the electorate as a whole, the rural majority being royalist in sentiment. This, however, does not necessarily mean that the deputies did not represent a very considerable body of opinion when they established the Republic in September 1792; for Louis XVI was at best discredited, his sole surviving son was but a child, his two brothers were hated as the leaders of the *émigrés*, and his disreputable cousin Orléans[2] had become a Jacobin deputy. In short, whatever men might feel about the monarchy, its restoration was not then a practical possibility. In choosing republicanism rather than some risky compromise with the *ancien régime* the Convention was hardly failing to represent France.

The fact remained that revolutionary republicans were in a minority in France, and this meant that the Convention had either to attract men to the new régime by moderation or to impose and maintain it by force. The division which appeared amongst the deputies in September 1792, and which practically paralysed the assembly and the nation for the next nine months, had many aspects, but this distinction between constitutional and coercive government was certainly essential to it. On the one hand the majority of the deputies, led by a group which later became known as the Girondins,[3] showed themselves exceedingly hostile to

---

[1] This should not be read to mean that the national elections were dominated by the Jacobins of Paris through correspondence with the affiliated local societies. Rather did the Jacobins in Paris neglect their correspondence for a month after 10 August, probably while they concentrated on the electoral campaign in the capital: see the circular to the affiliated societies of 12 September, J. Hall Stewart, *A Documentary Survey of the French Revolution* (New York, 1951). Subsequently, however, the men who might be called 'the provincial Jacobin deputies' failed to gain control of the Paris Club.

[2] *Biog. Notes:* ORLÉANS.

[3] Since Vergniaud and other deputies of the Gironde were notable opponents of the deputies and municipal authorities of Paris—as well as of the *sans-culottes* of the capital—the name Girondins is commonly used by historians to identify all deputies who were of that opinion. It is used here for convenience and without

what they regarded as the illegal and dictatorial powers of the Commune and Sections of Paris.[1] The true individuality of these men was soon to be obscured by much misrepresentation, but they seem to have been alike in expressing the widespread belief that the fall of the monarchy had finally brought the Revolution to an end, so that all that remained to be done was to repress agitation—which had now become counter-revolutionary by definition—and to complete the organisation of the Republic by a minimal amount of moderate legislation. Not surprisingly, the constitutional committee which was appointed on 11 October 1792 to prepare proposals for a new constitution was almost wholly composed of men of this opinion. On the other hand, the Jacobin deputies of Paris and their adherents, who were known as the Montagnards because they habitually occupied the loftiest seats in the assembly, formed from the first a powerful minority group. Led by Robespierre in the Convention, they were strongly supported outside it by the revolutionary authorities of Paris and by the Jacobin movement as a whole—for they soon succeeded in excluding their opponents from the Club in Paris and in re-asserting their own influence over most of the affiliated societies throughout France. Like Robespierre himself, these men generally felt that constitutional questions were less vital than the immediate security of the state; indeed, where the 'Girondins' prided themselves on their principles, the Montagnards gloried in demanding drastic action to defend the Revolution.

In the event, the Montagnard minority gradually imposed its control upon the Convention, and hence upon the nation. The first stage in this process was the protracted campaign which these deputies fought to secure the execution of the deposed King. Significantly dismissing as irrelevant all the legal issues which perplexed the assembly, Robespierre insisted that the King had already been tried and condemned by the people, and that for this reason as well as others his execution was a matter of political necessity. The death of Louis XVI on the guillotine on 21 January 1793 was the first political triumph of the Montagnards: intended in part to pacify Paris and prove the revolutionary ardour of the Convention, it was also deliberately designed to inaugurate a new order

---

prejudice to my own reluctance to accept generalisations about the characteristics of those members of the Convention who were not Montagnards. See my *The Girondins* (London, 1961).

[1] Although the Commune of 10 August was eventually replaced by an officially elected body, this remained composed of delegates from the 48 Sections into which Paris was divided. Virtually autonomous, these Sections were predominantly controlled by the *sans-culottes* in 1792–1794.

and to set the regicides—387 of the 721 deputies who voted—apart from royalists at home and abroad, including their own more moderate (and consequently counter-revolutionary) colleagues. It was therefore in a new situation and in an atmosphere poisoned by suspicion that the proposals of the constitutional committee were brought forward in February 1793 by the philosopher Condorcet.[1] Whatever its merits, this so-called 'Girondin' constitution was inevitably scorned and rejected by the Montagnards, who could not have accepted it without repudiating their own aspirations and admitting that the Revolution was at an end. Moreover, even though the Montagnards still remained a minority of the assembly, the increasingly desperate position of the nation made it comparatively easy for them to obstruct constitutional decisions.

In the spring of 1793 the ill-organised military forces of the Republic were in fact so greatly over-extended that they stood in danger of complete defeat. Flushed by the first successes of the French armies in the autumn of 1792, when they had repulsed the Prussian invasion, invaded the Rhineland and over-run the Austrian Netherlands, the Convention as a whole had enthusiastically agreed to offer aid to all who sought liberty. It had also begun the process of expansion by declaring Savoy, Nice and the Austrian Netherlands to be parts of France, and asserting the right of the Republic to expand to its 'natural frontiers'—the Pyrenees, the Alps and the Rhine. As a result of this forward policy and of the execution of the King, the French were faced in the early months of 1793 with the combined power of Austria, Prussia, Sardinia, Spain, Holland and Britain. An attempt to advance further, into Holland, then ended ignominiously, the French armies being forced to withdraw hastily from Belgium and from all the Rhineland save for Mayence. As a general allied assault on all the frontiers of France gathered momentum, counter-revolutionary activity within the Republic spread swiftly, and in western France a revolt in the Vendée soon grew into a savage civil war.[2]

---

[1] *Biog. Notes:* CONDORCET.

[2] Very varied points of view have been, and are still being, developed about the fundamental causes of this great insurrection and the protracted guerilla war which followed it. No single general statement about its nature can be wholly satisfactory, but it may be helpful here to say that the revolt seems to have begun as a spontaneous rural reaction to encroachment, interference and exploitation from the towns (tiny though many of these were) in the name of 'the nation'. It would also seem that since this urban pressure, partly 'progressive' and partly commercial, was particularly directed against the possessions, influence and faith of the Catholic Church, the insurrection was very rapidly identified with the cause of the Church against the Revolution.

These terrible circumstances, which coincided with a new period of scarcity and rising prices, gave ever-increasing force to the Montagnards' demand that unity of direction should be secured by the exclusion of their principal opponents from the Convention. By the end of May 1793 this solution had become acceptable to a sufficient number of minor deputies; and by then Paris, repeatedly roused to anger by military failure and economic hardship, was ready for another insurrection. On this occasion the combination of the Commune and the *sans-culottes* with the Jacobins and the Montagnards proved irresistible. Surrounded by the armed forces of the Sections, the Convention was compelled to agree to the arrest of 29 of its leading 'Girondin' deputies, men who had in one way or another come to be regarded as the chief enemies of Paris and the Montagnards. This event, afterwards known as the Revolution of 31 May,[1] undoubtedly marked a turning point in the history of the Republic. By encouraging the rising the Montagnards gained control of the Convention and began the long process of wresting victory from defeat; but to many people the Republic was henceforth identified with exclusive minority government, and even its friends felt that its nature had been violently distorted. To Thibaudeau, who had at first been attracted to the Montagnards' benches, the fall of the Girondins later seemed to be the transition from light to darkness; in his view it would have been an hundred times better if the deputies had allowed the people to murder them in their seats, since the Convention would at least have kept its honour and its moral authority intact.[2]

At this time the means of effective government already existed in undeveloped form. In response to the succession of crises, the Convention had established a small body, the Committee of Public Safety, with the general responsibility of supervising and invigorating the executive; and a second Committee, that of General Security, had become powerful in matters of police. The practice of despatching deputies to the frontiers and the provinces had been begun, and these Representatives of the People, armed with unlimited powers, could work through the local Jacobin Clubs and 'revolutionary committees' of *sans-culottes*. Moreover, the Revolutionary Tribunal existed in Paris to deal expeditiously with suspected traitors and counter-revolutionaries. But before the Montagnards could give cohesion to these various *ad hoc* creations, the crisis confronting them intensified. Their seizure of power inflamed

---

[1] The insurrection began on 31 May, but was not successful until 2 June.

[2] Thibaudeau, *Mémoires sur la Convention*, Vol. I, pp. 36, 43. Thibaudeau was in his own Department, Vienne, at the time of the insurrection, having been sent there as a commissioner of the Convention.

provincial resentment of the domination of France by Paris, and a number of the arrested deputies and their friends escaped from the capital to urge the country to rise and rescue its national assembly. Thus as a succession of frontier fortresses fell to the Austrians and the Prussians, and as the insurgent peasantry of the Vendée widened royalist power in the west, many towns and cities repudiated the authority of the 'purified' Convention. These revolts, which the Montagnards misrepresented as 'federalist'[1] attacks upon the unity of the Republic, were initially republican in inspiration; but being directed by socially conservative forces, they soon attracted royalist support, and in the course of the summer of 1793 both the great city of Lyons and the naval base of Toulon became in practice royalist strongholds.

The surrender of Toulon to British naval forces at the end of August 1793 then became what was probably the severest single blow to freedom in the Republic. Although coercive government was already developing apace, it was this event which led directly to the formal inauguration of the Terror. Outraged by the seemingly universal success of counter-revolution, sensing treason on every hand, infuriated by rising prices and fearful of famine, a great crowd of unorganised *sans-culottes* surged into the Convention on 5 September to demand 'food—and, to have it, force for the law!' Consequently Terror was put, as the phrase went, 'on the order of the day'. The law which established general price controls, the *maximum* of 29 September, was accompanied by a substantial increase in the size and activity of the Revolutionary Tribunal, and Vergniaud and other deputies arrested on or after 31 May soon afterwards followed Marie Antoinette to the guillotine. The Committee of Public Safety, too, was virtually forced to accept as new members Billaud-Varenne[2] and Collot d'Herbois,[3] two of the most fanatical and ruthless of the Montagnards. Composed now of 12 men,[4] all as resolute

[1] Since it is common practice to call the revolts of 1793 against the authority of the Montagnards in Paris 'federalist', it should be said here that almost all concerned on both sides were devoted almost above all else to the idea of the essential unity of the nation. It was, of course, for this very reason that the Montagnards' description of their opponents as 'federalists' was so politically effective. It follows that if the word federalist is used at all in this context, it should be used only with the implication that many people, particularly in the greater provincial towns and cities of France, were reluctant to identify their new democracy with dictation from Paris, particularly once the authority of the Convention was weakened by the expulsion of so many representatives of provincial France in the early summer of 1793.

[2] *Biog. Notes:* BILLAUD-VARENNE.

[3] *Biog. Notes:* COLLOT D'HERBOIS.

[4] The 'Great Committee' which ruled France from July 1793 to July 1794 is

as Robespierre and all united in their determination to save France no matter what the cost might be, the Committee in fact greatly increased its powers by yielding to popular pressure on 5 September. As Robespierre was quick to perceive, the Law of Suspects, passed on 17 September, put a particularly potent weapon into the hands of government. Legalising the imprisonment of all persons whose loyalty to the Revolution was doubted, this law was to be made effective by the *sans-culottes'* local 'revolutionary committees': but since disloyalty was defined by the Committee of Public Safety, any criticism of its proposals could easily be represented as counter-revolutionary, even though it came from the Convention itself.

The Montagnards in the Convention and in the two great Committees of Public Safety and General Security were now in fact in a position to organise the nation for war, and in the process they created a new and fearful form of revolutionary despotism. They did this gradually, in response to circumstances; as the events of 5 September show, they did it in part under pressure from the streets; but they nevertheless did it deliberately, and the argument of some modern writers that they were themselves comparatively moderate men is one that requires rather sharper definition.[1] Thus their acceptance of the general *maximum* in September, like their acceptance of a controlled price for grain in the previous May, was evidently more the outcome of expediency than of conviction, and the probability is that most of them remained free-traders at heart. Similarly, they did little between May and September

---

commonly classified as: Robespierre and his two friends, Couthon and Saint-Just; Billaud-Varenne and Collot d'Herbois, extremists of the left; Lazare Carnot, Robert Lindet, Jeanbon Saint-André, Prieur of the Marne and Prieur of the Côte-d'Or, 'moderates' who concentrated on particular aspects of national military and civil organisations; Barère, the Committee's usual spokesman in the Convention; and Hérault de Séchelles, who was retired in December 1793 and executed as a Dantonist in April 1794, without being replaced. The distinctions, though useful, can also be misleading: all the Committee's actions were the collective responsibility of all its members.

[1] Although historians generally, and more particularly Albert Mathiez, have long regarded the Montagnards as the most politically and socially advanced of the Revolutionaries, recent concentration upon 'seeing the Revolution from below' has led to emphasis upon their middle-class characteristics. Professor Soboul, in particular, has argued forcefully that the *sans-culottes* were 'the mainspring of the Revolution' and that the Montagnards were often driven to action by pressure from below: see, for example, *La Ire République, 1792–1804* (Paris, 1968), pp. 74–80. My own impression is that the acceptance of much of this argument should be tempered by the recollection that all committed patriots had much in common.

to meet the social aspirations of the *sans-culottes* who had helped them to acquire power. Politically, however, such moderation as they showed in that period was imperative because they had to reconcile as much of France as possible to their rule; and decrees like the one which in August ordered the devastation of the Vendée had already indicated sufficiently clearly what sort of treatment the recalcitrant might expect. More particularly, it may be thought most unlikely that many of them ever intended their much-advertised 'Constitution of 1793' to be put into effect, although Robespierre himself probably believed in it. That Constitution had in fact been produced on 10 June, a few days after the Montagnards' seizure of power, by the hasty revision of Condorcet's original proposals. Extremely democratic in substance, and presaging the social-welfare state in principle, the plan was presented to the electorate for approval, and this undoubtedly contributed considerably to the Montagnards' success in overcoming provincial hostility. Always masters of propaganda, they even organised a great Festival of Unity on the first anniversary of the Revolution of 10 August, when it was announced that an overwhelming majority of the voters had approved the Constitution.[1] This, however, remained in its ark of cedar-wood, and the Terror prevailed in reality. Indeed, all pretence of constitutional rule was abandoned on 10 October, when a decree declared that the government of France would remain revolutionary until the return of peace.[2]

That same decree also marked an important stage in the reconstruction of the system of government, a process which was completed by the so-called 'Constitution of the Terror' on 4 December (14 Frimaire). Then 'all constituted bodies and public functionaries' were placed under the immediate inspection of the Committee of Public Safety, to which they were required to report in writing every ten days. Only the Finance Committee and the Committee of General Security retained any real independence, and in the following April the various ministries were

---

[1] The Constitution was accepted by 1,801,918 votes to 11,610, these figures representing less than a quarter of the electorate.

[2] It is of course possible to suggest that the Montagnards were more moderate than they pretended to be, and that the fact that they did not actually put their ultra-democratic Constitution into effect is evidence of this. To the present writer the truth seems rather that they paid lip-service to one type of democracy, but practised quite another. The view that the Revolutionaries in general, and the Montagnards in particular, really respected constitutional government so deeply that they deliberately created extraordinary institutions to deal unconstitutionally with a temporary emergency is more plausible, but see below, pp. 22-3.

abolished altogether and replaced by commissions composed of nominees of the Committee of Public Safety.[1] Local government was also
reorganised, being fragmented as far as possible: the powers of the
departmental directories were largely transferred to the smaller district
authorities, whose elected officers became, or were replaced by, nominated 'National Agents'. These Agents, again, were required to purge the
councils to which they were attached, and to report regularly every
tenth day.

In what was perhaps its most permanently significant aspect, therefore, the Terror was a striking anticipation of twentieth-century centralisation. This was not simply a matter of the deliberate use of the
guillotine as an instrument of state policy, but also one of the endlessly
energetic direction of an ever-expanding administration. If delays were
inevitable when every order had to be carried by courier, if the evil of
local inertia was matched by that of the excessive independence of
deputies, such as Fouché,[2] who became practically pro-consuls in the
provinces to which they were sent as Representatives of the People, the
Committee of Public Safety at least made its will prevail wherever it
willed strongly. The war-effort, moreover, involved an astonishing
increase in state activity. In August 1793 the *levée en masse* (a measure
prematurely forced upon the Convention by popular pressure) had
placed the whole population and all the material resources of France at
the disposal of the Committee, and the selection, training and equipping
of the conscripts demanded both military organisation and economic
regulation. If a great deal was done by exhortation and by the voluntary
efforts of innumerable local committees, it was not without an enormous
expansion in the size of the War Office that Lazare Carnot[3] and Prieur
of the Côte-d'Or[4] were able to become the organisers of victory.
Similarly, the attempt to enforce price controls and the effort to maintain a regular flow of food and supplies to the armies and the big towns
led to the development of a Commission of Trade and Supplies, and
under the direction of Robert Lindet[5] this rapidly became a vast and
complex network of offices. In short, conscription, requisitioning,
compulsory purchase, rationing and 'revolutionary' taxation were as

---

[1] Strictly, the members of the Commissions were named by the Convention
on the presentation on the Committee of Public Safety. In the circumstances,
this was equivalent to nomination by that Committee.

[2] *Biog. Notes:* FOUCHÉ.

[3] *Biog. Notes:* CARNOT.

[4] *Biog. Notes:* PRIEUR OF THE COTE-D'OR.

[5] For Lindet: see Note to p. 97.

fundamental to the Terror as was the guillotine, and together with boundless self-sacrifice and patriotism these sent the Republican armies into the field some three-quarters of a million strong by the early summer of 1794.

Not surprisingly, the deployment of force on this scale brought victory to the Republic. In October 1793 the collapse of the 'federalist' revolts was symbolised by the surrender of Lyons, which had withstood the siege of an army of 35,000 men for over two months, and in December the main force of the 'Royal and Catholic Army' of the Vendéans was destroyed at Savenay, near Nantes. In December, too, the French won the decisive battle of Landau in the Rhineland, and the fall of Toulon to General Carteaux marked an important step in the career of the young Bonaparte, who had been appointed through a series of chances to the command of the Republican artillery there.[1] Moreover, 1794 saw spectacular victories attend French arms in the Netherlands: after Pichegru had routed the Duke of York's British and Hanoverian army at Tourcoing in May, Jourdan defeated the Austrians decisively at Fleurus on 26 June, and by 10 July these two commanders had joined hands in Brussels. As other armies crossed the frontiers into Spain and the Kingdom of Sardinia, this main advance continued, bringing Pichegru to Antwerp and Jourdan to Liège on 27 July, the day of Robespierre's fall in Paris. By then the Republic was free from all invasion and well on the way to conquests of its own.

The Terror, however, was much more than this startling manifestation of what national power could achieve. If for the next decade men recoiled from any measure which seemed to herald a revival of the Terror, this was not simply the reaction of an essentially individualistic society to direction, regulation and controls; what men remembered with the deepest horror was a social and political revolution, often anarchical but ultimately enforced by the ruthless application of the power of the state.

While it is all too easy to exaggerate the extent of class-conflict in the French Revolution, which occurred in a society largely composed of small property-owners, one important aspect of the Terror was undoubtedly the bitter hostility of the urban poor towards the wealthier bourgeoisie. This was very largely a direct consequence of the fact that

---

[1] Bonaparte, an artillery captain, was attached in July 1793 to the force charged with the suppression of revolt against the Convention in Marseilles; when this force subsequently moved against Toulon, its artillery commander Dommartin, was wounded, and Bonaparte was appointed to act in his place (with the rank of major) by the Corsican deputy Saliceti. See also chapter 3.

throughout the year 1793–4 Paris and other large towns were seldom far from famine. The poor, who suffered most acutely from hunger, not unnaturally suspected that a great part of their suffering was caused by hoarding and profiteering, for which they held the wealthier people responsible. Moreover, as the necessities of national defence compelled the government to mobilise the man-power of the masses, so patriotism tended to become equated with poverty; in the tension of war-time, effort was easily identified with simplicity in living, as was apathy with ostentation. Since neither love of France nor belief in the Revolution were ever in reality the monopoly of any particular social class, these natural suspicions and antagonisms might perhaps have been assuaged by a government capable of representing or attracting general support for the common cause. The Revolutionary Government, however, was essentially that of a minority, founded on force and dependent for much of its period of power on the active support of the *sans-culottes*. Many of its measures, particularly those concerning price-control and taxation, consequently tended to aggravate class-hatred, as did the means of denunciation and intimidation which were employed.

All this meant that for almost a year the social order in France seemed to have been turned upside down. Men of education, property and position were inevitably regarded as suspect. Not only had they to accept, or risk trying to evade, a searching system of economic controls which was in their eyes incompatible with property-right and real prosperity, but they were also subject to a good deal of petty persecution as well as to most of the weight of crippling taxation. They were, moreover, liable to lose their freedom, and even to be in danger of their lives, at the will of the *sans-culottes* on the local 'revolutionary committees'. The Committee of Public Safety indeed eventually succeeded in curbing and controlling even the *sans-culottes:* but it did so only by recognising and regulating the position they had won, both as individuals and as organised bodies, in the administration of the state. Thus it happened that educated men, if they were not themselves active Jacobins, were commonly swept aside by the poor and illiterate, either being dismissed from office or being compelled to accept the direction of strangers or subordinates. At the height of the Terror ignorance, coarseness and brutality seemed to have become sufficient qualification for responsible office.[1]

[1] See, for example, the experiences of Miot de Melito when the Ministry of Foreign Affairs was suppressed in 1794, and the new Commissioner of External Relations, 'ignorant, ill-mannered and stupid', had to be fetched from the billiard-hall whenever important papers required his personal signature.

Moreover, where subjugated areas were in question, the viler type of man, whether Jacobin or *sans-culotte*, naturally came into his own. Being passionately at war with their enemies within France as well as abroad, few of the revolutionaries had much compunction about killing them. Indeed, all those taken in arms were by definition outlaws, to be put to death on recognition,[1] and ruthless intimidation was often the only way in which the victorious republicans of 1793 could impose their will upon a hostile population. Repression, however, easily became sadistic fanaticism in an atmosphere in which anything short of enthusiastic zeal was held suspicious in itself, and the names of certain deputies and their *sans-culotte* allies soon became notorious. The firing squads by which Barras[2] and Fréron[3] supplemented the work of the guillotine at Marseilles and Toulon, the mass-murders by cannon-fire which Fouché and Collot d'Herbois favoured for a time at Lyons, the drownings employed by Carrier[4] at Nantes, these were but the most ill-famed episodes in the protracted repression of rebellion. Nor was retribution alone involved. In many parts of France the Terror meant the literal terrorisation of the countryside by armed bands of *sans-culottes* in search of food and counter-revolutionaries, as well as a widespread vilification of Christianity in the name of the new religion of Reason.

To its credit, the Committee of Public Safety was as much concerned to restrain excesses as it was to stimulate the lethargic. The law of 4 December 1793 was indeed largely intended to curb the agents of government, and in 1794 the Committee gradually recalled its more notorious Commissioners and ordered that all persons accused of conspiracy should be brought to Paris for trial before the Revolutionary Tribunal. Yet this effort to control the Terror was by no means an effort to end it. On the contrary, in 1794 the Terror became synonymous with the complete domination of France by the Committee of Public Safety, some of the members of which were fanatically dedicated to the task of creating a new form of society. In theory, the true France was represented by the 'purified' Convention, and the Convention was represented by the Committee, the membership of which was formally renewed by the Convention every month: hence in theory its power was legitimate,

---

Memoirs of Count Miot de Melito (ed. Fleischmann, trans. C. Hoey and J. Lillie, New York, 1881), p. 29.

[1] Law concerning rebellion, 19 March 1793: J. M. Thompson, *French Revolution Documents* (Oxford, 1948), p. 225.

[2] Barras: see Note to p. 89.

[3] *Biog. Notes:* FRÉRON.

[4] *Biog. Notes:* CARRIER.

being no more than a justifiable departure in emergency from normal constitutional practice. In reality, however, the time soon came when any criticism of the Committee was treated as treachery. In March 1794 the Hébertists, a group of shady politicians who championed social and anti-religious extremism, were sent to the scaffold despite their popularity with the *sans-culottes*; on the other hand, in April Danton and his friends, who had dared to advocate 'economy in human blood', were also executed, men of '89 and '92 though they were. Each group was destroyed because it represented not only a policy, but also a real challenge to the power of the Committee, which was thereafter unassailable. The Terror, moreover, was in fact intensified, not diminished, as the French armies advanced and the immediate emergency receded. As the speeches of Robespierre and Saint-Just, to name no others, reveal, some at least of the Committee were convinced that a combination of organisation, intimidation and propaganda would eventually and inevitably produce a perfect society. Believing that men could be and had to be made morally better if civic virtue was to prevail and democracy survive, they held mere indifference to be a capital crime and were sure that, as Saint-Just put it, it would one day be possible to 'kill the last enemy of liberty'.[1]

Although the extent of this tendency towards totalitarianism is still disputed, the rule of the Great Committee was associated everywhere with the predominance of a single political party, the rigid and puritanical Jacobins, and with an iron régime which clamped at least outward conformity upon all classes and conditions of men. After 10 June 1794, when the terrible Law of 22 Prairial[2] practically deprived the victims of the Revolutionary Tribunal of every possible means of defence, the execution rate in Paris reached appalling proportions, and the capital became a city of spies and fear and silence, in which men denounced others simply in order to avoid being denounced themselves. Where crowds had gathered to listen to orators, small groups of men now met furtively, dispersing as soon as any stranger approached. So far had uniformity become a condition of life that even in the Convention itself deputies met only for short and formal sessions, and many of them made

[1] Report on the Dantonists, 31 March 1794: H. M. Stephens, *Orators of the French Revolution* (Oxford, 1892), Vol. II, p. 536; cp. Report on the provisional government of France, 10 October 1793: '*la compression de tout mal amènera le bien*'—P. Mautouchet, *Le Gouvernement Révolutionnaire* (Paris, 1912), p. 200.

[2] Many deputies feared that one of the clauses in this law was designed to end what remained of parliamentary immunity—the right of deputies not to be arrested save on impeachment by the Convention itself. The arrest of Danton had, indeed, preceded his impeachment by the Convention.

a practice of keeping constantly on the move in order to avoid voting or giving any appearance of association with others.

This unhappy state of affairs came to an end after the dramatic days of 27–28 July 1794 (9–10 Thermidor), when Robespierre and his closest friends were suddenly overthrown and executed. Although an English agent in the service of the French government had despondently noted earlier in July: 'All hope of resistance seems at an end: the yoke is to be eternal',[1] the military successes of the Republic had in fact eased the pressure on the Committee sufficiently to allow long-suppressed quarrels to break out amongst its members. This division, and that which developed between the two Committees of Public Safety and General Security, enabled men like Fouché, Carrier, Tallien[2] and Barras, who had good reason to suppose that Robespierre was about to indict them for the acts of terrorism they had committed, to conspire against him in the Convention; and in this they had the support of the more violent of the Committee members, particularly Billaud-Varenne and Collot d'Herbois. Thus on 27 July when Robespierre and Saint-Just attempted to speak they were persistently howled down. Placed under arrest, together with the crippled Couthon, they were released from prison by the Commune of Paris and taken in triumph to the City Hall. In the course of the night, however, the authority of the Convention outweighed that of the Commune. The armed forces of the Sections of Paris either stood aside or rallied to the Convention, a column commanded by Barras seized the City Hall, and Robespierre and the others were executed next day on identification as men who had been proclaimed outlaws. Immediately afterwards more than a hundred others, including 83 members of the Commune, were also guillotined as Robespierrists.

Only then did the victors, themselves the principal terrorists, begin to discover that they had unleashed forces far beyond their own control. So much had Robespierre, as the principal political spokesman of the Committee, been identified by public opinion with the policy of Terror that his death was universally regarded as the hour of liberation. As Thibaudeau, who had for some months past prudently busied himself with 'obscure but useful service' in connection with education, put it: 'General joy burst forth, in the departments as in Paris. . . . Oh, what sweet and wonderful emotions overwhelmed our long-oppressed souls!'[3]

[1] Raoul Hesdin, *The Journal of a Spy in Paris* (London, 1895), p. 195 (entry for 4 July 1794).

[2] *Biog. Notes:* TALLIEN.

[3] Thibaudeau, *Mémoires*, Vol. I, pp. 83, 88.

The conspirators, moreover, had only won the day by enlisting the support of the individually insignificant members of the Plain, the 'honest men' to whom Robespierre had appealed in vain, and these now realised their potential power and began, with the full backing of public opinion, to destroy the whole apparatus of Revolutionary Government.

Thus Thermidor, itself the result of hazardous conspiracy, became so much of a turning point in the history of the Revolution that it is often regarded as its conclusion. Certainly it marked the end of an attempt by some members of an extraordinarily powerful government to thrust France forwards to a sort of democratic paradise; for Robespierre had undoubtedly been the principal prophet of a regenerated France, that great Republic in which equal citizens would live together in austere fraternity. Certainly, too, the days of Thermidor marked the end of the work of the Committee of Public Safety in saving France from famine, disruption and conquest. Yet great as were these achievements, Revolutionary Government and Terror had accomplished nothing constructive and durable: on the contrary, all that was progressive in the purpose of the Montagnards was almost irretrievably compromised by the bloody means they had employed. Far from ending the Revolution, Thermidor left all the work of founding a generally acceptable constitutional republic to be begun again.

2. The Reaction Against the Terror, July 1794-May 1795

The last year in the life of the National Convention has had short shrift from historians. The word 'Thermidorian', generally applied to the deputies who strove to govern France in the period between the fall of Robespierre in July 1794 and the dissolution of the Convention in October 1795, is indeed commonly used less as a convenient means of identification than as a term of opprobrium. The year, it would appear, was one in which a dismal clique of bourgeois politicians encouraged economic chaos and social reaction in order to perpetuate their own rule and consolidate that of their class. This representation of the period as no more than the depressing aftermath of the progressive Revolution of 1793-4 is so commonplace that it is a matter of astonishment to find a contemporary, Miot de Melito, writing in his *Memoirs* that the year 1795 was 'one of the most brilliant in the history of the nation'.[1]

Wherever the truth may lie, Miot de Melito's further comment that France had 'overcome the revolutionary madness' is at least a useful reminder that after Thermidor French affairs were no longer dominated by a single body of men devoted to a single doctrinaire interpretation of the Revolution. This of course made the task of government far more difficult than before. Where the Convention had been silenced by repeated purges and constant intimidation, majority decisions had now to be obtained by argument and debate amongst men whose recent experiences had made them highly suspicious of each other. More than ever, deputies were identified according to their past associations; and although, as the Terror was relaxed, a succession of groups re-appeared, each representing an earlier stage in the evolution of the Republic, none of these was sufficiently strong or stable to provide the Convention with a firm basis for consistent policy.

[1] *Memoirs of Count Miot de Melito*, p. 34. A. F. Miot, comte de Melito (1762–1841), was a successful diplomat who became a Councillor of State to Napoleon Bonaparte, whom he also served at the Ministry of Police. He was, however, closer to Napoleon's brother, Joseph, for whom he was Minister of the Interior first at Naples and then at Madrid.

In this complex situation a political problem so great as to seem almost insuperable confronted those moderate men who sought to establish a liberal constitutional republic in France. Not surprisingly, the Convention swung steadily to the Right in its reaction from the Terror; and public opinion, constantly reinforced by the re-appearance of people who had been in prison, in hiding or in exile, constantly demanded more and more measures of emancipation. But while almost all were united in their determination to destroy the Terror, none could tell how far it was safe to go. In the matter of justice, for example, the universal call for liberation and rehabilitation could all too easily become one for compensation and retribution, and the danger of encouraging a new form of terrorism, that of reprisals and revenge, was perpetual. The way of reaction, moreover, led inexorably towards royalism, and on 28 January 1793, immediately after Louis XVI's execution, his brother Provence[1] had openly identified the royal cause with violence. Assuming the title of Regent of the Kingdom on behalf of 'Louis XVII', the captive Dauphin, Provence had made it plain that he intended to restore the old order in its entirety and to inflict condign punishment on all who had committed crimes in the name of the Revolution.

While this made compromise with the royalists impossible for all republicans (whether or not they were actually regicides), the rapid revival of a Right, passionate, vengeful and vindictive, inevitably caused a resurgence of the Left. Although before Thermidor the Jacobin Club had been reduced to a rostrum for the reading of official reports; although the Montagnards had been regimented in the Convention, and the *sans-culottes* themselves subordinated by bureaucracy, the Terror came in retrospect to seem to these revolutionaries to have been a time when the people were supreme, when food-supplies were assured and when offices high and low were to be had for the asking. To them, therefore, a return to the 'Constitution of 1793', with its promise of democracy and social welfare, seemed sufficient to re-establish the sovereignty of the people and guarantee an age of gold, and for this they were eventually to rise again in insurrection.

Throughout the Year III (1794–5) moderate republicans had in consequence to walk with extreme circumspection along the narrow path separating one form of anarchy and terrorism from another. Amongst men who had survived the Terror because they were cynical and unscrupulous, moderates had to sustain high purpose and faith in the future; amidst scenes of passion and peril, they had not only to show and advocate restraint, but also to work out, and persuade others to accept,

[1] *Biog. Notes:* PROVENCE.

a reasonable and practical republican constitution. Whatever their achievement, their endeavour should command respect.

The first step, the destruction of the power of the recent Revolutionary Government, proved astonishingly, and indeed dangerously, easy. On 28 July 1794 the surviving members of the Committee of Public Safety, who failed to realise that Robespierre's fall was being hailed as the ending of tyranny, sent the persuasive Barère[1] to inform the Convention that the events of the previous day had left authority unimpaired. 'Invigorated and purified', he cried, 'the Revolutionary Government will be an hundred times more effective!'[2] But Barère also said: 'The Convention is everything;' and the fact was that the disrupted Committee had become dependent upon the deputies, who seized the opportunity to re-assert their own control. Next day the official proposal, that the Committee should replace its three dead members by candidates of its own choice, was brushed aside in favour of a motion by Tallien by which both the Committee of Public Safety and that of General Security were to be renewed by one quarter each month, retiring members not being eligible for immediate re-election. Moreover, when Barère tried to insist that Terror must remain 'on the order of the day' and that the Revolutionary Tribunal should retain its former personnel, he was met by uproar, and the assembly ordered the impeachment of Fouquier-Tinville, the infamous Public Prosecutor of the Terror. The choice on 31 July of no fewer than six new men to restore the Committee of Public Safety to its full complement of 12 meant that the power of those who had ruled France during the Terror was effectively broken.[3] Within a month the Committee had been stripped of its supreme responsibility for supervising the work of government and had become but one of the more important of 16 committees amongst which that responsibility was now distributed.[4]

---

[1] *Biog. Notes:* BARÈRE.

[2] A. Soboul, *La I*re *République* (Paris, 1968), p. 148; see also G. Lefebvre, *The Thermidorians* (trans. R. Baldick, London, 1964), pp. 7–8.

[3] In addition to replacing Robespierre, Saint-Just and Couthon, the Convention now filled the vacancy created by the death of Hérault de Séchelles, who had been executed with Danton, and dispossessed Jeanbon Saint-André and Prieur of the Marne on the ground that they were away from Paris *en mission*.

[4] Twelve of these committees were each responsible for one of the twelve commissions which had replaced the executive ministries on 1 April 1794. The other four were the Finance Committee and the Committees of Public Safety, General Security and Legislation. The last three, which were of major importance, were commonly called 'the Committees' or 'the Three Committees'. See P. Mautouchet, *Le Gouvernement Révolutionnaire* (Paris, 1912), p. 326.

A re-orientation of local government accompanied these changes at the centre. In Paris itself the powerful Commune which had been destroyed at Thermidor was simply not re-established, much of the administration of the capital being taken over by the national government. The 48 Sections of the city, with their General Assemblies, were allowed to survive, but for administrative purposes they were grouped into 12 *arrondissements*, each of which had only one 'revolutionary committee'— the members of which were nominated by, and responsible to, the Convention's Committee of General Security. In the provinces, too, the number of the 'revolutionary committees' was drastically reduced, only one being allowed in each district; and the power of the Jacobins and the *sans-culottes* was generally curbed by the requirement that only the literate were to be eligible for membership of these committees, and then only for three months at a time. Beyond this, the centralised structure of local government established by the Montagnards was little changed, though new commissioners were sent out by the Convention to begin the long process of replacing one set of government nominees by another.

The initial measures of the Convention after Thermidor were thus strangely compounded of a renewal of centralisation in local affairs and a diffusion of power in central government itself. The effect of this 'moral federalism', as Barère contemptuously called it, was moreover greatly enhanced by the assembly's simultaneous endeavour to stamp out the abuses associated with Revolutionary 'justice'. On 1 August the terrible Law of 22 Prairial was repealed; on 5 August the Convention ruled that only men against whom specific charges had been brought were to be held in custody; and from 10 August a re-organised Revolutionary Tribunal became bound to consider each prisoner's motives as well as his actions.[1] Well-meant though they were, these measures at once weakened government and increased the strength of the forces of reaction. Deprived of what Professor Lefebvre called its 'coercive force',[2] the Convention was in practice unable to exercise effective control of affairs either in the provinces or in Paris: but at the same time the rapid release of 'suspects' from imprisonment gave rise to a growing demand for the pursuit and punishment of all who could be called terrorists.

---

[1] Operative from 10 August, the rule as finally written in the law of 28 December 1794 was that each juror should pronounce: 'On my honour and conscience, the fact is established; the accused is convicted; he is convicted of having committed the deed with such intent.' J. Hall Stewart, *A Documentary Survey*, p. 546.

[2] *The Thermidorians*, e.g. p. 71.

So strong, indeed, was the public reaction against the Terror that the maintenance of any sort of legality soon began to appear as at least as difficult a problem as the uprooting of 'Robespierre's tyranny'. The fall of the Revolutionary Government inevitably implied the denunciation and arrest of men who, like Joseph Le Bon,[1] had enforced the Terror to the last hour in the departments of France, and these arrests as inevitably led to a further wave of denunciations against minor officials. At the same time, the wholesale expulsion of Jacobins and *sans-culottes* from positions of authority revealed abuses and opened the way for the persecution of these men by their successors. In Paris and other great towns like Lyons and Marseilles this sort of conflict had particularly strong class connotations, for more prosperous people returned in increasing numbers to the General Assemblies of the Sections, expelling the *sans-culottes* and initiating investigations intended to pay them back in their own coin.[2]

This mounting social evil was, moreover, aggravated by the irresponsible and ambitious conduct of many of the deputies. At first, when it seemed as if Thermidor might mean no more than the emancipation of the Montagnard deputies from the control of the Revolutionary Government, second-rate men like Duhem and Fayau tried to rally support amongst the *sans-culottes* by demanding that suspected persons should be deported and measures of social reform begun. The removal of the remains of Marat,[3] the 'Friend of the People', to honourable re-burial in the Panthéon then seemed proof that a new form of Terror was about to be inaugurated. On the other hand, some of those who had been associated with Danton openly encouraged the reaction, and several prominent Terrorists—particularly Tallien and the almost insanely violent Fréron—deliberately placed themselves at its head, openly exploiting public anger and anxiety in order to save their own skins. As soon as some freedom for the press was re-established, Fréron revived his *Orateur du peuple* as a virulently anti-Jacobin organ, using it to incite violence by street-gangs known as *la jeunesse dorée de Fréron*. Affecting flowing square-cut collars, earrings and long hair turned back at the neck *à la victime*, these middle-class clerks and draft-dodgers assaulted

[1] *Biog. Notes:* LE BON.

[2] The General Assemblies of the Sections were now only permitted to meet at ten-day intervals, and citizens were no longer allowed to claim the payment of 40 *sous* which had been granted for attendance in September 1793.

[3] Jean-Paul Marat (1743–93) had acquired immense popularity with the people as a fearless and disinterested champion of their cause. After his assassination by Charlotte Corday he was revered as a martyr, and the treatment of his corpse symbolised the status afforded to popular democracy.

Jacobins and *sans-culottes* in the streets, abusing legality to the cry of '*Vive la Convention!*'

The Thermidorians, however, were not all alike. Against the activities of men like Fréron must be placed the persistent endeavour of the moderate republicans to restrain vindictiveness and prevent new persecutions. Although this central part of the Convention[1] was not strong enough to establish the general amnesty called for at intervals by men like Robert Lindet and Cambacérès,[2] it at least succeeded in delaying the development of retributive justice and new forms of penal legislation. Thus on 29 August and 3 October attempts to indict the surviving members of the old Committee of Public Safety were defeated; and although the three men who were most commonly associated with the excesses of the Terror, Barère, Collot d'Herbois and Billaud-Varenne, found it wise to resign from the reconstituted Committee on 1 September, they remained secure throughout the autumn. Nor was this policy of restraint merely an expedient dictated by the strength of the Left: Joseph Le Bon, for example, was arrested on 2 August 1794 as one of the most notorious agents of the Terror, but despite the repeated demands of the reactionaries and the virtual elimination of the Montagnards in the spring of 1795, he was not sent for trial until 10 July of that year. Incalculable though it necessarily is, the significance of the moderates' opposition to the new counter-terror is clearly considerable. While it is true that the physical weakness of government during the year 1794–5 made popular reprisals against 'terrorists' possible and even commonplace, it is also true that the reaction in France only involved extensive bloodshed in one area, the south-east. Elsewhere legal processes generally prevailed,[3] a fact which may not be unrelated to the leisurely and careful proceedings of the reformed Revolutionary Tribunal, which sent only 63 people to the scaffold between July 1794 and the end of May 1795.[4]

The pressures which the moderates had to resist nevertheless increased

---

[1] Although here and elsewhere I have named some individuals as being 'moderate' on particular occasions and with regard to particular issues, I have not attempted any serious assessment of the numerical strength and political distinctiveness of 'this central part of the Convention'. This might well be the subject of a much more searching investigation than is possible here.

[2] *Biog. Notes:* CAMBACÉRÈS

[3] G. Lefebvre, *The Thermidorians*, pp. 119–22).

[4] As compared with more than 1,300 between the middle of June and the end of July 1794. The principal trials conducted by the Revolutionary Tribunal after Thermidor were those of the Revolutionary Committee of Nantes, of Carrier and of Fouquier-Tinville, the Public Prosecutor.

as the reaction gathered strength and more and more of the horrors of the Terror became known. On 9 Thermidor there were in Paris 94 prisoners from Nantes, the survivors of 132 citizens sent to the capital as 'federalists' in the middle of the previous winter. When they were eventually placed on trial on 8 September, they accused the principal witnesses against them, the 'revolutionary committee' of Nantes (who had also been sent to Paris as prisoners just before Thermidor) of responsibility for the executions and drownings which had occurred at Nantes during the Terror. This trial was exploited to the full by the anti-Jacobin press as revealing an atrocity story, which indeed it did, and the revelations undoubtedly served to give the reaction new momentum. Those originally accused were soon triumphantly acquitted, but within a month the Convention was compelled to agree that the members of the revolutionary committee should be sent before the Revolutionary Tribunal. These in their turn accused Carrier, saying that they had only acted on the orders he gave when he was sent to the area as a Comissioner of the Convention; and the deputies were then driven into the perilous course of appointing a commission to examine his conduct.[1] When the commission reported in mid-November, Carrier's record left the Convention no alternative but to send him before the Tribunal, which quite rightly sent him to the scaffold on 16 December. Even in so notorious a case as this, however, the dangers implicit in retribution were evident: one step more, and the whole Convention and even the Republic itself would be in jeopardy. Carrier, indeed, told the assembly outright that he had helped to save the Republic by his severity, and asserted that every man present was as guilty as he was himself.[2]

The reaction, however, was as yet far from its climax. At this stage it was the Jacobin movement, the original source of the Terror, which was the principal target of the reactionaries' attack, and in the climate of opinion built up by the exposure of what Terror had meant at Nantes the attack proved an easy victory. Initially the moderates tried to preserve a balance: a decree passed on 16 October did not forbid the existence of political societies, but simply struck at the roots of Jacobin

---

[1] By a new procedure, adopted *ad hoc* on this occasion, accusations against deputies were to be referred first to the Three Committees, then to a commission of enquiry, and finally to the Convention as a whole, which would hear both the commission and the accused before deciding whether to refer the latter to the Revolutionary Tribunal for trial.

[2] '*Tout est coupable ici, jusqu'à la sonnette du président*': Thibaudeau, *Mémoires*, I, p. 143. Carrier was executed on 16 December, but the Tribunal only convicted two of the members of the Revolutionary Committee of Nantes, releasing 30 others.

power by banning all affiliation and collective action.[1] In Paris, however, the Jacobins were so harassed by the press and goaded by the gangs that they made a fatal attempt to re-assert themselves. On 3 November Billaud-Varenne broke a long silence to warn opponents of the Club that 'The lion is not dead when it dozes, and when it awakens it exterminates all its enemies!'[2] This rash and ill-timed pronouncement gave the reactionaries sufficient excuse to cry: 'Conspiracy!' On the evening of 9 November the *jeunesse dorée* assaulted the Club, smashing its windows and dispersing its members, the men being beaten up and the women whipped from the galleries. The Jacobins appealed to the Convention in vain, being simply told to suspend their meetings, and the performance of the 9th was repeated on 11 November under the personal leadership of Tallien and Fréron. Under orders of the Convention the Club was then closed, the doors being sealed on 12 November. Thus the once mighty Society of the Friends of Liberty and Equality perished ignominiously. As an expression of faith in political and social democracy, Jacobinism was indeed to retain substantial support in the cities and towns of France, and it was eventually to re-appear in the days of the Directory as a major political force; but as a movement, effectively unified by centralised control, its power was broken, and the very name 'Jacobin' became for many no more than a term of abuse which was loosely applied to all radical democrats and popular extremists.[3]

In this matter, as in others, the Convention was evidently being hustled towards reaction by organised pressure from the streets: but it was not on that account 'completely under the control of public opinion', as the royalist observer Mallet du Pan[4] soon afterwards concluded.

[1] Men who had watched the growth of Jacobin power since 1789 would of course recall that measures of this sort had been attempted on previous occasions.

[2] G. Lefebvre, *The Thermidorians*, p. 39.

[3] For the revival of Jacobinism after 1795, see I. Woloch, *Jacobin Legacy: The Democratic Movement under the Directory* (Princeton, 1970). In what follows (chapters 4–6) I suggest that Professor Woloch may perhaps have over-estimated the extent to which these 'new' Jacobins had set the élitist and dictatorial tendencies of the original Jacobins behind them. It is appropriate to add here that Jacobinism in the wider sense of belief in both social democracy and powerful emergency forms of government survived as an essential strand in the French revolutionary tradition.

[4] Written in Mallet's letter of 18 February 1795, this passage is cited with gusto by both Mathiez and Lefebvre (A. Mathiez, *La Réaction Thermidorienne* (Paris, 1929), p. 112, and Lefebvre, *The Thermidorians*, p. 58). Jacques Mallet du Pan (1749–1801) was a Swiss journalist who, as an ardent advocate of constitutional monarchy, represented first the interests of the French Court in Germany and then those of the more moderate *émigrés*.

Rather did the great majority of the deputies share the general conviction that the Terror, in its every aspect, was the worst of all evils excepting only an unconditional and abject surrender to the royalists of the *ancien régime*. Their point of view was well expressed by Reubell, himself once an ardent Montagnard, who said in the Convention on 10 November: 'Where was tyranny organised? At the Jacobin Club. Who made the Republican system so odious that a slave laden with fetters would have refused to live under it? The Jacobins.'[1]

Essentially the same point of view is apparent in the Convention's unwillingness to resist the widespread demand for the restoration of freedom in matters of trade. Although on 7 September 1794 the assembly decided to maintain general price controls for a further year, those controls remained commonly identified with the Terror, just as the army of officials and agents employed by the various governmental commissions were generally assumed to be the creatures of Robespierre. Partly for this reason, the scale of state activity was considerably reduced during the autumn. In October, manufacturers recovered the right to import materials freely; in November, the penalties imposed on peasants who failed to supply their specified quotas of grain were relaxed, and the national maximum price of grain gave way to local price controls. At the same time, state production diminished, the national armaments workshops being closed down or returned to private enterprise. Eventually, after a long debate on a committee report, the Convention abolished the *maximum* outright on 24 December 1794. Requisitioning to feed the towns was to remain in force, but nominally only for a transitional period,[2] and even the Commission of Trade and Supplies only retained its rights of priority in purchases for the armies on condition that its agents paid the full current price for all they bought. Foreign trade, except in respect of the export of grain, was similarly freed from all controls on 2 January 1795.

For these decisions the Thermidorians have been severely censured by historians,[3] who point to the fact that the return of private enterprise was followed by frenzied speculation, disastrous inflation and the near-famine conditions of the spring of 1795. The Convention, it is suggested,

[1] *Ancien Moniteur*, 20 Vendémiaire, An IV.

[2] This transitional period was in fact repeatedly extended: see, for example, G. Lefebvre, *The Directory* (trans. R. Baldick, London 1965), pp. 29–30 for the attempt to end it in the early spring of 1796.

[3] Particularly by Mathiez, *La Réaction Thermidorienne*, by Lefebvre, *The Thermidorians*, and by Soboul, *La Iʳᵉ République*, p. 162ff. The details given here, though not the interpretation placed upon them, are principally derived from Lefebvre, op. cit., chapter 6.

was swayed by the class-interest of a resurgent bourgeoisie to abandon the beneficent controls which had been democratically maintained during the Terror. This interpretation of developments is certainly not one to be dismissed. Thibaudeau, who was now becoming one of the most influential deputies of the moderate republican centre of the assembly, has left us in his memoirs[1] a vivid vignette of the new society which began to form after Thermidor as impoverished members of the old *noblesse* mingled with wealthy bankers and businessmen at the supper-tables or in the salons of ladies like Madame Récamier and Madame Tallien, 'Our Lady of Thermidor'.[2] His account makes it quite clear that every effort was made to attract deputies to these gatherings, both in order to enlist their support for particular interests and to undermine political idealism for the Republic. Equally, however, the conventional picture of an assembly exclusively concerned with its own class-interest can be condemned as over-drawn. Certainly Thibaudeau, who can be considered Tallien's principal political opponent, did not succumb to the blandishments of the new royalists, and, so far as state control of the economy is concerned, it may be doubted whether any persuasion was necessary to make him oppose it. Rather is it significant that he prided himself for the rest of his life on having been one of the first deputies to denounce the *maximum* in open debate.[3] Abhorred as an integral aspect of the hated Terror, the system of state control and the evasions and abuses associated with it were also commonly believed to be the prime cause of economic distress.

In this matter the contrast between the Terror and its aftermath can easily be exaggerated, as indeed it usually is. Whatever the symbolic significance of their legislation, however high their vision of an harmonious society, the Montagnards of the Terror were not *in practice* either democrats or socialists. Their control of the economy, first forced upon them by popular unrest and military necessity, had always been used primarily to maintain a flow of supplies to the armies and to keep Paris and certain other great towns supplied with bread; all else was left to local control, and everywhere the black market had flourished. Moreover, despite the fair harvest of 1793 and the remarkably mild winter which followed, even the Revolutionary Government had barely held famine at bay in 1794; quite apart from the policy and action of government, the frightful economic situation of 1795 would seem to be a direct consequence of the wet summer and poor harvest of 1794, as well as of

[1] Thibaudeau, *Mémoires*, Vol. I, pp. 128–31.
[2] *Biog. Notes:* MADAME RÉCAMIER; MADAME TALLIEN.
[3] Thibaudeau, *Mémoires*, Vol. I, pp. 105–7.

the cruel severity of the winter of 1794–5, which was one of the worst of the whole century.

The Terror, too, had always had a predominantly political purpose. When the Republic ceased to be in danger, the organisation which had saved it was increasingly directed towards the foundation of a Republic of Virtue, and even Robespierre regarded popular concern with what he once called 'paltry merchandise'[1] as an irritating distraction from this great task. Expediency had in fact re-asserted itself strongly in Montagnard economic policy in February 1794, when Barère had introduced a revised price-list with the words: 'We must cure commerce, not kill it'. This revision, and the liquidation of the Hébertist group in March, had coincided with, and probably helped to cause, a renewal of inflation. After recovering from approximately 25% to approximately 50% of its face value between August 1793 and December of that year, the *assignat* had sunk back to 30% of its value by June 1794, and the ending of the Terror in July in fact stimulated a slight recovery. Thereafter the decline continued, the value of the *assignat* being only 20% in December 1794, when the *maximum* was abolished. These figures suggest the existence of a general trend that was little affected by the destruction of the Montagnard dictatorship;[2] and if after December the fall was both continuous and catastrophic, one may at least suspect that the return to a free economy had only precipitated an already inevitable collapse.[3] At the time, the deputies expected and believed that after a passing period of adjustment the restoration of economic freedom would be generally beneficial, and in this estimate they were appallingly wrong: but their mistake does not seem either unnatural or dishonourable.

[1] At the Jacobin Club, 25 Feb. 1793: Aulard, *Société des Jacobins*, Vol. V, pp. 44–5.

[2] Professor Lefebvre suggests that the Thermidorians early made all economic controls meaningless by depriving the government of 'coercive force' instead of simply 'moderating and regularising' that force—a thing easier said than done. Yet he himself writes: 'price limitation . . . soon forces the State to take over control of the national economy. From then on, dictatorship, police supervision and intimidation become indispensable to the State if it is to exact obedience.' *The Thermidorians*, p. 72.

[3] Cp. J. Godechot, *Les Institutions de la France sous la Révolution et l'Empire* (Paris 1951), p. 336, where it is suggested that despite the 'moderated' decline in values in the spring of 1794, the energetic policy of the Montagnards was *on the point of stabilising* the value of money at Thermidor (the present author's italics). Amongst other causes of the growth of inflation in 1794–5 must be reckoned the ending of the confiscations of property (the capital which the *assignats* nominally represented), and the reluctance of people to purchase such property at a time of reaction; one may however wonder just how much security there had been for anyone during the Terror.

Another aspect of the endeavour to establish a liberal Republic in France at this time was a protracted campaign to rehabilitate the surviving 'Girondins'. This was of course a delicate matter, for the return to the Convention of all the deputies who had been proscribed for opposing the Montagnards' seizure of power in 1793 seemed certain to effect the balance of forces in the assembly. The Montagnards naturally opposed this; the more ardent reactionaries hoped that it would strengthen their own position and many men of the centre dreaded the possibility that a new element of vindictiveness might be introduced into the assembly if men who had been persecuted were restored to their places. Other moderates, however, were convinced that the question was one of right,[1] for if the Montagnards and the Jacobins were identified with Terror and tyranny, their first opponents were evidently the victims of injustice. The conscience of some men therefore marched with the calculations of others to carry the reversal of the Terror one stage further. As a first step, 67 deputies who had signed a secret protest against the events of 31 May 1793,[2] and spent 12 months in prison in consequence, were re-admitted to the Convention on 8 December 1794, along with 11 others—including the English republican Tom Paine. Although old Dusaulx[3] promised on behalf of these men that they would not seek revenge, their return inevitably called the Revolution of 31 May 1793 more openly into question, and this cast doubt upon the validity of all subsequent revolutionary legislation—including the seizure and sale of the estates of the 'federalists'. The second stage of the campaign, intended to rehabilitate the men who had fled from Paris and been proscribed as outlaws after 31 May, therefore progressed but slowly, and it was not until 8 March 1795 that it succeeded. 'You are about to rouse every passion', cried the Montagnard Bentabole on that occasion; 'if you attack the insurrection of 31 May,[4] you attack the 80,000 men

[1] See, for example, Durand de Maillane, *Histoire de la Convention nationale* (Paris 1825), pp. 261–2.

[2] Originally signed by 75 deputies, the protest was denounced and its authors imprisoned in October 1793, when the principal opponents of the Mountain were indicted. They were on various occasions preserved from execution by Robespierre personally.

[3] *Biog. Notes:* DUSAULX.

[4] The use of the word 'insurrection' here is of some importance. According to the current belief, sovereign authority naturally reverted to the people in an emergency, and the people recognised this by declaring themselves to be 'in insurrection'. The repudiation of 31 May 1793 by the Convention in 1795 may be seen as tantamount to a repudiation of this interpretation of popular sovereignty, although—as Sieyès' words show—this was to some extent con-

who concurred in it.' Sieyès[1] however, replied: 'The fatal 31 May was not a work of patriotism, but an outrage of tyranny.' The recall of the proscribed deputies was then accepted with only one contrary vote—a fact which should not conceal the furious conflicts which had raged around this disinterment of the past—and men like Louvet, Lanjuinais and LaRevellière-Lépeaux (the future Director) resumed their seats.[2]

By that time (March 1795) the forces of both reaction and revolution were coming more and more violently into conflict, despite the moderates' well-meant efforts to end the state of emergency in France. To these efforts the pacification of western France was crucial. In the area of the Vendée, the Republicans' crushing victories over the main royalist armies at the end of 1793 had led only to perpetual guerilla war, for the repression which followed victory had been so savage that thousands of men had no hope left save for revenge, nor any means of livelihood save spoliation. In Brittany, in particular, disorder had been rife ever since the Vendéans had crossed and recrossed the province in the autumn of 1793. There flourished the *chouannerie*, a resistance movement compounded of local crime and genuine royalism, of Breton separatism and the desperation of both Vendéan refugees and deserters from the republican armies. In September 1794 the Convention became alarmed by the efforts of a famous royalist, Count Joseph de Puisaye,[3] to organise the *chouan* bands into a coherent fighting force which would be subsidised and supported from England. New generals were therefore sent to the west. Hoche,[4] the new commander of the Army of the West, had himself been imprisoned as a suspect by the Committee of Public Safety, and through him the Convention initiated a policy of conciliation. Hoche undoubtedly showed himself as able in the field as he was generous and humane after victory, and after the Convention had offered a general amnesty to all who would lay down their arms, hostilities were formally ended in January 1795. A negotiated peace was then concluded with the

---

cealed by the allegation that that insurrection was a false one, engineered by the Jacobins.

[1] 'who . . . thought the time was now ripe once more to ascend the tribune which he had deserted for nearly two years': Mathiez, *The Thermidorian Reaction* (trans. as *After Robespierre* by C. A. Phillips, New York, 1965), p. 115. *Biog. Notes:* SIEYÈS.

[2] Those deputies who had been outlawed in 1793–4 were granted amnesty, but not reinstated, on 17 December 1794. Others, like Isnard, simply re-emerged from the places of hiding to which they had retired before being officially proscribed. *Biog. Notes:* LOUVET; LANJUINAIS.

[3] *Biog. Notes:* PUISAYE.

[4] *Biog. Notes:* HOCHE.

Vendéans at La Jaunaye on 17 February and with the *chouans* at La Prévalaye at 20 April. In effect, however, these were practically peace treaties between equal powers.[1] The rebel leaders openly wore the white cockade, and almost dictated their own terms: the amnesty was to apply to all, and was to be accompanied by financial compensation for lands which had been seized and sold, or by subsidies for the re-establishment of damaged farms. There was also to be complete freedom of worship, exemption from service in the republican armies, and recognition of the right of the rebels to retain their arms for the policing of their own territory. These remarkable concessions may have served to show France, as the Convention hoped, that the Republic was not necessarily a régime of bloodshed and repression, but in practice they proved too generous to be durable. Whether driven by necessity or inspired by idealism, the moderates in Paris had gained a respite from open warfare in the west only by condoning armed defiance, and lawlessness not only continued in the area but also spread steadily eastwards into Normandy.

This settlement also influenced the deputies' decisions in their effort to end the conflicts over religion which had distracted France and endangered the Revolution ever since the Civil Constitution of the Clergy had been introduced in 1790; for if freedom of worship could be granted to rebels under arms, it could hardly be withheld from people who had remained loyal to the Republic. The religious question, however, was one which involved not merely the excesses of the Terror, but the whole nature of the Revolution itself. France had indeed learnt much from the fearful experiences through which she had passed: in 1794–5 the 'Dechristianisation' movement, those open attacks on Christianity against which Robespierre had set his face, gradually died away; and the Thermidorians made no effort to maintain the Worship of the Supreme Being, through which Robespierre had himself attempted to impose conformity in civic virtue and the fundamentals of faith upon all Republicans. The authorities, however, continued to insist upon observance of the *décadi*, the tenth day of rest and civic ceremony which had replaced Sunday in the Revolutionary Calendar, even although this was often no more than a convenient occasion for local meetings and administrative announcements. As for those priests who had never accepted the Civil Constitution, they were still treated as counter-revolutionaries, legally liable to the death penalty if they were discovered.

[1] See M. Hutt, 'La Prétendue Pacification de l'An III: Considérations critiques sur la situation en Bretagne à la veille de Quiberon', *Annales historiques de la Révolution française*, XVIII (1966), pp. 485–521.

The Convention nevertheless now tried to disassociate the Republic from religion. It first withdrew all financial assistance from the 'Constitutional' Church, and then on 21 February 1795 it passed a decree establishing freedom of worship for all the clergy of that Church and for those other priests who had compromised with the Revolution to the extent of swearing the 'little oath' of loyalty to Liberty and Equality. The new freedom was yet severely circumscribed, for where priests were concerned even moderate republicans became passionately prejudiced. As in 1790, the best that an assembly anti-clerical and rationalist in outlook could achieve was no more than an utterly unsatisfactory compromise. The churches being reserved for the formalities of the *décadi*, religious worship was only permitted in private meetings; and even then, no donations were to be collected and no outward display of any sort was permitted, even the appearance of a name or a symbol on a building being banned. Still, restrictive as it was, this law opened opportunities for many faithful Catholics to resume their attendance at church, often with the tacit consent of the local authorities, and it enabled the courageous revolutionary bishop Grégoire[1] to begin his great work of reorganising the Constitutional Church.

Here again, the attempt to follow a liberal course increased the strength and potential danger of reaction. As religion revived, so did the influence of the 'refractory' clergy who had never compromised with the Revolution. Many of these non-jurors now came out of hiding or returned from exile in defiance of all the legislation against them, giving Mallet du Pan good reason to believe that: 'In re-creating Catholics, the Convention is re-creating Royalists.'[2] If this was partly wishful thinking, Mallet was right in recognising that royalism was reviving rapidly in France. The first news of Thermidor had encouraged many exiles to return to their homes regardless of the laws, while the friends and relatives of fugitives strove by every means to have their names struck off the lists of those proscribed as emigrants. Moreover, although the penal laws against *émigrés* remained essentially unaltered, the alleviation of the Terror provided opportunities of which many royalists took full advantage, returning particularly as 'peasants and workers', to whom re-entry was permitted by a decree of 11 January 1795. The return to the Convention of the 'Girondins' or 'federalists' opened the doors still wider, for as a logical consequence of their rehabilitation all those who had been driven into exile since 31 May 1793 were reinstated in their

---

[1] *Biog. Notes:* GRÉGOIRE.
[2] 17 March 1795. See Lefebvre, *The Thermidorians*, p. 69.

civil rights,[1] and this category included the great mass of ordinary people who had fled from the Terror. In the Convention itself, too, some of the deputies who had returned to their seats from prison were embittered and disillusioned men who scarcely concealed their desire for the restoration of some form of constitutional monarchy. Mallet du Pan therefore had some grounds for optimism, particularly as in September 1794 he had brought a first approach from the almost forgotten leaders of the Feuillants to the notice of the British government. Indeed, by December of that year William Wickham, as British chargé d'affaires in Berne, had begun his efforts to encourage action by the constitutional monarchists in France and to effect a reconciliation between them and the 'pure' royalists of the original emigrations.[2]

But while the early months of 1795 were perhaps the most favourable opportunity that was ever to occur for the restoration of sound constitutional monarchy in France, the young Dauphin[3] being then still alive in Paris, all those who hoped that this solution would meet the nation's crying need for legal and acceptable authority were pursuing an illusion. In Berne, Wickham soon discovered that the émigrés who followed the dead King's brothers, regarding the Count of Provence as 'Regent of the Kingdom', were completely intransigent in their adherence to the principles of the ancien régime. To these men, the Feuillants and other constitutionalists were renegades who had betrayed their King and dishonoured their own nobility;[4] only after their complete capitulation could they be permitted to begin negotiations with the 'pures'—who in any case preferred to continue to think in terms of reconquering France through some combination of invasion and insurrection. On the other hand, the type of royalism that began to come into the open in France in the beginning of 1795 was so flagrantly violent that the possibility of compromise between the constitutionalists of the

---

[1] A recognition which was extended even to de Précy, the royalist count who had led the revolt of Lyons in 1793. On the general subject of the return of emigrants at this time, see: D. Greer, *The Incidence of the Emigration during the French Revolution* (Gloucester, Mass., 1966), pp. 96–102.

[2] This mission is the subject of the detailed study: Harvey Mitchell, *The Underground War Against Revolutionary France* (Oxford, 1965). See also chapter 5, below.

[3] '*Louis XVII*': Louis Charles, the second son of Louis XVI and Marie-Antoinette, b. Versailles 1785, became heir to the throne on the death of his elder brother on 4 June 1789 and was regarded as King after the execution of his father on 21 January 1793. Imprisoned in the Temple when the monarchy was overthrown in August 1792, he died in captivity early in June 1795.

[4] See, for example, W. R. Fryer, *Republic or Restoration in France: 1794–97*, (Manchester, 1965), pp. 26–27.

royalist and the republican parties soon became remote. This aspect of the reaction first became apparent in Lyons early in February 1795, at the very time when the Convention extended an amnesty to that city, which had been under emergency government ever since its surrender in October 1793. Devastated, impoverished and embittered, Lyons had become a centre of royalist activity and a haven of refuge for deserters, draft-dodgers and criminals on the run; and since the local authorities were disarmed, as well as being obsessed by fears of a new Jacobin revival, the murder of real or supposed 'terrorists' was condoned until killing became commonplace and gangs of self-styled royalists began to dominate most of the Midi.

Although throughout the greater part of France the reaction was far more restrained than this, men being generally content to ostracise the 'terrorists' and to prosecute them in trials which often broke down for want of evidence, the threat to the Republic from the Right mounted relentlessly. As soon as the Jacobin Club had been closed and Carrier had been executed, the reactionaries renewed their demands for the indictment of Barère, Billaud-Varenne and Collot d'Herbois.[1] In this they were now supported by some of the deputies recalled to the Convention on 8 December 1794, including moderate men who believed that the impunity enjoyed by the three Terrorists was a stain on the reputation of the Convention and an abiding indication that the Terror might yet be renewed. On 27 December the Convention at last agreed to appoint a commission to examine the conduct of the accused; but as on previous occasions, the commission procrastinated, anxious to avoid a major political trial in which not only the Terror but the Republic itself would be the real target of attack. In the meanwhile, the *jeunesse dorée* ran wild in Paris, particularly contending with the Jacobins in attempts to dominate theatre audiences and excite demonstrations of political opinion. So considerable were the tumults they raised that the Convention was compelled to repudiate some of the symbols of the Republic: after many busts of Marat had been destroyed by hooliganism, his remains were officially removed from the Panthéon—and then cast by the gangs into the common sewer of Paris. Even the Marseillaise had now to be banned in favour of the new battle-song of reaction, *Le Réveil du peuple contre les terroristes*.[2] At the same time the old *sans-*

[1] This campaign was also directed against Vadier, who had been a prominent member of the Committee of General Security during the Terror: being in hiding, he was eventually condemned *in absentia*.

[2] The music of this song was composed by Gaveaux, who sang it for the first time before the General Assembly of the William Tell Section (previously Place

culottes were persecuted both legally and illegally by the 'honest men' who now controlled most of the Sections of the capital. Required by law to produce accounts of the money they had handled during the Terror, they were examined by hostile committees of enquiry, and a great many were deprived of all political rights and held up to public obloquy as 'levellers' and 'drinkers of blood'. They were also manhandled in the streets and cafés by young thugs 'of the quality', and repeatedly denounced to the Convention as 'tigers' and 'cannibals', people who ought to be deprived 'of the air they have already infected for far too long'.

Goaded by persecution of this kind, the poor of Paris, and indeed of all of France, had also to endure the worst effects of soaring prices and a desperate dearth of essential supplies. Once the *maximum* had been abolished, prices rose steeply. The government, which had now to purchase supplies for the armies at current prices, aggravated the evil by issuing more and more *assignats*, 7,000 million of which were printed between January and May 1795.[1] As the value of the *assignat* dropped from 20% in December 1794 to 14% in early March 1795 (when headlong inflation really began) and then to 8% in April and perhaps 3% in July, prices rose even more steeply: by comparison with an index figure of 100 for 1790, the cost of living in Paris rose from 580 in January 1795 to 720 in March and 900 in April. More specifically, although the official

---

Louis XIV, to the north of the Palais Royal) on 19 January (30 Nivôse) 1795. The words, by Souriquières, may speak for themselves:

1. Quelle est cette lenteur barbare?
   Hâte-toi, peuple souverain,
   De rendre aux monstres de Ténare
   Tous ces buveurs de sang humain!
   Guerre à tous les agents du crime!
   Poursuivons-les jusqu'au trépas,
   Partage l'horreur qui m'anime!
   Ils ne nous échapperont pas.

2. Voyez déjà comme ils frémissent,
   Ils n'osent fuir, les scélérats!
   Les traces du sang qu'ils vomissent
   Décèleront bientôt leurs pas.
   Oui, nous jurons sur votre tombe
   Par notre pays malheureux
   De ne faire qu'une hécatombe
   De ces cannibales affreux!

The official republican festival of 21 January, the anniversary of the execution of Louis XVI, with which the advent of this song coincided (and to which 'votre tombe' probably refers) was accompanied by a demonstration at the Palais Royal, where the effigy of a blood-stained Jacobin was burnt and its ashes conveyed in a chamber-pot to the sewers.

[1] As compared with a total issue of 5½ thousand millions up to March 1794, or of 10–11 thousand millions by December 1794. The number of assignats actually in circulation probably increased from 8 to 11 thousand millions in the first half of 1795. These figures may be further compared with the initial issues on the security of the Church lands of 1,900 millions up to June 1791.

prices of bread and meat in Paris—where their sale was still subsidised and controlled—remained at 12 *sous* for the 4lb loaf and 21 *sous* for 1lb of meat, prices for these quantities on the open market had risen by late April to 6 *livres* and more than 7 *livres* respectively. Nor was the problem merely one of high prices: the paucity of the previous harvest, the difficulty of moving supplies during a winter in which severe frost was followed by widespread floods, and the universal reluctance of farmers to surrender good grain for depreciated paper currency, all combined to impose famine conditions on all but a minority of fortunate speculators. In the provincial towns conditions were generally even worse than they were in Paris, and the position of the poor may be gauged by the words which the relatively well-to-do Charles Sérizat wrote to his brother from Lyons: 'We are short of everything . . . a thousand francs are not worth a hundred at current prices . . . In a word, I am spending 12 to 15 thousand francs a month, and I am dying of hunger.'[1] Although the government extended requisitioning month by month, the difficulty of supplying Paris with food was such that on 15 March the president of the Convention's Subsistence Committee, Boissy d'Anglas[2] (whom the people called 'Boissy-famine'), had to ask the assembly to introduce ration-cards for every family for bread. At a time when a working-man would eat as his staple diet two pounds or more of bread each day, the ration was fixed at one and a half pounds for manual workers and one pound for all others. Even so, by 27 March this ration had to be cut by half, the balance being made up in part by rice—which could not be cooked for want of fuel—and by the end of the month some Sections were receiving only sufficient supplies to distribute quarter rations.

Remarkably, these fearful conditions did not reduce the poor of Paris to silent subservience. Despite all that they had suffered since their first great rising in 1789, their faith in the Revolution was still sufficiently strong for them to believe that their plight might be remedied by democratic demonstration or insurrection. On 17 March a deputation supported by 800 men from the Observatoire and Finistère Sections appeared at the Assembly with the pathetic words: 'We lack bread and we are on the verge of regretting all the sacrifices we have made for the Revolution . . . When you have satisfied our demand, we will cry "*Vive la République!*" ' Hungry, ostracised, persecuted, but not yet wholly disillusioned, such crowds now came again and again to the Convention to demand: 'Bread and the Constitution of 1793'. This resurgence of the revolutionary

[1] Quoted by Renée Fuoc, *La Réaction Thermidorienne à Lyons* (Paris 1957), p. 51.
[2] *Biog. Notes:* BOISSY D'ANGLAS.

movement in the capital, commonly considered[1] a direct consequence of the Thermidorians' failure to control either the reaction or the economy, might equally well be thought the almost inevitable outcome of earlier Revolutionary fanaticism and financial failure: but whatever its origin, it clearly placed the Republic in appalling danger. Already menaced by lawlessness from the Right, the centre of the Convention now faced the prospect of being overwhelmed by violence and disorder from the Left. The situation is epitomised in the dramatic scenes which marked the opening on 22 March of the long-delayed debate to decide whether Barère, Billaud-Varenne and Collot d'Herbois should be sent to the Revolutionary Tribunal as Terrorists. On that occasion, the *jeunesse dorée* and the 'patriots' fought for possession of the public galleries, the *Réveil du Peuple* and the *Marseillaise* being sung in conflicting chorus across the chamber. The debate itself, moreover, soon became a battle royal: on the one hand, the Right made it clear that they regarded everything about the great and terrible year of 1793–4, including the Republic itself, as being under indictment; and on the other, as the Mountain strove to reply, the mighty administrators of the fallen Revolutionary Government—Robert Lindet, Prieur of the Côte-d'Or and Lazare Carnot—spoke boldly from the centre to identify themselves with their accused colleagues and remind the assembly that every one of its deputies was sworn to the defence of democracy.[2]

Here, as in so much of the Revolution, the fundamental difficulty lay in the definition of democracy. If the masses were now being moved to action by hunger; if—as Professor Rudé says[3]—'economic hardship was the primary cause of the movement', the more politically conscious *sans-culottes* were still moved also by the hope of realising their own long-cherished dream of democracy. As a police observer wrote of the culmination of the popular movement in the rising of 1 Prairial (20 May):

---

[1] See the works of Mathiez, Lefebvre and Soboul, as already cited, and *inter alia*, G. Rudé, *The Crowd in the French Revolution* (Oxford 1960), chapter 10, and R. Cobb and G. Rudé, 'The Last Popular Movement of the Revolution in Paris: The *Journées* of Germinal and of Prairial of Year III', originally in the *Revue Historique* (CCXIV, 1955) and reprinted in J. Kaplow, ed., *New Perspectives on the French Revolution* (New York, 1965), pp. 254–76. While in what follows I am heavily indebted to all these authorities, the interpretation given here is my own.

[2] Lefebvre, *The Thermidorians*, pp. 101–2: 'On all occasions you did what you had to do; you could not have followed a different course without shattering the foundations of the democratic system you were sworn to defend.' (Carnot).

[3] G. Rudé, *The Crowd in the French Revolution*, p. 157.

'Bread is the material cause of their insurrection; but the Constitution of 1793 is its soul'.[1] Nominally only temporarily suspended, that Constitution symbolised for the people both social security and the inherent right of every free man to participate personally in local and national political decisions; and despite some indications to the contrary, the probability is that only a very few desperate men had any desire for a return to the Terror. To the great majority of the deputies and all who could be called middle-class, however, popular democracy, social anarchy and the Terror were by now synonymous terms: the former, in their experience, led so inexorably to the others that any attempt to distinguish them would have seemed inconceivable folly. Such was the lasting legacy of the Terror; and if in this the Thermidorians were wrong, they had at least good reason to know that something more than manhood suffrage was involved. The Constitution of 1793 in fact enshrined the principle of the sovereignty of the people, and as the long record of dictatorial delegations, demonstrations and insurrections showed, in revolutionary Paris that concept left little place for the authority of a national parliament.

For these reasons—and not, as is sometimes suggested, simply on account of class-interest—the Thermidorians repelled the people of Paris in the spring of 1795. The Constitution of 1793, which Fréron had described as 'the work of a handful of scoundrels', was really written off in mid-March as beyond revision;[2] and when on 21 March a great crowd from eastern Paris called upon the Convention to put it into effect and so 'end all political storms', the Committee of General Security accepted the aid of the *jeunesse dorée*, who cleared the area of the Tuileries with their cudgels.[3] The reactionaries in the assembly saw the growing unrest as their opportunity to destroy the remnant of the Montagnards; the latter were above all fearful of compromising themselves by seeming to support the people; and the republicans of the centre, whom Thibaudeau at this point courageously represented as President of the Convention, held it their highest duty to defend the

[1] G. Rudé, op. cit., p. 155. It should be said here that R. Cobb and G. Rudé, in the article cited above, describe this as a 'convenient and reassuring theory', their contention being that in this instance and some others the police were writing with a view of supporting the deputies' belief that the Montagnards were really responsible for a politically inspired rising. Kaplow, op. cit., p. 274.

[2] Lefebvre, *The Thermidorians*, pp. 101–2; A. Soboul, *Précis d'histoire de la Révolution française* (Paris, 1962), p. 368.

[3] Compare Rudé, *The Crowd in the French Revolution*, p. 147, citing an earlier suggestion that the Committee, 'having no means of repression, no armed force on which it can rely' should accept such aid.

independence of the assembly against external pressure. Thibaudeau, indeed, seems to have been convinced that the repeated demonstrations were part of a 'terrorist' campaign to prevent or prejudice the debate on the indictment of Barère, Billaud and Collot,[1] and was as ready as anyone to disperse them by force.

Since the disturbances continued, becoming ever more threatening, the deputies may be forgiven for supposing that the full fury of the Revolution was about to be resumed. Indeed, the Quinze Vingts Section again appeared before the Convention on 31 March to denounce the abolition of the *maximum*, the closure of the Commune and the popular clubs, and the imprisonment of patriots,[2] and on 1 April the Convention was almost overwhelmed. On that day, 12 Germinal, a huge crowd from eastern and central Paris[3] inundated the Tuileries and forced its way into the chamber of the assembly, the people again calling for 'Bread and the Constitution of 1793!' For four hours this intrusion continued: but an appeal to the Montagnards by Vanheck, the spokesman of the Cité Section, evoked no response. Indeed, as the sound of the tocsin over the Tuileries[4] brought the armed forces of western Paris to the rescue of the assembly, the Montagnards themselves helped to persuade the people to leave the hall.

Although some writers[5] have alleged that this affair was only allowed to continue because the leaders of the Right hoped that the Montagnards would compromise themselves irretrievably, there seems no need to look for sinister forces to explain either the event or its aftermath. To the majority of the deputies it was an outrage, reminiscent of the days of

---

[1] Thibaudeau, *Mémoires*, Vol. I, pp. 143–56. The view that Thibaudeau held is now rejected by historians: see, for example, Lefebvre, *The Thermidorians*, p. 102. It nevertheless seems likely that the Convention's post-mortem on the Terror may have served to aggravate popular anger amongst the *sans-culottes*.

[2] This deputation, which asserted the duty of citizens to rise against oppression (as prescribed in the Declaration of Rights of 1793), announced the fact of insurrection in the words: 'We are risen (*debout*) to uphold the Republic and Liberty'. The closure of the Jacobins had been followed in February by the closure of other more popular societies in the sections, and this and the call for the re-opening of the municipality suggest that the insurgents had political as well as economic motives.

[3] The *sans-culottes* regained temporary control of some ten sections in eastern, south-eastern, central Paris and Montmartre at this time. See Rudé, op. cit., p. 158.

[4] It was by the Police Law introduced by Sieyès on 21 March that the bell on the Unity Pavillion of the Tuileries was established as the sole tocsin in Paris, to be rung when the Convention was itself in danger.

[5] E. G. Mathiez, *La Réaction Thermidorienne*, p. 207.

1792 and 1793 when first the Crown and then the Convention had had to accept the dictation of the Sections of Paris. Certainly they did not hesitate to strike hard at those they regarded as the potential leaders of a new Terror, whether these were actually compromised or not. On that same night Barère, Billaud-Varenne and Collot d'Herbois were condemned without further enquiry to deportation to Guiana, and they were immediately packed off to the Ile d'Oléron to await transportation.[1] At the same time, eight Montagnards were arrested as 'terrorists' and removed at once to the fortress of Ham. Paris itself was placed under martial law, command of its armed forces being given to General Pichegru, by now renowned as the conqueror of Holland as well as of Belgium; next night, having dispersed all the *sans-culottes* who had rallied in the hall of the Quinze Vingts Section, he curtly informed the Convention that its commands had been obeyed. Within the next few days warrants went out for the arrest of eight more deputies, some of whom had in fact been active opponents of Robespierre at Thermidor.[2] On 10 April, moreover, the Convention ordered the 'disarming' of men known in their Sections as 'having participated in the horrors committed during the tyranny which preceded Thermidor'. In practice, this meant that some 1,600 of the most vigorous of the *sans-culottes* of Paris were identified by those who had most reason to dislike them; deprived of their civic right to carry arms and excluded from all public employments, they also became men marked down for persecution and arrest.

The crisis, however, was far from over. The news of the rising in Paris gave the reactionaries of south-eastern France an additional incentive for their oppression of 'terrorists'; the decree about 'disarmament' enabled them to intensify it. Beginning at Bourg on 19 April, a succession of atrocities occurred as alleged terrorists were slaughtered in, or on the roads to, the principal prisons of the area between Lyons and Marseilles. Lyons, Aix, Marseilles and Tarascon, to name only the most important places, all witnessed scenes of this sort. These murders were marked by particularly horrid deliberation, for while the number of those killed seldom exceeded 100 on any one occasion, the gangs sometimes returned to the prisons to surprise and slay anyone who had contrived to survive the initial massacre. Tolerated by the National Guard, the activities of such bands as the Marseilles 'Company of the

---

[1] Collot died from fever soon after reaching Cayenne in 1795. Billaud survived, became a farmer, and eventually moved to Haiti in 1817 with the slave girl Virginie; there he died respected in 1819. Barère contrived to remain in France, and eventually sought office under Bonaparte.

[2] Such as Cambon, long the director of French finances.

Sun' were openly encouraged by certain Commissioners of the Convention, notably the recently reinstated 'Girondin' Isnard. Apart from these major massacres, the 'patriots' of the Midi were hounded down remorselessly, being killed, as one contemporary put it, 'like game in the fields, wherever they could be found'.[1] Goaded into revolt, the *sans-culottes* of Toulon eventually marched in force to the relief of their comrades in Marseilles; but they were routed by the military under Isnard's direction, and a military commission soon sent 52 of them to their deaths.

To the Convention, it now seemed as if France stood on the brink of a new civil war.[2] While White Terror raged in the south, reports came in daily from all parts of the country of both food-riots and royalist demonstrations. On the other hand, revolution in Paris remained unsubdued: the constant interference with food-convoys made it ever more difficult to feed the capital, and evidence soon accumulated that another insurrection was being prepared. Caught thus between revolution and reaction, the more moderate deputies strove desperately to establish stability. On 1 May legislation was introduced against returning *émigrés* and priests, and against all who tried to bring about a restoration of the monarchy—a clause aimed particularly at the virulent right-wing press. At about the same time, however, the law which forbade troop-movements in the vicinity of Paris was suspended, and all armed forces in the area, including the National Guard, were placed under one command as the 17th Military Division.[3] To Thibaudeau in particular the inability of government to enforce the laws seemed the principal evil of the day, and on 26 April he even proposed that the whole executive power should be entrusted to the Committee of Public Safety, all other committees being confined to proposing legislation. This attempt to avoid both the dictatorship of 1794 and the decentralisation of 1795, by concentrating executive authority in a committee without legislative rights, excited prolonged debate, but led only to some extension of the powers of the Committee of Public Safety, a compromise solution proposed by Cambacérès. Reluctant to revive any forms of provisional government, the Convention was drawn rather to expedite the com-

---

[1] Durand de Maillane, *Histoire de la Convention nationale*, p. 277.

[2] Cp.: 'I saw the civil war start in the Vendée—there was nothing as terrifying as I have seen here in Lozère and Vaucluse.' Goupilleau de Montagne, cited by Mathiez, *La Réaction Thermidorienne*, p. 232.

[3] Steps to purge the Army staffs and to re-organise the National Guard (with the re-establishment of cavalry and other units recruited from the well-to-do) were also initiated at this time, but the effect of these was not apparent until after 1 Prairial.

pletion of a Constitution, which alone seemed likely to assuage party conflicts and calm public opinion, and to this end a Commission of Eleven was established on 18 April,[1] again at Cambacérès' instigation.

To the *sans-culottes* of Paris, however, the immediate implementation of the Constitution of 1793 now seemed the only hope of salvation.[2] During April the daily distribution of bread declined until a ration of 4oz, sometimes supplemented by rice, became normal for the poor, and on 16 May this was reduced to 2oz. In these famine conditions, suicides and deaths from malnutrition became commonplace, and reports of illegal assemblies and an impending march on the assembly mounted daily. On 19 May a widely-circulated pamphlet in fact announced: 'The Insurrection of the People to obtain Bread and Reconquer their Rights'. This called first for Bread; but it also specified a political programme— the immediate release of all imprisoned patriots, the application of the Constitution of 1793 and the prompt convocation of a new legislature. Next day, on 20 May (1 Prairial) there began the last and perhaps the most remarkable of the great popular risings of the Revolution. From first light, drums called the people to arms throughout the old revolutionary faubourgs, Saint-Antoine and Saint-Marcel. Led, as in October 1789 by groups of women, crowds gradually gathered strength and converged upon the Tuileries until the assembly was besieged and its galleries packed with women crying repeatedly for bread. At the command of André Dumont, then acting as President in place of the elderly Vernier, these women were evicted by a few soldiers and some 'young men' armed with whips. As the galleries were being cleared, another part of the crowd burst into the chamber itself, having battered its doors open with a bench. These people, too, were hustled out, this time by a detachment of the National Guard from the Section of Grenelle. About an hour later, however, when the insurgents had been reinforced by the arrival of the three battalions of the National Guard from the Saint-Antoine Sections,[3] the people again broke into the hall. On this occasion shots were fired, and one deputy, Féraud, was killed.[4]

[1] The first of these commissions was established in Frimaire (Nov.–Dec. 1794); this abandoned its task on 15 March, and was replaced by a Commission of Seven on 30 March, after Thibaudeau had called for action on the 21st. The Commission of Eleven, which finally revised the constitution, replaced the Seven; it was created on 16 April and its members were named on the 18th.

[2] Soboul, *Précis d'histoire de la Révolution française*, p. 371, where Levasseur of the Sarthe is also quoted to the same effect.

[3] I.e., Quinze Vingts, Montreuil and Popincourt.

[4] Probably by accident. It was once supposed that he was killed deliberately, the people mistaking him for Fréron, and it is sometimes suggested that he was

1 Robespierre
from a lithograph by Delpech

2 The condemned 'Girondins' leaving the Palais de Justice after condemnation by the Revolutionary Tribunal, 31 October 1793

Although Boissy d'Anglas, who was now in the chair, did not abandon it even when Féraud's head, impaled on a pike, was waved before his eyes, complete tumult followed for about three hours, the uproar being so great that even the insurgents themselves could not effectively voice their own demands. Only at about seven o'clock in the evening did Vernier, having returned to the chair, persuade the people to clear a space so that the deputies could descend from the comparative safety of the higher tiers of benches in order to resume their function. Hedged in by the crowd, they had then to sanction a series of proposals made by a few Montagnards, including the release of imprisoned 'patriots' and the creation of an emergency Food Council. Ultimately these motions extended to the abolition of the Committee of General Security and its replacement by an extraordinary commission: but no sooner had four Montagnards been named as members of this commission than other deputies entered the hall at the head of detachments of the National Guard of the western Sections, notably that of Lepeletier. Since for some time past the people had been allowed to leave the hall, but prevented from re-entering it, there was little resistance; but only at midnight was the assembly free to see its secretaries burn the record of the Montagnards' decrees. At Thibaudeau's demand, the Montagnards who had most obviously compromised themselves were then denounced and arrested, as were others who were assumed to have been in conspiracy with them.[1]

Throughout the day the Governing Committees had been left at liberty to organise forces for the suppression of the rising, which—by accident or design[2]—was frustrated at the very moment when the reluctant

---

particularly disliked on account of responsibilities he had concerning the food supply of Paris. The probability is that he was particularly active in trying to protect the President of the Assembly, Boissy d'Anglas, and that he was shot in the general scuffle round the steps leading to the latter's chair.

[1] These being Duroy, Duquesnoy, Bourbotte and Prieur of the Marne, the four members of the commission; Soubrany, who had accepted command of the armed forces of Paris; four others who had been prominent in the debate and four others who were named as notable Terrorists in 1793–4.

[2] It has been alleged that this rising, too, could have been ended earlier had not the authorities allowed it to continue to tempt the Montagnards into committing themselves: see Mathiez, *La Réaction Thermidorienne*, pp. 250–2. According to Thiers (*The French Revolution*, Vol. II) the four members of the new commission were actually leaving the hall to assume authority when the government force entered. Compare Cobb and Rudé (Kaplow, op. cit., p. 271): 'the leaders of the majority, having let the Montagnards compromise themselves, were able to rally the loyal sections. . . .'

Montagnards had at last accepted the responsibility of supplanting the government. Still greater danger, however, had yet to be overcome. Early next morning, 21 May, the alarm bells rang again and an attempt was made to re-establish a committee of insurrection at the City Hall. In the afternoon a loyal force found that the Hall had been deserted, but it had soon to retire before the advancing battalions of the Faubourg Saint-Antoine, now marching fully armed and free from impeding crowds. Soon this insurgent army, reinforced as it marched by the contingents of central Paris, stood on the Place du Carrousel some 20,000 strong; and there it was confronted by the still more powerful military forces[1] mustered by the Convention, the 'good citizens' ready to oppose the 'rabble'. This was a situation without precedent in the Revolution, and for a while all trembled in the balance. The insurgents' cannon were loaded and trained on the Convention; the Convention's gendarmerie and gunners went over to the insurgent forces; and in the assembly the deputies waited in expectation of bombardment and assault.[2] Again, however, the insurrection petered out. Declaring themselves unwilling to shed blood or fail in their respect for the National Convention, the delegates of the people agreed to present their petition peacefully to the assembly, and their supporting battalions retired when the call for bread and the Constitution of 1793 had been answered with fair words and promises by Vernier.

As remarkable in their scale as in the determination shown by the insurgents, these two insurrections, like that of 12 Germinal, show clearly the fundamental weakness of the *sans-culottes*' movement. Without effective support from the Montagnards in the Convention, without the alliance of the Jacobin organisation, without even a City Council to capture and control, the *sans-culottes* were impotent. They might compel the parliament of the nation to agree to their demands, but they could never ensure that action ensued: after each transient triumph, their forces melted away and left the road clear for repression. This was now to be severe. On 22 May the forces of the Convention, commanded by General Menou and strongly reinforced by units of the regular army, surrounded the Faubourg Saint-Antoine. By the evening of the 23rd, the threat of assault and the pressure of public opinion compelled even

---

[1] These are estimated by Rudé to number 40,000 men (*The Crowd in the French Revolution*, p. 154); other estimates are still higher, as was that of Rovère, who wrote of 50,000 men apart from the *jeunesse dorée* (see Mathiez, op. cit., p. 253).

[2] 'Let us be calm and remain at our posts; nature has condemned us all to death, what matters it whether it be sooner or later.' (Legendre).

the most intransigent men in the local battalions to submit: the barricades were dismantled and the Faubourg surrendered all its arms and cannon.[1] In defiance of all precedent, a military commission was then established to deal summarily with the principal 'rebels', and in the next few weeks this tried 149 people, of whom 36 were condemned to death.[2] At the same time the destruction of the Montagnards was completed, the Convention eventually authorising the arrest of more than 40 deputies. Robert Lindet and Jeanbon Saint-André,[3] once members of the great Committee of Public Safety, were amongst those proscribed, and even Carnot was only saved by the intervention of a deputy who cried out: 'He organised victory!' The second anniversary of the Revolution of 31 May was then marked by the abolition of the Revolutionary Tribunal and by the establishment of a new day of festival. As Thibaudeau saw it, this was the final triumph of virtue over the crime which had killed such men as Vergniaud in 1793.[4]

Public passion, however, was not as easily placated as Thibaudeau wished. At the invitation of the Convention, the General Assemblies of the Sections met daily from 24 May until they were satisfied that their 'bad citizens' were either imprisoned or disarmed. Since nearly all the Sections were now dominated by 'decent people', the reaction had free rein, and it is likely that in addition to the 2–3,000 arrests ordered by the government, the Sections disarmed some 1,700 *sans-culottes* and committed about 1,200 others to prison without trial or specific sentence.[5] Moreover, to deprive the capital of further revolutionary potential, all the Sections were encouraged to give up their cherished cannon, and the poor were for all practical purposes excluded from the ranks of the

---

[1] Earlier on the 23rd a mixed force of 'young men', National Guards and dragoons had entered the Faubourg; this force, however, was surrounded in the street and compelled to retire ignominiously. Conversely, the surrendering of the cannon was highly humiliating to the whole district, these hand-drawn weapons being the pride of élite detachments of the local battalions.

[2] The use of military commissions had hitherto been restricted to areas of open civil war and to crimes committed by soldiers; indeed, 18 of those condemned even by this tribunal were gendarmes who had defected to the insurgents on 21 May. The commission which tried the *sans-culottes* of Toulon (*above*, p. 49) was established a few days later, on May 27.

[3] *Biog. Notes:* SAINT-ANDRÉ.

[4] Thibaudeau, *Mémoires*, Vol. I, p. 171.

[5] Tonnesson, K. D., *La Défaite des Sans-culottes* (Paris, 1959), p. 339, and Hampson, N., *A Social History of the French Revolution* (London, 1963), p. 245. Rudé (*The Crowd in the French Revolution*, p. 156), referring to the figure of 10,000 prescribed given in the *Gazette française* of 28 May, says 'the eventual total of arrested and disarmed must have been considerably larger. . . .'

National Guard.[1] Before the end of August 1795, too, the National Guard was placed under the orders of a military committee, the old gendarmerie was replaced by a new Police Legion and the administration of the police was entrusted to a commission of three men. All this foreshadowed the imperial system for the control of the capital later developed by Bonaparte.

Like Thermidor ten months before, the repression which followed the rising of Prairial is often regarded as the ending of the Revolution. As Professor Soboul has it, the defeat of the insurrection eliminated the people from the political scene and destroyed the popular hope of an egalitarian social democracy; thereafter 'the bourgeois rule of the notables began'.[2] Even if the events of May 1795 are seen more as the culmination of a process which began early in 1794, they undoubtedly mark the final stage in the destruction of the social-democratic movement in the Revolution: henceforth there would be no comparable movement, but only conspiracy.[3] The despair of the Montagnards is symbolised by the fate of the six deputies who were tried by the military commission for their part in the belated attempt by the Mountain to assume power on the night of 20 May: condemned to death, they stabbed themselves in succession as they descended the steps from the courtroom.[4] As for the *sans-culottes*, who had been abandoned by the Revolutionary Government in 1794 and isolated after Thermidor by the dispersal of the Jacobins, they were now bereft even of the leadership of the most active and vigorous of the men of their own kind. Those who were imprisoned or disarmed after Prairial were exposed for the rest of their lives to preventive arrest whenever any crisis threatened.[5] This extended repression ensured that the masses of Paris did not rise in arms against the government until more than 50 years had passed: but it also eventually bred a new type of professional prison-trained conspirator.

[1] They were, amongst other things, 'excused from service'. Moreover, while respectable citizens were allowed to retain their muskets, the pike, that supreme symbol of men's equality in patriotic citizenship, had now to be returned to the store. See Tonnesson, op. cit., pp. 343–4.

[2] Soboul, A., *Précis d'histoire de la Révolution française*, p. 376.

[3] Professor I. Woloch—*Jacobin Legacy: The Democratic Movement under the Directory* (Princeton, 1970)—considers that 'the disappearance of *sans-culottism* as an autonomous movement' resolved a fundamental ambiguity in Jacobinism and enabled middle-class democrats to welcome 'the *sans-culottes*' (*sic*) as participants and followers in revived Jacobin activity under the Directory (p. 20).

[4] Romme, Goujon and Duquesnoy succeeded in killing themselves; Duroy, Bourbette and Soubrany were executed despite their wounds.

[5] R. Cobb, 'Note sur la répression contre le personnel sans-culotte de 1795 à 1801, *Annales historiques de la Révolution française* (t. XXVI, 1954), pp. 23–49.

Thus in the sense that political and social power remained in the hands of men of position and property, the days of Prairial were indeed decisive. This, however, was by no means as clear at the time as it has since become. Fear of a revival of the Terror was, indeed, to remain for years a lively and ever-present anxiety to those who experienced and suffered it. Moreover, if the republicans of the centre had at least temporarily mastered the popular movement, they had had to rely on very discreditable allies to do it, and the danger of unrestricted reaction was consequently greater than ever. To those who regarded themselves as the true republicans, the Revolution would not be over until the danger from the Right had also been warded off. Only then could the period of emergency be ended by the establishment of legitimate constitutional government.

3. The Achievement of the Constitution, May-October 1795

In the late spring and early summer of 1795 the Thermidorians were still gradually substituting free institutions and procedures for those of the Terror. On 12 June, indeed, a brief but significant decree forbade any public authority to designate itself 'Revolutionary'; the remaining 'revolutionary committees' were in future to be known only as 'watch committees'. This process of gradual change, however, inevitably caused a great deal of administrative confusion, particularly after the departmental and district councils had been reinvested on 17 April with the powers of which they had been deprived by the 'Constitution of the Terror' in December 1793.[1] In the circumstances of the time, too, freedom could easily lead to new forms of retaliatory terrorism, as it had already done in the south-east. On the other hand, the 'Constitution of the Terror', eroded though it was, still remained the basis of government for the Republic. At root, all was still provisional. Public officers and councils were still nominated, not elected. The Convention still sent deputies armed with emergency powers to points of danger, and in the south-east some of these in fact outdid the reactionaries by trying to lead a sort of legalised White Terror. In Paris itself, the rising of Prairial and the ensuing repression of the *sans-culottes* similarly showed very clearly that if the position of government was highly precarious, its powers were still fundamentally arbitrary.

After Prairial, however, the endeavour to formulate a final constitution for the Republic began to take precedence over the process of piecemeal change. Freed at least temporarily from the threat of insurrection, the Convention was now more conscious than ever of the nation's need for an established law and an enduring form of government.

Some historians have indeed asserted that immediately after the rising in Prairial the assembly was so dominated by the Right that a royalist

---

[1] P. Mautouchet, *Le Gouvernement Révolutionnaire* (Paris, 1912), pp. 367, 372; see also pp. 361, 371, 375.

triumph was rapidly approaching.[1] This is, of course, in large part a matter of conjecture. If, as seems likely enough, there were many deputies who would have welcomed a return to constitutional monarchy, given sufficient safeguards, there were clearly very few upon whom even the most optimistic royalists could confidently count to promote it. Moreover, the measures which are alleged to mark the 'fever of reaction' would seem in reality to be no more than further examples of the assembly's desire to make the Republic as free and as just a society as it could. Apart from the disarmament and imprisonment of 'terrorists'— whom the Committee of General Security and the local authorities began to release in mid-June wherever offences against common law were not involved[2]—the two measures principally in question were the re-establishment of freedom of worship and the compensation of relatives of victims of the Terror.[3] At the end of May, Lanjuinais—who is sometimes called a royalist, but would be better recognised as a courageous moderate and a sincere Catholic—persuaded the Convention to approve the opening of all available churches for public worship as well as for the ceremonies of the *décadi*, the only proviso being that priests should submit to the laws of the Republic. Then on 5 June Boissy d'Anglas, whose political position was closely akin to that of Lanjuinais, introduced a decree (drafted in committee) by which compensation would be paid to the relatives of those victims of the Terror whose property had been confiscated at the time of their execution—a concession which could hardly be withheld at a time when the 'terrorists' were themselves in prison.

As had happened before, however, both these measures were exploited by the royalists. The delight of the 'Constitutional' clergy in the reopening of the churches was matched by that of avowed opponents of the Revolution, and it was not in fact long before 'refractory' Catholic priests were openly officiating at services and consciously or unconsciously promoting the royalist cause. This was certainly not Lanjuinais' intention: rather had he hoped that the religious freedom of the *simultaneum* would help to reconcile all Catholics to the Republic. Similarly, the granting of compensation to the victims of the Terror at once stimulated a demand in the rapidly-expanding royalist press for the payment of comparable compensation to the families of *émigrés*, and this

---

[1] E.g., A. Mathiez, *La Réaction Thermidorienne* (Paris, 1929), p. 259.

[2] G. Lefebvre, *The Thermidorians* (trans. R. Baldick, London, 1965), pp. 125, 153. It should be said that much more of the present chapter than can be explicitly acknowledged is derived from the work of Lefebvre.

[3] Mathiez, op. cit., pp. 260–6.

in turn implied the recall of all royalists to France. In all probability, developments such as these would soon have alarmed even deputies of royalist sympathies and made a reconciliation amongst constitutionalists of all parties unlikely. Certainly a semi-official article published on 6 June forcefully repudiated rumours that a renunciation of republicanism was imminent:

> Because the Convention has won a great victory over the terrorists, the successors of Robespierre, it would appear that nothing remains for it but to proclaim the monarchy ... No! The national representatives cannot share in these criminal intentions ... (They) will not betray the confidence of virtuous citizens, who detest equally the arbitrary, perfidious and deceitful government of a single man, and the bloody anarchy of an unreasoning, unenlightened and unbridled mob.[1]

At this point, moreover, the hopes of the more moderate royalists were blighted by death. Ever since August 1792 the nine year old son of Louis XVI and Marie Antoinette had been held a closely-guarded prisoner in the grim tower of the Temple, and while he lived it was always possible that he might be restored as a constitutional prince with a Council of Regency made up of respected liberals, whether 'royalist' or 'republican'. On or about 8 June, however, the boy perished miserably in prison. Although stories were at once put about—and have ever since continued—that 'Louis XVII' had in reality succeeded in escaping, the fact is not in doubt: rather is it remarkable that the child, bereaved and brutalised, should have survived so long.

As a recent historian of French Royalism has written, this event 'fatally embarrassed' projects for a reconciliation between the nation and its traditional kingship.[2] Henceforth there could be no king but Louis XVI's brother, the exiled Count of Provence, who at once assumed the title of Louis XVIII; nor could the heir to the throne be anyone save his brother, Charles, Count of Artois. In consequence, the loyalties of all but the most intransigent, or blindly faithful, royalists were to remain distressingly divided, for neither prince could yet countenance any real compromise with the Revolution. The Declaration of Verona, which Louis issued on 24 June, is itself indicative of the abyss which separated the constitutional royalists within France from their king and his fellow exiles. To Louis, this document was moderate and conciliatory, for in

---

[1] A. Mathiez, *After Robespierre: The Thermidorian Reaction* (trans. C. A. Phillips, New York, 1965), p. 222.

[2] W. R. Fryer, *Republic or Restoration in France? 1794–7* (Manchester, 1965), p. 17.

it he promised forgiveness to all save regicides and terrorists, recognised the availability of all offices to all Frenchmen, and undertook to rule France in accordance with its 'ancient and venerable Constitution'. To many potential moderate monarchists, however, this seemed but to say that the *ancien régime* was to be restored with no more than minimal concessions to paternalism and the thinking of the old aristocracy. To promise that no new taxation would be imposed without the consent of an Estates-General was little short of ludicrous in 1795. Of the vitally important question of the lands that had been sold and re-sold since 1789, the Declaration said nothing, though Louis' insistence on the re-establishment of religious worship implied a great deal; and the promise that abuses would be met and rectified was clearly conditional upon 'the restoration of the royal authority to the plenitude of its rights'. The Declaration in short repudiated despotism only to insist upon the recognition of divine hereditary right, and it assumed that all the achievements of the Revolution could be casually cast away.[1] The practical consequence was that the great majority of French royalists remained isolated and impotent between the absolutism of the old order and the republicanism of the new. As Mallet du Pan wrote, their only consolation was the promise that they were not to be hanged[2]—and even that concession was one which many of the more frenzied of the *émigrés* would certainly have denied them.

If after this anyone retained any illusions about the possibilities of some swift compromise between royalist and republican moderates, these were promptly to be shattered, for in pursuance of the *émigrés'* lunatic determination to recover their inheritance by force of arms the advance-guard of an expeditionary force had already been landed in Brittany. Moreover, although this was not fully realised at the time, this invasion was but part of an elaborate plan for the reconquest of France from east and west simultaneously. As Wickham, the British agent at Berne, saw it, the Austrians were to initiate an advance through Savoy to Lyons; the triumph of counter-revolution at Lyons would then lead to an uprising in Franche-Comté, which in turn would enable the *émigrés* under the prince de Condé[3] to advance across the Rhine. The

[1] Ibid., pp. 13–15; F. A. Aulard, *A Political History of the French Revolution* (London, 1910), Vol. III, p. 249.

[2] Cited by Fryer, op. cit., p. 16.

[3] Louis Joseph de Bourbon, prince de Condé (1736–1818): The cousin of Louis XVI and the grandfather of the ill-fated duc d'Enghien, Condé emigrated immediately after the fall of the Bastille and, after a period at Turin, became the organiser and leader of the *émigré* army in the Rhineland. When this force was finally disbanded in 1801 the prince retired to England.

activities of numerous royalist cells throughout France—including those of the Secret Agency established in Paris—would also distract the republicans, and in the west a second royalist army would disembark from British ships as the *chouans* and Vendéans rose again in their support.[1]

Needless to say, much of this plan remained a pipe-dream, a vast deal of British gold disappearing uselessly into the pockets of obscure but imaginative secret agents. On this occasion, however, something of substance had been achieved by the counter-revolutionaries, and for four weeks after the Declaration of Verona the situation of the Republic seemed critical. Lyons, as the deputy Chénier told the Convention on 24 June, was recognisably a focal point of royalism and an abiding threat to the Republic. Further, some of the sums expended by Wickham had found their way into the ready hands of the new commander of the French Army of the Rhine, General Pichegru.[2] Lionised as the conqueror of Holland, this spendthrift young general was now disgruntled by the evil conditions which prevailed in his ill-supplied army; perhaps, too, his experiences in Paris in Germinal had served to disillusion him about the merits of republicanism. At any rate, from 23 May onwards he was at least sufficiently disaffected to receive visits and money from Condé's agents and to assure them of his own good intentions.[3] More important still, in April Count Puisaye had at last succeeded in persuading the British Government to finance and convey to France a force of some 12,000 men, both French royalists and released prisoners-of-war. When at the end of June this expedition made its way to the peninsula of Quiberon, on the southern coast of Brittany, the *chouans* were in fact already in the field against the army of Hoche.

If in 1793, when France was ringed with foes and rent by civil war, plans like these had received even the half-hearted help that the British were now giving, the counter-revolution might perhaps have been successful. In 1795, however, the allied coalition had crumbled, and despite political instability and economic disaster the Republic had become the predominant power in western Europe. After the great victories of the early summer of 1794, the French forces had continued to advance more gradually during the rest of the year. The various armies of the Republic had occupied Holland, pushed the Austrians back across the Rhine, invaded the Palatinate, attained the lesser passes of the Alps (Mount Cenis and the Little St Bernard) and advanced into Spain on

---

[1] H. Mitchell, *The Underground War against Revolutionary France* (Oxford, 1965), pp. 51–64. For the activities of the Paris Agency, *see also* p. 69ff.

[2] *Biog. Notes:* PICHEGRU.

[3] Mitchell, op. cit., pp. 62–3.

both sides of the Pyrenees. The King of Prussia, always primarily interested in the partition of Poland, had then withdrawn his forces from the war: negotiations for peace, begun in November 1794, were concluded by the Treaty of Basle on 5 April 1795. The Dutch, despite their newly-established republic, had no alternative but to accept the stringent terms of the Treaty of the Hague on 16 May, and negotiations with Spain were soon to be resolved at Basle on 22 July. Since lesser states like Tuscany—whose duke was in fact the first of the allied rulers to recognise the French Republic[1]—had also made their peace, only Britain and Austria remained effectively at war with France at the time of Louis XVIII's 'accession'.

In practice neither of these two powers had sufficient confidence in the *émigrés* to risk much in their support. Indeed, neither was even prepared to recognise Louis as King of France, since to do so would be to destroy whatever chance there was of negotiation with French moderates. In consequence the projected assault upon the Republic from the east proved a mirage. There was no advance through Savoy. Franche-Comté remained quiescent, and Pichegru naturally did nothing. In the west, however, the British at least compromised: if they did not commit their own forces in support of the *émigrés*' cause, they did enable them to land in France in strength. Lord Bridport's fleet first penned Admiral Villaret-Joyeuse's ships into Lorient, and then covered the disembarkation of the royalist army, together with an immense quantity of stores, near Carnac on 27 June and 15 July.

Although *chouan* bands had seized Auray, which commanded the approaches to the Quiberon penninsula by land, and Charette[2] had at once resumed the war in the Vendée, the royalists soon lost the initiative. Disputes—possibly stimulated by the Paris Agency in order to discredit the constitutionalist Puisaye—paralysed their command during the first few vital days, and Hoche, who had known since the end of May that a landing was imminent in the area, soon appeared with forces strong enough to brush the *chouans* aside. The republicans then constructed earthworks across the neck of the peninsula, enclosing the royalists, as Hoche reported to the Convention, like rats in a trap. After successfully repulsing two attempts by the invaders to break through these lines, the republicans in their turn then advanced under cover of a storm on the night of 20 July. Aided by the defection of some of the French whom the *émigrés* had pressed into service from the British prison hulks, they first captured the Fort de Penthièvre and then swept forward to the end of

[1] On 10 February 1795.
[2] *Biog. Notes:* CHARETTE.

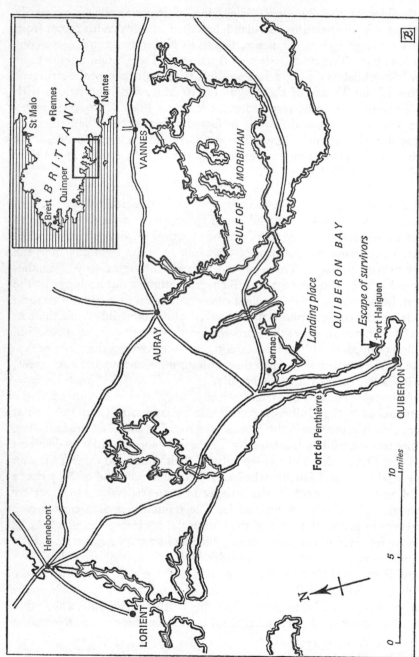

The Landings at Quiberon, June–July 1795

the peninsula on the morning of 21 July. While some of the royalists, including Puisaye, managed to regain the ships, the majority—pressed prisoners-of-war, *chouans* and about a thousand *émigrés*—fell into the hands of the Republic.

Although the Convention had only recently repealed the law of 27 March 1793 by which rebels found under arms were outlawed, this being described as 'one of the means used by tyranny to establish the terror',[1] it had responded to the renewal of the *chouans*' activities in May by decreeing on 18 June that all such rebels would be condemned to death. In consequence of this and of the existing penal legislation against all *émigrés*, military commissions tried the captives. The pressed men were almost all acquitted, as were about a third of the *chouans*; but 748 of the *émigrés*, including Sombreuil, one of the commanding officers, and Mgr de Hercé, the Bishop of Dol, were shot. Since Hoche himself, and both Tallien and Blad, the two deputies whom the Convention had ordered to the scene of the invasion, explicitly denied that any formal terms of capitulation had ever been offered to those who surrendered, it has been argued that these executions were justified by the laws of war as well by those of the Republic. Some, too, suggest that Blad, who had responsibility after Hoche and Tallien had left the scene, was right in supposing that military necessity dictated severity, the republican army being encamped in hostile territory and in danger of attack.[2] Whatever may be thought about this, or about the fact that Charette promptly retaliated by massacring all the republicans he had captured, it was— and is—evident that the ruthlessness of the Revolution towards royalists had not diminished perceptibly since 1793.

The King in whose name these *émigrés* fought and died in Brittany remained remote from their enterprise; the part played by his brother Artois, who landed belatedly in the Ile d'Yeu on 30 September and returned to England a month later, was at best trivial. The royalist cause was nevertheless profoundly compromised by the fact that these princes and their supporters had again unleashed violence in France. Time after time Mallet du Pan had warned the emigrant courts that an unconditional restoration of the *ancien régime* was inconceivable, and that to associate the monarchy with civil war and with hated foreign enemies was the height of folly. After Quiberon he could only report that no one 'had dared to speak of royalty when the *émigrés* in alliance with the English were advocating it in Brittany with arms in their hands'.[3]

[1] Mautouchet, op. cit., p. 366.
[2] Mathiez, op. cit., p. 279; Lefebvre, *Thermidorians*, p. 149.
[3] Fryer, op. cit., p. 39, n. 1.

Although Charette's men remained in arms and guerilla warfare dragged on in the west, the principal result of the landing at Quiberon was a resurgence of revolutionary fervour throughout France. Even before the landing took place an alarmed Convention had at last intervened to check the White Terror in the Rhône Valley by suspending the local authorities in Lyons and disarming the National Guard there.

In Paris, too, the end of June saw the beginning of the 'war of the black collars', in which soldiers and *sans-culottes* together began to harass the *jeunesse dorée*, clipping the hair and soiling the clothes of all whom they could catch.

During the period of the emergency the Convention finally washed its hands of these affected hooligans, a number of whom were successfully rounded up for military service. On the anniversary of 14 July the playing of the Marseillaise in the Convention symbolised the sterner spirit prevailing in the assembly, and in that month, as the release of imprisoned 'terrorists' continued, something was done to curb the right-wing press and to subsidise such republican papers as Louvet's *Sentinelle*.

Although all this hardly amounts to the 'decisive change of policy' which Mathiez called it,[1] it is convincing evidence that in July 1795, when proposals for a new constitution were under discussion, the deputies in the Convention were less inclined than ever to countenance royalism or any other form of extreme right-wing reaction. Rather did they expect those who were associated with constitutional monarchism to abandon the King and his *émigrés* and to rally to a constitutional republic. As Doulcet de Pontécoulant somewhat dramatically cried in the Convention on 1 July: 'Republicans, Anglomaniacs of '89, Constitutionalists of '91, the same fate awaits you, the same flag must unite you; march all together to exterminate those who have no other desire but that of vengeance!'[2] In reality, the position of the constitutional royalists in France could hardly have been more embarrassing: horrified by the slaughter of the captured royalists, who were themselves Frenchmen with friends and relatives in France, they were also as hostile as any republican to the armed invasion of their country. In the circumstances those deputies who sympathised with these feelings had no alternative but to support the more convinced republicans of the centre in establishing a conservative Republic.

The Constitution which was to be the legal foundation of that Repub-

[1] Mathiez, op. cit., pp. 280–1.
[2] Ibid., p. 272. The term 'Anglomaniacs' refers to those deputies who were said in 1789 to favour a constitution similar to that of Britain.

lic was long and elaborate.[1] Prepared during May and June by the Commission of Eleven appointed shortly after the rising of Germinal, and debated at length in the Convention in the weeks between 4 July and 22 August, it was filled with clauses intended to safeguard the future against particular abuses characteristic of the Terror and the more recent past. The significance of the Constitution of 1795 was nevertheless far greater than the sum of its clauses, a point which the marxist historians who condemn it as typically 'bourgeois' tend to forget. In contrast to the monarchical Constitution of 1791, which was for a while regarded with almost religious reverence, that of 1795 was commonly admitted to be imperfect.[2] In contrast to that of 1793, 'the constitution of anarchy' which it was designed to supersede, it was avowedly hostile to democratic and socialist ideas; but this much-laboured comparison is somewhat academic, for no matter what it may have represented, the Constitution of 1793 had not become operative. The men of 1795, mindful of the fact that there had never been any form of lawful republican government in France, were above all concerned to create one which could be put into immediate effect. Sickened by provisional régimes and arbitrary authority, of Terror and counter-terror, of 'royalism' and 'anarchy', they had come to see constitutional government as the sole hope of salvation for the Republic.[3]

The members of the Commission which drafted the Constitution were moderate men,[4] and they were of course profoundly influenced both by their past experiences and by the democratic storm which had so nearly destroyed parliamentary government during their deliberations in Prairial. Their Republic indeed retained the fundamental features of the Revolution—the abolition of privilege, the guarantees of personal freedom, the independence of the judiciary, the public responsibility of officials, and the control of local and national affairs by elected officers

[1] Printed in English in J. H. Stewart, *A Documentary Survey of the French Revolution* (New York, 1951), pp. 572–612. See also Aulard, *A Political History*, Vol. III, chapter 7.

[2] But compare references to the contrary in R. Guyot, 'Du Directoire au Consultat', *Revue historique*, Vol. CXI (1912), p. 1.

[3] See, for example, Thibaudeau, op. cit., Vol. I, p. 173ff; Durand de Maillane, *Histoire de la Convention nationale* (Paris, 1825), p. 277.

[4] According to Thibaudeau (op. cit., p. 179) 3 members of the Commission of Eleven were royalist in sympathy, and various historians (e.g. A. Mathiez, *La Réaction Thermidorienne* (Paris, 1929;) translated as *After Robespierre* (New York, 1965), p. 236) extend this proportion. This does not, however, appear to have had much practical effect on the Constitution, which was particularly the work of the republican Daunou; nor is the term 'moderate' here used as one of contempt.

and assemblies; but they made every effort to preserve it from the evils they associated with popular sovereignty and the dictatorship of a man or a committee. A Declaration of Rights and Duties restricted the meaning of equality to the absence of any distinctions based on birth, the law being the same for all, and it asserted the sanctity of property right as the foundation of 'the entire social order'. The Constitution itself then similarly related effective political power to the possession of substantial property. The franchise was liberal, extending to all male taxpayers over 21 years of age and resident in France for 12 years; but a process of indirect election restricted the effect of this considerably. Not only had electors at the second level to meet the same high property qualification that had been required in 1791, but the primary assemblies could only choose one elector for every 200 citizens, in place of the 100 of 1791. In consequence, the final voice in elections fell to some 30,000 people, these being only a proportion even of the local notabilities who met the property qualification.

This system, which has been severely criticised by some historians as an undemocratic device designed to perpetuate the rule of the rich, has been seen by others as providing a foundation on which a more broadly-based democracy might have developed. As Madame de Staël was to write in 1799, 'The Constitution can be made more democratic as people become more public-spirited'.[1] At the time, however, few people would have gone even so far as that. Democracy in the sense of universal suffrage and popular political power was something men had learned to abhor as synonymous with the exercise of arbitrary authority by some organised political minority, and as such it was regarded as the antithesis of true liberty. Rejecting it with hardly a dissenting voice,[2] the Convention turned instead to an effort to ensure that the old aristocracy of birth should be replaced by a real aristocracy of wealth and talent. As the spokesman of the Commission of Eleven, Boissy d'Anglas, put it in introducing their report on 23 June: 'We ought to be governed by the best elements among us. The best are the most educated and those most interested in the maintenance of the laws. Now, with very few exceptions, you will find such men only amongst those possessing property.'[3]

---

[1] Madame de Staël, *Des Circonstances actuelles qui peuvent terminer la Révolution* (ed. J. Viénot, Paris, 1906), cited by J. Godechot, *La Pensée Révolutionnaire 1780–1799* (Paris, A. Colin, 1964), p. 286. The Constitution itself included provision for the extension of the franchise to the literate after 1804. (Title II, Cl. 16).

[2] Aulard, *A Political History*, Vol. III, pp. 279n., 281–2.

[3] Cited, for example, by Mathiez, op. cit., p. 237.

If today this identification of wealth with wisdom seems either naive or narrow-minded, it may be recalled that Boissy d'Anglas had presided over the Convention of 1 Prairial and had had the newly-severed head of Féraud waved before his eyes. After six years of Revolution, it was the maintenance of law which seemed all-important, and to liberally-minded men real democracy meant above all the rule of law. As Thibaudeau had said on 21 March: 'I know of only one democratic Constitution: it is that which would offer the people liberty, equality, and the peaceful enjoyment of its rights'.[1]

The Constitution-makers were equally concerned to safeguard the hard-won freedom of Frenchmen by diffusing political power as widely as possible. Their Declaration of Rights laid down as a fundamental principle: 'The social guarantee cannot exist if the separation of powers is not established, if their limits are not determined'; and in the Constitution precise provisions were made for the application of this principle. In order to avoid the dictatorship of any legislative committee, the national parliament or Legislative Body was to consist of two houses. One, a Council of Five Hundred, would be responsible for proposing laws and taxation; the other, a Council of Elders numbering 250, would either reject these proposals or give them the force of law, there being no possibility of amendment. To guard also against any personal dictatorship, the executive power was to be held by five Directors simultaneously, these being elected by the Legislative Body. Further, the Treasury as well as the judiciary were to remain independent; all communication between the two Councils, and between them and the Directors, was to be conveyed in writing by messengers; and both the Legislative Body and the Directors were to be subject to partial annual re-election—the deputies retiring by one third in annual rotation, and one Director retiring each year in accordance with the outcome of a draw.

In retrospect it is not difficult to decry these stipulations. Annual elections are not conducive to stability in government, nor does the strict separation of powers produce harmony and strength of purpose amongst the leaders of a nation. The carefully thought-out checks and balances, the devices intended to ensure that there would be gradualness in all things, these may now be seen as far more appropriate to a united people in times of peace than to a deeply-divided nation which was still involved in war. But although their Constitution was framed at a time of insurrection and debated during a period of invasion, the men of the day still had faith in regulated freedom, as well as boundless belief in institutions. The most serious defect of the Constitution of 1795 was,

---

[1] Aulard, op. cit., p. 272.

indeed, the provision which was most characteristic of their determination to establish a law that would not be lightly altered. Understandably reluctant to trust the unknown men of the future with too much freedom of action, they made their Constitution so rigid that nine years would have to elapse before it could be legally revised in any respect.

Accepted by the Convention on 22 August, this Constitution was then submitted to France for approval by plebiscite. Although in practice priests, nobles and all prominent local 'terrorists' were disenfranchised, the voting in this (as in the elections which ensued) was by universal suffrage, and the national verdict announced at the end of September showed that the Constitution had been accepted by 1,057,390 votes to 49,978.[1] To some unkind historians, this result seems only to show that France was determined at all costs to rid itself of the Convention, doubly discredited as that assembly was by the ruthlessness of the Revolutionary Government in 1794 and by the approach of anarchy in 1795. Disillusionment of this kind no doubt contributed to the decision, but it can hardly account for it: rather does the size of the majority suggest a general desire for stability and tranquillity under an established law. If the great majority of Frenchmen were countrymen, more royalist than republican in sentiment, the material interests of peasants and townsmen alike were at this time inseparable from the survival of the Republic, and to all but a few a constitutional Republic was infinitely preferable to the illegitimacy implicit in any revolutionary régime. Partly for this reason, and partly in consequence of the disillusionment and suppression of the *sans-culottes*, the abandonment of popular democracy appears to have passed almost unremarked.[2] As for the constitutional royalists, these seem to have been happy to approve the Constitution, being convinced that their cause would be greatly benefited by the free election of a new parliament.[3]

The Convention, however, was well aware of this possibility and was fully determined to avoid it. Asserting on 18 August that the election of an entirely new legislature would mean that the Constitution would be violated within six months, one member of the Commission of Eleven, Baudin of the Ardennes, asked the vital question: 'Into whose hands is

[1] The total electorate being estimated at over six millions (J. Godechot, *Les Institutions de la France sous la Révolution et l'Empire* (Paris, P.U.F. 1951), p. 252), it is clear that there was, as Soboul says, 'massive abstention' (A. Soboul, *Précis d'Histoire de la Révolution Française* (Paris, 1962), p. 398). The plebiscite about the Constitution of 1793 had, however, only been approved by comparable figures: 1,801,918 to 11,610.

[2] Aulard, *A Political History*, Vol. III, p. 284.

[3] Mathiez, op. cit., p. 245.

the sacred trust of the Constitution to be placed?'[1] Deeply impressed by the example of 1791[2]—when the National Assembly had accompanied its Constitution by a self-denying ordinance disqualifying its deputies from the first Legislative Assembly, and a new revolution had followed within a year—the Convention on 22 August accepted Baudin's proposal that no less than two-thirds of the first Legislative Body should be elected from its own ranks. Since the Constitution itself provided that the Legislative Body was to be renewed annually by one third, this supplementary decree meant that three years would elapse before a completely new parliament could come into existence. In the meanwhile, the men of the Convention, who were assumed to be committed to the Republic and who were indisputably experienced in the ways of revolution, could continue to exercise a controlling influence upon developments.

Although the names of a good many deputies in the Convention—men, like Fréron, who had succeeded in living through and even leading the Terror and the Reaction alike—have become synonymous with unscrupulous opportunism, there were many others who sincerely believed that the two-thirds device was an essential means of protecting the Republic in its first formative years. As will appear, they were indeed quite correct in anticipating that the opponents of the Republic would persistently endeavour to dominate the successive elections to the new parliament. The outcry against the decree was nevertheless furious. The royalists, thwarted in their hopes of an immediate victory at the polls, were of course enraged. As the Count of Vaublanc, one of the many émigrés who had returned to France since Thermidor, wrote later in life: 'This decree sickened the whole of France'.[3] Many who were not royalists, however, were equally resentful of the drastic restriction imposed on their freedom to elect representatives of their own choice, a restriction which was regarded as an infringement of the principle of the sovereignty of the people. Beyond this, too, there was undoubtedly

---

[1] G. Lefebvre, *The Thermidorians* (trans. R. Baldick, London, 1965), p. 169.

[2] Durand de Maillane, *Histoire de la Convention nationale*, p. 288; Thibaudeau, op. cit., Vol. I, p. 187.

[3] *Mémoires de M. le comte de Vaublanc* (ed. Barrière, Paris 1857), p. 302. The career of Vincent Marie Vienot, comte de Vaublanc (1765–1845) reflects much of the Revolution. A right-wing deputy in the Legislative Assembly, he went into hiding after the fall of the monarchy, but returned to Paris after Thermidor. Condemned to death for his part in the Vendémiaire rising, he was able to take a seat in the Legislative Body in 1797, only to be proscribed as a royalist at 18 Fructidor (Sept., 1797). Returning to France in 1800, he again became a deputy, and was a Prefect in 1805.

general anxiety lest the Convention, in perpetuating its power, really planned to renew and perpetuate the Terror. As Vaublanc also recorded, 'The horrible tyranny with which the assembly had crushed France was in every mind'.

The agitation which ensued, and which eventually culminated in an armed attack upon the Convention on the day of 13 Vendémiaire (5 October 1795), is commonly described as 'royalist', although of late historians have been more inclined to emphasise its socially conservative character. While closer consideration may suggest that neither of these interpretations is wholly satisfactory in itself, the movement was clearly very different in both leadership and composition from previous Parisian insurrections. As we have seen, since the fall of Robespierre in 1794, and still more since the great popular uprising in Prairial, the active leaders of the poor had been persecuted and oppressed. Once proud to bear arms as patriotic *sans-culottes*, they were now cursed as 'terrorists', deprived of the right to carry arms,[1] excluded from public employment, and prevented from attending the General Assemblies of their Sections. Many, indeed, were still in the prisons to which they had been consigned after Prairial. On the other hand, the more prosperous and better-educated people, who had gradually returned to the Sectional assemblies since Thermidor, were now predominant in them, particularly in the wealthier districts of western Paris. As the royalist journalist Lacretelle put it: 'The well-to-do succeeded to the power of the multitude, and called themselves "the people" in their turn'.[2]

By the late summer of 1795, too, the leadership of this middle-class resurgence was in several Sections, and particularly in the wealthy Lepeletier Section to the north of the Palais Royal, in the hands of avowed constitutional monarchists. Deeply divided amongst themselves, lacking leadership and organisation alike, these men have been described by one modern authority as 'an army, or rather a mob, of individuals, united (only) in a common negative aim.'[3] Since they could not in practice have given their whole-hearted support to a king who had repudiated constitutional monarchy, that aim was simply the destruction of the Republic which they hated and despised, and their irresponsibility

---

[1] Not by legislation alone, but also by various forms of pressure in the Sections themselves. See Note 2 to p. 78 above and K. D. Tonnesson, *La Défaite des Sans-culottes* (Paris, 1959), pp. 343–4.

[2] C. Lacretelle, *Dix années d'épreuves pendant la Révolution* (Paris, 1842), p. 247. See also G. Rudé, *The Crowd in the French Revolution* (Oxford, 1960), pp. 143, 166.

[3] Fryer, op. cit., p. 42.

in fact anticipated that right-wing wrecking policy which was so often to be the plague of later political life in France. Louis XVIII, for his part, would have no truck with them, and even ordered his agents in Paris to do everything possible to thwart their plans.[1] Their number, however, included several unusually able journalists, and these had no difficulty in exploiting the anger and anxiety aroused amongst republicans by the Two-Thirds Decree. The deputies were in consequence universally represented as self-seeking placemen whose only desire was to perpetuate their own monopoly of power—a point of view still reflected in modern writing on the subject.

Much might in fact be said for the view that the real fault of the deputies at this time lay in their failure to have sufficient confidence in the electorate. Through an exaggerated, if understandable, fear of insurrection, they themselves did much to foment it. Whatever may be thought about the wisdom or folly of the Two-Thirds Decree itself, the precautions which were taken against royalism as the plebiscite approached were certainly excessive. The Convention clearly attempted to influence the outcome of the vote by renewing existing legislation against priests and *émigrés*, while at the same time relaxing the laws which prevented 'terrorists' from voting. Further, it ordered units of the regular army into the suburbs of Paris, and detachments were soon to be seen in the principal streets. Although in practice the Sections of Paris admitted or excluded people from the poll more or less as they pleased,[2] and although not more than 5,000 regular soldiers were available in the city when the crisis came, these measures undoubtedly caused widespread alarm. Since the status of citizenship was then held inseparable from the acceptance of responsibility for civic defence, the appearance of the soldiers seemed at best insulting and at worst sinister, just as the re-appearance of the 'terrorists' seemed ominous. Many peaceful and conservative republicans, people who were naturally the Convention's strongest allies, were thus convinced that the Terror was coming again and so gave their support to the protest movement which the royalists rapidly organised.

The announcement of the results of the plebiscite at the end of September made matters far worse, for according to the official figures the electorate—which had been expected to sanction the Two-Thirds Decree as well as the Constitution—had approved the Decree only by 205, 489 to 108,754 votes. It was, and still is, uncertain how far these

[1] H. Mitchell, *The Underground War Against Revolutionary France* (Oxford, 1965), pp. 83–7.
[2] Lefebvre, *The Thermidorians*, p. 173.

astonishingly small figures were falsified, or how far the voters had simply failed to distinguish between the decree and the Constitution itself, both of which were before them simultaneously. In Paris, however, the majority of the Sections had certainly treated the Decree as a separate proposal and rejected it outright, and the official figures were at once condemned as fraudulent.[1] Moreover, as the outcry about this mounted in the Sections, the Convention again aggravated the situation by calling for further aid from the 'terrorists'. Nor was this call unanswered. Despite the desperate condition to which the poor were by now reduced through the appalling rise in the cost of living,[2] and despite the persecution that the 'terrorists' had suffered since Prairial, these men now showed that they still preferred the Republic to any sort of counter-revolution, and three battalions of volunteers, the 'Patriots of 1789', were formed for the defence of the Convention. Further, on the night of 3 October, when the assembly believed a royalist insurrection to be imminent, it not only appointed a Commission of Five to organise its defence, but also authorised the 'terrorists' generally to re-arm themselves.

Since this last measure in particular caused something akin to panic in Paris, on the morning of 4 October the royalists of the Lepeletier Section felt sufficiently confident of success to call the city to arms. Only a few adjacent Sections and the traditionally turbulent Théâtre-Français Section on the southern bank of the Seine were with them wholeheartedly, and even amongst themselves their enterprise seems to have been curiously compounded of desperation and carefree recklessness. If someone gave a lead, they seemed to think, perhaps the multitude might follow. In fact most Sections stood to arms, and many sent detachments to march with the men of Lepeletier: but in all probability only a fraction of those concerned in the insurrection of Vendémiaire shared, or even appreciated, the royalists' purpose. If Paris rose it was not for the royalists and against the Republic, but because men supposed that the Terror was about to be re-imposed upon them.[3]

[1] 33 of the 48 Sections of Paris simply reported that they had rejected the Decree unanimously (as did at least 269 assemblies in France as a whole) and the Convention was then, and is now, condemned for not taking this into account—though it is not easy to see how the tellers could have counted figures not submitted to them. See Lefebvre, *The Thermidorians*, p. 175.

[2] Bread, distributed in Paris at this time at the controlled price of 3 *sous* per 1 lb.—the official ration—was actually selling on the open market at between 15 and 20 *livres* the lb. Rudé, op. cit., p. 162.

[3] H. Zivy, *Le Treize Vendémiaire, An IV* (Paris, 1898), p. 108. On 6 October Merlin de Douai reported to the Convention (*Ancien Moniteur*, 14 Vendémiaire)

This supposition was certainly a tragic error. If the Convention had gradually reinforced itself by enlisting a strictly limited amount of support from the men it had previously suppressed, it had done so partly because it over-estimated the seriousness of the royalist threat. Beyond this, however, it more correctly recognised in Paris in September 1795 a situation with which bitter experience had made it familiar. Essentially its authority, which it believed to be that of the nation as a whole, was being challenged by some of the Sections of Paris, which were again acting on the assumption that there could not possibly be any principle or authority superior to that of the sovereign power of the people in their own assemblies. As had so often happened since 1792, this principle was held to justify every stage of opposition to parliamentary authority, and in its campaign against the Two-Thirds Decree the Section Lepeletier had followed a familiar path. Through arrogant petitions to the Convention, through the exchange of speakers and delegations with other Sections, through the attempt to form a central committee of the Sections and eventually through open defiance of the Convention, Lepeletier had moved steadily towards insurrection. In reply to a direct order from the Convention to concern itself only with its proper duties—at that time the election of delegates to the assembly which was to choose new deputies for Paris in the Legislative Body—it had, moreover, given the classic reply: 'The powers of every constituted body cease in the presence of the people'.[1]

The insurrection of Vendémiaire, while differing sharply from previous insurrections in the social standing of the people concerned, consequently posed the same political problem as before. If, as seems likely, the Convention over-reacted when it was insulted and defied, precipitating a crisis by assuming too quickly that a new 31 May 1793 impended, it may nevertheless be thought right in its determination to resist the Sections. The constitutional Republic it had laboured so long to create was about to be inaugurated: representative democracy had to be made to prevail over the direct democracy of the people in their local assemblies, regardless of what the social or political complexion of these

---

that seven sections (Lepeletier, Butte des Moulins, Théâtre Français, Brutus, Poissonière, Temple and Contract Social) and some others had declared themselves to be in revolt against the Convention on the night of the 4th; but only Lepeletier openly avowed a royalist aim. See also Rudé, op. cit., pp. 170–2, and Lefebvre, *The Thermidorians*, p. 176.

[1] Thibaudeau, *Mémoires sur la Convention*, Vol. I, p. 190. See also Rudé, op. cit., pp. 169–70, where the attempt of the Sections to co-ordinate their actions is described as a 'direct challenge to the authority of the Convention'.

local assemblies might be. As Thibaudeau told the Convention: 'We will never consent that the Convention should allow its authority to be challenged by a tiny fraction of the people. We are the representatives of the nation. We will fight the anarchy of the royalists with the same courage that we fought that of the *sans-culottes*.'[1]

Both sides now had recourse to force. After the Section Lepeletier had called Paris to arms on the morning of 4 October, the Convention's Commission of Five ordered General Menou[2] to disarm the Section and occupy its meeting-place, the convent of the Filles Saint-Thomas (which stood where the Bourse is now). Menou had had no hesitation in making a display of force against the *sans-culottes* of the Faubourg Saint-Antoine in Prairial, but he now proved unreliable. Being more in sympathy with the insurgents than with the 'terrorists', he refused point-blank to march with the 'Patriots of '89', whom he described as 'a pack of ruffians and assassins'.[3] After wasting much time in bickering about this, he then advanced at nightfall with regular troops alone; but having crowded all his men, guns and horses into a single narrow street, the rue Vivienne, he contented himself with parleying with the insurgents—and then withdrew his force again on the worthless understanding that the insurgents would also retire.

When the Convention heard of this 'victory of eloquence', as Lacretelle later called it,[4] Menou was promptly put under arrest and his command of the Army of the Interior entrusted to Paul-Jean Barras, the principal deputy on the Commission of Five. Once an officer in the royal army, Barras was reputed a strong man. In the time of the Terror he had been notably ruthless in his repression of opposition to the Convention in south-eastern France, and when he and others of his ilk had joined forces to overthrow Robespierre in July 1794, it was he who had been charged with organising the defence of the Convention against the Robespierrist Commune of Paris. To assist him now, five generals were put under his orders and one of them was Bonaparte, a young artillery commander in search of proper employment.

Bonaparte, who was then 26 years of age, had held commissioned rank as a regular soldier since 1785. Initially much preoccupied with the involved political strife of his native Corsica,[5] he had advanced rapidly

---

[1] Thibaudeau, loc. cit.

[2] *Biog. Notes:* MENOU.

[3] Mathiez, *La Réaction Thermidorienne*, p. 304.

[4] Lacretelle, op. cit., p. 259.

[5] In 1768, one year before the birth of Napoleon, the Republic of Genoa had sold the island of Corsica to France, which had already been aiding a Corsican

in his career after the expulsion of his family from that island in 1793. First distinguishing himself by his part in the recapture of Toulon from the royalists and the British in that same year, he had been described by his general as 'a most rare officer'[1] and promoted from the rank of captain to that of a general. Under the patronage of Robespierre's younger brother, Augustin—who similarly reported him to be 'an artillery officer of transcendent merit'[2]—he soon became commanding General of Artillery to the Army of Italy, and the plans he put forward for the operations of that army were such that its commander ascribed its success in September 1794 to his abilities.[3] But as he had been advanced during the time of the Terror, so its sudden ending in July 1794 had almost ruined him. Although he was only imprisoned for two weeks before being cleared of any suspicion of complicity in the 'plots' which were then being alleged against the Robespierrists, many continued to distrust him as a 'terrorist' general who had been promoted prematurely, and there were also some suggestions that he was unduly ambitious.[4] At least partly for these reasons, he had been recalled to Paris in the spring of 1795 and appointed to the command of an infantry brigade in the Army of the West. Evading this somewhat ignominious appointment, he had contrived to attach himself instead to the Topographical Bureau in Paris, where he was concerned with military intelligence and planning. His position at the end of September 1795 was nevertheless ambiguous: he was doing important work, and he had influential friends in the governing Committees; but, impoverished and obscure, he was neither fully reinstated nor on active service. While it would be an exaggeration to say that he was 'haunting the corridors of the Committee of Public Safety' in the hope of picking up a post,[5] he was

---

revolt against Genoa since 1764. When French aid became French annexation, the patriot leader Pascal Paoli (1725–1807) took refuge in England; but the Bonaparte family supported the French interest. Divisions in the island were made more intense by the Revolution: Paoli returned, but he and the patriots were alienated as the new régime became more violent. In 1793 the failure of Bonaparte's attempt to seize control led to the expulsion of his family, and at Paoli's request the British occupied the island in his support until the French returned in 1796. Paoli himself died in England.

[1] Du Teil, cited by F. Markham, *Napoleon* (London, 1964), p. 12.

[2] *Correspondence de Maximilien et Augustin Robespierre* (ed. G. Michon, Paris, 1926), p. 274.

[3] T. M. Hunter, *Napoleon in Victory and Defeat* Historical Section, Army HQ., Ottawa, 1964), p. 26.

[4] H. Calvet, *Napoléon* (Paris, P.U.F., 1966), p. 18.

[5] Ibid., p. 20.

certainly toying with the possibility of leading a military mission to Turkey.

The day of 13 Vendémiaire Year IV (5 October 1795) was consequently as momentous for Bonaparte as it was critical for the Convention and the Republic. The precise part played by the future Emperor on this occasion is, indeed, still somewhat conjectural: according to the account Barras gave in his later (and extremely prejudiced) *Memoirs*, Bonaparte was no more than an *aide-de-camp* who only acted on Barras's own orders;[1] Bonaparte himself, however, subsequently asserted that his influence was decisive: 'They asked for my advice. I answered, for my part, by asking for guns . . . Next morning the news looked very bad. Then they put me in charge of the whole thing.'[2] The truth would seem to be that Bonaparte was indeed Barras's lieutenant, and that if he was not (as he immediately afterwards claimed) officially second-in-command of the Convention's forces, he acted as if he were.[3] According to Thiébault, who was present as a captain, he appeared as a puny and unimpressive person, with long lank hair and ill-fitting shabby clothes; but Thiébault also wrote: 'From the first his activity was astonishing; he seemed to be everywhere at once . . . He surprised people by his laconic, clear and prompt orders, imperative to the last degree. Everybody was struck by the vigour of his arrangements, and passed from admiration to confidence, from confidence to admiration'.[4]

Despite torrential rain on the night of 4 October, the commanders appointed after Menou's arrest took energetic measures to repel the attack on the Tuileries which there was then every reason to expect. On the instructions of Barras,[5] Bonaparte despatched Major Murat of the 21st Chasseurs[6] with 300 horsemen to the gun-park at Les Sablons, and

[1] Barras, *Memoirs* (ed. Duruy, London, 1895), Vol. I, pp. 321–6.

[2] *Mémoires de Mme de Rémusat* (Paris, 1803), Vol. I, p. 270.

[3] Lefebvre, *The Thermidorians*, p. 178. Bonaparte's assertion that he had been second-in-command was immediate: see his letter to Josephine of 6 October (*Corres.* I, p. 91), cited in Stewart, *A Documentary Survey*, p. 647, and the *Memoirs of Bourrienne* (Hutchinson edn., London, s.d.), p. 20.

[4] *The Memoirs of Baron Thiébault* (trans. Butler, N.Y., 1896), Vol. I, pp. 258–60. Born in Berlin in 1769, Paul, baron Thiébault was a prominent member of the National Guard in the fashionable Feuillants district of Paris until his dislike of political extremism drove him to enlist as a regular. A captain in 1795, he became a general in 1800 and saw much service without being favoured by fortune. He died in Paris in 1846.

[5] Bourrienne, loc. cit. Napoleon's letter to Bourrienne: 'General Barras ordered the artillery to be brought from the camp at Sablons . . .'; see also J. H. Rose, *The Life of Napoleon I* (6th ed., London, 1916), p. 70 fn.

[6] *Biog. Notes:* MURAT.

Murat, forestalling the insurgents, succeeded in returning with 40 pieces of artillery. By morning, the Tuileries had been converted into a veritable fortress. About 8,000 men—some 5,000 regulars, with 1,500 of the 'Patriots of '89' and 1,500 armed police and pensioners—were disposed to command all the approaches to the Palace.[1] Some guarded the Place du Carrousel to the east; others held the narrow streets and alleyways which led northwards into the Rue Saint-Honoré; and others again dominated the opposite bank of the Seine, both from the quays alongside the Louvre and from the southern end of the Pont Royal, the only bridge which then led directly to the Tuileries from the south. A reserve force, moreover, was stationed on the Place de la Révolution, where it commanded the possible avenues of retreat to the west—for which a further covering force of cavalry was also held available.

In Paris, meanwhile, some 25,000 to 30,000 men of the National Guard had answered the Section Lepeletier's call to arms. Although many, perhaps even the majority, of these remained in their own districts in anticipation of a revival of 'terrorist' activities, those who advanced against the Tuileries outnumbered the defenders considerably.[2] They could, moreover, concentrate their attack where they chose, and at about nine o'clock in the morning of 5 October their battalions debouched from the northern side-streets into the Rue Saint-Honoré, confronting the troops there with a massive display of force. The insurgents, however, were without canon, for by the irony of fate the Lepeletier Section itself had set other Sections an example after Prairial by surrending its guns to the Convention. Since both sides were equally reluctant to begin bloodshed, long hours of inactivity ensued; and as negotiations proceeded, fraternisation threatened to sap the strength of the defence.

At about 3.30 in the afternoon, however, someone fired a shot at the men of the Sections, either from the window of Venua's restaurant or from the entrance of the passage which led through that building to the Tuileries.[3] Danican, the disgruntled general who commanded the

---

[1] See map, p. 78.

[2] Sources and secondary authorities agree that between 25,000 and 30,000 men of the Sections were under arms, but vary considerably about the number of those who actually took part in the attack on the Tuileries. Rudé, op. cit., p. 173, follows Zivy, H., *Le Treize Vendémiaire, An IV*, pp. 84–5, and Lacretelle, op. cit., p. 260, in giving the figure of 7–8,000; but Lacretelle subsequently speaks of a column of 15,000 men, and all accounts suggest that the defenders were out-numbered.

[3] According to Lacretelle, op. cit., p. 261, and others, this was a deliberately provocative shot fired from the window of the restaurant by the Montagnard

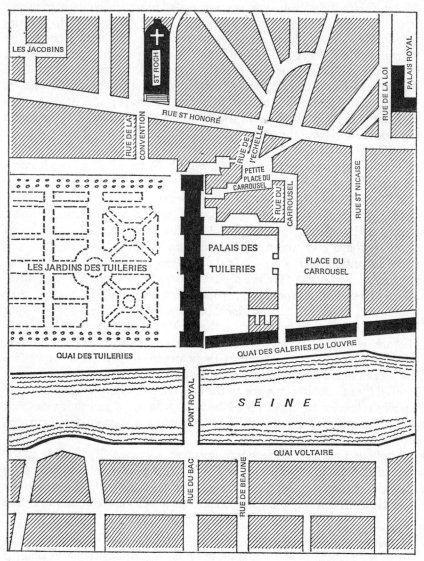

Plan to Illustrate the Attack on the Tuileries, 13 Vendémiaire An IV

attacking force,[1] then ordered his men to attempt to force their way through the nearby Rue de la Convention to the Tuileries, this attack being covered by musket-fire from men posted on the steps of the Church of St Roch. The assault, however, was met by a discharge of grape-shot and countered immediately by a charge of the 'patriot' battalions. After a short, fierce fight the assailants were scattered and driven to take refuge inside the church and in the Palais Royal.

A little later, after more desultory fighting across the Place du Carrousel, the insurgents made a second major attack from the south. Advancing in a long broad column along the open Quai Voltaire, they sought to cross the Pont Royal and take the defenders of the Tuileries from the rear. In this, their leaders were at least not lacking in courage, although they probably did not appreciate the fact that their march would take them straight across the front of the troops lining the *quais* on the northern bank of the Seine, and directly into the mouths of the guns posted at the head of the bridge. The column of marchers was in fact greeted with grape-shot and caught in a crossfire of musketry, and its mass dispersed so swiftly that those in the lead looked back to see the long sweep of the *quai* deserted behind them.[2] Not surprisingly, the remnant of the formation turned off abruptly into the shelter offered by the buildings in the Rue de Beaune, a block short of the head of the bridge.

Utterly disheartened by these reverses, the leaders of the insurrection scattered during the night, and on the morning of 6 October the regulars were able to occupy such strong points as the Church of St Roch[3] with-

---

deputy Dubois-Crancé; Thiébault, p. 262, however asserts positively that it was fired by the Adjutant-General Solignac, who fired from the head of the passage, being goaded past endurance by the bravado of the National Guardsmen opposite.

[1] Danican, 'whose public life began and ended that day' (*Memoirs of Chancellor Pasquier* (trans. C. E. Roche, New York, 1893), I, p. 132) was an elderly general who had once been an ardent revolutionary, but who had recently resigned his command after being disgraced for reactionary activities.

[2] Lacretelle, op. cit., p. 263.

[3] Engravings which depict Bonaparte directing the storming of the Church of St Roch, and accounts which suggest that this was a central event in the fighting, are inaccurate. The facts are obscure, but the account given by Thiébault seems to reconcile difficulties. According to this, the insurgents' attack across the rue St-Honoré on the regulars at the head of the rue Dauphin (de la Convention) was covered by the fire of a strong body of men stationed on the steps of the church, and the artillery fire which broke the assault also struck down some of these men on the western end of the steps. The counter-attack of the 'patriots' then cleared the steps, but the Church itself remained a place of refuge for the insurgents throughout the night, being taken without difficulty next morning.

out difficulty. Before long, detached columns were transversing the city in peace, and commissioners from the Convention were able to tour the Sections to restore confidence. Thus, at the cost of some 300 killed and wounded on either side, a rising in Paris was shattered by military force for the first time since the Revolution began.

To Bonaparte, this victory brought renewed opportunity. Although the importance of his ability and resolution was not officially acknowledged by Barras in his first report, this had evidently been considerable. The artillery, which was his particular responsibility, had been employed with devastating effect, and Barras's second report recognised generously enough that: 'it is to him, and to his wise and prompt dispositions, that the safety of this area is due'.[1] With the patronage of Barras—now, as in Thermidor, applauded as the saviour of the Convention—he was again promoted rapidly. Confirmed as second-in-command of the Army of the Interior on 10 October, he succeeded Barras as its commander on the 26th, being by then a full General of Division.

For France, too, the day of 13 Vendémiaire was full of consequence. Although fear of a renewal of the Terror had been a principal cause of the insurrection, the royalists who had exploited this social anxiety had done so to strike at the Republic: but now their cause, like that of the 'pures' who had been defeated at Quiberon, really seemed irretrievably ruined. Mallet du Pan, who had constantly opposed any recourse to force, was in complete despair, and Vaublanc, one of those who marched, subsequently wrote: 'This day was fatal to liberty'.[2] The moderate republicans, on the other hand, now had good reason to believe that the Revolution was at last ending in the triumph of their cause. Paris was, and was to remain, firmly under military control, its National Guard being disarmed and incorporated in the organisation of the Army of the Interior. Moreover, when Barras first reported to the Convention on 6 October, he rightly announced: 'Citizen-Representatives, the sovereignty of the Lepeletier Section no longer exists'.[3] Far from simply dispersing a mob, the guns employed in Vendémiaire had completed the process begun in Prairial whereby the sovereignty of the Sections, long both the strength and the bane of the Revolution, was destroyed.

The moderates, to their credit, did not exploit their victory. Although three military commissions were set up to judge the leaders of the in-

[1] *Ancien Moniteur*, 18 Vendémiaire An IV.

[2] Mallet du Pan to Wickham, 13 October 1795, cited by Fryer, op. cit., p. 43; Vaublanc, *Mémoires*, p. 303.

[3] *Ancien Moniteur*, 14 Vendémiaire An IV.

surrection, only two executions took place, for no serious efforts were made to seize those who were accused, and the royalists generally were allowed to remain in more or less open retirement. This leniency has been contrasted unfavourably with the harsh treatment of the poor after Prairial, but it was not due merely to social partiality: led by Thibaudeau, the moderates deliberately determined to remain moderate and to avoid compromising the coming constitutional régime by initiating a new wave of persecutions.[1] Thibaudeau, too, was also principally responsible for defeating a last-minute attempt by Tallien to postpone the inauguration of the Constitution. Despite the insurrection, the election returns for the new Legislative Body soon showed that the Right would be far stronger in future than it had been in the Convention; on 22 October, Tallien, foreseeing the danger that royalism would re-appear in a new cloak of constitutional respectability, demanded that the elections should be annulled and the Commission of Five authorised to act as an emergency government. Thibaudeau, however, attacked Tallien furiously as one who had been by turns a Terrorist, a Counter-terrorist and a Royalist, and he successfully appealed to the assembly to maintain its republican solidarity and to avert a revival of terrorism by establishing legality. The long-awaited Constitution consequently came duly into effect,[2] and on 26 October the President of the Convention formally announced that the assembly's mission was accomplished and its session at an end.

The significance of this apparently mundane announcement was much greater at the time than it may now appear in retrospect. The operation of the Two-Thirds Decree of course meant, as it was intended to mean, that there was at first comparatively little change between the personnel of the Convention and that of the first Legislative Body of the new constitutional Republic. To a considerable extent, as unsympathetic historians indicate, the same men, with the same tarnished reputations and the same political passions and social prejudices, had still to grapple with the same problems.[3] Nor did the Convention bequeath any easy legacy to its successor. If the rigours of the Terror had been abolished, if the shedding of blood was almost ended, the Revolution and the

---

[1] 'Restons donc dans un juste milieu': Thibaudeau, Mémoires, Vol. I, p. 216; for the stormy session which followed Tallien's proposals, see also pp. 246–61.

[2] Tallien had nevertheless ensured that some important 'revolutionary' powers were retained, and it may be argued that these in effect invalidated the new constitutional régime from the beginning. See Lefebvre, The Directory (trans. R. Baldick, London 1964), pp. 4–8, and below, chapters 4 and 5.

[3] E.g., G. Lefebvre, The Directory, p. 1.

collapse of the currency had reduced France to a ruinous condition. Moreover, despite the military victories of 1794 and the diplomatic triumphs of 1795, the Convention had not succeeded in securing a general peace. On the contrary, in the last weeks of its life it had not only ratified the annexation of Belgium, the French occupation of which practically precluded peace with either England or Austria, but it had identified that annexation with the new order by making it an integral part of the new Constitution.

Yet if at the end of October 1795 the situation of France was still revolutionary, to contemporaries it appeared that the advent of the Constitution was indeed the end of the Revolution. True, the Constitution was uncompromisingly Republican, and there were certain highly significant exceptions to the general amnesty which the Convention announced in its last official act. These, however, were seen at the time as reinforcing rather than compromising legality, and many men undoubtedly shared Thibaudeau's conviction that the greatest difficulties of the nation would disappear once a lawful system of government had been begun. To contemporaries, too, the closure of the Convention was in itself an occasion of profound significance. As Thiébault wrote, the assembly which had saved France and freedom when both seemed certain to be overwhelmed by the armies of despotism, had also exercised for a time a tyranny so terrible that it seemed to have demanded the sacrifice of an entire generation.[1] The disappearance on 26 October 1795 of the body whose name was so fraught with wonder and with fear consequently seemed to mark nothing less than the ending of an era. It was not by chance that the Convention itself ordered at this time that the Place de la Révolution should henceforth be known as the Place de la Concorde.

[1] Thiébault, *Mémoires*, Vol. I, p. 266.

3 Thibaudeau at the age of 67

4 Sieyès
from a lithograph by Delpech

5 Carnot
engraving by
W. H. Mote

6 Pichegru
after a drawing by
Gaildrau

Part Two
The Constitutional Republic, 1795-1798

*'If our speeches now are compared with those of 1793 or
even 1795, it will be found that we have in fact
changed our language. But times have also changed, and
all revolutionary habits must yield little by little to
the constitutional régime. The nature of things imposes
this upon us. Yet while the Legislative Body accepts
this as a matter of honour and duty, the Directory
remains obstinately immovable. They will not move
forward with us, and we cannot go back to meet them.
It is this lack of communication* (mésintelligence)
which gives the royalists all their importance.'

A. C. Thibaudeau, *Mémoires sur la Convention et le
Directoire* (Paris, 1824, Vol. II, pp. 245–6)

4. The Repudiation of the Left, October 1795-May 1797

On 26 October 1795, the day on which the Convention was dissolved, elaborate proceedings began for the formation of the executive and legislature of the new constitutional republic. It was, in the first place, necessary to ensure that, as the Two-Thirds Decree required, no less than 500 members of the Convention should become deputies in the new Legislative Body. Only 379 of these places, however, had been filled by the elections, for although the voters had conformed with the Decree, they had in fact returned many of the more conservative deputies for several constituencies at once.[1] Those who were elected had in consequence to form an *ad hoc* electoral college, 'The Electoral Assembly of France', and co-opt more than 100 of their old colleagues. Next day, when these 500 deputies had been joined by the 250 newly-elected deputies (the 'new third'), two separate Councils were created: 250 of those of more than 40 years of age were separated by lot to form an upper chamber, the Council of the Elders, and the remainder constituted themselves as the Council of the Five Hundred. The Legislative Body being thus established, on 29 and 30 October the Five Hundred drew up a list of 50 candidates for the five appointments required to form the Executive Directory, and from this list the Elders chose the names of LaRevellière-Lépeaux, Reubell, Sieyès, Letourneur and Barras. With the exception of Sieyès, who refused to serve and was subsequently replaced by Carnot, these Directors assumed office on 2 November.

These complex proceedings were not without significance. They might, indeed, almost be said to epitomise the future history of the régime, for although in all things the letter of the law had been scrupulously observed, no spirit of compromise had governed its application. In particular, the deputies drawn from the Convention, who of course held the majority in both the new Councils, had pre-determined the choice of the five Directors: by ensuring that the list of 50 names would

[1] E.g., Thibaudeau, Lanjuinais, Boissy d'Anglas.

include those of 45 nonentities,[1] a caucus had in fact forced the Elders to choose an executive wholly composed of men of the Convention, and *all of them regicides*. Since the newly-elected deputies naturally resented treatment of this sort, the inauguration of the constitutional republic was marked by division and distrust. The newcomers, for their part, were almost by definition men who had not been directly associated with revolutionary republicanism. Some—particularly General Mathieu Dumas and his friends—were Feuillants who had been prominent in public life before the constitutional monarchy was destroyed, and had suffered correspondingly during the Terror. A few—a very few—would certainly have welcomed a restoration of the Old Order. All, however, were regarded by most of the men of the Convention with profound suspicion as committed or potential royalists. Consequently, although some regrouping occurred as old and new conservatives, and old and new moderates, drew together, a broad rift remained between most of the new third on the one hand and most of the men of the Convention and their Directors on the other.[2] Although few historians have much hesitation in describing this rift as one between a republican majority and a royalist minority,[3] it may well be that mutual mistrust, far more than any fundamental difference of principle, was really the distinguishing feature of the political life of the time.

Beginning thus inauspiciously, as time progressed this new period in French history acquired an increasingly evil reputation. The name of the Directory, which should signify the reviving importance of government, has become synonymous with mis-government, licentiousness and corruption. After six full years of Revolution, society was certainly in a state of flux. The currency being totally discredited, speculation and financial racketeering were rife, and the popular passions for dancing and gambling, buying and selling, were to some extent symbolised by the immodesty and immorality of a small section of the fashionable world, greatly though popular writers have exaggerated the importance of the latter.[4] More serious historians, seeing that the fundamental

---

[1] Thibaudeau, *Mémoires*, II, p. 5.

[2] The composition and character of the new chambers are discussed by Thibaudeau, op. cit., p. 12; see also, *inter alia*, Lefebvre, *The Directory*, pp. 15–16, and Fryer, *Republic or Restoration in France? 1794–97* (Manchester, 1965), pp. 51–4.

[3] E.g., A. Soboul, *La Ire République* (Paris, 1968), p. 210.

[4] On the atmosphere of the period in general, see Lefebvre, *The Thermidorians*, chapter 11 (particularly pp. 191 and 201) and *The Directory*, chapter 4. For 'the passion of buying and selling' see Lacretelle, *Dix Années d'Epreuves* (Paris, 1842), pp. 280–1.

problem was one of government, have generally recognised that the Directors and the Councils were bound to be unpopular: amidst a population politically apathetic and anxious only for the return of peace and some measure of prosperity, they were forced to meet almost insuperable domestic and military problems with inadequate financial and administrative means. As yet, however, the extent of their achievements and failures can hardly be said to have been adequately investigated. To most of the great writers of the Revolutionary or the Bonapartist traditions, the period has been one to be either dismissed or damned. Where some have seen it merely as a drab prelude to the brilliance of Napoleonic power, others have condemned it as a sordid aftermath of the Revolution, a period in which the 'bourgeoisie' and the 'notables' consolidated their power and completed the suppression of the social revolution associated with Robespierre or (more recently) with the *sansculottes*.[1] Moreover, while increasing attention is now being attracted to the relatively little-known years between 1795 and 1799, recent research has been principally concerned with the forces of opposition to the constitutional republic. In short, a sympathetic history of those who strove to make the constitution work remains to be written.

If it is true, as is here suggested, that what would now be called a crisis of confidence was really the greatest difficulty of the day, it would also seem that the irresponsibility of those who incited the insurrection of Vendémiaire did immeasurable harm to France. By their resort to force, they revived both a fear of royalism and a fear of a new Terror at the very moment when the advent of the constitution might have opened the way to reconciliation. Although, as we have seen, Tallien's attempt to retain some form of emergency government had been defeated by Thibaudeau—an occasion when, as Thibaudeau put it, he remained 'clamped to the tribune' amidst a furious political storm[2]—the Convention had soon afterwards accepted Tallien's alternative proposals for stringent security measures.[3] On 25 October 1795, just before the Convention was dissolved, the law known as that of 3 Brumaire reviving the savage revolutionary legislation of 1792 and 1793 against non-juring Catholic priests, who were now again subjected to banishment under pain of death. By the same law, all close relatives of the 120,000 people

---

[1] Or, more specifically: 'Between Mathiez, who spent a lifetime in defending the Jacobin leader, and Madelin, equally intent upon eulogising Bonaparte, the Directors have come in for a good deal of unmerited abuse.' A. Goodwin, 'The French Executive Directory: A Revaluation', *History*, XXII (Dec. 1937), p. 202.

[2] Thibaudeau, op. cit., II, pp. 246–61.

[3] See also Lefebvre, *The Directory*, pp. 2–6.

who were officially—but by no means accurately—listed as emigrants[1] were excluded from any form of public service, as were all those who were known to have participated in the agitation in the Sections before Vendémiaire. It need scarcely be added that when the Convention next day concluded its session by proclaiming a general amnesty for 'all acts simply connected with the Revolution', the 'Vendémiairists' were excluded from its benefits. At the same time, as if to underline the impartiality of the new régime, the 'terrorist' deputies who had been deported were also excluded from the amnesty. No further proceedings were taken against those other Montagnards who, like Robert Lindet, had been indicted or arrested after the risings of Germinal and Prairial, but these men—of whom there were finally 68[2]—still remained ineligible for election to the new Councils.

Like the rigged election of the Directors which followed, this 'exceptional legislation' may be explained by the deputies' understandable anxiety lest excessive liberalism should allow unavowed royalists to acquire so much influence in local and national government that either reaction would triumph or the Terror would have to be revived to prevent it. The measure may nevertheless fairly be condemned as class legislation of the worst type—i.e., that which penalises large numbers of people by classes, whether social or otherwise. While it may be an exaggeration to suggest, as do Mathiez and Lefebvre, that the Two-Thirds Decree and the Law of 3 Brumaire together made the rule of the Directory no more than a concealed form of dictatorship, they undoubtedly weighed heavily against the possibility that the operation of the new constitution would effectively end the Revolution. The Two-Thirds Decree meant, in effect, that the Directors and their supporters in the two Councils had until the next election, a period of eighteen months, in which to reconcile the 'new third' and the electorate to the new order; the Law of 3 Brumaire and the related exceptional legislation, however, meant that a host of potential supporters was gratuitously alienated. Not only did this law deprive the Directory

---

[1] The émigrés remained liable to the death penalty on identification in France, their property being confiscated and sold. While many had returned to France after Thermidor and had their names provisionally struck off the lists, the Constitution forbade further exceptions, and those temporarily struck off were excluded from public office. The figure of 120,000 is that in Aulard (*A Political History*, III, p. 334) as the official estimate early in 1797; Mathiez (*Le Directoire*, Paris 1934, p. 31) has 170,000; D. Greer, the best authority, cautiously estimates a maximum of 145,000 in 1800 (*The Incidence of the Emigration during the French Revolution*, Glous., Mass., 1966).

[2] Mathiez, *Le Directoire*, p. 25.

of the services of a great many capable men at a time when there was a desperate dearth of local officials, it also perpetuated revolutionary discrimination and political rancour. So long as it existed, no moderate republican could speak convincingly of the merits of the constitution: but anyone who advocated a repeal of the Law of 3 Brumaire was at once exposed to the accusation of disloyalty to the Republic. The pattern of parliamentary life in the constitutional Republic was thus distorted from the outset, and the executive Directory, even before it had begun to act, was identified with oppression.

Most unfortunately, too, the Directors themselves were men incapable of magnaminity. Despite their reputation, they were not, with the exception of Barras, dishonest; nor need they be thought incompetent, or insincere in their determination to consolidate the Republic.[1] Apparently, however, only one of them, Lazare Carnot, could conceive that their definition of republican policies might require modification if constitutional government was ever to prevail. Elected to preserve and protect the political position upheld by the Convention after the Terror, they were an ill-assorted set of men, amongst whom old antagonisms smouldered. Inflexibility alone was their common characteristic.

Of the five, Letourneur[2] was certainly the least important. Competent as an expert on naval affairs, he was nevertheless a colourless character who was ever content to conform to Carnot's position on all matters of policy. Carnot[3] himself, the only really outstanding man in the Directory, was clearly temperamentally unsuitable for a position which demanded consistent cooperation with others. A natural administrator with a genius for military organisation, he unhesitatingly involved himself in unfamiliar responsibilities, but brought to them an autocratic and even dictatorial attitude. Difficult as a colleague, he had a high regard for authority, and was as sensitive to public opposition as he was to private criticism. Barras and Reubell, on the other hand, were both aggressive men. The former was one who, as has well been said, 'united in one person the worst characteristics of a licentious and insolent noble of the time of Louis XV and those of a truculent patriot of the Terror'.[4] Shifty, unprincipled and corrupt, he was primarily interested in his own power and prosperity, and while his readiness to abandon intrigue and act decisively in emergencies gave the Directory strength, his innate

---

[1] Goodwin, op. cit., p. 203.
[2] *Biog. Notes:* LETOURNEUR.
[3] *Biog. Notes:* CARNOT.
[4] G. K. Fortescue, 'The Directory', *Cambridge Modern History* (Cambridge, 1914), Vol. VIII (*The French Revolution*), p. 491. *Biog. Notes:* BARRAS.

inability to credit the sincerity of any opponent undoubtedly helped to make it intransigent. Reubell,[1] too, was notoriously domineering. Able, well-informed and resolute, he was nevertheless an abrupt and often an offensive man, strangely personifying in his manner the republican policy with which he was particularly identified, that of conquest and expansion to the 'natural frontier' of the Rhine. In much the same way, little LaRevellière-Lépeaux,[2] apparently a conservative republican whose deepest interest lay in the development of education, really represented a good deal of the true revolutionary's fundamental fanaticism. Intellectually convinced that human progress depended on the emancipation of men's reason, he too was an ardent believer in the extension of the new enlightenment, a process which to him implied the continuation of republican propaganda and conquest. He, moreover, abhorred aristocracy and popular democracy alike, and his hatred of priests and of Catholicism almost amounted to an obsession.

These men, who accepted the responsibilities of office in circumstances which symbolised the desperate situation of their country, immediately made their attitude plain. The Councils being established, the Elders in the Manège and the Five Hundred in the Tuileries, the four original Directors moved to the Luxembourg palace on 2 November: but to such straits was France reduced that all four were forced to travel in a single carriage, and the soldiers of their escort were all more or less in rags. As for the Luxembourg itself, the palace which had once been the home of the Count of Provence had since his emigration been used as a political prison, and although more than a year had elapsed since Thermidor it was still in so sad a state that the newcomers had to borrow firewood, four straw-seated chairs and a rickety table from the hall-porter before they could begin to act.[3] On 5 November, after Carnot had joined them, they nevertheless informed the nation that it once again had got a government. This first Manifesto[4] was in part a wise appeal to France for patience, the Directors recognising that if they were to put 'social order in place of the chaos which is inseparable from revolutions', their chief need was for time. In part, too, it was an expression of the Directors' wholly commendable determination to govern resolutely and to do everything possible to restore public prosperity and internal peace.

[1] *Biog. Notes:* REUBELL.

[2] *Biog. Notes:* LAREVELLIÈRE-LÉPEAUX.

[3] LaRevellière-Lépeaux, *Mémoires* (Paris, 1895), I, p. 317.

[4] Printed in translation in L. Gershoy, *The Era of the French Revolution 1789–99* (Princeton, 1957), p. 176.

Yet at a time when, as Thibaudeau later remarked,[1] France's greatest need was the ability to rise above the past, the Directors showed that they regarded their political position as fixed and inflexible. Resolved 'to maintain liberty or to perish', they announced that they would 'wage active war on royalism' and 'repress all factions vigorously'. This intention, a re-assertion of the attitude adopted by the Convention after Thermidor when its motto was 'War to the Royalists and to the Terrorists',[2] evidently implied that the Directors, like most of the men of the Convention, still defined the Republic in the narrow terms which had been imposed upon it by the execution of Louis XVI and the crises of 1793–5.

Moreover, as time was soon to show, the Directors were themselves divided by their recollections of the Terror. Thus Reubell believed that Carnot, as a member of the great Committee of Public Safety, had been at least partially responsible for his own recall in disgrace from his mission to Mainz, where he was alleged to have been feathering his own nest.[3] Similarly, Barras, who had been a notorious Terrorist at a time when Lépeaux was living in concealment as an opponent of the Terror, had been one of those most responsible for the destruction of the Committee of Public Safety's power. Old antagonisms like these were inevitably fostered by the strains of office, for the Directors undoubtedly worked furiously in their endeavour to reorganise France. Being quite literally the directors of the executive, they never allowed the ministers to be anything more than their agents, simply summoning them separately to hear their reports and give them their instructions. For more than six months, too, the long daily councils of the Directors were regularly resumed each evening, and frequently continued far into the night, and this practice prevailed whenever any critical situation occurred.[4] Each day, moreover, whichever Director happened to be acting as their president—an office which each man held in turn for three months at a time—had to hold public audience in the Luxembourg, the main rooms of which were fairly soon redecorated and refurnished from the store-rooms of the old monarchy. Nor were these audiences unexacting, for at each a crowd of petitioners and spectators had to be received with elaborate ceremony, intended to impress

---

[1] Thibaudeau, *Mémoires*, II, p. 10.

[2] Aulard, op. cit., III, p. 242.

[3] G. D. Homan, 'Jean François Reubell, Director', *French Historical Studies*, No. 1 (1960), p. 422.

[4] Lépeaux, *Mémoires*, I, p. 363; see also *Mémoires de Barthélemy, 1768–1816* (Paris, 1914), pp. 180–4.

Frenchmen and foreigners alike with the gravity and grandeur of the first magistrates of the Republic. Worst of all, perhaps, the Directors lived in close proximity to each other: since the private rooms of the Luxembourg were appropriated by Barras and the heterogeneous crowd of courtiers who surrounded him, the other four Directors and their families occupied apartments in the adjoining Petit Luxembourg, where private strife accentuated political differences. Such being their way of life, it is small wonder that each Director in turn fell ill, or that the increasing opposition their rule aroused should have made them ever more quarrelsome, domineering and intractable.[1]

In the circumstances of 1795–6 it was probably also inevitable that the Directors' initial measures should have made them unpopular without achieving anything more than partial success. Their first task, as onerous as it was invidious, was that of selecting the administrative personnel of the new constitutional régime. At the national level, the appointment of ministers proved relatively easy, the main problem being that of finding men of ability who were prepared to serve. Sieyès, for example, not only refused the Ministry of External Affairs personally, but he also dissuaded Gaudin, a prodigious worker and an expert financier who was later to be invaluable to Bonaparte, from accepting the Ministry of Finance in 1795.[2] After some weeks of reshuffling, however, the Directors succeeded in making stable appointments: Bénézech became Minister of the Interior, Delacroix Minister of External Affairs, Petiet Minister of War, Truguet Minister of Marine, Ramel Minister of Finance and Merlin of Douai Minister of Justice. Significantly, a new Ministry, that of Police, was also created in January 1796, and to this Cochon was eventually appointed. Of these men it may be said that at least Merlin and Ramel were remarkably able, and if they were obnoxious to the Right, Bénézech and Cochon were equally detested by the Left.[3] The Directors also soon succeeded in establishing an efficient

---

[1] Even allowing for the fact that the memoirs of the various Directors were written after a succession of crises, the extent to which these are permeated by the authors' dislike and distrust of each other is remarkable.

[2] Mathiez, *Le Directoire*, p. 51. On p. 39 Mathiez remarks that Sieyès maintained 'tenacious opposition from the shadows throughout the whole regime'.

[3] Of these men—some of whom are more particularly identified in the Biographical Notes—three (Pierre Bénézech (1749–1802), Claude Petiet (1749–1806) and Admiral Laurent J.-F. Truguet (1752–1839)) had already distinguished themselves in the public service, while four (Charles de Lacroix (1754–1808), Cochon de Lapparent (1749–1825), Philippe A. Merlin de Douai (1754–1838) and Jacques Ramel de Nogaret (1760–1839)) had all been regicide members of the Convention. All save Ramel and Merlin, who became a

secretariat: organised by one man, Lagarde, for the whole of the Directorial period, this was eventually to be available to Bonaparte as the basis of his own secretarial service.

The organisation of local government proved far more difficult. According to the provisions of the Constitution, there were no longer to be any local assemblies except for electoral purposes; but local officers were to be elected and to have wide powers in a country considerably decentralised. Like the nation, each Department was to have its own executive directory of five elected members, and as sub-divisions of the Departments there were to be similar 'municipal' bodies. Parity of size amongst these last was to be obtained in part by sub-dividing the four major cities of France (Paris, Lyons, Marseilles and Bordeaux), and in part by grouping into 'municipalities' the many small communes which had populations of less than 5,000. Each of these smaller communities would then be administered by an elected 'municipal agent', who would also be its representative in the 'municipality' of the area. Finally, to supervise and coordinate the activities of all these elected officers, the Directors of the Republic were required to appoint a commissioner to each municipal and departmental directory.

These provisions in fact imposed a gigantic task upon the Directors, for no sooner were they in office than they were required to find some 10,000 commissioners,[1] who obviously had to be men who were both politically trustworthy and capable of accepting considerable responsibility. This, however, was but the beginning of the matter, for in practice the Directors found that most of the local administrations were either very hostile to the new government, or were only partially formed. While some few areas were markedly Jacobin in sympathy, as were Dijon and Toulouse,[2] the electors generally had returned men who were far more 'moderate' than the central government. Moreover, the brevity of the time allowed for the elections, the resignations of many new officials who found themselves excluded from office by the Law of 3 Brumaire, and the general apathy of the electorate—which practically amounted to a nation-wide electoral strike—had combined to leave a

---

Director, were to be dismissed in 1797, and all save Ramel were to be Councillors of State or Prefects to Bonaparte. Of the four regicides, one, Cochon, was to move far enough from his earlier associations to incur odium as a 'royalist', as did his friend and associate, the Director Carnot.

[1] To say nothing of those other commissioners attached to judicial tribunals, and innumerable police officers and fiscal officials.

[2] J. Godechot, *Les Institutions de la France sous la Révolution et l'Empire* (Paris, 1951), p. 412.

large part of France in a state of administrative anarchy comparable to the more notorious conditions of 1799.[1]

For France the consequences of this situation, which of course came as the culmination of a long period of war, rebellion and disorder, were appalling. Quite apart from the fact that civil war still continued in the West, and to a lesser extent in the Rhône Valley, taxes went unpaid, military service was evaded, and highway robbery and brigandage were rampant. For the Directors, too, the immediate results of the confusion were, to say the least, unfortunate. On the one hand, they were long compelled to give far more attention to appointments than to the formulation and direction of policy;[2] on the other, the corridors of the Luxembourg were soon regularly thronged with place-hunters, and the Directory almost inevitably became associated with the jobbery and graft implicit in a spoils system. Moreover, in their search for reliable men, the Directors—who for this purpose divided France between them, each taking responsibility for the area they knew best—naturally tended to consult those deputies who had come from the Convention; these as naturally recommended men of strongly republican persuasion; and as result, the conservative local administrations of France found themselves saddled with hostile and uncompromising commissioners. However this situation may be interpreted—whether one thinks that the Directors deliberately loosed upon France a horde of scoundrel Jacobins, or that the new nobility of a bourgeois republic now entered upon its inheritance, or that loyal republican officials now found themselves confronting local administrations composed of thinly-disguised royalists—the certain fact is the Directors were generally held to have been offensively partial in their choice of commissioners. No sooner were the appointments made than the Directory's agents and the local administrations were almost everywhere at loggerheads.

The ultimate consequences of this initial crisis (which extend well beyond the range of the present chapter) may also conveniently be indicated here. Since so many elections had been incomplete, the Directors in November and December 1795 were compelled to ask the Legislative Body to authorise it to fill the vacancies by still more official appointments. This request, made in succession regarding the departmental and the municipal administrations and even the local judges and justices of the peace, was in each instance approved by the Councils.[3]

[1] Mathiez, op. cit., p. 65.
[2] Lépeaux, *Mémoires*, I, pp. 402–5.
[3] Legislation of 16 November, 13 and 16 December 1795: Godechot, op. cit., pp. 412, 415.

This, however, only aggravated political tension. To some deputies, particularly those of the new third, this legislation seemed clear proof that the Directors were already violating the strict separation of powers prescribed by the Constitution, and doing so in order to extend their oppressive discrimination against the Right. Further, the process of nomination grew apace, considerably extending the powers of government. By the Constitution the Directors were empowered to suspend or dismiss local administrative officers either individually or collectively, and if all five seats on a local directory were vacant, the Directors could fill them by nomination until the next elections. As might be expected, this right was soon being used extensively.[1] Moreover, in the West and in the Rhône Valley all local officers were nominated as a matter of course as the authority of the Republic was restored. Very gradually, therefore, more uniformity was imposed upon local administration: but since the electorate, limited though it was at the secondary level, had so largely abdicated its function, this was only achieved by the steady growth of nomination and centralisation. Though the impoverished Directory was far from enclosing France in the iron bands which Bonaparte finally forged for her, the commissioners of the Directors, themselves in some respects the heirs of the National Agents of 1794, were eventually to be the predecessors of the prefects of the Consulate and the Empire.

In 1795, however, while the unfortunate Directors were still without adequate means of action, they had to cope as best they could with the problems the nation had inherited from the past. Of these, the war and the collapse of the currency were the most serious, and neither was susceptible of any easy solution. Despite all its diplomatic triumphs, the Convention had not succeeded in re-establishing a general peace in Europe. In August, the protracted negotiations with Austria—significantly influenced by Sieyès and Reubell, both of whom were firm believers in the extension of the French frontier to the Rhine[2]—had been abandoned, and early in September the French armies had resumed the offensive across the Rhine. At first all had gone well: with the connivance of the Elector Palatine, the fortresses of Mannheim and Düsseldorf were surrendered to Pichegru and Jourdan respectively, and Jourdan had advanced with the Army of the Sambre and the Meuse while Kléber

---

[1] Thus between 12 January and 30 March 1796, 11 departmental administrations were wholly or partially purged: Godechot, op. cit., p. 410. It should be added that in Mathiez' view (op. cit., p. 67) the Law of 3 Brumaire banning the acceptance of office by the relatives of *émigrés* was practically a dead letter.

[2] Lefebvre, *The Thermidorians*, p. 183.

had besieged Mayence. This offensive, however, had soon collapsed. While Jourdan advanced, Pichegru's Army of the Rhine remained suspiciously inactive, and the French forces, depleted and ill-supplied as they were, were soon confronted by such powerful Austrian reinforcements that they were forced to retreat. At the end of October, when the Directors were assuming office, the French again retired behind the Rhine, and in December an armistice on this front ended hostilities for the winter.

Although General Schérer, who commanded the Army of Italy, was more successful in his advance towards Genoa, the Directors seemed to have inherited a war which was not to be won without exhausting and expensive effort: yet by breaking off negotiations and approving the annexation of Belgium, the Convention had practically prohibited peace. From this impasse there arose in the course of 1795 one of the most fundamental political divisions of the period. Belief in the prosecution of the war for the attainment of the Rhine frontier became a hallmark of loyalty to the principles of republicanism prescribed by the Convention, with which the Directors were identified. Conversely, anyone who advocated a resumption of negotiation, which necessarily implied a withdrawal by France to her 'former limits', was immediately damned as a royalist, no matter how firmly he may have believed in the Republic.

Since the waging of war was inextricably entangled with the financial problems of France,[1] this same stigma of royalism was eventually to be attached indiscriminately to all those who criticised the government's expenditure and resisted or evaded taxation. Initially, however, the most serious opposition to the Directors' financial measures came not from the Right but from the Left, i.e. from those dispossessed revolutionaries who still maintained that more stringent control of the economy could even now save the *assignat*. This assertion, though politically effective, was almost certainly invalid, for the inflation which had begun soon after the outbreak of war in 1792 had by now reached its climax and was probably beyond control. When the new régime began, the *assignat* of 100 francs was worth less than 20 *sous*,[2] the daily expenses of government were at least ten times its receipts, and the Directors were hard put to it to have enough paper money printed each night for the needs of the following day.

---

[1] See Lefebvre, *The Directory*, chapter 3.

[2] Lefebvre, loc. cit., gives 15–16 *sous*; Mathiez, op. cit., p. 88, gives 70 *sous*; and Godechot, op. cit., p. 433, gives 30 centimes in February 1796. The essential point would seem to be that the *assignat* was not worth the paper it was printed on.

As one of many attempts to remedy this situation, the Convention in its closing session had decreed a measure of severe emergency taxation. Abandoning this, the Directors determined to abolish the *assignat* altogether, and at their request—for by the Constitution they had neither any control of the Treasury nor any right to initiate legislation— the Councils on 6 December 1795 agreed to impose a forced loan on all the wealthiest taxpayers, this being so designed as to encourage payment in coinage. While the results of this endeavour to replenish the Treasury and to restore confidence in the currency were awaited, and while all sales of national property (the original security for the *assignat*) were suspended, the Directors took up a proposal for the replacement of the *assignat* by a reliable bank-note. In return for a substantial grant of national property, a number of prominent bankers proposed to establish a new bank which would be capable of issuing notes both to redeem the *assignat* and to supply the Treasury. Sensible though it was, this scheme was wrecked by an impassioned Press campaign fought against it by Robert Lindet: furiously resentful of his own exclusion from public office, he argued that corruption must be implicit in any proposal to replace public finance by private enterprise.[1] The forced loan, too, proved a failure. So effectively was this obstructed by the local administrative bodies that almost a year elapsed before it produced some 300 million francs, about half the expected total. Moreover, only 12 millions of this were paid in coin, and the Directors had in any case had to stave off their creditors by granting them the right to receive the revenue as it came in. Despite these reverses, however, they held firm to their resolution, and on 19 February 1796 the plates from which the *assignats* were printed were publicly destroyed in the Place Vendôme.

Since there were at that time still *assignats* in circulation to the nominal value of 34 billion francs,[2] one further attempt was made to replace these by a valid paper currency. In March 1796 a law agreed between the Directors and the Councils created a new government issue of paper known as the *mandats territoriaux*. These notes were strictly mortgage debentures entitling the bearer to immediate possession of national property, a corresponding amount of which was specifically set aside as security for the issue. They were also to be legal tender, exchangeable for *assignats* at the rate of 30 francs *assignat* to one franc *mandat*, and so high was the hope that this issue would restore confidence in the currency that the ban previously imposed on the sale of national property was withdrawn. In fact, however, experience soon

---

[1] See A. Montier, *Robert Lindet* (Paris, 1899), p. 332ff. *Biog. Notes:* LINDET.
[2] Mathiez, p. 105 and Godechot, p. 433; Lefebvre, p. 26, gives 39 billions.

showed that while the *mandat* was reasonably valued in terms of property, the price of which was taken at approximately 20 times that of 1790, it was quite wrongly valued in terms of the *assignat*, which then stood at the most at $\frac{1}{4}$%. Consequently the *mandat* depreciated so rapidly that by July 1796 it, too, was almost useless. As a last desperate measure the Directors then sold a private company, the Dijon Company, the right to collect the issue of *mandats* for a down payment of $2\frac{1}{2}$ millions in cash, and at the price of a vast profit to the company, a protracted law-suit and a major public scandal, the paper money of France practically disappeared. On 4 February 1797 both the *assignat* and the *mandat* ceased to be legal tender.

By then the revolutionary paper money was so completely discredited that its abandonment, which would once have seemed tantamount to the repudiation of the Revolution itself, scarcely caused comment. Nor, indeed, did it do much to help the Directors, for in spite of all the devices they adopted to bring coinage back into circulation, this remained rare. In a word, grave financial difficulties persisted throughout the first critical 18 months of the Constitutional Republic, and these certainly seriously compromised the possibility of establishing it securely.

Amongst other things, the constant shortage of money poisoned the Directors' relationship with the Councils even while the majority of deputies were still men of the Convention. The Directors perpetually demanded funds and constantly complained that the Councils and the Treasury were hampering their work and weakening the armies by quibbling over details and procrastinating over grants; and the Councils, for their part, became increasingly convinced that it was folly to keep on supplying money to men who neither could nor would account for its perpetual disappearance. Driven to desperate expedients, the Directors sold off all the national assets they could, from woods and forests to the crown jewels, and yet they became ever more dependent upon dubious contractors to keep the armies supplied. Further, although it would be wrong to suppose that the civil government was at this time dominated by its generals, the influence of the latter was undoubtedly increased by the contributions which came in cash to the French Treasury from the conquered territories.

As might be expected, the collapse of the revolutionary currency also had profound social repercussions. Those who were in a position to speculate were able to make enormous profits and to purchase national property for such derisory sums that the Councils were convinced that the Directors were deliberately dissipating the national inheritance. To take one instance alone, in 1796 a man purchased a piece of woodland for 63,000 francs *mandat*, the equivalent of 3,000 francs in coin, and promptly sold the timber alone for 25,000 francs in coin.[1] As Benjamin Constant had remarked in 1795, when on his first arrival in France from Switzerland he had bought for 30,000 Swiss francs an estate which gave him a steady income of 8,000 francs a year: 'What things might a man do here with 200,000 francs in cash!'[2] What could be accomplished may be seen from the fortunes of Fouché: being discredited and practically penniless at the close of the Convention, he joined Tallien and Réal in a company dealing in military supplies and in 1799 possessed a château and an annual income of 20,000 francs.[3] On the other hand, all those who were in government service on a fixed salary, or who were dependent on annuities paid in paper, suffered very severely, as may be seen from the instance of the judge who in the fall of 1795 was found dead in his chambers from starvation.[4] As for the urban poor, their conditions were now more miserable than ever. Prices, even in metal currency, were in 1795–6 more than twice those which had preceded the great Parisian rising of 1789.[5] Moreover, another poor harvest in 1795, and the persistent reluctance of countrymen to exchange good grain for worthless paper, kept the cities near starvation level throughout that winter. In these circumstances the Directors not only continued the food-controls established in 1793, but enforced them more strictly than ever. Millions of francs were spent in supplying Paris and other big towns with grain, which was obtained by taking it from the peasants in lieu of taxation; and bread, meat and rice were distributed to the population at purely nominal prices. Outright famine was thus avoided, but its proximity is apparent in the increase of 10,000 in the death-rate in the Department of the Seine alone.[6]

Although these evil conditions, aggravated as they were by the most startling contrasts of poverty and prosperity, inevitably engendered bitterness and unrest, the urban masses were no longer capable of a great uprising. For them, life had become mainly a matter of endurance. To

[1] Mathiez, *Le Directoire*, p. 108.

[2] J. C. Herold, *Mistress to An Age: A Life of Madame de Staël* (N.Y., 1958), p. 161.

[3] Mathiez, op. cit., p. 129. It is said that Fouché ultimately left a legacy of 14 million livres.

[4] Mathiez, op. cit., p. 89.

[5] 'In December 1795 bread was selling in Paris at 50 francs a lb., or seven sous in metallic currency.' (Lefebvre, *The Directory*, p. 28). Thus the quartern loaf, if it could be obtained, would have cost 28 sous in coin, whereas in the spring of 1789 its price was dangerously high at approximately half that amount.

[6] Lefebvre, op. cit., p. 29.

the men of the governing classes, however, any agitation which coincided with a subsistence crisis was a portent of peril: so lively were their recollections of the past that, to them, insurrection always seemed imminent.[1] Since the Directors themselves were already extremely sensitive to criticism, the first political test which the constitutional régime encountered, a revival of the challenge of the Jacobins, had far more serious consequences than its real importance warranted at that time.

As we have seen, Jacobinism as an organised political movement had been effectively broken in 1794, and after Prairial the remaining deputies of the Mountain had been persecuted and ostracised. Democracy, too, had become so discredited by the Terror and by insurrection that the property-owners' Constitution of 1795 had been accepted by France almost without dissent. Constitutional government, on the other hand, had been begun at a time when the threat of counter-revolution seemed serious: the royalist landings at Quiberon had but recently been repulsed, the *chouans* in western France were still under arms, and royalists in Paris had just initiated the bloody rising of Vendémiaire. The new government, therefore, while disavowing 'anarchy', had from the first been inclined to lean towards the left. The Convention's Law of 3 Brumaire, the Legislative Body's choice of regicide Directors, and the Directors' own subsequent selection of 'Jacobin' commissioners had all been aspects of this 'Union of Republicans'; and all had been correspondingly offensive to the deputies of the 'new third' and presumably to the greater part of the political nation. The Directors, moreover, did not hesitate to subsidise radical republican journals; and, as the Constitution required, they permitted the re-establishment of political clubs, subject though these were to those constitutional articles which strictly forbade any form of affiliation or collective action.

The opening of the constitutional period consequently offered considerable opportunities for compromise and reconciliation. The Directors, who could have endeavoured to associate the conservative deputies of the 'new third' with their work, had also the prospect of rallying wider support amongst those Frenchmen who were still faithful to the democratic tradition. Nor, despite all the difficulties of the situation, is it inconceivable that really able leaders might not have been capable of accomplishing both these things. For to the Jacobins, too, the time was potentially one of opportunity. If, being tolerated, they could successfully rid themselves of the taint of Terrorism—which is often said to have been only a transitory characteristic of their movement—they could

[1] Ibid., p. 3: ' "Social" fear dominated the history of the Directory.'

at least uphold, and perhaps influence the government towards, their belief in limited state intervention in the economy and full public participation in public affairs. Something of this sort certainly appears to have been in the minds of many of those who attended the most important of the new clubs, the 'Reunion of the Friends of the Republic', which is more commonly known from its place of meeting as the Panthéon Club.[1] Though attended from its foundation by upwards of a thousand members, it observed the law meticulously and was most careful not to occasion the government any anxiety. As one journal put it early in December 1795: 'As of now the Constitution of '95 is our veritable source of order and energy; every good citizen owes it, not the sacrifice of his opinion nor his ultimate views, but a public respect, a sincere submission and the tribute of his efforts, without losing, for all that, the right to prepare its reform or improvement.'[2]

This potentially promising position was, however, cast away by the activities of a minority of extremists. In the first instance, the uncompromising hostility of Robert Lindet blighted the possibilities of cooperation between the Jacobins and the Directors. Although personally approached by Carnot, once his colleague on the great Committee of Public Safety, he flatly refused to serve the Directors as a commissioner, replying to Carnot with the words: 'I do not wish to be responsible for the organisation of bankruptcy and famine';[3] and as has been said, it was he who was primarily responsible for the frustration of the plan to establish a form of national bank. In the words of Mathiez, indeed, 'No-one did more than he to wreck the policy of reunion, and no-one was more tenacious in trying to revive the passions of the past'.[4] At the same time another of the excluded Montagnards, Jean-Baptiste Amar,[5] a man of considerable wealth, encouraged a group of malcontents and extremists to meet in his apartment and to discuss plans for a new insurrection. According to one of those involved, the Italian Buonarroti,[6] these men regarded the Constitution of 1795 as 'illegitimate in its origin, oppressive in its spirit and tyrannical in its intentions', and as the winter wore on they were increasingly successful in penetrating the Panthéon Club,

---

[1] It met in the great hall of a disused convent, l'Abbaye de Ste Geneviève, near the Panthéon.

[2] J. Woloch, *Jacobin Legacy: The Democratic Movement under the Directory* (Princeton, 1970), p. 25.

[3] A. Montier, *Robert Lindet* (Paris, 1899), p. 322.

[4] Mathiez, op. cit., p. 149.

[5] *Biog. Notes:* AMAR.

[6] *Biog. Notes:* BUONARROTI.

which was to them no more than a convenient cover for the design of destroying the Directory.[1]

Amar and his associates, moreover, also encouraged, and probably actually financed, violent attacks upon the Directory by a journalist who called himself Gracchus Babeuf.[2] A man of humble origins about whom a huge historical literature has been built up in recent years, Babeuf may best be described here as one whose passionate hatred for social injustice had been perpetually inflamed by what was to him personal misfortune and unmerited political persecution. Repeatedly imprisoned and perpetually in opposition to all régimes, he had by this time become a professional revolutionary who was convinced that a further, final, revolution was imperative to consolidate the welfare of mankind.[3] Resuming publication of his paper, *The Tribune of the People*, in mid-November 1795, he first denounced the Constitution of 1795 as a violation of the plebiscite which had sanctioned the 'democratic' Montagnard Constitution of 1793, and demanded an insurrection and an immediate return to revolutionary government. The second number, which appeared on 30 November, went still further. Repudiating those who supposed that his only desire was to substitute one constitution for another, he repudiated also the whole existing social order and called for its complete destruction; only thus, he maintained, could private property, the ultimate source of all oppression and injustice, be eliminated, and only thus could true democratic freedom and equality be established.

In the circumstances of 1795–6 the publication of ideas such as these infallibly initiated a chain reaction of repression and resistance. The Directors ordered the arrest of Babeuf, who escaped. The Jacobins, disregarding his communism but secretly delighted by his 'democratic' indictment of the Directory, praised him as a persecuted patriot,[4] particularly after his wife was arrested in the hope that she would reveal her

[1] P. Buonarroti, *Babeuf's Conspiracy for Equality* (trans. O'Brien, London, 1836), pp. 61, 63.

[2] *Biog. Notes:* BABEUF.

[3] For Babeuf, see D. Thomson, *The Babeuf Plot* (London, 1947); some extracts from his writings are available in J. Godechot, *La Pensée Révolutionnaire, 1780–1799* (Paris, Colin, 1924), pp. 250–76, and a stimulating assessment of their significance may be found in J. L. Talmon, *The Origins of Totalitarian Democracy* (London, 1961), pp. 172–200. More detailed study may be approached through the bicentennial issue of the *Annales historiques de la Révolution française*, No. 162 (Oct.–Dec. 1960) which begins with a bibliographical study by J. Godechot.

[4] Woloch, op. cit., pp. 32–42.

husband's hiding-place. Becoming increasingly critical of authority, the Jacobins were also more and more inclined to demand stringent measures of price-control to counter the economic crisis, and at the end of February 1796 the Directors retaliated by ordering Bonaparte, since Vendémiaire the commander of the Army of the Interior, to close down the Panthéon Club as well as various minor right-wing societies. There then began a general harassment of the Jacobins,[1] in the course of which the Councils passed the Law of 27 Germinal (16 April 1796) to make it a capital offence for anyone to advocate either the restoration of the monarchy or a return to the Constitution of 1793. Bonaparte, meanwhile, had married Josephine and departed to assume command of the Army of Italy—an appointment which is sometimes alleged to have been intended to remove from Paris one still suspected of Jacobin sympathies, but which was probably made on purely military grounds.[2]

The ultimate consequences of the pursuit of Babeuf are also remarkable. Being silenced, he and his closest associates once again became conspirators, devoting themselves to the preparation of that final insurrection which they had so often discussed in prison. In the event, this plot, the notorious 'Conspiracy for Equality', was scarcely even an episode: betrayed to the Directory by one of their agents, the conspirators were arrested on 10 May before they were ready to act, and the police also seized a mass of documents which enabled them to initiate a round-up of scores of supposedly incriminated persons. But though it failed completely, the Conspiracy has since been seen to mark a most important stage in the development of the theory and practice of Revolution. From his perception of popular misery, together with his appreciation of the significance of the economic controls of 1793–4 and his knowledge of the abstract egalitarianism of certain of the *philosophes*, Babeuf had compounded a fierce and uncompromising communism. If this was in some respects more relevant to the conditions of that time than of ours, it was nonetheless as far-reaching as it could be; if production did not interest Babeuf, distribution did. As he put it, 'Stomachs are equal', and his unqualified condemnation of all private ownership was matched by his insistence that freedom is chimerical unless it is accompanied by absolute economic equality. Moreover, as Lefebvre wrote, Babeuf had 'arrived at a clear conception of . . . popular dictator-

---

[1] Ibid., pp. 46–7.
[2] Appointed on 23 February, Bonaparte married Josephine—herself probably previously a mistress of Barras—on 9 March, and left Paris on 11 March. According to Lépeaux (*Mémoires*, II, p. 23), the appointment was made by the Directors unanimously.

ship':[1] the Equals, though prepared to pay full homage to the sovereignty of the people, would of necessity have to exercise it themselves until such time as the annihilation of opposition should permit enlightenment to reach the apathetic masses. To the attainment of this end the Babeuvists had given much thought, and they had arrived at an astonishingly advanced technique of revolution. By extensive propaganda and by the careful allocation of agents, the masses were to be prepared for action and the military and the police subverted from their duty; but only the innermost ring of the conspirators, the six or seven men who formed the Secret Committee, would comprehend the whole of the initial plan and something of the ultimate purpose of the insurrection.[2] In 1796 these methods, like the theoretical ideas of the conspirators, soon ceased to bear any relation to reality. Treasured by Buonarroti throughout his long years of imprisonment and exile, they were, however, eventually to be transmitted by him to the revolutionary underground of France in the 1830s, and from thence they ultimately became an integral part of the revolutionary experience which was inherited by Lenin.

More immediately, Babeuf's conspiracy proved a fatal blow to whatever possibility remained of reconciliation between the re-emergent democratic movement and the Directory of 1796. The Directors themselves of course made things worse than they need have been by exaggerating the extent of the danger. According to Barras, who had typically insured himself against all eventualities by intriguing with the malcontented, only Reubell and himself had kept their heads, the other three being seized by terror. As Barras also remarked, Carnot in particular viewed the affair with 'singular passion'.[3] Probably because Carnot's whole being was outraged by opposition to government,[4] he identified himself with the work of repression. On 12 May all those Montagnards who had been persecuted after Prairial in the previous year were banished from Paris, and every effort was made to capture those of them who, like Amar and Robert Lindet, had been foolish enough to countenance some part of Babeuf's plans. Moreover, since one Montagnard deputy who still retained his seat—Drouet, the man

---

[1] Lefebvre, *The Directory*, p. 32.

[2] It is in fact likely that even in the central secret committee few knew all that Babeuf had in mind. Buonarroti himself, for example, was probably more interested in the extension of revolutionary democracy to Italy than in anything else. See R. R. Palmer, *The Age of the Democratic Revolution*, II, pp. 237–40.

[3] Barras, *Memoirs* (ed. Duruy), II, pp. 147–50; compare Lépeaux, *Mémoires*, I, pp. 418–21.

[4] M. Reinhard, *Le Grand Carnot* (Paris, 1950–2), II, pp. 184–5.

who, as a stable-master, had first recognised Louis XVI at the time of the Flight to Varennes in 1791—had actually been arrested, a full state trial had to be arranged for all those seized in connection with the conspiracy. While this was being prepared in accordance with the Constitution, which required that a High Court should be especially convened at a distance from Paris, the Directors intensified their surveillance of the Jacobins throughout France and replaced many of their own commissioners with men who were far more conservative in character. This repression, which deprived the Jacobins of almost all their influence, would seem to have been quite indiscriminate, for in reality most of the Jacobins had ignored Babeuf's communism and deplored his incitement of violence; but to men of LaRevellière-Lépeaux's mind, all democrats were alike in being simply 'the most ferocious agents of the Terror'.[1]

Like the other Directors, Lépeaux later indignantly rejected the common charge that the Directors never did more than throw their weight aimlessly from side to side in order to counteract whichever political peril seemed most pressing. In their own eyes, their policy was one of pure republicanism, which they maintained consistently by striking hard at all who challenged them. In this there may well be more truth than is commonly allowed, just as it is probably also true that despite the occurrence of conspiracy and repression there was throughout the period of the Directory an imperceptible but steady growth in organised administration and in public acceptance of legally constituted authority.[2] Yet the Directors' determination to maintain the political position they had inherited had the result that that position became ever more identified with their own personal survival. They consequently became increasingly savage in their measures of repression.

This tendency is all too evident in the long-drawn sequel to the Babeuf affair. On the night of 9 September 1796, shortly after Babeuf and his fellow-prisoners had been sent to Vendôme to await trial, a 'Jacobin' crowd appeared at the military camp at Grenelle, on the outskirts of Paris, and endeavoured to incite the troops there to action against the Directory. Since Carnot had again been forewarned, the immediate reply was a cavalry charge. Some of the crowd were killed outright, and subsequently 31 of those who were arrested were shot after being illegally tried by a Military Commission. If this 'massacre' was not, as is sometimes suggested, the result of deliberate provocation by the government, it certainly seems to have been something that

---

[1] Lépeaux, loc. cit.; compare Woloch, loc. cit.
[2] Aulard, *A Political History*, III, p. 327.

Carnot could easily have prevented had he so wished.[1] Similarly, the government clearly went to endless lengths to secure the conviction of Babeuf and all those accused with him in the protracted proceedings at Vendôme in the spring of 1797. By brilliant self-defence,[2] Babeuf succeeded in his assertion that neither he nor anyone else had actually done anything more than publicise permissible opinions, and he and all the others were eventually acquitted on the general charge of conspiracy. The government, however, had the charge altered at the last moment, so that seven of the accused, including Buonarroti, were sentenced to deportation,[3] and two, Babeuf and Darthé,[4] were condemned to death for advocating the restoration of the Constitution of 1793. Both the condemned men at once attempted to commit suicide, but both were nevertheless carried to the scaffold and executed (27 May 1797). If the initial acquittal stands in striking tribute to the ultimate efficacy of the Constitution of 1795, the final verdict must also mark the ruthless partiality of the Directory. To the democrats Vendôme, like Grenelle, was henceforth to be a name hallowed by the blood of martyrs.

[1] Lépeaux, *Mémoires*, II, pp. 7–9; Reinhard, *Le Grand Carnot*, loc. cit., and Mathiez, *Le Directoire*, pp. 231–34.

[2] See *The Defense of Gracchus Babeuf before the High Court of Vendôme* (ed. and trans. J. A. Scott, Univ. of Massachusetts Press, 1967).

[3] 65 persons were indicted, of whom 47 were present in court. Drouet, whose involvement was the ostensible reason for the state trial, escaped in advance of the proceedings and lived to become a Sub-prefect in Sainte-Ménehould for Bonaparte.

[4] *Biog. Notes:* DARTHÉ.

5. The Loss of the Middle Way, May 1796-September 1797

By crushing the Jacobins, the Directors accelerated the process of political change which was continuing around them. Even before Babeuf was arrested on 10 May 1796 it was evident that the repudiation of the Left would be accompanied by a corresponding revival of the Right. Conservative republicans and would-be constitutional monarchists alike were then highly optimistic about the future. As Dupont de Nemours saw it on 7 May: 'The Directory is rallying more and more every day with the honest and imposing mass of the Nation which wants the Constitution, laws, order and internal peace, and which detests in equal measure the Counter-Revolution and a prolongation of the Revolution.'[1] In that same month the *Moniteur* began to publish instalments of a work in which Benjamin Constant[2]—and in all probability the exiled Madame de Staël[3]—urged all honest men to recognise that since the intransigence of the Bourbons made a restoration impossible, the nation's best hope lay in the formation of a strong republican party which could support the Directory in a policy of toleration and compromise. 'Men of all parties', he cried, 'rally to a government which offers you liberty and peace and which cannot crumble without burying you in its ruins.'[4] At the beginning of June, moreover, Carnot—probably the only one of the Directors to believe that the government should make concessions to the Right in order to win the support of moderate men—received Mathieu Dumas[5] and several of his friends at dinner in the Tuileries. According to Dumas's own account, these ex-Feuillants had now no thought of serving the royal cause, but wished only 'to prevent the return of anarchy and to bring republican government, such as they found it and such as usurpation had made it, to legitimise itself

[1] *L'Historien* of 18 Floréal An IV, cited by Mathiez, *Le Directoire*, p. 219.
[2] *Biog. Notes:* BENJAMIN CONSTANT.
[3] *Biog. Notes:* MADAME DE STAËL.
[4] H. Nicholson, *Benjamin Constant* (London, 1949), p. 130.
[5] *Biog. Notes:* DUMAS.

by the probity and morality of its actions'.[1] This meant in practice the replacement of obnoxious ministers by more congenial men, and the modification or repeal of the 'exceptional legislation' of 3 Brumaire Year IV (by which the introduction of the Constitution had been accompanied by the exclusion of the relatives of *émigrés* from public office and by the revival of the penal laws against priests). Above all, perhaps, it meant the conclusion of the war by 'a safe and honourable' peace.

The difficulties of establishing a strong centre party of the sort which was envisaged were, of course, considerable. On the one hand, those who thought of themselves as the men of the Revolution immediately took alarm. On 9 June Tallien assailed the Directors for simultaneously persecuting patriots and encouraging reactionaries, and this attack at once revived recrimination and suspicion. Although Tallien was unsuccessful in the assembly, he and Sieyès were soon able to attract upwards of a hundred deputies to meetings at the Hôtel de Noailles, where the necessity of preserving the Law of 3 Brumaire inviolate was nothing less than an article of faith. On the other hand Dumas and his friends stood in constant danger of being compromised by the activities of the *émigrés*. Thus when Wickham, the British agent in Switzerland, succeeded in establishing Antoine d'André as a principal representative of the cause of constitutional monarchy,[2] the latter's first move was to send messengers to make contact with Dumas and his friends, who had once been his colleagues in the Constituent Assembly. Asked about the possibility of reaching some agreement with 'Louis XVIII', the Dumas group carefully reiterated the necessity of supporting the existing government against the Jacobins, and as carefully explained that 'nothing was to be done for the present'; but their reply was nevertheless reported to Wickham with one from another group of deputies who were more extremist and far less non-committal.[3] Whatever the real intentions of Dumas and his friends—and it would not be surprising or discreditable if, like many others, they saw some need to anticipate the possibility of a restoration—their policy was certainly alarming. It was, for example, they who later arranged for the readmission to the Council of Five Hundred of the deputy Vaublanc, who had been condemned to death *in absentia* for the active part he had played in the rising of Vendé-

---

[1] Lieut.-Gen. Mathieu Dumas, *Memoirs of His Own Time* (2 Vols. London, 1829), Vol. II, p. 64.

[2] See below, p. 121ff.

[3] W. R. Fryer, *Republic or Restoration in France? 1794–97* (Manchester, 1965), pp. 129–36.

miaire.[1] As this episode shows, the conservative revival could easily open a road for a far more fullblooded royalist reaction.

Further, although 'Louis XVIII' had in fact dismissed as 'wholly inadmissible' all suggestions that he should make some temporary concessions to constitutionalism,[2] the men whom his intransigence drove into the Directors' arms were treated by all save Carnot with profound distrust. As Dumas wrote: 'It was not with us, but against us, that the majority of the Directory wished to govern'.[3] Indeed, according to Barras the attitude of Reubell to moderates like Thibaudeau was: 'They all ought to be thrust into a sack and pitched into the river'. The Directors, for their part, had some reason to suppose that the conservatives really regarded them as nothing but Terrorists who were only worthy of temporary toleration.[4]

Deep-seated distrust of this sort was in fact already dividing the Directory against itself. In general, Carnot and Letourneur seem to have been agreed that cooperation with the Right and strong measures against the Jacobins were imperative, whereas Reubell and (to a lesser extent) Barras believed that the real danger to the Republic came from the royalists and their sympathisers on the Right. This division, embittered by recrimination and aggravated by a general resentment of Carnot's unfortunate tendency to arrogate the authority of his colleagues, easily led each pair of Directors to suspect that the other was acting in connivance with the worst enemies of the Republic. Even Lépeaux, who as yet stood somewhat apart from these conflicts, was intensely suspicious of the others, having no doubt that Barras had been involved with Babeuf, or that Carnot had deliberately provoked the Grenelle affair in order to promote a royalist reaction.[5]

For all these reasons it proved impossible at this time to form an effective alliance between the 'old' republicans who supported the Directory and those men who were prepared to accept the Republic but believed that some real relaxation of the restrictive revolutionary legislation was imperative. This failure was particularly unfortunate, for the period before the elections of 1797, when some 250 of those deputies who had previously been members of the Convention were due to retire from the Councils, was a vital transitional one. The original requirement

---

[1] Vaublanc, *Mémoires* (ed. Barrière, Paris, 1857), pp. 306–8; Fryer, op. cit., p. 140, n. 2. Vaublanc took his place on 30 August.

[2] Fryer, op. cit., p. 106.

[3] Dumas, *Memoirs*, II, p. 71.

[4] Barras, *Memoirs*, II, pp. 177, 159–61.

[5] Lépeaux, *Mémoires*, II, pp. 4, 7–9.

that two-thirds of the initial membership of the Councils should be drawn from the Convention had of course been justified by the argument that experienced men should be in a position to protect the Constitution during its infancy: but such temporary tutelage would evidently be pointless if it were not accompanied by some sincere endeavour to win support for the new order.

To historians in the revolutionary tradition it has seemed that this failure to achieve reconciliation in 1796 was primarily due to the impossibility of satisfying a reactionary Right. According to this view, the 'concessions' which were made by well-meaning but misguided republicans were exploited without scruple by their 'royalist' opponents, who immediately made fresh demands.[1] This view, however, would seem to derive from the continuation of conflict about the selection of local administrators, and from the fact that few local authorities were now seriously enforcing the laws against the clergy and the *émigrés*. In the Councils themselves, the more striking thing is the inability of the Right to win any real concessions. Despite protracted debates during the final months of 1796, they did not succeed in establishing a realistic law about the Press (which was nominally free, but actually restricted by the laws against conspiracy).[2] Nor did equally lengthy discussion of the Law of 3 Brumaire lead to its amendment in any significant way: all that the Right could secure was the repeal of the article which ordered the enforcement of the revolutionary legislation against dissident priests, a 'concession' which did not seem to affect the validity of the penal laws themselves.[3] Yet even this was enough to alarm the violently anti-clerical Lépaux, who henceforth tended to join Barras and Reubell in opposition to Carnot. Thus at the end of 1796 the Directory and the Councils were still both so deeply divided that something like stalemate ensued, all concerned looking more and more to the outcome of the spring elections.

During 1796, too, military events made it ever more difficult for the government to conclude that 'safe and honourable' peace which was a principal objective of the so-called 'royalists' in the Councils. Carnot, who was still primarily responsible for the direction of the war, had for this year planned a major attack on Austria through Germany. The

---

[1] E.g., Mathiez, *Le Directoire*, pp. 256, 263–5, 273–5; Lefbvre, *The Directory*, pp. 37–41.

[2] Aulard, *A Political History*, III, pp. 274–5.

[3] It was also agreed that the 'terrorists' who had benefited by the amnesty of October 1795 should be excluded, like the relatives of *émigrés*, from all public offices. This, the Law of 14 Frimaire Year IV (10 December, 1796), was a further blow to the Jacobins rather than a positive gain by the Right.

Army of the Sambre and the Meuse, under Jourdan, and that of the Rhine and the Moselle, the command of which had passed in April from Pichegru[1] to Moreau, were to cross the Rhine at Düsseldorf and Strasbourg, to advance simultaneously to the Danube, and then to move as a united force upon Vienna. The Army of Italy, a much smaller force, was meanwhile to move forward in support of these operations in order to prevent the enemy from concentrating his forces in Germany.[2] As it happened, however, success eluded France in the main theatre of war, but attended her arms in astonishing measure in Italy.

Failure and success were largely due to the appearance on each side of men of military genius. In Germany the French generals, able as they were, were outmatched by a new Austrian commander, the young Archduke Charles. When the armistice made in December 1795 was broken late in May 1796, the forces of Jourdan[3] advanced rapidly from Düsseldorf, but had to retire in equal haste when the Archduke moved in strength against them. Moreau,[4] meanwhile, had had great difficulty in breaking through on the Rhine; but when he succeeded on 20 June, he quickly defeated Condé and the *émigrés* at Ettlingen and swept forward to Stuttgart and the Danube. By 24 August his army was directly threatening Munich, and as the Archduke returned southwards to meet him, Jourdan was also able to take the offensive and advance almost to Ratisbon. By this time the German states of the Holy Roman Empire were recommending the Emperor to make peace, and the Emperor himself was preparing to leave Vienna. The Archduke Charles, however, had contrived to retain a central position between the converging French armies, and from Ingolstadt he suddenly struck hard towards Nuremberg in Jourdan's rear. So began a disorderly French retirement and an Austrian pursuit which ended only when Jourdan was compelled to recross the Rhine at Düsseldorf at the end of September. Moreau, who had for a time continued to advance alone, eventually realised the danger of doing so and fell back also, his retreat being rightly famed as a major feat of arms. As the Austrians constantly sealed off the successive routes to the north, he was compelled to retire along the Danube to the Black Forest; and finally, as the Archduke came down the Rhine to cut him

---

[1] Pichegru had been dismissed in March 1796 and offered an appointment to the Swedish embassy. Apparently the Directors had doubts of his loyalty and zeal, but did not know the full story of his relationship with Condé. See H. Mitchell, *The Underground War against Revolutionary France*, pp. 121, 191.

[2] M. Reinhard, *Le Grand Carnot*, II, pp. 193, 202. Bonaparte's Army of Italy had some 37,000 men as compared with Jourdan's 95,000 and Moreau's 85,000.

[3] *Biog. Notes:* JOURDAN.

[4] *Biog. Notes:* MOREAU.

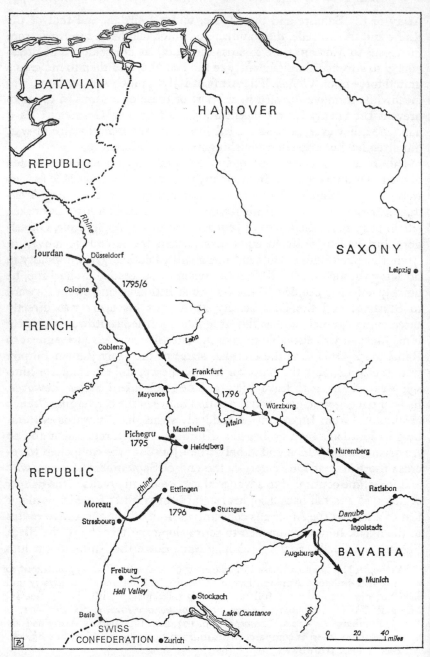

BATAVIAN

HANOVER

REPUBLIC

SAXONY

Rhine

Jourdan   Düsseldorf   Leipzig •

1795/6

Cologne •

FRENCH

Lahn

Coblenz

Frankfurt

Mayence   1796

Würzburg

Pichegru   Mannheim
1795   • Heidelberg   *Main*

REPUBLIC   • Nuremberg

Rhine   • Ettlingen   Ratisbon

Moreau   1796   • Stuttgart   *Danube*
Strasbourg •   Ingolstadt

Augsburg •   BAVARIA

Freiburg •
Hell Valley   • Munich

Basle •   • Stockach   *Lech*
SWISS   *Lake Constance*
CONFEDERATION • Zurich

0   20   40
miles

The French Campaigns in Germany, 1795, 1796

off, he regained that river by forcing his way through a narrow defile known as the Valley of Hell. The return of his army to France on 24 October nevertheless marked the complete collapse of the principal French attack.

On the other hand, the spectacular success of the Army of Italy, the smallest and worst-provided of the French armies, made the year 1796 immortal in military history. Even before his appointment as its commander, Bonaparte, reporting daily to the Directory on the situation of Paris, had constantly proffered advice about the Italian front; and General Schérer, the man on the spot, had eventually told the Directors outright that whoever was responsible for their proposals ought to come to Italy and put them into effect himself.[1] This, and much more besides, Bonaparte did. When he assumed command at Nice on 27 March he promptly ordered Berthier,[2] whom good fortune had assigned to him as his Chief of Staff, to move his headquarters forward 60 miles, a move in itself symbolic of a campaign remarkable for rapid marches and sudden concentrations of force. The French, whose effective strength was 37,600 men, were at first confronted by a most formidable obstacle: the arc of the Maritime Alps, which descend from the heights of Savoy to the sea near Genoa, was held by 25,000 Piedmontese from the Col de l'Argentière to Carcare, and by 31,000 Austrians from Carcare to the coast. Acting against all precedent, Bonaparte broke through this shield in a fortnight. Diverting the main Austrian army by a feint towards Genoa, on 11 April he struck at the junction of the allied lines at Carcare. After scattering Austrian forces at the battles of Montenotte and Dego on 12 and 14 April, he turned against the Piedmontese, defeating them at Mondovi on 21 April and advancing on their capital, Turin. Less than a week later the emissaries of King Victor Amadeus accepted the Armistice of Cherasco, by which the French acquired control of the fortresses commanding the route from France through Piedmont to Lombardy. As Bonaparte said when at one o'clock in the morning of 27 April he gave the Piedmontese emissaries one further hour to accept his terms: 'It may happen to me to lose battles, but no

---

[1] Reinhard, op. cit., II, p. 201. Bonaparte's Italian campaign, and the question of the extent to which his genius was influenced by his teachers and earlier military thinkers, have been the subjects of much historical writing. The books which I have found most useful are: F. Markham, *Napoleon* (London, 1964); Lt-Col. T. M. Hunter, *Napoleon in Victory and Defeat* (Historical Section, Army H.Q., Ottawa, 1964); and S. Wilkinson, *The Rise of General Bonaparte* (Oxford, 1930).

[2] *Biog. Notes:* BERTHIER.

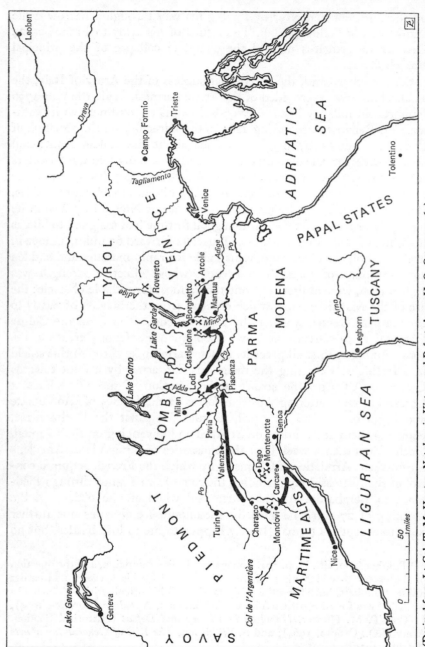

(Derived from Lt-Col. T. M. Hunter, *Napoleon in Victory and Defeat*, Army H.Q. Ottowa, 1964)

7 Barras

8 Mme de Staël
*after a painting by
Gérard*

9 Triumphal entry of monuments of the sciences and the arts, 27 July 1798

one shall ever see me lose minutes either by over-confidence or sloth'.[1]

Yet all this was but a preliminary step for Bonaparte, whose purpose was to destroy the Austrian army, occupy Lombardy and carry the war through the Tyrol into Bavaria.[2] When the Austrian commander, Beaulieu, managed to retire across the River Po at Valenza before he could be cut off from the north, Bonaparte avoided direct pursuit, which would have involved him in crossing the many tributaries which feed the Po from the Alps. Instead, he sent a picked force forward into neutral territory (the Duchy of Parma) to seize a bridgehead at Piacenza, a threat which forced Beaulieu to abandon Milan and retire behind the Adda. Here on 10 May the French caught the Austrian rearguard and seized the bridge at Lodi—a battle in which Bonaparte took personal command whilst under heavy fire, though he did not, as legend relates, charge the enemy at the head of his grenadiers. Only when Beaulieu stood on the Mincio, a short front protecting the fortress of Mantua and resting at its ends on the Po and Lake Garda, did Bonaparte pause to refresh his men and occupy Milan. Even so, the respite was short: on 30 May—the day before Jourdan opened his initial attack in Germany—the Army of Italy surprised and smashed Beaulieu's defences at Borghetto, an engagement which compelled the Austrians to retreat again to the Adige. At this point the Directory, conspicuously failing to co-ordinate the campaigns in Germany and Italy, prohibited further pursuit and ordered Bonaparte to turn southwards and assert French power in Italy: British trade was to be excluded from Leghorn, the Kingdom of Naples was to be forced from the anti-French alliance, and the Papacy brought under French domination. For the remainder of 1796, while Jourdan and Moreau were being beaten back from Bavaria to the Rhine, Bonaparte's principal military task was to maintain the siege of Mantua. This city successive Austrian generals with apparently overwhelming forces attempted to relieve, only to be outmanoeuvred and defeated at the battles of Castiglione (5 August), Roverto (4 September) and Arcole (15–18 November).

Victory on this scale, unexpected and unforeseen, inevitably shifted the political problems of France to a new scale of magnitude. For one thing, Bonaparte and his army suddenly emerged as a new and powerful factor in the situation. The general, who in Paris had written of his marriage with Josephine as 'a pledge of my firm intention to seek honour

[1] Wilkinson, op. cit., p. 132.
[2] Hunter, op. cit., p. 57, citing *Correspondence de Napoléon Ier*, I, pp. 236–7 (No. 257).

only in the service of the Republic',[1] had indeed 'consistently sub-ordinated tactics and strategy to French policy'[2] in 1796: but in the course of his campaign he nevertheless steadily emancipated himself from civilian control by presenting the Directory with a series of *faits accomplis*. Only once did the government whose cause he seemed to serve so well seriously attempt to assert its authority. Immediately after the battle of Lodi—that conflict which Bonaparte later said had first awakened in him a full awareness of his powers—when the Directors ordered the abandonment of the pursuit of the Austrians, they also indicated their intention of dividing the Army of Italy and appointing General Kellermann to the command in the vital northern sector. Obey-ing the military order, Bonaparte objected vehemently to this proposed reorganisation. His letter of 14 May, a well-justified and effective protest against civil interference in successful military operations, was also a threat of resignation, and the Directors at once capitulated to it.[3] Soon afterwards Bonaparte, who had never hesitated to accept diplomatic responsibilities, was determining policy and dictating treaties from a headquarters which had many of the characteristics of a court. Wor-shipped by his soldiers, he was by the summer of 1796 virtually the ruler of Italy, whence his reports to Paris were accompanied by advice to the Directors about the suppression of factions in France.

More immediately, the Directors had to decide what use was to be made of the new power which France had acquired. Bonaparte himself, while he regarded the rich plains of Lombardy as a fruitful field for requisitioning and robbery, found it expedient to encourage the aspira-tions of Italian revolutionaries, at least up to the point of creating petty republics which would be the satellites of the French Republic. It was in accordance with this policy that in October 1796 he reorganised the northern states into three republics, the Cisalpine (Milan), the Cispadane (Modena and Reggio) and the Transpadane (Bologna and Ferrara). Amongst the Directors, however, only Lépeaux was really in sympathy with this policy, the others being primarily interested in the immediate exploitation of Bonaparte's conquests. This, in the first instance, meant filling the depleted coffers of France with the wealth of Italy. Bonaparte, who had been told on his appointment that 'the raising of very consider-

---

[1] Ibid., p. 36, citing *Correspondance*, I, 117–18 (No. 89): '*de ne trouver de salut que dans la République*'.

[2] Ibid., p. 42.

[3] Ibid., pp. 61–3. See also J. M. Thompson, *Napoleon Bonaparte, His Rise and Fall* (Oxford, 1963), pp. 71–2, and Reinhard, op. cit., II, pp. 205–6—where Carnot's acceptance of Bonaparte's action is ascribed to 'feebleness or error'.

able sums of money will be imperative',[1] consequently imposed upon the Italian states a swift succession of settlements which were nothing less than brigandage on a grand scale. At an early stage in the process, too, the inadvisability of resistance was made manifest: when a tax of 20 million livres and the surrender of invaluable art-treasures was imposed upon Lombardy, the city of Pavia rose in revolt; but Bonaparte (whose communications were admittedly jeopardised) returned in person to supervise the storming of its walls, and then gave the place over to his troops for a three-hour period of massacre, lust and rapacity.[2] In all, it is thought that some 50 million livres were extorted from Italy,[3] the Papacy in particular being mulcted of 15½ millions in cash, and of pictures, statues and manuscripts worth more than as much again. How much of this plunder reached France is, however, another matter.

Although Lépeaux subsequently described these depredations as shameful, many Frenchmen felt rather, as did Thibaudeau, that it was right and proper for France, the centre of the new republican civilisation, to acquire and preserve the treasures of antiquity. To Thibaudeau, indeed, it seemed that in 1796 the Republic was at last winning European recognition, and that it was 'a very fine thing to be a French citizen'.[4] But while Bonaparte's victories naturally had an intoxicating effect in France, they also made the conclusion of a moderate and judicious peace more remote than ever. This was no longer only a question of determining where the frontier of France should lie; explosive as that issue remained, the future of what was incontestably foreign territory, beyond the Alps, had now to be decided also. To Carnot, this was no more than a complication: to secure a permanent settlement in Europe, the sacrifice of all conquests was worthwhile.[5] To Reubell, however, the lands of Italy were invaluable as means to an end: in exchange for them, Austria would certainly surrender its rights in Belgium and recognise the extension of French territory to the Rhine. Nor was this all, for a third Director,

---

[1] Mathiez, *Le Directoire*, p. 120. Civilian commissioners were attached to the French armies at this time, but they had but a shadow of the power once wielded by the former Commissioners of the Convention. According to Melito, Bonaparte said of them in June 1796: 'They count for nothing in my policy'. (Melito, *Memoirs*, p. 52.)

[2] The phraseology here derives from that of J. Holland Rose, *The Life of Napoleon I* (6th ed., London, 1916), p. 98.

[3] Lefebvre estimates that about one-fifth of this sum reached the government (*The Directory*, p. 75).

[4] Lépeaux, *Mémoires*, II, p. 25; Thibaudeau, *Mémoires*, II, p. 129, 133–5.

[5] According to Barras (*Memoirs*, II, p. 255), Carnot had said: 'I would not delay peace a single hour for the sake of the whole of Italy'.

Lépeaux, represented the cosmopolitan tradition of the Revolution: seeing the peoples of Italy as liberated from tyranny and clericalism, he believed—like Bonaparte, but more altruistically—that it was the duty of France to assist them to attain manly republican independence.[1] Thus while all wanted peace, the possession of northern Italy aggravated the profound differences that divided the Directors and the deputies alike; for conquests, whether won by the sword or inspired by idealism, were identified by the Right with Jacobinism, just as a compromise peace was equated by the Left with royalism. The temptation to temporise was consequently strong, and it was made the more so by the humiliating collapse of the campaign in Germany. As the year ended men awaited the fall of Mantua in much the same way as they awaited the outcome of the elections in France.

Peace, however, had already become something more than a matter of controversy amongst statesmen. In mid-November Carnot himself tried to anticipate events by persuading the Directory to despatch a special agent, General Clarke, to Italy to negotiate an armistice with Austria. But while Carnot, now increasingly the representative of the Right, sought peace without conquests, Bonaparte's attitude was very different. Being determined to renew his assault upon Austria at the first opportunity, he suspected with some reason that Clarke had been sent to report on his activities.[2] He was, moreover, extremely hostile to the proposal that Lombardy, which he regarded almost as a personal possession, might be exchanged for the Rhineland. Clarke, who was repulsed by the Austrians, was therefore also snubbed and rebuffed by Bonaparte, his failure being indicative of the widening rift between the soldiers in the field and the conservatives in Paris. Purged by desertion and refined by battle, the Army of Italy was ardently republican, as were, in varying degrees, the other armies of France. They were, moreover, increasingly convinced that many of the politicians were indistinguishable from royalists.

It was on this account doubly unfortunate that the Directors should at this time have brushed aside an approach for peace from Britain, the country whose finances gave the royalists as well as the Austrians all their means of action. To the British it was reasonable at least to attempt negotiation: while they themselves seemed unable to accomplish anything in Europe, the advent in France in 1795 of an apparently stable and respectable government had seemed to suggest that the outward march of the Revolution might at last be at an end. The Directors, how-

[1] Lépeaux, *Mémoires*, II, p. 34.
[2] Reinhard, op. cit., II, pp. 213–14. Reinhard suggests that all the Directors were united in their desire for peace at this time.

ever, had before them the far more entrancing prospect of destroying British independence altogether. By the Treaty of Basle in 1795 France had secured the friendly neutrality of Prussia, which presaged the possibility of neutralising the Baltic and severing Britain from a vital source of her naval supplies. By another treaty, that of San Ildefonso in August 1796, the Directors had secured an alliance with Spain, which compelled Britain to withdraw her fleet from the Mediterranean (and, incidentally, ended a dangerous threat to Bonaparte's lines of communication with France). Great plans were therefore afoot for the combination against England of the formidable fleets of France, Spain and Holland, a country already subject to French domination; and, as a preliminary step, General Hoche was assembling 13,000 veterans of the Vendée at Brest in readiness for an invasion of Ireland, where rebellion was imminent. From the French point of view it was therefore little short of ridiculous that in November 1796 the British should send Lord Malmesbury, a diplomat of the old school, to Paris to discuss the possibility of making peace by restoring Belgium to Austria, and he was in fact ordered to leave the country on 20 December, four days after Hoche's army had been embarked for Ireland. Military considerations aside, however, the arrogance of the Directory towards Malmesbury, as well as the general contemporary conviction that his mission was merely a façade for British double-dealing, show sufficiently clearly that Britain was still regarded as the implacable enemy of the Republic.

In believing this the Directors were in error, for, as the fact of Lord Malmesbury's presence in Paris showed, the British did not regard the republican form of government as being in itself prohibitive of peace. Nor, as it soon appeared, were the British Isles to be overwhelmed so easily. Hoche's expedition indeed reached the Irish coast at Bantry Bay on 6 January 1797, but furious gales made a landing impossible and eventually drove the fleet back to Brest;[1] and when shortly afterwards the great ships of Spain entered the Atlantic to join the French, they were decisively defeated by Sir John Jervis off Cape St Vincent (14 February 1797). Thus while Duncan kept the Dutch locked in the Texel and while the Spanish lay crippled at Cadiz, Hoche's army marched away from the west to reinforce the armies on the Rhine—and the mighty operations against England dwindled down to a pathetic foray by four small ships and a handful of convicts, who finally surrendered tamely enough to the Volunteers at Fishguard.[2]

[1] E. Desbrière, 1793–1805: *Projets et Tentatives de débarquement aux iles brittaniques* (4 Vols., Paris, 1900), I, p. 135ff.
[2] Ibid. for Pluviôse An V.

Yet although the Directors, as over-confident as they were distrustful, were foolish to reject the British offer to negotiate, they were correct in their assumption that Britain was the source and fountain-head of the royalist conspiracy which caused them so much anxiety. It had in fact long been the British belief that the return of peace to Europe depended less on military victories than on the re-establishment of settled government in France: what was wanted above all was a legally constituted and generally accepted authority, at once respectable enough to recognise and strong enough to uphold the sanctity of international law. From 1795 onwards the British had hopes that the Constitutional Republic might itself prove to be just such an authority; but the continuing aggrandisement of France and the intransigence of the Directors more constantly confirmed them in their earlier judgement that peace would only be attained by the restoration of the legitimate monarchy. To achieve that end William Wickham had, as we have seen, been sent to Berne in December 1794, and through him considerable sums of money had for some time been expended in the endeavour to stimulate and organise royalist opinion and activity.[1]

Britain's sympathy for a restoration in France was, however, always subject to the proviso that the monarch should be restored with at least a very substantial measure of public consent, and subject to whatever constitutional limitations should be agreed between himself and his people. So vital did Britain consider this proviso that she constantly evaded giving any formal recognition to the Pretender, Provence; and although, as at Quiberon, the British sometimes directly aided the more extreme royalists, they always remained as reluctant to associate themselves with absolutism as they were loath to identify the monarchy with alien arms. On the other hand, the Pretender and his Court, as well as a great many of the *émigrés*, remained determined never to depart in any particular from the principles of the *ancien régime*, which they were constantly more inclined to reassert by the sword than by any measures which might imply some element of concession. Throughout 1795 and much of 1796, therefore, Wickham's task was singularly unrewarding. Entrusted with great responsibilities, but forced to rely on dubious men and still more dubious information, he strove persistently to reconcile the interests of the 'pure' royalists with those of the constitutional monarchists in France; but the suspicions of each of these groups towards the other was matched only by their common belief that there must be some ulterior motive behind any advice emanating from the British.

[1] See p. 121, n. 1.

In the course of 1796, however, Wickham was fortunate enough to find both a means of action and a man capable of winning the confidence of the constitutionalists while receiving some support from the Court. The plan was, in essence, a simple one. British influence and British money, which had hitherto been devoted to fruitless attempts to affect the course of the war, were henceforth to be used to control French political developments. In the first instance, a party sympathetic to the monarchy would be built up within the Legislative Body in 1796–7. Then in the spring of 1797, when the elections to replace the retiring third of the deputies took place, every effort would be made to ensure that sufficient monarchists were returned to give that party effective control of both the Councils. Thereafter it should be possible to effect a restoration more or less legally and with a minimum of violence, though how soon this should be done, and whether it would be expedient to await the outcome of the elections of 1798 also, remained to be determined. As this suggests, the whole plan was one which evolved gradually as contacts grew between Wickham at Berne and the deputies of the Right in Paris; and, as we have seen, the man principally responsible for making those contacts was Antoine d'André, who had once been a prominent and respected member of the National Constituent Assembly of 1789–91. Having been persuaded by Wickham to make his peace with 'Louis XVIII', d'André became Wickham's most valuable agent in the development of their 'Great Design' to restore the monarchy by legal action.[1] He was, indeed, subsequently described by Reubell as the most dangerous man he had ever known.[2]

The idea of effecting a restoration in this way was not, of course, an original one. The danger of some such development had been foreseen by Tallien before the Constitution of 1795 had come into force; the Law of 3 Brumaire had, indeed, been passed in an attempt to anticipate it. Moreover, the Pretender's own agents in Paris (who acted independently of Wickham, although they too were subsidised from London) had also come to realise in 1796 that more was to be gained by subverting deputies than by inciting armed rebellions against the Republic. Up to

---

[1] For the development of British relationships with the royalists in France, and for the activities of Wickham and d'André in particular, see: H. Mitchell, *The Underground War against Revolutionary France: The missions of William Wickham, 1794–1800* (Oxford, 1965) and W. R. Fryer, *Republic or Restoration in France? 1794–97: The Politics of French Royalism, with particular reference to the activities of A. B. J. d'André* (Manchester, 1965). As these titles suggest, both authors examined substantially the same subject, but with significant differences of emphasis and interpretation.

[2] Mitchell, op. cit., p. 130. *Biog. Notes:* D'ANDRÉ.

a certain point this was most helpful to Wickham and d'André. Since these royal agents were not compromised by constitutionalism, their recognition that nothing further could be expected of the royalists in the Vendée carried considerable weight with the Pretender, and this certainly inclined him to countenance Wickham's plans. Further, in the autumn of 1796 one of these men, Despomelles, had begun to develop The Philanthropic Institute, ostensibly a harmlessly conservative body but in reality a cover for a royalist secret society. Although this was as yet far from fully formed, it had an increasing number of local branches; and since one of its main objectives was the organisation of electoral support for royalists and their sympathisers, its support was, at the least, encouraging for Wickham.[1]

The benefits to Britain of cooperation with the 'pure' royalists were, however, accompanied by considerable disadvantages. The Institute, though nominally composed of 'The Friends of Order', had its inner ring of 'Legitimate Sons' whose ultimate objective was armed insurrection. The members of the Agency, too, were constantly inclined to abandon the long road of political infiltration in favour of conspiracy and some swift stroke of violence, a course more congenial to the Court itself than was any manipulation of the democratic processes.[2] In fact, a piece of folly of this sort led directly to the arrest of most of the members of the Agency on 30 January 1797. Two of them, the abbé Brottier and one other, had approached two well-known republican officers in Paris, either with the intention of enlisting their support for the future, or, as the police asserted, to persuade them to take part in an immediate *coup d'état* against the Councils and the Directory. Whatever their motives, the agents were twice betrayed. One of their confidants, the ne'er-do-well prince de Carency, had already revealed many of their secrets to Barras; and the two officers—Colonel Malo and Adjutant-General Ramel, the commander of the Grenadiers of the Guard of the Councils —informed the Directors of everything that occurred in their interviews with Brottier.[3]

Strangely, the immediate consequences of this affair were slight. The public attitude towards the official account of the plot was one of some incredulity, and the Agency itself was quickly reconstituted under new leadership. The arrested men, too, received relatively mild treatment.

---

[1] Fryer, op. cit., p. 194; Lefebvre, *The Directory*, pp. 55–6.

[2] Lefebvre, loc. cit., and Fryer, p. 183.

[3] Mitchell, op. cit., pp. 112–17. The prince de Carency was the ne'er-do-well son of the duc de La Vauguyon, one of the most loyal of the Pretender's ministers.

Of the 18 who appeared in court, only four were convicted, and only two of these, Brottier and Duverne du Presle, were sentenced to long terms of imprisonment. This leniency, which is sometimes contrasted with the severity previously shown to the Jacobins and so treated as proof of the Directors' natural affinities with the Right, is however misleading. The Directors in fact became involved in a protracted dispute about the trial with the judiciary, and the verdict undoubtedly reflected the judges' resentment of what one recent authority has called 'the Directors' flagrant violation of judicial procedure and independence'.[1] A few months later, indeed, the Directors found an opportunity to deal far more drastically with the convicted men.[2] Ultimately, too, the effects of this conspiracy were considerable. In all probability, knowledge of it contributed to the growth of anxiety in the Councils about the dangers of a royalist revival, a feeling which had an adverse effect upon the efforts of moderate men to create a strong conservative party. Still more important, one of the principal agents, Duverne du Presle, talked freely in order to save his own skin, so that from February onwards the Directors were well-informed about the Agency, the 'Institute' and the Anglo-Royalist attempt to penetrate and dominate the Councils. Although for the time-being the Directors kept these revelations to themselves, they were certainly influenced by them, and they were eventually to use them to devastating effect.

To the royalists, as to those who hoped to establish a strong conservative party within the republican constitution, the elections in March and April 1797 now became of crucial importance, and d'André was able to persuade the moderates associated with Dumas that all opponents of the Directors should set their differences aside to win a majority for the Right.[3] In wider perspective, too, it is clear that the hour was momentous. Threatened as the Constitutional Republic was by several different forms of arbitrary authority—the absolutism of the extreme royalists, the type of revolutionary government to which the Directors and the men of the Convention were inclined, and the independent militarism of the runaway General Bonaparte—it had so far survived in a state of suspended animation. Consequently, just as the success of the counter-revolution depended on the strength to be won by the supporters of the monarchy, so—democracy being discredited—the future of legal republican government depended on the emergence of a strong but moderate conservative coalition.

[1] Mitchell, op. cit., p. 113.
[2] See below, chapter 6.
[3] Mitchell, op. cit., p. 152.

It is on this account the more remarkable that although the Directory and the royalists alike spent money freely and resorted to every available device to organise the electorate—a political development which is notable in itself—the number of those who voted was probably only a little larger than it had been in 1795.[1] This was, no doubt, in part a consequence of the disillusionment of the Jacobins and the fact that the well-to-do were often able to exclude them from the primary assemblies. Even so, the French electorate's readiness to allow its political powers to lapse by default is a significant, though apparently a little-noticed, feature of the election. Much more attention has been given to the campaign organised by the royalists, to which 'Louis XVIII' was somehow induced to contribute. On 18 March 1797 the Pretender, who had for some time past been residing at Blankenburg with the Duke of Brunswick, issued from there a new Declaration to disassociate the monarchy from any thoughts of despotism or revenge. At this critical time, moreover, the lilies of France yielded ever so slightly to circumstance: without making any concession to constitutionalism in principle, the Pretender unbent far enough to authorise, at least by implication,[2] the use of democratic and parliamentary machinery as a means of promoting the royal interest. Heartbreaking as its rigidity was to some of the more realistic believers in constitutional monarchy,[3] the Declaration at least allowed the royalists to advance their cause under the thinnest of anti-Jacobin disguises.

Promoted by press and pulpit, advocated by the agents of d'André and of the 'Institute' alike, the royalist attack merged naturally into the wider reaction of France against economic dislocation, political instability and apparently perpetual war. The result was a resounding defeat for the Directory. According to the law, 250 of the 500 deputies who had come into the Councils from the Convention in 1795 were bound to retire in 1797; of that number, only 216 were in fact still sitting at the time of the elections; of these 216, only 11 were re-elected; and of the 11, perhaps only five or six were convinced republicans. Thus whereas before the elections the Directors were supported by approximately two-thirds of the Councils, after them that support was reduced to approximately one third. Whatever else the election meant, it undoubtedly

---

[1] For the elections, see Fryer, op. cit., pp. 192–6; Mitchell, op. cit., chapter 8 (particularly pp. 143, 150–6); Mathiez, *Le Directoire*, pp. 278–82; and Lefebvre, *The Directory*, p. 58.

[2] 'Direct men's suffrages to men of substance, the friends of order and peace': Aulard, *A Political History*, IV, p. 52. See also Fryer, op. cit., pp. 179–80.

[3] R. Palmer, *The Age of the Democratic Revolution*, II, p. 249.

deprived the government of its majority in parliament, and for this situation a Constitution founded squarely upon the principle of the separation of powers—which implies the absolute independence of both government and parliament—provided no obvious solution. Further, at the local level the newly-elected administrators and judges are generally agreed to have been almost entirely hostile to the Directory. According to Mathiez, the Directors could henceforth only count with confidence on the support of the army and of a minority of men who had a strong financial interest in their survival.[1]

To ask to whom the victory went is, however, to enter a historical hall of mirrors, in which contemporaries and historians alike have seen their own images enlarged and those of their foes distorted. The common belief has always been that the royalists won the election. This party, it is said, controlled a substantial minority of seats in the Councils before the elections, and won so many more by them that the majority in parliament became, as Lefebvre puts it, 'specifically royalist'.[2] On the other hand, as a few historians—including Aulard—have persistently pointed out, in 1797 the word 'royalist' was practically meaningless.[3] Used as a term of approbation in the optimistic calculations of the Court, it was for the Directors and their supporters a word of opprobrium particularly appropriate for the collective condemnation of all their critics. What is more, the assertion that the royalists controlled the Councils, which enabled the Directors to justify their own conduct in the following months, has ever since profoundly influenced many of those who have written about the period.

The best approach to a truer appreciation of the situation would seem to lie in a recognition that the word 'royalist' was for many men a relative, not an absolute, term. Since in a time of continual change few could afford to divorce allegiance from circumstance, political loyalty often had to be related to political realities. Although to avow royalism was still technically a capital offence, many men would certainly have been happy to see a restoration of a constitutional monarchy:[4] but since the legitimate monarch still steadfastly refused to accept this solution,

[1] Mathiez, *Le Directoire*, p. 289.

[2] Lefebvre, *The Directory*, p. 59.

[3] Aulard, *A Political History*, IV, pp. 31–2, and G. K. Fortescue, *Cambridge Modern History* (Cambridge, 1914), VIII, p. 496. Fryer, op. cit., pp. 199–210 provides a well-balanced modern assessment.

[4] See for example Lally-Tollendal's *Défense des émigrés adressée au peuple français* (summarised in Palmer, *The Age of the Democratic Revolution*, II, pp. 227–8), in which it is suggested that the restoration of a constitutional monarchy would make it easier to bring the war to an end.

and since a restoration would involve a redistribution of property quite unthinkable even in terms of compensation, these constitutional monarchists had of necessity to be constitutional republicans. They remained, moreover, deeply divided amongst themselves, both about the conditions on which monarchy might conceivably be restored, and about the legitimacy and possibility of discovering an alternative successor to the throne. The election result was consequently essentially negative: the electors returned men who were opposed to the Directors and who were anxious to end the war and to curtail or abolish the restrictive legislation against the *émigrés*[1] and the clergy. In so far as anyone can be said to have won the election, victory went to a loose coalition of conservative groups which d'André had done much to create, and which, as he himself was quick to recognise, began to disintegrate almost as soon as the results were known.[2]

Somewhat more specifically,[3] it seems reasonably certain that when the new deputies took their seats the two Councils together fell broadly into three parts. On the one hand, the Directorial group constituted about one third of the parliament, and this may be thought of as being composed of staunchly anti-clerical republicans who were reluctant to end the war prematurely. On the other hand, there was a Right wing of approximately equal size, which came to be called, from the club which was its place of rendezvous, the party of Clichy. Amongst these men there were certainly a few out-and-out royalists, whose presence and irresponsibility caused alarm wholly disproportionate to their numbers;

---

[1] The general term *émigrés* is used at this point to refer to a. the relatives of *émigrés*, and b. those *émigrés* who had returned to France and secured partial but not complete rehabilitation. Whatever some men had in mind, the rehabilitation of the people who were still in exile was not openly in question, except in so far as some clarification of the classification was known to be necessary.

[2] Fryer, op. cit., pp. 199, 203; see also Aulard, *A Political History*, IV, p. 53.

[3] Readers familiar with the field will readily recognise that in this review of the situation which resulted from the elections of 1797 I have sedulously avoided citing specific figures or referring to particular deputies. This is because, for the reason indicated above, I am deeply distrustful of classifications based on the assumption that a particular deputy (or a particular number of deputies) was (or were) positively royalist *at this particular time*. It follows that I have not incorporated in the text the conclusions of J. Suratteau, and that I differ from those scholars who have accepted his findings, notably Harvey Mitchell, op. cit., pp. 157–8 and A. Soboul, *La Ire République*, p. 242. *Vide:* J. Suratteau, 'Les Elections de l'an IV' and 'Les Elections de l'an V aux Conseils du Directoire', *Annales historiques de la Révolution française*, XXIV (1952) and XXX (1958). Further investigation of the problem may well be thought necessary.

by far the greater number, however, were would-be constitutional monarchists who were in practice eager to end the war on almost any terms and to rehabilitate all who were ostracised as '*émigrés*' or disaffected priests. Between the two main groups to Right and Left stood a more heterogeneous Centre, which was probably slightly larger than either and which was sometimes crudely described as the Belly. Either by conviction or by necessity, these men of the Centre shared the republicanism of the Directorials; but they sympathised strongly with the determination of the Right to compel the government to modify its policies. Amongst them there was nevertheless much disagreement about the terms on which the war should be ended and about how, and how far, the restrictions on the *émigrés* and the priests should be relaxed.

The general situation was therefore one in which the Directors were certain to be confronted, *in some matters and to some extent*, by an overwhelmingly hostile majority; but since the barrier between the Republic and the monarchy was ultimately insurmountable, some hoped that it might be possible to convert that hostile alliance into one in which stable and progressive government might be based on the cooperation of the Directors with an increasingly influential Centre. With varying degrees of emphasis, this course was the one which people as different as Carnot, Benjamin Constant, Madame de Staël, Mathieu Dumas and Thibaudeau advocated and sought to follow. Its successful pursuit, however, depended in part on the willingness of the Directors to meet the moderates, and in part upon the ability of the latter to establish and maintain a reasonable measure of unity amongst themselves.

The necessity for flexibility on all sides was demonstrated immediately after the election, when events occurred both in France and in Italy which greatly restricted the possibilities of compromise. By one of the most inane provisions of the Constitution of 1795, a document permeated by its authors' fears of the executive, one of the Directors was bound to retire each year, the choice being determined by the drawing of lots. Since the Directory—as might well have been foreseen—was already deeply divided, this meant in practice that the balance of forces within it, and consequently the whole orientation of its policy, was ultimately dependent upon chance alone. Had the lot fallen on Barras, Reubell or even Lépeaux, the reconstituted Councils' choice of a new Director would have given Carnot and Letourneur effective control, and this would have gone far to establish a harmonious relationship between the government and the parliament. As it happened, however, the lot which was drawn in public on 14 May fell on Letourneur; and although on 20 May, when the new deputies took their places, the Councils at once chose a man of the Right, François de Barthélemy,[1] to replace him, the fact remained that only two of the five Directors were in sympathy with the new majority. Barthélemy was justly renowned as an unusually able diplomat who had negotiated the Treaties of Basle with Prussia and Spain; but he was not a man whose character could contribute to the restoration of concord in the Directory. Dignified and formal, he speedily shrank from his colleagues' impassioned conflicts; and although he took his stand beside Carnot, he scarcely troubled to conceal his view that they were all four scoundrels, whose present conduct was as indecent as their records were appalling.[2]

Barthélemy's position was, in truth, an impossible one, for by the time of his election the function he was best fitted to fulfill had ceased to bear any relationship to reality. In electing him, the Councils certainly chose a man whom they expected to contribute to the making of an honourable and durable peace: but by the summer of 1797 the issue of peace or war was no longer being determined by diplomacy, but by Bonaparte. On 14 January, at the battle of Rivoli, that amazing general had for the fourth time frustrated an Austrian attempt to relieve Mantua, which fell to the French a fortnight later. Anticipating the Directory's wishes, Bonaparte had at once invaded the Papal States and compelled the Pope to accept the Treaty of Tolentino (19 February).[3] Then on 10 March he had resumed his long-delayed offensive against Austria itself. As the Army of Italy had by this time been strongly reinforced from the Rhineland armies, the Austrians were heavily out-numbered, and even the Archduke Charles, who had at last been sent to command them, could not prevent Bonaparte from forcing a crossing of the Tagliamento and advancing rapidly through the Alps towards Vienna. By 7 April, when the French were within a hundred miles of the capital, the Austrians were compelled to sue for peace; and on 18 April—after the conclusion of the elections in France, but before the new deputies had taken their seats—a preliminary treaty of peace, which Bonaparte negotiated personally, was signed at Leoben.

Provisional though this agreement was, it nevertheless effectively deprived the Directors of control of war and peace alike. As it so

---

[1] *Biog. Notes:* BARTHÉLEMY.

[2] *Mémoires de Barthélemy* (ed. J. de Dampierre, Paris, 1914), pp. 168–9.

[3] On 3 February 1797 the Directors had written a notable letter to Bonaparte, describing 'the Roman religion' as 'the irreconcilable enemy of the Republic' and instructing the general to do everything possible to destroy the Papal government. By the time Bonaparte received these instructions (about 14 February) his campaign was practically complete: but in making the treaty he of course deviated from them. J. M. Thompson, *Napoleon Bonaparte*, p. 81.

happened, the conclusion of Bonaparte's campaign coincided with the opening of a new French offensive in Germany. Two days before the Peace of Leoben, Hoche, who was now in command of the Army of the Sambre and the Meuse, had begun a triumphant advance towards Frankfurt; two days after it, Moreau's Army of the Rhine also crossed that river; but both armies were halted by the arrival of couriers sent by Bonaparte from Italy. Similarly, by ensuring that news of the peace, and particularly of the Austrian surrender of Belgium, was widely known in France, Bonaparte practically compelled the Directors to accept the terms he had arranged.[1] Precariously placed as their government was, they were certainly in no position to repudiate an immensely popular peace. To accept the Austrian surrender of Belgium, however, was to accept the secret conditions on which it had been made—and Bonaparte had in fact solved the immediate problem of French foreign policy by a thoroughly discreditable bargain: in return for ceding both Belgium and Lombardy, Austria was to be given a substantial part of the territory of the Republic of Venice, which had for centuries been an independent state.

One of the prime purposes of the new deputies in the Councils was thus frustrated even before they had assembled in Paris. They had hoped to contribute to the conclusion of an honourable peace: they were to be confronted instead with solutions founded on force and buttressed by brigandage. Worse still, it soon became apparent that the conclusion of a definite treaty with Austria, entrusted by the Directory to Bonaparte, was still to be governed by events in Italy, where the general saw to it that he had an ever-increasing area of land available for barter. While much of the reorganisation he imposed upon Italy at this time was, indeed, as enlightened as it was efficient, there was never any doubt about where power lay or whose interests had priority. Coming to visit Bonaparte at Montebello, Miot de Melito encountered, not the general of a triumphant Republic, but one who was a conqueror on his own account.[2] Now the three republics created in the previous autumn were merged into one, the Cisalpine, which was eventually to be further enlarged at the expense of both the Papacy and Venice. The treatment afforded to the latter was, of course, particularly shameful: since its territory had been violated by both Austria and France, it had long been easy enough for Bonaparte to press claims for compensation against it; but not content with this, he had instigated a rising against the French in Verona, declared war against the Republic on his own responsibility

[1] Lefebvre, *The Directory*, pp. 81–2.
[2] Melito, *Memoirs*, p. 92.

on 2 May, and for all practical purposes destroyed its ancient independence.[1] It thus became possible for Bonaparte to increase the 'compensation' to be offered to Austria, and so to win Austrian recognition of the Rhine as the frontier of France.

Despite this, and despite the fact that in July Pitt again sent Lord Malmesbury to France with proposals for peace, negotiations with both Britain and Austria remained inconclusive throughout the summer. This was partly because the triumph of French arms in Europe not unnaturally increased the Directors' intransigence. Lord Malmesbury now offered to recognise the French acquisition of Belgium and to restore to France and her allies all their overseas possessions save for the Spanish island of Trinidad and the Dutch possessions, Ceylon and the Cape of Good Hope; but the French called for the return of these vital bases also, as well as demanding that King George III should repudiate his antique title to the throne of France. Powerful individual interests, too, militated against peace. In Paris, the intrigues of Barras and Talleyrand (who became Foreign Minister on 16 July) did much to obscure understanding of the British position, for both men apparently hoped to profit financially if agreement could be reached at a time of their own choosing.[2] As for Bonaparte, he made no bones about telling Miot de Melito that peace was not in his interest. As he explained, he had not yet really finished with Austria, and the prospect of paying court to the lawyers in the Luxembourg did not attract him; only when he could play a part in France equivalent to the one he had played in Italy would he be ready to return.[3] Still more important, both Britain and Austria were well aware that they would be able to treat with France on much more equal terms if the political instability which had followed the elections was to be ended by the triumph of either the moderates or the extreme Right. In 1797, in short, the true peace of Europe depended to a very considerable degree upon the outcome of the conflict in Paris.

Now, more than ever, that conflict was represented as one between republicans and royalists. Many, indeed, so regarded it, believing not only permanent peace but the very survival of the Republic to be poised in precarious balance. Whilst widely accepted both then and later, this view is recognisably a delusion born of distrust. There were indeed in the Councils a number of deputies who were—or who subsequently

---

[1] It may be remarked that the Directory's declaration of war on Venice reached Bonaparte after he had signed the Treaty of Milan which concluded it.

[2] A. Goodwin, 'The French Executive Directory · A Revaluation', *History*, XXII (Dec. 1937), p. 212.

[3] Melito, *Memoirs*, p. 95.

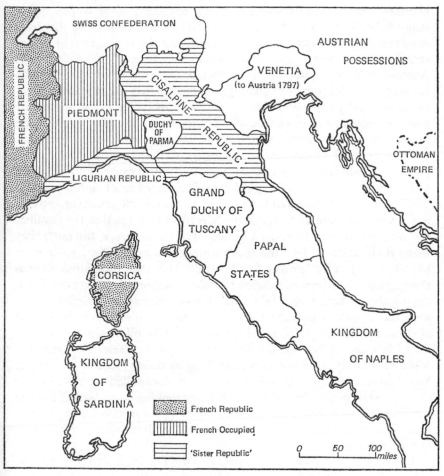

SWISS CONFEDERATION

AUSTRIAN

POSSESSIONS

FRENCH REPUBLIC

PIEDMONT

CISALPINE

DUCHY
OF
PARMA

REPUBLIC

VENETIA
(to Austria 1797)

OTTOMAN
EMPIRE

LIGURIAN REPUBLIC

GRAND

DUCHY OF

TUSCANY

PAPAL

CORSICA

STATES

KINGDOM

OF NAPLES

KINGDOM

OF

SARDINIA

French Republic

French Occupied

'Sister Republic'

0   50   100
                    miles

French Penetration of Italy, 1797

became—outright and uncompromising royalists: some would say as many as 80. There were, too, a substantial number who hoped that freedom and loyalty might soon be reconciled by the restoration of a constitutional monarchy: some would say as many as 200. The reality of the Anglo–royalist conspiracy is, moreover, indisputable: with full British backing, d'André sought unceasingly to ensure that the new strength of the Right and Centre was used to the best advantage of the monarchy and the cause of peace; and he also did his utmost to plan and prepare for the armed insurrection which he believed must one day either consolidate political victory or anticipate political failure. Yet while suspicion and half-knowledge of these secret activities caused endless alarm to the Directory and to all republicans, it remains most significant that Wickham and d'André sought above all to restrain the exultant extremists. As they recognised well enough, the plain fact was that the royalists did *not* have a majority in the Councils. On the contrary, the more they made their presence felt, the more support they lost. No sooner were the election results known, for example, than the influential Dumas group, which had been persuaded to make common cause with the Right during the contest, took fright and hastened to resume its relationship with the Directory through Carnot. In brief, as d'André realised, any obvious recrudescence of royalism immediately filled most men with dread lest the Terror should be restored to counteract it, so that the Right could only hope to achieve anything by doing practically nothing. Wickham and d'André therefore constantly counselled caution, urging all to proceed gradually and to await the probable elimination of the last survivors of the Convention in the elections of the next year, 1798.[1] The much-vaunted strength of the royalists in the Councils in 1797 was in fact an illusion.

The division between the deputies and the Directors was nevertheless very real. Quite apart from the question of how the war was to be concluded, a matter about which the Councils were remarkably ill-informed, the conflict involved an issue of fundamental importance, that of reconciling the Constitution with the will of the majority. In the first instance, the problem was that which had been central to political life ever since the inauguration of the Directory: by 'exceptional legislation', particularly the Law of 3 Brumaire, the Convention had imposed certain rigid restrictions upon the operation of the Constitution, and these the Directors had as rigidly retained; but as circumstances and the com-

[1] For the political situation which followed the elections of 1797 in France, and for the reactions of Wickham and d'André, see Fryer, op. cit., pp. 207–24, and Mitchell, op. cit., pp. 174–5, 182–5.

position of the Councils changed, an ever-increasing number of deputies had become convinced that these restrictions would have to be repealed, or at least modified, if France were ever to become a truly constitutional republic. Beyond this there was the still deeper issue of whether the Constitution, which could not legally be altered for at least nine years from 1795, could be so modified in practice that the will of a parliamentary majority would in some degree be reflected in the conduct of the executive. These vital questions were not, of course, unrelated to the threat of royalism, for provincial France was already strongly influenced by reaction, and the sway of royalist priests and returning *émigrés* could be expected to increase if the stranglehold the Convention had imposed upon the country were relaxed.[1] To recognise the reality of reaction and even violence in the provinces in 1797 need not, however, imply that all who sought to make France a genuinely constitutional state were unconsciously promoting an inevitably successful counter-revolution. While much was, and always has been, made of this argument, it is essentially a highly speculative one, which presumes that gradualness was bound to fail and that, as three of the five Directors held, the controls imposed on certain classes of Frenchmen since 1792 had to be kept operative indefinitely. Many, if not most, of those who were called 'royalists' were in reality men who believed that in one way or another the experiment of widening the range of constitutional freedom, which had been begun in 1795, would have to be resumed.[2]

Since in this the interests of the Right and the Centre coincided, a whole series of measures to emancipate the supposedly counter-revolutionary classes were passed in rapid succession during the early

[1] This brief statement summarises the review to be found in Lefebvre, *The Directory*, pp. 63–4. While that survey is necessarily general in character, it provides an interesting illustration of the way in which the author, recognising the breakdown of an argument at the parliamentary level ('The relative impotence of the majority', p. 63) at once moves to a wider field of assertion. While some more specific detail may be found in Mathiez, *Le Directoire*, pp. 307, 309–10, or in studies like that of M. Reinhard (*Le Département de la Sarthe sous le régime directorial*, Saint-Brieuc, 1936), the subject is one which still requires wider investigation.

[2] It should be noticed that Lefebvre rules this alternative out of court from 1795. In his view, the events of that year had shown that if 'the Constitutionalists' became influential, their reluctance to curb reactionary violence and their willingness to negotiate with the foreigner would lead directly to a White Terror and the restoration of absolutism: 'the experiment of Year III was conclusive'. He consequently sees the Directory as an essentially contradictory régime which professed liberalism but which was always bound to be despotic and exclusive. *The Directory*, pp. 7–8.

summer of 1797. Notably, the Law of 3 Brumaire, which had barely survived attack before the elections, was at last repealed; and although the religious question, as always, excited long and often heated debates, on 14 July the penal legislation of 1792 and 1793 against priests was also abrogated by the Council of Five Hundred. Two days later, indeed, that Council even agreed to abandon the long endeavour to impose an oath of allegiance upon the clergy, from whom no more than a simple declaration of obedience to the law was to be required in future.

From the beginning of this process it was nevertheless apparent that the path of moderation would not be easy to follow. Long condemned to impotence, and even now frustrated in all that concerned foreign affairs, both the Centre and the Right were at first inclined to an impetuosity not uncharacteristic of new majorities; and despite d'André's counsel, the extremists on the Right acted independently and irresponsibly. One evident sign of this was the election on 20 May of Pichegru, now a deputy, as President of the Council of Five Hundred. Another was the recall, on that same day, of those notoriously royalist deputies who had been excluded from their seats for their share in the rising of Vendémiaire. Still more significant was the attempt of Gibert-Desmolières, one of the most intransigent members of the Clichy group, to deprive the Directory of all control of national expenditure. His proposals, which the Council of Five Hundred accepted on 18 June, were not perhaps wholly illegitimate, for the perpetual bankruptcy of the government seemed explicable only by the prevalence of racketeering by official contractors; but his plan would have made it impossible for the Directors to continue the war, or even to govern, and this was clearly the real purpose behind it. On 23 June, moreover, a particularly loquacious deputy, Dumolard, launched himself—apparently entirely on his own initiative—into a long and well-justified attack upon the secrecy surrounding events in Italy and upon the increasingly obvious iniquity of Bonaparte towards Venice and other independent states.

Not surprisingly, developments such as these alarmed and alienated all but the intransigents themselves. To Thibaudeau, even the repeal of the Law of 3 Brumaire now seemed premature, and he began to feel that the Councils were preparing an attack upon all the men who had made the Revolution and the Republic.[1] The division in the Directory itself also became more bitter than ever: according to Barthélemy, scarcely a day passed without some horrifying outbreak of table-banging and bad language; and from the end of June the three Directors most hostile to change—Reubell, Barras and Lépeaux—began to meet separately and

[1] Thibaudeau, *Mémoires*, II, pp. 179–80, 183.

in secret to consider what steps should be taken 'to save the Republic'.[1] The most startling reaction to the course of events came, however, from the military. As all the reports which reached the armies from Paris were filled with accounts of the extravagant language and ill-considered conduct of the Councils, the soldiers soon supposed that these were wholly controlled by royalists, and during July the Directors consequently received—and published—a remarkable series of addresses from the armies. Nominally messages in commemoration of 14 July 1789, these were in reality impassioned protestations of republican ardour and declarations of the readiness of the soldiers to intervene in Paris in order to exterminate the royalists and save the Constitution. Only in the Army of the Rhine was opinion more restrained, for its officers, who had once followed Pichegru, now prided themselves on Moreau's non-political professionalism.[2] Bonaparte, on the other hand, had no doubts about what should be done. Infuriated by Dumolard's indictment, he privately urged the Directors to act decisively to destroy foreign influences in France, writing: 'If this needs force, summon the armies'. His proclamation of 14 July, too, included the frank and famous passage: 'Soldiers! . . . Mountains divide us from France; if need arise, you will cross them with the swiftness of the eagle to maintain the Constitution, to defend liberty, to protect the government and the men of the Republic.'[3]

The fervour of these exhortations in all probability surprised the Directors themselves, revealing as it did the ease with which they might effect a *coup d'état* without re-igniting the fires of Jacobinism. But preparations for the use of military force against the Councils were well advanced even before the feelings of the armies were fully known. Initially, in April, Reubell had simply but vainly proposed that the Directory should annul the elections altogether and arrange new ones under stricter control. In June, however, Barras began to seek military

---

[1] Barthélemy, *Mémoires*, p. 208; Barras, *Memoirs*, II, p. 562.

[2] A favourable interpretation of Moreau's position, which was ambiguous and has been regarded as 'royalist'. Since succeeding Pichegru he had acquired evidence (from the capture of an Austrian baggage wagon) which revealed Pichegru's contacts with Condé; but this he kept to himself until the last possible moment—by which time the Directors were fully informed of Pichegru's conduct from other sources. It is a matter of opinion how far Moreau's silence indicates political sympathy, natural indecisiveness, or personal or professional loyalty to Pichegru.

[3] See J. M. Thompson, *Napoleon's Letters* (Everyman, London, 1964), No. 30, p. 60; and *Napoléon Bonaparte: Proclamations, Ordres du Jour* (Paris, 1964), p. 20.

aid. Nor was this hard to find. Bonaparte not only promised Barras's agent his support, but also sent him back to Paris with a copy of the confession of the comte d'Antraigues, a prominent royalist agent who had been arrested at Trieste and who had revealed the full details of Pichegru's treasonable trafficking with Condé. Barras nevertheless preferred to act through Hoche, a republican hero who was nearer at hand, and on 1 July this general began to move some 10,000 men of the Army of the Sambre and the Meuse towards Paris, ostensibly in preparation for a new embarkation from Brest for Ireland.

This resort to force was certainly unnecessary. As d'André had anticipated, the recklessness of the extreme Right had soon alarmed the more moderate deputies, and by July the number of potential supporters of cooperation between the Directory and the Councils was obviously increasing rapidly. For one thing, the Council of Elders was already showing itself to be an upper chamber which was quite capable of checking irresponsibility in the Council of Five Hundred. Desmolières' financial proposals, for example, were quickly quashed by the Elders; and although on that occasion the majority was small, the Council delayed its approval of the emancipation of the priests throughout six increasingly critical weeks.[1] Moreover, whilst the Five Hundred had been almost unanimous in abolishing the hated Law of 3 Brumaire and in ending the persecution of the clergy, it soon appeared that the passage of more far-reaching legislation was quite another matter. Thus when the Right objected even to holding the clergy to a declaration of loyalty, they were defeated by 210 to 204 votes; and their various attempts to rehabilitate at least some groups of *émigrés* were almost entirely unsuccessful.[2]

At this time the influence of the more notable moderate groups was also growing apace. In May, Benjamin Constant, renewing his earlier call for republican unity, had published *Des Réactions politiques* and *Les*

---

[1] The Elders accepted the annulment of the Law of 3 Brumaire, which was passed by the lower house on 9 June, on the 27th; Desmolières' plan was rejected on that same day; and the legislation about the clergy, passed by the Five Hundred on 14 and 16 July, was only approved on 24 August.

[2] It may be necessary to recall here that the *émigrés* were officially those whose names were listed as non-resident in returns made by local authorities, and the Constitution itself explicitly forbade both their re-admission to France and any new legislation in their favour. It being common knowledge that the 120,000 names involved were grossly inaccurate, the practical question was one of promoting rapid revision of the lists by something other than individual erasure. See Lefebvre, op. cit., p. 63 and D. Greer, *The Incidence of the Emigration during the French Revolution* (Glous., Mass., 1966).

Effets de la Terreur, classic statements of liberalism in which the government was urged to avoid all illegal measures as alien to the true tradition of the Revolution.[1] In June, moreover, Madame de Staël was once again in Paris and welcoming to her salon 'Jacobins in the morning, *émigrés* at mid-day, and all the world at dinner';[2] and with her enthusiastic support, Constant at the end of the month helped to found the Constitutional Circle, a club that soon attracted 'all that is estimable and distinguished in the Republican party'[3]—including, curiously, Sieyès, Talleyrand and even Barras. At the same time, Mathieu Dumas and his friends, who stood to the right of the Constitutional Circle but were fully as anxious to reach some working agreement with the Directors, drew still closer to Carnot, the Director who now felt more strongly than ever that the will of the nation as represented in parliament must be respected even by the lawful government. To him, and to Barras, the Dumas group now made a positive proposal: suggesting that there was a real need to consolidate constitutional government by increasing public confidence in it, they asked these Directors to secure the dismissal of those ministers whom the majority of the legislative distrusted, and to appoint others in whom it could have faith.[4]

At this juncture therefore, the government had before it a clear choice. Although in all probability only Barras knew enough to appreciate the position fully, the advance of Hoche on the one hand, and the advances of the moderates on the other, offered it the alternative of coercing the Councils or of cooperating with them. The proposed compromise, too, was one which might well have solved a permanent problem: the rigid separation of powers prescribed by the Constitution, with all its attendant train of misunderstandings and conflict, might have been surmounted by the growth of a convention making ministers dependent in some measure upon the confidence of the deputies. To Carnot, this solution held strong appeal on practical grounds, and on 14 July he formally proposed that the Directors should replace four ministers— Merlin de Douai (Justice); Ramel (Finance); Delacroix (Foreign Affairs); and Truguet (Marine)—in accordance with the wishes of the Legislative Body. Challenged by Reubell, who asserted that the adoption

---

[1] E. Schermerhorn, *Benjamin Constant* (London, 1924), p. 166.

[2] R. MacNair Wilson, *Madame de Staël et Ses Amis, 1766–1817* (trans. G. Roth, Paris, 1934), p. 201.

[3] E. Schermerhorn, op. cit., p. 164 (citing Constant's letter to his uncle of 11 July).

[4] See, *inter alia*, Barras, *Memoirs*, II, pp. 561–2, 568, and Reinhard, *Le Grand Carnot*, II, pp. 227–8, 230–1.

of any such principle would lead to complete anarchy in government, Carnot reiterated his belief that good government depended on goodwill between the executive and the majority in parliament. Barthélemy agreed. Lépeaux, however, joined Reubell, maintaining that the executive was itself the representative of the people and that it must remain independent if it were to be consistent. Thus all depended on Barras, who—if Dumas is to be believed—had previously promised him his support 'on the honour of a republican gentleman'; but Barras now briefly dismissed the plan as unworthy of consideration. As soon as this point was reached, the five Directors reviewed all the ministerial appointments, and in less than 20 minutes the three men closest to the parliamentary majority—Bénézech (Ministry of the Interior), Cochon (Police) and Petiet (War)—were dismissed, and the two most repugnant to that majority—Merlin and Ramel—were reinstated. Throughout, it need scarcely be said, Carnot and Barthélemy were consistently outvoted by three to two. Thus the Directory, or as it is now more accurate to call it, the Triumvirate, deliberately rejected the way of conciliation.[1]

Since Barras did not have to employ the force which he had available, this crisis ended in anti-climax. When the Councils learnt of the proximity of Hoche's forces, which were actually within a distance of the Legislature forbidden to unauthorised armies by the Constitution, deputies as diverse as Vaublanc, Pichegru, Dumas and Thibaudeau prepared to impeach the Triumvirate. For this, however, word from Carnot that a *coup d'état* was imminent was awaited, and Carnot failed them—almost certainly because Barras chose this moment to inform him of Pichegru's treason. The affair consequently petered out in banalities: Carnot merely wrote to explain that the march of the troops had been misdirected through a clerical error, and the Councils confined themselves to ordering that signs be posted to mark the limits of the forbidden 'constitutional zone'. Still more astonishingly, Hoche, who had supposed himself to be acting for all the Directors, found himself summoned to Paris and cross-examined by an indignant—and surprisingly formidable—Lépeaux, whilst Barras sat silently by.[2]

But although the use of force was avoided in July, events moved inexorably towards its employment later. The Independents and the Right, feeling with Dumas that the Directors' treatment of the Councils

---

[1] See the *Memoirs* of Barras, II, pp. 568–71; of Lépeaux, II, p. 88; and of Dumas, II, p. 91; also, Reinhard, op. cit., II, pp. 231–2, and G. Robison, *Revellière-Lépeaux, Citizen-Director, 1753–1824* (Columbia, 1938), pp. 144–7. The date of this meeting is usually give as 16 July.

[2] Mitchell, *The Underground War against Revolutionary France*, pp. 193–6.

was 'an injury to the Nation',[1] fell back on a policy of resistance. From 20 July onwards much consideration was given to draft legislation about the re-establishment of the National Guard in Paris, this having been practically disbanded after Vendémiaire, and attempts were also made to strengthen the Guard of the Councils. D'André meanwhile redoubled his efforts to gather and organise an unofficial force of disaffected soldiers, émigrés and chouans. These preparations, however, were perpetually marred by division and vacillation: as always, opinion varied about whether it would be better to take the offensive at the first opportunity, or to wait until danger recurred—or even to remain entirely on the defensive until after the elections of 1798. Consequently little was accomplished beyond the 'provisional' closure of all political clubs, including the Constitutional Circle—a measure which the Directory probably accepted through fear of a Jacobin revival, and which had the effect of intensifying the general atmosphere of conspiracy and suspicion.

On the other hand the Triumvirate, who had of course the advantage of executive authority, were able to advance their measures as they pleased. Hoche's army, nominally despatched, actually hovered in the vicinity of Paris, and Bonaparte's offer of assistance was accepted. But Bonaparte, who had already told Miot de Melito that 'the nation must have a chief, and one made illustrious by glory',[2] was cautious. He simply sent to Paris his swash-buckling, sabre-trailing lieutenant, General Augereau,[3] who on 8 August was appointed to the command of the troops in the capital. Outbreaks of violence between his men and d'André's black-collared royalists inevitably followed.

While these preparations proceeded, political life stagnated, such overtures as were made for conciliation seeming superficial and futile. It is, indeed, remarkable that almost all accounts of the time record despondency and despair, apathy and lassitude.[4] Pichegru, in whose military ability the Councils once placed much confidence, seemed overcome by inertia—perhaps because Barras had warned him that his past conduct was now well-known to the Directors. Wickham and d'André, whose high hopes of a peaceful restoration were now fading fast, were at one in deploring the disarray and incompetence of the Councils. In all this, sheer exhaustion no doubt played its part; for, as both Barras and Thi-

---

[1] Reinhard, op. cit., II, p. 232.

[2] Melito, *Memoirs*, p. 94.

[3] *Biog. Notes:* AUGEREAU.

[4] See, for example, Thibaudeau, *Mémoires*, II, p. 220; Reinhard, *Le Grand Carnot*, II, p. 231.

baudeau noted in their memoirs,[1] one great defect of the Constitution of 1795 was that it made no provision for any dissolution or prorogation of the Councils—and both men had been at the centre of affairs for five tumultuous years. Even Carnot, who on 14 July had vigorously appealed to all to follow *le juste milieu*, now disassociated himself from events: on 10 August, in his final public speech as President of the Directory, he repudiated royalism as well as terrorism; and both he and Barthélemy now kept away from meetings of the Directory, at which their presence simply occasioned abuse and even—as on 4 August—actual blows.[2]

To the indefatigable Madame de Staël, however, one hope of her longed-for 'middle way' remained. As she realised, the great weakness of the Centre had always been its disunity: indeed, the reorganisation of the ministries in July, which Dumas had found so frustrating, had been hailed with delight in the Constitutional Circle, from the ranks of which the new ministers, and most notably Talleyrand, had been chosen. If the use of force was to be avoided, which Madame de Staël (but not Benjamin Constant) still believed to be possible, she saw that this breach must be healed, and she was sure that Thibaudeau alone could accomplish this. In him she recognised one who not only held the balance in the Five Hundred but also remained on good terms with men of all parties. All this she told him frankly enough at a meeting between them on 13 August,[3] and she appealed to him to rally his friends to the support of the Directory and so help her to prevent a *coup d'état* which might well culminate in a revival of the Terror. This, however, Thibaudeau refused to do. In his view, it was for the Directors to make the first move, since it was they who had persistently clung to policies of persecution at home and aggrandisement abroad; to agree to support them unconditionally would not be a gesture of goodwill, but agreement in advance to condone imminent violence. Thus a most consistent champion of moderate republicanism refused to the last to sacrifice principle to expediency and 'to join the Directory in renewing the Revolution'. Thibaudeau nevertheless wrote of these days as a time when he and his small circle of friends met and parted in death-like despondency.[4]

[1] Thibaudeau, op. cit., II, pp. 163, 168; Barras, *Memoirs*, II, p. 617.
[2] Reinhard, *Le Grand Carnot*, II, p. 236.
[3] Thibaudeau, op. cit., II, pp. 243–8. While the interpretation here is my own, I should like also to acknowledge my appreciation of many helpful conversations about the attitude of Mme de Staël at this time that I have had with Miss F. S. Montgomery, a graduate student of Carleton University. See M. J. Sydenham and Frances S. Montgomery, 'Madame de Staël and the French Revolution', *History Today* (Feb. 1971), p. 89.
[4] Thibaudeau, op. cit., II, pp. 261; 265–7.

Strangely enough, it was little Lépeaux who finally took the initiative in effecting the *coup* which all expected. As he himself wrote afterwards, this 'would never have taken place without me'.[1] Angrily indignant about the state of affairs, and completely convinced that his own conduct had always been beyond reproach, he somehow seemed to personify the upright middle-class republicanism of France. Becoming President of the Directory on 23 August, he promptly took the swaggering Augereau to task, and so over-awed him that the street-brawling of the soldiery ceased forthwith. Next day, moreover, all his prejudices were confirmed by the action of the Council of Elders, who at last gave their approval to the abolition of the revolutionary legislation against the priests. After that, Lépeaux took the first opportunity to make his attitude plain in public, this being the occasion on 27 August of his reply to addresses by Visconti, the representative of Bonaparte's newly-created Cisalpine Republic, and by General Bernadotte, the bearer of Austrian flags captured in Italy. Speaking in unusually strong tones, but being evidently much moved by emotion,[2] he said plainly enough that the Directory was fully prepared to risk all perils to defend the Constitution from those hidden royalists who invoked its protection even as they violated it.

This being seen as a declaration of intent,[3] the Councils again prepared to impeach the Triumvirate and again sought Carnot's aid. Carnot, however, had given up the struggle, and he merely replied that although the Constitution was certain to be attacked, he preferred to see the republicans triumph;[4] and in the event, it was the government which struck first. Although the strain of the crisis had been too much for the tough Reubell, whose nerve temporarily failed,[5] on the night of 3 September Lépeaux and Barras incarcerated themselves with him in a heavily-guarded apartment at the Luxembourg.[6] From these rooms, to which various ministers and officers were called but which no one could leave freely, orders were issued for the arrest of Carnot and Barthélemy; and Augereau was called in and instructed to occupy the halls of the Councils at the Tuileries. Possessing overwhelming strength and acting

---

[1] Lépeaux, *Mémoires*, II, p. 85.

[2] Barras, *Memoirs*, III, p. 6; Lépeaux, *Mémoires*, II, p. 126.

[3] Thibaudeau, *Mémoires*, II, p. 256; see also Robison, op. cit., p. 154.

[4] A. Meynier, *Les coups d'état du Directoire: Le Dix-huit Fructidor An V* (Paris, 1927), p. 134.

[5] G. D. Homan, 'Jean-François Reubell, Director', *French Historical Studies* (I, 1960), p. 428.

[6] For the *coup d'état*, see the works cited above, particularly Mitchell, Fryer and Meynier. See also: V. Pierre, *18 Fructidor: Documents pour la plupart inédits* (Paris, 1897).

in accordance with carefully prepared plans (for which, needless to say, Barras later claimed all the credit), Augereau then fulfilled his mission faultlessly. At four o'clock on the morning of 4 September (18 Fructidor), a single cannon-shot signalled action, and shortly afterwards Augereau appeared in the Tuileries Gardens with an entourage of some 400 officers. To him Ramel at once surrendered command of the Guards of the Councils, the men of which were in any case evidently unreliable. The few deputies who had remained on the alert within the building[1] were then placed under arrest, the only moment of drama being the seizure of the physically powerful Pichegru, whom the soldiers were loath to arrest and who resisted them with a bayonet which he tore from an assailant's grasp.[2]

So effective was the military control of the capital that d'André's royalists were completely frustrated: only about 13 of his officers responded to his call,[3] and these had to be told at once to save themselves as best they could. Nor was there even any disorder, for the Directory chose this moment to placard Paris with the detailed statements in which Duverne du Presle and the comte d'Antraigues had previously exposed the Anglo-royalist plot and revealed Pichegru's disloyalty. These startling revelations were moreover reinforced by a proclamation that anyone advocating either royalism or a return to the Constitution of 1793 would be shot on the spot, as would anyone found looting. The Triumvirate clearly feared that the crushing of the Right might encourage a resurgence of popular democratic agitation: but in fact so much military force was deployed that—to Lépeaux's immense relief—the belated appearance of a token force from the faubourgs, complete with two cannons and a keg of brandy, was superfluous and harmless.

These drastic measures, together with the process of proscription and repression which began next day, effectively ended the most serious of the many royalist conspiracies against the internal security of the Republic. Such conspiracies of course continued, on occasion causing considerable alarm; but the defeat of the 'Great Design' in 1797 proved to be decisive for more than 15 years. Only when France was exhausted by perpetual war would the monarchy, itself grown far more amenable

---

[1] After the crisis of July the Councils had created two security commissions, collectively known as the Commissions of the Inspectors of the Halls. These were, at least potentially, rival executive bodies to the Directory, and as it was they who had taken the lead in opposing the Directory, so it was against them that the Triumvirate struck first.

[2] Meynier, op. cit., p. 153.

[3] Mitchell, op. cit., p. 211.

to compromise, appear as a tolerable alternative to Napoleonic despotism. The price that had to be paid for this much immunity was nevertheless a high one. As the extent of the danger from the royalists in 1797 was greatly exaggerated, so the reaction of the government was excessively violent; and as its intransigence was matched by the disunity of more moderate men, an unusually good opportunity for cooperation between the Directory and the Councils was almost casually cast away. On 18 Fructidor the Executive, repudiating parliamentary government in the conviction that its own authority was at least equally representative of the real will of the people, used the army to make itself independent of, and superior to, the Legislature; and in so doing the Triumvirate, whose only policy was the preservation of a discredited and inefficient order, called an abrupt halt to the natural process of political change and severed themselves from moderate conservative opinion. To men like Thibaudeau, who had striven for so long to establish a state in which the rule of law would prevail, real republicanism seemed to have been wantonly destroyed by a minority of short-sighted and self-interested men. Though he himself was not proscribed, Thibaudeau practically retired from public life; and when on 5 September the Directors offered to provide him with a passport, he replied that he would rather eat grass in the streets than accept any gift from their hands.[1]

[1] Thibaudeau, *Mémoires*, II, p. 278.

6. The Abandonment of Legality
September 1797-May 1798

The *coup d'état* of 18 Fructidor was an event of great consequence for France and Europe alike. By their sudden seizure of power the Triumvirate of Barras, Reubell and LaRevellière-Lépeaux had certainly frustrated a royalist project for the restoration of the monarchy; and since that project had had the backing of Britain and, indirectly, of Austria, its abrupt failure had also ended a period of procrastination during which France and her enemies had made neither peace nor war. But although royalism was repudiated, so also was much that was more moderate. Consequently it still remained to be seen whether France was to be a republic in anything but its name.

In international affairs, the first consequence of the *coup* was the collapse of the negotiations for peace between France and Britain. This is not to say that Barras, Reubell and Lépeaux were blindly bellicose. On the contrary, they were probably well aware of the advantages of concluding a creditable peace. In the circumstances, however, it is scarcely surprising that Reubell, who at once took charge of foreign affairs over Talleyrand's head, should have adopted a high-handed attitude towards Lord Malmesbury, the British negotiator at Lille. His demand that Britain should immediately agree to restore the colonial possessions of France's allies, Spain and Holland, was apparently made in good faith, for he was unaware that Talleyrand had already led Lord Malmesbury to suppose that this unacceptable condition would be waived in favour of a cash settlement; but it was nonetheless worded as an ultimatum, and Lord Malmesbury left Lille on 17 September, little more than a week after 18 Fructidor.[1] To Britain, which had been ready to recognise a respectable French Republic, this apparent volte-face by the Directory seemed clear proof that the Revolution was resurgent,[2] and the British were confirmed in this opinion by an immediate French attempt to com-

[1] A. Goodwin, 'The French Executive Directory—A Revaluation', *History* (Dec. 1937), p. 213.
[2] As Canning put it, 'This cursed Revolution has baffled our good intentions'.

pel them to capitulate. Under pressure from Paris, the Dutch Republic ordered its fleet at the Texel to put to sea and destroy the British North Sea squadron in order to open the way for landings by French forces in England or Scotland. Yet although 1797, the year of the naval mutinies at Spithead and the Nore, had been a critical one for Britain, this French stroke led only to disastrous failure: on 11 October the Dutch fleet was almost entirely destroyed by Admiral Duncan at the battle of Camperdown.

The *coup d'état* in France was also followed by the conclusion of a peace between France and Austria, the provisional agreement of Leoben being made definitive on 17 October by the Treaty of Campo-Formio. This treaty, however, was the work of Bonaparte, and for all its apparent grandeur as a French triumph it left the future fraught with possibilities of further conflict. Immediately after 18 Fructidor Bonaparte had assured the Triumvirate that he stood ready to support them with 100,000 men; but he had nevertheless promptly proceeded to test his position by a display of temperament, threatening to resign if Augereau was rewarded for his part in the *coup* by being given command on the Rhine. In this situation the Directors had no alternative but to placate him, for it was to his support above all else that their success was due. Augereau was set aside, and Bonaparte, assured of his strength, at once concluded the negotiations with the Austrians at his own pleasure and in direct contravention of instructions sent from Paris; and the Directors had again no alternative to accepting an immensely popular *fait accompli*.[1]

Superficially this settlement seemed to be greatly to the advantage of France, for Austria now not only accepted the French annexation of Belgium (i.e., the Austrian Netherlands) and the French establishment in Lombardy of the nominally independent Cisalpine Republic, but also recognised the extension of the eastern frontier of France to the left bank of the Rhine. Yet these gains were purchased at a considerable price. For one thing, a central feature of the treaty was the agreement to partition the ancient Republic of Venice—a partition which the Directors had expressly forbidden Bonaparte to make. As Austria thus acquired the city of Venice and a considerable share of its territories,[2] her power was

[1] Lefebvre, *The Directory*, p. 94 and Goodwin, op. cit., pp. 214–15. See also Lépeaux, *Mémoires*, II, pp. 272, 277, and G. D. Homan, 'Jean-François Reubell, Director', *French Historical Studies*, No. I (1960), p. 431, where Reubell is quoted as saying: 'The triumph and glory of Bonaparte have compromised all opinions'.

[2] I.e., Istria and Dalmatia and all Venetian territory east of the Adige River. The remaining lands, to the west of the Adige, went to the Cisalpine Republic, to which Modena, Ferrara, Bologna and the Romagna were also added.

effectively re-established in Italy despite all her defeats there, it being, indeed, augmented by her new means of access to the Adriatic. Further, the partition profoundly shocked much European opinion and did immeasurable harm to the reputation of the French Republic even in France itself. Many liberally-minded men might approve those French conquests which seemed to emancipate oppressed peoples from autocratic rule, but few could condone the callous sacrifice of a free and comparatively democratic state to the ambitions of Bonaparte and the interests of Austria. If it be added that the treaty necessarily committed France to the support of Bonaparte's Cisalpine Republic, and even— since it included the annexation to France of the Ionian Islands—involved France in Bonaparte's nascent Eastern aspirations, the Directors' extreme reluctance to ratify it can well be understood.

Nor was this all, for the arrangement that was made about the Rhine frontier was similarly unscrupulous and inconclusive. In Germany, as in Italy, Austria had successfully safeguarded her own position by disregarding the rights and interests of others, the French advance to the Rhine being made in fact at the expense of those German princes of the Holy Roman Empire who possessed lands on the left bank of the river. What is more, while it was agreed that a congress should meet at Rastadt to arrange for compensation to be made to these princes in Germany, particular provision was made that Prussia should not be entitled to any such compensation. In this way Bonaparte involved France in what amounted to an attempt to re-organise the states of Germany, and yet at the same time he offended Prussia, which was potentially France's most powerful supporter. This again displeased the Directors; but the advance to the Rhine was nevertheless in full accordance with their policy, and their immediate reaction to the news of Campo-Formio was to order a special military force to be prepared for the capture of Mayence, the only citadel west of the Rhine which was not already in French hands. That the troops of the Elector of Mayence, left in the lurch by the Austrians, should have been compelled to surrender to the French in December 1797, a month after the Congress of Rastadt had assembled, may well be thought symbolic of the way in which the *coup d'état* of 18 Fructidor and the treaty of Campo-Formio drew France towards further expansion and further warfare.[1]

Not surprisingly, all these developments were accompanied by a revival of militant revolutionary enthusiasm in France. As the Directors and their supporters denounced royalism, and as new *départements* were rapidly established in the newly-acquired areas, Republicans 'began

[1] On the treaty, see the works cited above by Lefebvre and Goodwin.

10 Public audience by the Directors in the Luxembourg, 21 November 1795

11 Bonaparte at Milan, 1797 (aged 28)
after a portrait by Andrea Appiani

priding themselves on belonging to the 'Great Nation', whose mission was to free the world'.[1] This idealism was now evidently associated with an immediate national interest, for the French had to consider how best to consolidate their new eastern frontier and how best to secure their communications with Italy. But whatever the main motivation, and however responsibility be divided between Bonaparte and the Directors, the fact is that after 18 Fructidor the Republic was once again revolutionary in international affairs. In 1797, as in 1793, Europe was still expected to learn the meaning of the law of nations from the mouth of the French cannon.

The situation within France after the *coup* is naturally rather more difficult to determine. As we have seen, Thibaudeau thought that real republicanism had been destroyed, and many others shared Miot de Melito's view that the *coup* was catastrophic and ruinous to the Constitution and to all regular government.[2] Even Madame de Staël, who had so hopefully supported the Directory and who was so soon to be forced to leave France again as a suspect, would one day write that freedom alone was conquered in Fructidor. Most modern historians, too, deplore the Directory's alliance with the army and condemn the new régime as a dictatorship. Lefebvre, for example, believed that the *coup* 'consecrated the failure of the constitutional and liberal experiment attempted by the Thermidorians'.[3] On the other hand, the Directors and their supporters consistently maintained that the resort to force was no more than what Benjamin Constant called a matter of regrettable necessity. According to this view, the Directors had been confronted by a majority of deputies determined to destroy constitutional government, and since they had no legal means of saving the Constitution, they had been compelled to use force. For its apologists, the day of 18 Fructidor was a memorable and a triumphant one: far from dealing the Republic a mortal blow, it had 'irrevocably established its existence'.[4]

That violence should be simultaneously condemned and condoned by different parties is not, of course, remarkable. Enough, too, has already been written here to suggest that the reality of the royalist threat before

[1] Lefebvre, op. cit., p. 96.
[2] Melito, *Memoirs*, p. 109.
[3] Lefebvre, op. cit., p. 93. It is, of course, somewhat surprising to discover Lefebvre regarding the Thermidorians as liberals, particularly as he remarks that their 'experiment with liberalism' had been abandoned in 1795 (ibid., pp. 6–7).
[4] E. W. Schermerhorn, *Benjamin Constant* (London, 1924), p. 171; J.-C. Bailleul (*Rapport sur la conspiration du 18 Fructidor, 26 Ventôse An VI* (B.M., F.R.1381.13); Barras, *Memoirs*, III, pp. 22, 58.

18 Fructidor was considerably, if perhaps unconsciously, exaggerated.[1] What is now more pertinent is the point that not only men like Barras, but even one so fanatically sincere as LaRevellière-Lépeaux, should have continued to insist that the Constitution of 1795 was still valid and effective despite the *coup*. That it had been abused, that the three Directors had, in Lépeaux's words, 'inflicted a serious wound' upon it, could not of course be denied, for the use of military force had been made manifest to all. On 18 Fructidor the Presidents of both the Councils had somehow contrived to slip into their seats for long enough to declare that the parliament was being dissolved by force; and somehow some 30 of the Elders had managed to march in procession towards their chamber, so compelling the cavalry to disperse them by the sword.[2] Lépeaux nevertheless maintained, and apparently believed, that the *coup* was unusual, perhaps even unique, in its essentially constitutional character. For him, the proof of this was that the use of force was brief and bloodless, and that as soon as the situation had been restored all was again done in strict conformity with the Constitution. As he himself put it: 'Never did men who had become absolute masters of the State divest themselves so swiftly and so completely of all extraordinary power'.[3]

Whatever the truth of this, it was certainly not immediately apparent. The Triumvirate, of course, lost no time in clothing its measures with some semblance of legality. On 18 Fructidor itself the two Councils were re-convened, the Elders being summoned to assemble in the School of Medicine and the Five Hundred being called to the Odéon. As soon as a sufficient number of selected deputies had been admitted to these buildings by the military, the Council of Five Hundred approved without debate a proposal for the appointment of an extraordinary Commission of Five. This Commission was nominally created to propose

---

[1] See above, chapter 5. For a summary of the contrary view, which suggests that the uncommitted deputies of the Right and Centre were so divided and irresolute that they in effect left the real royalists a clear field for subversive action against the Directory, see Harvey Mitchell, op. cit., pp. 214–16. The final official report on 'The Conspiracy of 18 Fructidor', presented to the Councils by Bailleul in March 1798 (Bailleul, op. cit.) certainly exposed a conspiracy—the activities of the Paris Agency and of the Institutes as well as the British payments to Pichegru being recapitulated—but it made no serious attempt to establish its extent in the Councils. As Bailleul said: 'No one seeks to prove the existence of light'.

[2] Meynier, *Le Dix-huit Fructidor, An V*, pp. 134–5. Still more strikingly, Hoche's men moved into Paris waving the signs so recently set up to mark the limits of the 'constitutional zone' in which military movement was illegal: Mathiez, *Le Directoire*, p. 335.

[3] Lépeaux, *Mémoires*, II, pp. 137, 142, 151.

measures 'for the preservation of public tranquillity and the Constitution of the Year III'; but it was in reality the agency through which the Triumvirate acted in the Council, and it is significant that it was composed of Sieyès and his closest associates. Sieyès, who in 1789 had been the principal exponent of the doctrine of the sovereignty of the nation, had for some time been convinced that a parliament's primary function was that of supporting the executive, and he had been deeply (if, as always, unobtrusively) involved in the Triumvirate's preparations for the *coup*.[1] Speaking for him and for the Commission, another deputy, Boulay of the Meurthe,[2] now assured the Five Hundred that 'the triumph of the Republic' was not to be marred by bloodshed, and so persuaded the Council to approve all the measures which the Commission proposed. When the Elders had reluctantly ratified these early next morning, they became effective as the Law of 19 Fructidor (5 September 1797).[3]

This piece of exceptional legislation, which was to be as important in the future as the Law of 3 Brumaire had been in the past, was in part simply a proscription list. By it, 42 deputies of the Five Hundred, 11 of the Elders and 12 other men, a total of 65, were sentenced to be deported, a form of punishment and political ostracism for the development of which Sieyès was believed to be particularly responsible. How many of these men can properly be called committed royalists is a matter of opinion. Some, perhaps as many as half, probably were.[4] The list, however, included the two Directors Carnot and Barthélemy, General Pichegru, the Police Minister Cochon, the two royalist agents Brottier and Duverne du Presle, and deputies as varied as Boissy d'Anglas, Dumas, Dumolard, Desmolières and Portalis, to name no others, and it is hard to believe that these men had much in common either with each other or with royalists like Imbert-Colomès, Job Aimé or Willot. Rather does it seem likely that the Triumvirate was primarily interested in ridding itself at a stroke of all its critics, tarring all with the same brush. As for the much-vaunted 'bloodlessness' of the proscription, it may be remarked that while no fewer than 48 of these men, including Carnot

---

[1] Bastid, P., *Sieyès et sa Pensée* (Paris, 1939), pp. 180–3, 187, 191–3.

[2] *Biog. Notes:* BOULAY OF THE MEURTHE.

[3] This is given in full in V. Pierre, *18 Fructidor* (Paris, 1893), pp. 59–72.

[4] Harvey Mitchell (op. cit., p. 211) accepts the analysis of Polissard, one of those who evaded arrest, by which 24 of 40 of those proscribed were really royalists; and Mitchell himself concludes that 32 of 48 of them may fairly be so described. Meynier (op. cit., pp. 173–5) earlier concluded that the 65 included 16 certain royalists and 16 near-royalists. V. Pierre, who gives the list of names in full (*18 Fructidor*, p. 64) regards it as an amalgam (p. xviii).

and Dumas, successfully evaded arrest, the remainder were shown no mercy. Within 24 hours Barthélemy and Pichegru and various others were being carted out of Paris in heavily-barred carriages[1] *en route* for Rochefort and French Guiana. In all, 17 of the 65 were so transported,[2] and with them there went by his own wish Barthélemy's valet, Le Tellier. Of these 18, eight escaped from Guiana in an open boat in May 1798, and six of these—including both Pichegru and Barthélemy— eventually returned safely to Europe. Of the other ten, however, seven died in captivity, nearly all within the first 12 months of their exile, and only three survived long enough to be recalled to France when Bonaparte became First Consul.[3]

The Law of 19 Fructidor also authorised a more general purge of parliament and the local administrations. By its first article the elections of 1797 in 49 Departments were declared illegitimate and invalid, and subsequent articles also determined the outcome of certain disputed elections at the Triumvirate's pleasure. At the parliamentary level, the *coup* consequently meant that the seats of 177 deputies (including those who were proscribed)[4] became vacant; and since no provision was made for filling these vacancies before the elections in the spring of 1798, the Legislative Body remained reduced by approximately one quarter of its numerical strength. The authority of the Directory was also considerably increased by the right it acquired to fill by nomination the many vacancies that occurred in the local administrations and law courts as a result of the annulment of the elections.

At the same time the triumph of the Executive over the Legislative was marked by an uncompromising reassertion of the 'exceptional legislation' of 1795. The Law of 3 Brumaire, which the Centre and Right had so recently succeeded in repealing, was reimposed upon France in a still more stringent form: the relatives of *émigrés* were now disenfranchised

[1] I here avoid the common expression 'iron cages', which suggests that these prisoners (and Babeuf before them) were transported in open cages like wild beasts. One should rather picture a closed carriage, heavily railed up externally.

[2] I.e. Barthélemy, Barbé-Marbois, Lafon-Ladebat, Pichegru, Willot, Tronçon de Coudray, Aubry, de la Rue, Ramel, Rovère, Murinais, Bourdon de l'Oise, Dossonville, Villeurnoy, Job Aimé, Gibert Desmolières and Brottier (Duverne du Presle, the informant, having been released).

[3] Those who escaped were: Barthélemy and his valet Le Tellier, Pichegru, Willot, Aubry, de la Rue, Ramel and the police agent Dossonville. Of these, Aubry and Le Tellier died, the latter on board the vessel which picked up the party and took them to England. See Pierre, op. cit., chapter 4. The three prisoners who survived life in French Guiana were Barbé-Marbois, Lafond-Ladebat and Job Aimé.

[4] But excluding those who resigned, as, for example, Dupont de Nemours.

as well as being excluded from all public offices.[1] Similarly, those *émigrés* who had returned to France were given 14 days to leave the country under pain of death, even if they had already obtained provisional reinstatement. The legislation of 1792 and 1793 against dissident priests was also reaffirmed, and all those priests who had returned from exile were ordered to leave again under penalty of deportation to Guiana. Sieyès, indeed, would have liked to enforce a still more barbarous system of class discrimination. Still, as in 1789, regarding the nobility as a cancerous growth which could only be excised from the body politic,[2] he sought to expel all those of noble birth from the soil of the Republic. Neither the Directors nor the deputies, however, were willing to go so far, and when on 24 September Boulay put forward proposals amounting to this proscription of a complete social class, he encountered indignant protests. Although the nobility were nominally deprived of civic rights, this particular piece of legislation was apparently allowed to remain incomplete and ineffective.[3]

The Law of 19 Fructidor was nevertheless sufficiently savage. In other provisions, it established military commissions for the trial and execution of *émigrés*, and it empowered the Directory to deport any priest it chose merely by an order duly made out in his name. Instead of an oath of submission to the law, one of hatred of royalism and anarchy was now required of all public officials; and by this and allied legislation, the Press was placed under the control of the police for one year, 42 journals being suppressed immediately. Political clubs were, indeed, permitted again, always provided that no-one in them ever professed principles contrary to those of the Constitution of 1795; but this concession seems only to indicate the new government's awareness of its own need for some public support.

Thus on 5 September 1797 subservient men set some stamp of legality upon the Triumvirate's resort to force; and thus armed, the Triumvirs subjected the Right, and all those whom they associated with it, to a new

---

[1] An indication of the attitude of the government, and a corrective to too casual a use of the term 'exceptional legislation', may be found in the fact that the relevant articles of the Law of 3 Brumaire were now to remain operative until *four years after* the conclusion of a general peace—which only the most optimistic could then have supposed to be imminent.

[2] 'It is impossible to say what place two privileged bodies are to occupy in the social order. It is equivalent to asking what place is to be assigned in the body of a sick man to a malignant affliction that saps and torments it. It must be neutralised.' Sieyès, E., *Qu'est-ce que le tiers état?* (trans. J. Hall Stewart, *A Documentary Survey*, p. 56).

[3] Bastid, op. cit., pp. 195–6; Lefebvre, *The Directory*, p. 103.

régime of repression. Legality, indeed, soon became of small account. With or without lawful authority, local commissioners and the police demanded identification papers, searched private houses and arrested men on suspicion of conspiracy. Nor was any means of expression secure, for letters were liable to secret inspection, and such journals as were not suppressed were increasingly filled with reports inspired by the government.[1] Moreover, military commissions, which were established in many parts of France after various outbreaks of royalist activity in the south-east, within a few months sentenced at least 160 people to be shot as *émigrés*.[2] Characteristic of the system, this kind of summary justice was soon extended, a law being passed in January 1798 to enable the commissions to deal with brigandage wherever two or more persons were involved. Yet as the military courts apparently acted with commendable caution, the number of those executed as *émigrés* is surprisingly small. The greater social evil was really the renewal of indiscriminate persecution, for although the classification of the *émigrés* was well-known to be highly haphazard, the government insisted that the laws against them must be enforced. Consequently a multitude of men and women who had returned to France earlier in the year had now again to seek refuge beyond the frontiers. From Marseilles alone some 15,000 people left the country in this new exodus.[3]

Equally harsh and arbitrary treatment was meted out to the clergy. Already divided and sub-divided by the demands of successive régimes for allegiance, the Catholic Church in France was now subjected to the further requirement that its priests should take the new oath of hatred to royalty. Apparently most of those who belonged to the 'Constitutional' or 'Gallican' Church—from which the Republic had withdrawn all support in 1795—conformed to this fresh demand, and about one fifth

[1] After Fructidor the established governmental procedure of subsidising selected journals was supplemented by the growth of a semi-official office for the preparation of approved articles. The suppression of offending journals—which were repeatedly re-established under new names—continued, 16 being suppressed at once on 17 December 1797. On this subject, see Lefebvre, op cit., p. 98; Godechot, J., *Les Institutions de la France*, pp. 426–30; and Aulard, A., *A Political History*, III, pp. 374–91.

[2] See V. Pierre, *18 Fructidor*, Introduction xxii–xxxvi and Section V.

[3] See D. Greer, *The Incidence of the Emigration during the French Revolution* (Glous., Mass., 1966), p. 102. According to Lépeaux (*Mémoires*, II, p. 176) the Directors attempted to organise a re-assessment of the classification of the *émigrés*, but were soon frustrated by the rascality of their own officials and informants. Greer (loc. cit.) cites one instance before Fructidor in which a man who offered 40,000 francs for the removal of his name from the list was met by the Minister of Police's demand for 80,000.

of the others, the 'refractory priests' also did so—no doubt feeling by now that all means were fair against the godless. About 11,000 priests consequently remained liable to deportation to Guiana as non-jurors, and in 1797–8 the Directors evidently devoted much of their time to the preparation of some 1,700 deportation orders against selected individuals amongst these. Partly because of the British blockade, only 263 of those so sentenced ever reached their destination—where 156 of them soon died. Almost a thousand others remained in internment on the Ile de Ré and the Ile d'Oléron off the western coast of France, and amongst these too the death rate was high.[1] Further, although deportation to Guiana, was also tacitly substituted for the death penalty for priests who were found in France despite previous banishment, between 40 and 50 of these were in fact executed locally as *émigrés*.[2]

Some of this severity may perhaps be regarded as inevitable whilst France was still at war with Britain. So far as Catholicism was concerned, however, the policy of the Directory after 18 Fructidor involved a great deal more than state security. As it happened, the first National Council of the 'Constitutional' Church had been meeting in Paris at the time of the *coup d'état*, and this in effect accepted its new situation: declaring that all French Catholics owed sincere submission to the laws of the Republic, it disavowed all those of its priests who should refuse to forswear royalism. The government nevertheless spurned such support and at once resumed the revolutionary attempts to suppress Christianity itself.[3] The 'Constitutional' Church was, indeed, tolerated; but the law of 1795[4] which forbade all external manifestations of religion was revived and extended, even public burials by the rites of the Church being banned. At the same time, the Ministry of the Interior initiated a new

---

[1] I follow here the figures given in Godechot, op. cit., pp. 454–5 and Lefebvre, op. cit., pp. 101–2. The matter is however complicated by the proscription in November 1798 of an additional 8,000 Belgian priests, of whom 350 were interned and 30 deported—these last two figures being included in those given in the text.

[2] As distinct, apparently, from those priests who had returned to France before the Law of 19 Fructidor, by which they were ordered to leave on pain of deportation to Guiana. The position of those who returned subsequently was obscure, for the Councils had now rescinded the repeal of the laws of 1792 and 1793 which imposed the death penalty on priests who returned from banishment. See Lefebvre, op. cit., pp. 92 and 100–2.

[3] See Godechot, op. cit., pp. 456–60; Lefebvre, op. cit., pp. 156–9; Meynier, A., *Les Coups d'Etat du Directoire*, II: *Le Vingt-deux Floréal An VI* (Paris, 1928).

[4] I.e., the law of 29 September 1795 (see J. Hall Stewart, *A Documentary Survey*, p. 547), this being a further development of that of 21 February 1795.

drive to establish the civic ceremonies associated with the Republican Calendar and the cult of the *décadi*. Consequently in 1797, when the celebration of midnight mass at Christmas was forbidden, the unfortunate priests were required to observe and sanctify the *décadi*; and after April 1798, when the use of the Republican Calendar was made compulsory, innumerable new conflicts arose over the observance of Christian, Republican and national festivals. Although the violence and vandalism characteristic of this campaign in 1793 were now uncommon,[1] its revival led directly to a multiplicity of minor acts of oppression, such as that which forbade the sale of fish on Fridays. If these measures were again effectively met by local resistance in some areas, in others the local authorities persecuted all priests without distinction. Thus the 'Constitutional' clergy, of whom about 100 were imprisoned during this period, secured little except survival by their acceptance of the Republic.

For some six months after Fructidor those priests who lived in or near Paris, or one of a few provincial towns, had also to contend with the challenge of yet another new cult, that of Theophilanthropy.[2] This was in many respects harmless enough, for its first adherents sought simply to encourage belief in those spiritual ideas (particularly, the existence of God and the immortality of the soul) and those moral precepts which they thought all religions to have in common. Although, as this suggests, their creed was derived from Robespierre's Cult of the Supreme Being, they expressly repudiated the view that belief should be regulated by the State. Theophilanthropy was nevertheless adopted enthusiastically by LaRevellière-Lépeaux, who so identified himself with it that he was long supposed to have been its founder; and he, as one who was both passionately anti-clerical and profoundly convinced that the new republican society stood in urgent need of a new morality, contrived to give the cult some official standing and a good deal of semi-official support. The 'Constitutional' clergy thus found themselves virtually compelled to allow these new rivals to make use of their churches, and by the beginning of 1798 all but two of the churches in Paris were being shared

---

[1] They were not, however, unknown. Since churches in which Mass was not regularly celebrated could be put up for sale, the Abbey of Cluny was so sold, and subsequently destroyed; and in 1799 the local administration in Finistère gave orders that any public assembly at the *pardon* of Sainte-Anne d'Auray was to be broken up by military force.

[2] See the works cited above by Lefebvre, Godechot and Meynier, and, for the attitude of Lépeaux, both his own *Mémoires* (particularly Vol. II, p. 158ff.) and Robison, G., *Revellière-Lépeaux, Citizen Director* (New York, 1938), p. 161ff. The standard work is Mathiez, A., *La théophilanthropie et la culte décadaire* (Paris, 1904).

between the two faiths—even if some priests secretly purified their buildings after every sacrilegious use of them by their rivals.

As it happened, Theophilanthropy soon declined. While it was always too intellectual and contemplative to attract much popular support, it became associated with Jacobinism,[1] and after the elections of 1798 the government abandoned it as dangerously democratic. Thereafter the Theophilanthropists survived only in isolated groups, and the cult of the *décadi* enjoyed a monopoly of official favour. Since the latter at least provided patriots with some opportunities for pageantry, it may have acquired some measure of popularity; but the greater probability is that the government made itself obnoxious to the majority of ordinary people by trying to sustain this singularly artificial form of civic morality.

Despite Lépeaux's insistence upon the constitutional character of the Second Directory (as the government established in September 1797 is usually called), that régime therefore seems to have been in many ways as revolutionary at home as it was in relation to Europe. Far from healing the wounds of France, it prolonged the nation's anguish by renewing the record of political persecution and by reviving the attempt to replace Christianity by unrealistic rationalism.[2] In the opinion of Lefebvre, its rule was indeed nothing less than a new manifestation of the Terror, akin to that of 1794 in its frank recognition that revolutionaries must maintain themselves by force.[3]

Nor can the new government be called republican even in the more limited sense that it really represented any progressive popular movement. Although the 'Directorial Terror' was aimed at the royalists, at the Right, and in all probability at much of the Centre, it was not effected from below but by the power of the police and the army. The extensive purge of local administrations naturally enabled a good many men of Jacobin sympathies to obtain office:[4] to Lépeaux's surprise, even the new Minister of Police, Pierre Sotin, turned out to be an enthusiastic

---

[1] Particularly during the period between 25 July and 5 September 1797, when political clubs were forbidden by law.

[2] This view may be compared with that of Lefebvre (*The Directory*, pp. 157–9), which is more indicative of the strength of the secular tradition in France. Noting that the Directors made themselves unbearable, Lefebvre remarks: 'In this way they compromised the process of de-Christianisation, which was in fact continuing of its own accord . . . If it (the Directory) had pursued a policy of secular indifference, it could have counted on time to do the rest.'

[3] Op. cit., p. 97.

[4] Meynier, op. cit., p. 28, according to whom 19 departmental and 462 municipal commissioners were replaced and 63 departmental and 178 municipal councils reconstituted.

Jacobin who promoted and protected militant democrats on every possible occasion.[1] Moreover, once the ban on political clubs was lifted there was a rapid proliferation of 'Constitutional Circles' throughout France, and most of these were in fact ardently democratic. But although these new Jacobins seem to have been men who had learnt by experience to eschew political violence and social extremism,[2] the Directors and people like Benjamin Constant regarded them from the first with considerable suspicion. If some minor legislation was passed in response to their wishes, they were still constantly harassed and kept under observation, and at least 35 of their clubs were closed down before the elections of 1798. As one official, evidently a 'vigorous republican' of whom the government could whole-heartedly approve, remarked: 'their exaltation must be limited if it is not to become misguided'.[3]

It would of course be misleading to suggest that the government of France by the Second Directory was never anything but purely repressive, or that some repression of indiscriminate brigandage and lawlessness was not urgently necessary. After the elimination of Carnot and Barthélemy on 18 Fructidor, the control of the executive by Barras, Reubell and Lépeaux was complete, and there was between them a working, if hardly an amicable, relationship. Their strength, moreover, was soon reinforced by the appointment of two new Directors, Merlin de Douai[4] and François de Neufchâteau.[5] Although the former was already well-hated as the author of the notorious Law of Suspects of 1793, both were men of marked ability and considerable administrative experience. This new Directory, being more united and more independent of parliament than its predecessor, was eventually able to begin to master local violence and to initiate, if not actually to complete, several important reforms. Indeed, one of its most far-reaching measures, the partial liquidation of the National Debt, was begun on the evening of 19 Fructidor itself, when the Legislative Body was reduced to a cypher.[6]

Yet even if the ultimate merit of much of the work of the Second Directory be recognised, the initial political position of the régime was as reactionary as its methods and objectives were revolutionary. Not

[1] I. Woloch, *Jacobin Legacy: The Democratic Movement under the Directory*, pp. 218–20.

[2] Ibid., *passim*. See also Godechot, op. cit., pp. 423–5 for some figures and details about the size and activities of the clubs 1797–9.

[3] Woloch, op. cit., p. 83.

[4] *Biog. Notes:* MERLIN DE DOUAI.

[5] *Biog. Notes:* FRANÇOIS DE NEUFCHÂTEAU.

[6] See below, chapter 7, for consideration of the financial and administrative measures of the government.

only was the *coup d'état* of 18 Fructidor a blow struck by a narrowly-based government which deliberately repudiated popular aid: it was also a successful repudiation of one possible way in which legitimate political evolution might have taken place within the framework of the Republic.[1] Lépeaux, Barras and their associates constantly claimed that they had acted to uphold the Constitution of 1795 against organised royalist infiltration; in fact they violated that Constitution, manipulating the law by a mixture of force and chicanery and so subordinating the parliament of France that it was henceforth compelled to devote much of its time to the consideration of trivialities.[2] What is more, they forced Frenchmen to conform again to the political pattern imposed upon them two years previously. To the Triumvirate, in particular, that pattern was now more synonymous than ever with their own monopoly of political power, and criticism of it, coming initially from the Right, was conveniently damned as 'royalism'. To such limits had the Republic shrunk by 1797. In short, the Constitution may have remained nominally operative in the period immediately following 18 Fructidor; but it certainly did not apply to the ostracised and supposedly alien Right, and its application to the rest of France was at best speculative.

The real weakness of the Directors' claim to legitimacy was their failure to follow their *coup* by a revision of the Constitution. Had they taken the risk of attempting this in a democratic direction they might well have rallied very substantial support, for the Jacobins were now once more living in the expectation that an attitude of cooperation and constructive criticism would eventually be so rewarded. Not surprisingly, nothing suggests that any such move was contemplated: to those in authority in France in 1797, the Jacobin was a terrorist not by circumstance but by nature. The Directors, however, were well aware of the desirability of constitutional change: their *coup*, indeed, could have been as well, and probably better, justified on the grounds that the independence of the Treasury, the indissolubility of the Councils and the regular recurrence of elections made good government impossible and revision

[1] Compare R. Palmer, *The Age of the Democratic Revolution*, II, p. 216: 'The difficulty was that the Directory occupied too narrow a band in the (political) spectrum. It was never able to broaden its base.' Relevant as this is to my own reading of the position, I am unable to see the Directory quite so much as the victim of circumstance. Rather is it the Directors' inveterate suspicion of all potential support which impresses me.

[2] It may, indeed, be argued that the *coup* of 18 Fructidor was little more than an incidental consequence of the decision taken in the previous July, when the Triumvirs rejected Ministers who might be representative of parliamentary opinion. See G. Robison, *Revellière-Lépeaux, Citizen-Director*, p. 131.

imperative. Sundry schemes to increase the legitimate authority of government by fundamental reform were indeed mooted during the autumn of 1797:[1] but the Directors did no more than toy with most of these, and by this inaction they inevitably prolonged instability and committed themselves to still further arbitrary action.

Crucial in itself, this matter is the more significant since both Bonaparte and Sieyès, the two men who were eventually to destroy the Directory, were at this time involved in a tentative move towards constitutional changes tantamount to just such a revolution.[2] Only a few days after 18 Fructidor Bonaparte received a letter from Talleyrand, the Minister of Foreign Affairs,[3] which was probably written at the instigation of Barras. This letter, which has not survived, apparently sought to sound out Bonaparte's reaction to further political change, and it suggested that he might confer with Sieyès if the latter were to come to Italy for consultations on the constitutional problems of the Cisalpine Republic. Bonaparte's reply,[4] which was written on 19 September 1797, was, to say the least, cordial. Outlining his attitude in general but sufficiently suggestive terms, he wrote that the French, who were afflicted by a proliferation of ineffectual laws, were so far organised only in outline. Given the principle of the sovereignty of the people, which he described as the only real advance the French had made in 50 years, he argued that 'the government, taken in the wide sense that I would give it, ought to be regarded as the real representative of the nation'; and since the powers of parliament, which had been evolved in England to curb 'the insolent tyranny of the court party', would then be superfluous, the Legislative Body should be transformed into a Grand Council of experienced administrators.

As Sieyès had long since identified himself with a proposal to establish a very similar sort of supervisory senate—the 'Constitutional Jury' which to his chagrin had been so decisively rejected when the Constitution of 1795 was being drafted—as well as with the idea that the legislative ought to be further subordinated to the executive, it is evident that there was already in 1797 sufficient ground for an alliance between the two men. That nothing came of their apparent readiness to act together at this time would seem to be a consequence of the Directors' suspicions of

[1] See Mathiez, *Le Directoire*, p. 338; R. Guyot, 'Du Directoire au Consulat: les Transitions', *Revue historique*, Vol. CXI (1912), p. 4.

[2] Mathiez, op. cit., pp. 351–2.

[3] *Biog. Notes:* TALLEYRAND-PÉRIGORD.

[4] *Napoleon's Letters*, ed. J. M. Thompson (Everyman, London, 1964), p. 65, citing *Corres.* III. 2223.

Bonaparte—whose views probably proved more far-reaching than Barras had anticipated. Lépeaux, it seems, was now determined to uphold the existing order of things, which he regarded as genuinely constitutional; and Barras abandoned the scheme when he realised that Reubell, who believed constitutional change to be necessary, was too distrustful of Bonaparte to cooperate by outvoting Lépeaux.[1] Thus if the Directors failed to revise the Constitution of 1795 at the time when they had the best opportunity and justification for doing so, they also kept Bonaparte, without whose assent they could scarcely act decisively, at bay.

Bonaparte's own ambitions, however, had still to be reckoned with. Having been appointed plenipotentiary of the French Republic to the Congress of Rastadt, he went there by way of Switzerland as soon as the Treaty of Campo-Formio was concluded. His objective, however, was France, and before he had been at Rastadt for a fortnight he got the Directors to approve his return to Paris, which he reached on the evening of 5 December 1797. There he was fêted as a national hero, and the street in which he lived was renamed *la rue de la Victoire* in his honour. He was, indeed, in a position of singular strength, for as it so happened his most formidable rival, the young hero Hoche, had died suddenly on 18 September;[2] and Moreau, France's other great military leader, had been deprived of his command soon after 18 Fructidor for covering up evidence relating to Pichegru's connivance with the royalists. That in this situation Bonaparte seriously considered acquiring some measure of political power seems practically certain. According to Miot de Melito, whom he had met at Turin in November, he had then said frankly that he had only supported the Directors in Fructidor in order to thwart the Bourbons; far from having anything in common with them, he regarded them as poor creatures who understood nothing of government: 'I am not their dupe . . . I have tasted command, and I cannot give it up . . . if I cannot be master I shall leave France.'[3]

Whether this idea of political mastery was already in Bonaparte's mind when he came to Paris, or whether it was suggested to him by what he saw and heard in the capital, he undoubtedly tried to see how far he could advance. On 10 December an official reception was given in his honour at the Luxembourg, and Talleyrand praised him effusively as the Champion of Liberty: but Bonaparte, in a brief and almost insolent reply, asserted that the conclusion of peace on the continent marked the opening of the era of representative governments. Further,

---

[1] Mathiez, op. cit., p. 353.
[2] Hoche was then aged 29, one year older than Bonaparte.
[3] Miot de Melito, *Memoirs*, pp. 112–13.

he ended his speech with the well-known comment: 'When the happiness of the French people is based on better organic laws, the whole of Europe will become free'. This remark may best be understood as an invitation to Barras, the next speaker, to announce the imminence of a revision of the Constitution, which would presumably have directed towards making the government more powerful and 'representative' in Bonaparte's sense. Barras, however, chose to disregard the gambit, and he concluded his enumeration of the general's exploits by urging him to crown his career by the conquest of England.

Bonaparte, who had in fact already been appointed Commander-in-chief of the Army of England, nevertheless remained for a while in Paris. Wearing civilian clothes, he sought, as he said, to probe the ground; but although he impressed the academic world and was elected a Member of the Institute, he was unable to rally sufficient support to make any alteration in the law which restricted eligibility for election to the Directory to men of at least 40 years of age. As he remarked to Bourrienne, the fact was that the Directors did not want him, and the time to overthrow them had not yet arrived.[1] As for the Directors themselves, they were in a similar situation: though they might resist Bonaparte, they dared not repudiate him, particularly as the approaching elections in the spring of 1798 might well renew their need for military support. Thus by what amounted to the tacit consent of both parties, Bonaparte's first tentative bid for political power was allowed to lapse, and the Republic remained at least nominally bound by the Constitution of 1795.

Any open conflict for power was the more easily avoided since foreign affairs afforded both Bonaparte and the Directors ample opportunities for action. At this time of uneasy peace between the powers of old Europe and the young Republic, the security of France seemed to depend on the establishment of sympathetic governments in all the small states along her eastern border. As we have seen, the treaty which Bonaparte had brought back from Campo-Formio gave France every incentive to consolidate her control of the Rhine, to increase her influence in the German states of the Holy Roman Empire, and to extend republicanism —and her own protective power—more deeply into Italy. Moreover, as Barras had reminded Bonaparte, England, the arch-enemy, had still to be defeated, and this implied a constant French endeavour to control every accessible centre of English trade and English influence. The political and strategic interests of the Republic, to say nothing of economic advantages both public and private, thus coincided with the revival

[1] F. de Bourrienne, *Memoirs of Napoleon Bonaparte* (Hutchinson Library ed., London, n.d.), p. 67.

of revolutionary enthusiasm which followed Fructidor, and a new phase of French expansion began in 1798. Of this, Bonaparte's restless ambition and the three principal Directors' most characteristic attributes— Barras's greed, Lépeaux's idealism and Reubell's preoccupation with the security of the Rhine frontier—were all in different ways representative.

The increase in French control of the affairs of the so-called 'Sister Republics', which was one well-marked feature of the renewed expansion, usually had some measure of justification. All too often, however, it was the interests of France which ultimately prevailed. Thus on 22 January 1798 French forces were employed to effect a purge of the Dutch Convention, and as a result the Batavian Republic, which had been distracted and divided ever since revolution had accompanied the French occupation of Holland early in 1795, eventually rejected federalism and accepted a unitary and democratic constitution by a referendum held in April 1798. That this solution was popular is not in doubt, for the majority was overwhelming;[1] but the principal concern of the French, particularly after Camperdown, was certainly to ensure that Holland would have a stable government and be more effective as an ally in the war against England. Similarly, when the legislative assembly of the Cisalpine Republic refused to ratify the exceedingly costly treaty of alliance which its government had concluded with France on 21 February, a purge of that assembly was effected by the French army of occupation on orders from Paris.[2] Here again, though local initiative was of considerable importance in a *coup* ostensibly directed against Austrian and 'aristocratic' influences in the Cisalpine, the French sought first to secure a reliable and a dependent ally. In brief, both these purges correspond broadly to that which had taken place in Paris on 18 Fructidor, and in this respect both are illustrative of the beginning of what has well been called 'the enslavement of the sister republics'.[3]

This process did not, of course, simply involve France's consolidation of her control of areas already occupied by her armies. Much more alarming to the other powers of Europe was the fact that within a few weeks of the conclusion of the treaty of Campo-Formio the French were using force to establish still more satellite republics. This was not,

[1] 165,520 to 11,597. For the Batavian Republic, see R. R. Palmer, *The Age of the Democratic Revolution*, II, chapter 6 (pp. 177–204).

[2] Ibid., chapter 10, particularly pp. 319–22. By the terms of the treaty the Cisalpine Republic was to pay 18 million lire a year to support the French army of occupation, whilst maintaining its own army and placing an embargo on all trade with England.

[3] Lefebvre, *The Directory*, p. 119.

indeed, wholly a consequence of French ambition. Since democratic republicanism was still a new and entrancing political faith, some men of all nationalities were eager to see their own countries adopt it, and some of these did their utmost to solicit French intervention. Feelings of this sort were naturally strong amongst progressively-minded men in the cantons of the Swiss confederation—an organisation which may perhaps best be briefly described as a particularly complex conglomeration of local oligarchies. Swiss patricians like Peter Ochs of Basle and La Harpe of the Vaud continually sought French aid to free the Confederation from domination by the canton of Berne, a step which they believed to be the essential preliminary to any effective reforms. As might have been expected, however, the French responded with much more than a mere demonstration of force, the Directors indeed being remarkably united in their enthusiasm.[1] After Fructidor they had compelled the Bernese to expel Wickham and the French *émigrés*; but they still regarded control of Switzerland as a matter of military necessity, for on this depended both the security of France's communications with northern Italy and her ability to block the most natural road of any invader from the east. Consequently as soon as it became clear that no spontaneous but far-reaching revolution was to be expected of the Swiss, the Directory ordered General Brune[2] to march on Berne. There, as an alien 'revolution', instigated by French agents and supported by French arms, swept the country, the Helvetic Republic was proclaimed on 22 March 1798. Resistance to the new unitary constitution and to the French exactions—which included the confiscation of the 6 million livres in the Treasury of Berne and an immediate levy of 15 millions on the cantons —then sufficed to justify the continuation of the French occupation.[3]

In Italy, too, French expansion continued despite the nominal conclusion of the war. Here again the Directors were to some extent victims of circumstance, for the more the French advanced, the more they were caught up in the conflicts of their own client states, so being drawn from conquest to conquest. But while the Directors in Paris sometimes seem less like the leaders than the led, they were not slow to take full advant-

[1] Reubell in particular recorded: 'I am pushing with all my strength': G. D. Homan, 'Jean-François Reubell, Director', *French Historical Studies*, No. 1 (1960), p. 433.

[2] *Biog. Notes:* BRUNE.

[3] For the Helvetic Republic, see Palmer, op. cit., p. 368 and chapter 13 (pp. 395–421). I should also record the benefit I have gained from my conversations on this subject with Mr R. Aksim, a graduate student at Carleton University (see unpublished M.A. thesis, *Reluctant Patriots: The Swiss Revolution of 1798 to 1803*).

age of some of the abundant opportunities offered to them. Of these, the most important was the instability of the Papal States, where local problems were aggravated by the presence of revolutionaries from the Cisalpine. The murder of a French general[1] in a political demonstration in Rome in December 1797 admittedly demanded redress; but it also allowed the Directors to act in conformity with their long-cherished hatred of Catholicism,[2] and in February 1798 a force commanded by Berthier occupied Rome on orders from Paris. Almost immediately a 'revolution' took place, the Roman Republic being proclaimed in the Forum on 15 February. The Papal States nevertheless remained under French military control, and, while the Pope took refuge in Tuscany, his people and his possessions were for a second time so ruthlessly exploited that some 70 million francs were extracted from them in little less than a year.[3]

Events such as these evidently portended a renewal of open war in Europe. To Austria in particular the continual augmentation of French power was quite intolerable, and public resentment of it became apparent in Vienna in April 1798, when angry demonstrations followed the flaunting of the French flag by General Bernadotte[4]—whose appointment as ambassador by Bonaparte had in itself been regarded as an insult. It is significant, too, that when hostilities began in the spring of 1799, the first clashes occurred in the Grisons in Switzerland, and this before war had formally been declared. The 'high tide of Revolutionary democracy'[5] which rose in 1798 was in fact coincidental with a renewal of French aggression and French aggrandizement. While it may be true, as Professor Palmer has written in his invaluable study of this complex scene, that the conflict which divided Europe was 'a war of democrats and republicans against monarchists and aristocrats',[6] it was also one brought about by the persistent refusal of the French Republic to accept the existence of any limitation upon its power and its possessions. However deep the ideological differences between the old order and the new, and however many European 'jacobins' sympathised with the 'demo-

[1] Léonard Duphot, who was about to marry Désirée Clary, the sister-in-law of the French ambassador Joseph Bonaparte and the future wife of Bernadotte.

[2] As was stated in chapter 5, above, early in 1797 Bonaparte had been ordered to destroy the papal government, since 'the Roman religion would always be the irreconcilable enemy of the Republic' (3 February 1797). He, however, had then been content to secure the peace of Tolentino.

[3] Palmer, op. cit., II, pp. 368–9 and 372–7.

[4] *Biog. Notes:* BERNADOTTE.

[5] Palmer, op. cit. *passim* and particularly chapter 11 (pp. 327–62).

[6] Ibid., p. 372.

cratic revolution', the fundamental fact remains that French influence
was infallibly followed by French military occupation, just as the introduction of French 'democratic' reforms was accompanied by remorseless
French exploitation. Consequently it is not so surprising as Professor
Palmer supposed that 'The British government seems actually to have
believed that in continuing the war with France it was working for the
liberation of 'Europe'.[1] Being, as always, more concerned with French
power than with French politics, the British were even less inclined than
others to accept a situation in which what Pitt called 'the Public Law of
Europe' was perpetually and flagrantly violated by a swollen and
insatiable state.

The British, the only people with whom the Republic was still officially at war, were in fact at this time standing to their arms in daily
expectation of invasion. In the face of fantastic rumours about the huge
rafts that were being prepared to bring vast forces against them, men of
all classes enlisted in Armed Associations and Volunteer Companies,
drilling and building blockhouses and barriers in a mood which Mallet
du Pan, who was in the country in May, described as one of 'unbounded
confidence almost amounting to presumption'.[2] For a short time the
danger was real enough, for as Commander of the Army of England
Bonaparte had at his disposal 50,000 men and—at least on paper—50
warships and all the small craft of northern France and the Low Countries. A concentration of these forces having been ordered for the end of
February 1798, the general left Paris early in that month to carry out a
whirlwind inspection of the northern ports. Only when this was completed did he report to the Directory on 23 February that as the naval
preparations were inadequate, the expedition would have to be abandoned as impossible for at least 12 months.[3] Although, as he recommended, the appearance of invasion was maintained, the French plans for a
direct assault upon the British Isles in fact dwindled away, and in the
event only one brigade under General Humbert briefly disturbed
Ireland in the following summer.[4]

[1] Ibid., p. 371.

[2] A comment quoted by Sir Arthur Bryant, *The Years of Endurance* (London,
1942), p. 228. Since the invasion threat of 1798 is commonly overshadowed in
British history by the still more dramatic danger of 1803–5, adequate accounts
of it are uncommon.

[3] *Correspondence*, III, 2419, cited in J. M. Thompson, *Napoleon's Letters*
(London, 1964), p. 72.

[4] Humbert's tiny force landed at Killala Bay on 22 August, routed a regular
force four times as large at Castlebar and covered 150 miles before being brought
to bay by Cornwallis on 8 September.

In abandoning invasion, Bonaparte was not however proposing peace. While that was mentioned in his letter as a last resort (and as a possible means of enabling France to increase her pressure on the German states), he was principally concerned to advocate an alternative plan which had long been in his mind, that of a great expedition to Egypt. By conquering that country, he suggested, France would threaten British commerce throughout the East. Bonaparte's own motives in pressing this proposal are not difficult to understand: recklessly oblivious of ultimate consequences, he saw only, on the one hand, an inevitable decline in his personal prestige if he remained passively in Paris, and, on the other, a splendid vision of glory in the Orient. What is more remarkable is that the Directors should have given their approval, a thing they were evidently most reluctant to do.[1] The common suggestion, that they welcomed the expedition as a means of ridding themselves of Bonaparte and his embarrassing pretensions to power,[2] cannot be considered as anything more than a possible contributory reason for their decision: for all their deficiencies, the Directors were not men likely to deprive France of a substantial army at a critical period simply in order to save their own skins. Rather does it seem that the influence of Bonaparte and Talleyrand (who in this matter proved a powerful ally) gradually wore away their doubts, convincing them that the conquest of Egypt would be both practical and advantageous. After all, if Bonaparte, of all men, had concluded that a direct attack on Britain was out of the question, what alternative remained but to destroy her trade, the basis of her power? Although France had already banned British goods from all the territories she controlled, and imposed punitive restrictions upon neutral ships found carrying them,[3] even men convinced that commercial

---

[1] This is, at least, the impression which all later independently strove to convey in their memoirs. According to Reubell, who probably mattered most, his opposition was most vigorous, and was taken to the point of responding to Bonaparte's threat of resignation by the offer of a pen (G. D. Homan, op. cit., and G. Robison, *Revellière-Lépeaux*, p. 207). The story that Lépeaux was won over by the prospect of establishing Theophilanthropy in the East seems to derive, as might be expected, from the account of Barras. See Barras, *Memoirs*, III, pp. 206–9, and Lépeaux, *Mémoires*, II, pp. 340, 345.

[2] 'Bonaparte must leave the country . . . his personality really weighs too heavily upon the Directorate': Barras, *Memoirs*, III, p. 255.

[3] Legislation to supplement the Navigation Law first passed by the Convention in September 1793 had been approved on 18 January 1798. This economic warfare was of course mercantilist, being aimed not at the starvation of Britain but at the destruction of her prosperity and financial credit by the restriction of her exports.

wealth was fictitious and fragile could see that the attainment of victory by this process alone was likely to be long-deferred.

By reasoning such as this, and perhaps because they dared not alienate Bonaparte and Talleyrand on the eve of the spring elections of 1798, the Directors eventually and with deep misgivings approved the Egyptian expedition on 5 March. Thereafter no effort was spared to ensure that it was successful. In order to baffle the British, who contrived on 2 May to restore a naval squadron under Nelson to the Mediterranean, the real objective of the enterprise was kept a closely-guarded secret; but substantial forces were mustered openly at Toulon, a great part of the money looted from Berne and Rome being spent for this purpose. By the middle of May, when the expedition was ready to depart, Bonaparte had under his command 38,000 soldiers and almost 300 transports, together with an escorting fleet which included 13 ships of the line. Further, since this was not merely a military operation, but also one of scientific, geographical and cultural investigation, there was in addition a well-equipped team of 187 scientists, artists and men of letters and learning.

But if the Egyptian expedition was a remarkable, perhaps even a unique, venture towards systematic conquest and colonisation, it was nonetheless a wholly unscrupulous one. Whatever may be thought about the rights and wrongs of European expansion in general, the fact remains that Egypt was nominally part of the possessions of Turkey, a power with which France was not at war; which was, indeed, traditionally its ally. Since war with Turkey and eventually also with Russia ensued, France was soon to be involved in another major European conflict. Yet it may be remarked here that the responsibility for this was by no means Bonaparte's alone. Having gravely prejudiced the prospects of permanent peace in Europe by his manipulation of terms and territories at Campo-Formio, he had indeed been closely associated with the establishment of both the Roman and the Helvetic Republics. With his encouragement Berthier had marched on Rome, and from his collusion with Peter Ochs and Reubell at a dinner given by the latter on 8 December 1797 sprang the French invasion of Switzerland. Yet if he be thought more to blame than anyone else for the results of all this,[1] there is no reason to suppose that either the Directors, who made the decisions, or Frenchmen generally, had been loath to sanction these acts of violence. The excursion to the East was admittedly a different matter, in which all the initiative came from Bonaparte: yet it may well be thought

---

[1] In this connection, see Lefebvre, *The Directory*, pp. 109, 121, 123.

that the European war which it occasioned was in reality a natural consequence of the whole policy of the Republic.[1]

It would also seem natural that the Directory, revolutionary in its foreign policy, should at this same time have again shown itself to be equally arbitrary at home. As we have seen, the repression of the Right after the *coup d'état* of 18–19 Fructidor had been advantageous to the Left, a good many democrats having succeeded in obtaining local office and in resuming their participation in political life through the new 'Constitutional Clubs'. As in 1796, these new Jacobins accepted the Constitution of 1795 although they hoped to see its practice become more democratic—particularly so far as the interpretation of the laws governing the franchise was concerned. As 'friends of the common good', too, they had inherited a good deal of the social vision of 1793. Believing in the progressive taxation of wealth and in some measure of state intervention in economic matters, they were forthright in their attacks upon the 'bloodsuckers' and 'vampires' who enriched themselves at the expense of the armies and the nation. Professor Woloch, whose study of this radical resurgence is indispensable to a proper appreciation of it, has concluded that in 1798 Jacobinism evolved into 'a constitutional movement for reform' and became 'an embryonic party of movement, anxious to revive the momentum of revolution without its violence'.[2] To all those who sympathised with this development, the elections of 1798 appeared as a time of great opportunity, for the seats of all those expelled as 'royalists' in Fructidor as well as those of the last surviving 'third' of the Convention—a total of 437, or almost three-fifths of the two chambers—had now to be filled. For all their attachment to the constitutional republic, however, the democrats (or 'anarchists') of 1798 fared little better than the moderates (or 'royalists') of 1797. Nor is this surprising, since in the second case, as in the first, the would-be reformers en-

---

[1] Compare Goodwin ('The French Executive Directory—A Revaluation', *History* (Dec. 1937), p. 215): 'the revival of the second Coalition must be ascribed not to Directorial incompetence, but to the initiation of the Egyptian expedition—a venture devised by Bonaparte and Talleyrand'. While this comment is really compatible with my own (if the occasion of the war is distinguished from its deeper causes), it would, I think, be wrong to suppose that the Directors (whether competent or incompetent) can be absolved from all responsibility for a war for which Bonaparte personally can conveniently be blamed. Miot de Melito, it may be added, returned to Paris in December 1797 convinced that the Directors were determined to revolutionise all Italy—*Memoirs*, p. 116.

[2] Woloch, Iser, *Jacobin Legacy, The Democratic Movement under the Directory*, pp. 150, 165 and *passim*.

countered a Directory which (as Professor Woloch rightly recognises)[1] was dogmatically opposed to all organised opposition and to political parties as such.

The Directors' suspicions of the Jacobins (which were probably increased by the tendency of the Dutch and Italians in the 'sister republics' to become more democratic and nationalistic than was convenient) seem to have been sharpened early in 1798, when the deputy Pons of Verdun brought a storm about his head by proposing various small but significant changes in the conditions of eligibility to attend the primary assemblies. Certainly a change of front by the Directors, who had hitherto been primarily concerned to restrict the Right, became apparent on 15 February, when Sotin, the Minister of Police who had favoured the Jacobins, was suddenly dismissed—a matter in which Bonaparte seems to have had some hand.[2] Sotin was replaced by Dondeau, a front-man for the Director Merlin de Douai, who now assumed a role of repression similar to that played by Lépeaux in Fructidor. Becoming President of the Directory on 25 February, Merlin promptly published a proclamation condemning faction and 'those wild exaggerators who by the abuse of their principles and their previous excesses spread alarm among citizens'.[3] In effect this message of 27 February began the Directors' electoral campaign by resurrecting an old bogeyman: the royalists, it was said, no longer dared to appear in their true colours, but were masquerading as ardent revolutionaries in order to spread dissension and destroy the Republic by extremism.[4]

By what seems something more than a coincidence, on that same day Benjamin Constant made a violent attack upon the Jacobins at the (conservative) Constitutional Club in Paris.[5] This was in part a reasoned appeal to Frenchmen to remember that the Jacobins of 1793–4 were men

[1] Ibid., pp. 272–6, 310, 347.

[2] Woloch, op. cit., p. 277 and A. Espitalier, *Vers Brumaire: Bonaparte à Paris, 5 déc. 1797–4 mai 1798* (Paris, 1914), p. 99.

[3] Woloch, loc. cit.

[4] '*Royalisme à bonnet rouge*'. While Woloch (p. 277) may be correct in describing this as 'a new metaphor', the identification of public agitation with royalist activity was of course commonplace after 1792; nor was this merely a matter of convenience, for (apart from the plain fact that royalist agents were constantly active in France) the men of the Revolution had no doubt that all their enemies to both Right and Left were alike in being counter-revolutionaries.

[5] I.e., the Constitutional Club or Circle of the Hôtel de Salm in the rue de Lille, since 1797 a stronghold of the Directorials. Originally opposed to the 'royalism' of the Clichy 'Club', it had remained apart from the democratic movement, the centre of which in Paris was the Constitutional Club in the rue du Bac.

whose intolerance had been matched by their determination to wrest victory from defeat. But though he called upon his audience, remembering this, to forget the bitterness of the past, Constant also drew a sharp distinction between the Jacobins of the Terror and those of 1798. The former, he asserted, had now died away and been succeeded by men who had all their vices but none of their virtues: these were merely criminals, followers of Babeuf and anarchists whose activities were directed against the sanctity of property, an institution fundamental to the whole social order and all the achievements of the Revolution. In a word, Constant's contribution to the electoral campaign was a potent battle-cry which might, without misrepresentation, be translated as: 'Peace to the ashes of Terrorism: war to the contagion of communism'.[1]

While this speech may now excite some scorn, both as 'an extreme apotheosis of property rights'[2] and for its identification of the new Jacobins with the extreme egalitarianism and desperate violence of Babeuf, it may yet be regarded as surprisingly enlightened for its own time. However moderate the Jacobins of 1798 may have been, they were commonly associated with social extremism, and they were in fact, as Lefebvre has said, 'quite capable of partially reviving the social democracy of the Year II (1793–4)'.[3] Moreover, even if liberal allowance be made for deliberate distortion, the language of the day indicates all too clearly that few men were capable of responding to Constant's call to forget the past. Reiterated references to the Jacobins as men of blood and pillage, as erstwhile agents of Robespierre who now sought to re-establish the régime of 1793, suggest rather that fear of the Terror was still a very real force in France, and this in the political as well as in the social sense. Nor, in all probability, did the conduct of the Jacobins seem as innocuous in 1798 as it may seem today. Restricted as they were, their revival was accompanied by proselytism and tendencies towards collective action,[4] and the highly-organised manner in which many clubs contrived to dominate the elections in their own districts is rather

---

[1] *'Paix aux cendres du terreurism: guerre au Babeuvisme renaissant.'* See A. Meynier, *Les Coups d'état du Directoire, II: le Vingt-deux floréal, an VI* (Paris, 1928), p. 35. The speech, there considered in some detail (pp. 32–5), is also reviewed in Woloch, op. cit., pp. 155–6.

[2] Woloch, p. 156; see also Lefebvre, *The Directory*, p. 129.

[3] Lefebvre, loc. cit.

[4] Particularly by the practice known as *ambulance* or perambulation, by which the members of a flourishing club went out as a body to visit nearby towns or villages and to encourage the Jacobins there to do the like. This practice, particularly strong in the Sarthe, was declared to be unconstitutional by the Directory on 7 March. See Woloch, *Jacobin Legacy*, pp. 136–44.

more than reminiscent of the techniques perfected by the original Jacobin movement from 1789 onwards.[1] These 'new' Jacobins, too, were evidently as exclusive as their predecessors had been, being as anxious to disenfranchise 'anti-republicans' as others were to disenfranchise the Jacobins themselves. Nor, again, were their expressions always those of constitutional democracy: setting out, as they did, to revitalise the political life of France, they soon had at least some of the primary assemblies re-asserting the old fundamental conviction that 'When the sovereign has risen, it receives no orders or advice from anyone whatsoever'.[2]

The Directors, for their part, responded to this Jacobin pressure both by repression and by a counter-campaign. Increasingly, offending officials were dismissed, particular clubs closed and specific newspapers suppressed, and on 14 March a more general measure of restriction appeared when all clubs were once again forbidden to organise collective petitions by their members. Eventually, too, the government resorted to more open repression, some suspected persons being arrested and such great cities as Lyons and Marseilles being placed under martial law. Rather more interesting, because more original, is the effort made by the Directors to dominate the elections directly. Agents were sent to the provinces to report on the activities of the opposition and to rally support for reliable men—often enough the agents themselves, who were thus in many instances the first officially-sponsored candidates for legislative office in France. Since this process was an innovation, it was carried out in great secrecy. The agents were represented as commissioners conducting a survey of the state of the roads throughout the country, and their reports were written in symbolic terms, the political reliability of a given district being expressed, for example, by the statement that 'all the roads in this department are in good repair'. One of the Directors nevertheless recorded his colleagues' activities with engaging frankness. According to Barras (who, as usual, was strongly inclined to discount the danger from the Jacobins), the Directory: 'while blushing with shame, determined on a distribution of money amongst those preparing and machinating the elections'. Barras also gives in his Memoirs what purports to be a list showing how the sum of 184,654 francs was distri-

[1] Ibid., pp. 267–71.
[2] This Professor Woloch dismisses as 'a mild hint of sans-culottisme' and 'rhetorical blasts at incipient paternalism' (pp. 264, 267). The reader need hardly be reminded that I should consider it more indicative of the continuation of a particular attitude of mind. For the exclusiveness of the Jacobins at this time, see, *inter alia*, Woloch, op. cit., pp. 253–4.

buted amongst the commissioners, and states that a list was drawn up 'of the deputies to be elected for Paris'.[1]

In these circumstances, and since the Jacobins were never more than an active and predominantly urban minority in France, it is scarcely surprising that the supporters of the Directory should have emerged victorious from the particularly confusing electoral processes of April 1798. If the Jacobins either captured or gained considerably in some 24 departments and approximately 50 towns,[2] the greater part of France remained almost untouched by the democratic revival. The significant point, however, is that this was not enough for the Directors, who had already made their intentions plain in an influential and widely-circulated proclamation. Personally drafted by Merlin de Douai as soon as the trend of the voting at the primary level appeared, this proclamation of 29 March indicated quite clearly that the election of 'men who are universally execrated ... persons ignominiously famous in revolutionary annals' would not be tolerated; as in 1797 the parliament had 'chased from its midst traitors who had already been seated for four months', so now 'it will surely know how to exclude those whom some are trying to bring in'.[3]

The Directors now in fact proceeded to act in accordance with preparations made well beforehand to eliminate effective opposition, whether from the Right or from the Left, from the Legislative Councils. Fundamental to these was the Law of 12 Pluviôse (31 January 1798), which seems to have been accepted by both the Councils almost without discussion.[4] This authorised the Councils, *as they were then constituted*, to check the credentials of newly-elected deputies as soon as the election results were known. Since in the circumstances of 1798 an abnormally large number of the seats in the chambers had to be filled, this meant in practice that an assembly largely composed of deputies who were due to retire—but who were eligible for re-election—would be able to decide disputes relating to the composition of the new parliament.[5] Further-

---

[1] For the activities of the 'Highways Commissioners', see Meynier, op. cit., pp. 43–50, and Barras, *Memoirs*, III, pp. 246–51.

[2] Woloch, op. cit., pp. 282–5.

[3] Ibid., pp. 287–8.

[4] Meynier, op. cit., p. 41.

[5] Or, as Lefebvre more succinctly puts it, 'the outgoing deputies would purge their successors' (*The Directory*, p. 126). In 1797 this process of verification had taken place *after* the new deputies had replaced those who were retiring, a procedure open to the objection that the newcomers were judges in their own cause. As this could be considered one of the things which had made the *coup d'état* of 18 Fructidor necessary, the change made for 1798 had some theoretical

more, Merlin de Douai had sent specific instructions to the Directory's local agents to organise the withdrawal of 'honest' electors from electoral assemblies which were clearly going to be dominated by a hostile opposition. In such circumstances the seceders were to reconstitute themselves elsewhere and proceed to complete their own elections independently. Technically, this was legal, for the Constitution authorised the Legislative Body to adjudicate upon disputes and irregularities in the proceedings of both the primary and the secondary electoral assemblies, and isolated examples of schisms are to be found in the elections of 1795 and 1797. The systematic exploitation of this device for political purposes was, however, an innovation, which Lefebvre describes as 'characteristic of Merlin's crafty mind'. Since the Jacobins also made extensive use of the same device, schisms abounded in the elections of 1798.[1] The consequence of all this was that the Directory, which had dominated the existing Legislative Body since Fructidor, was legally able to determine the results of the elections, and to do so without any resort to force.

In the event, the issue was determined by one particular case, that of Paris itself (i.e., the Department of the Seine). There, the 668 delegates to the secondary Electoral Assembly, which was the most influential electoral college in France, met initially at the Oratoire on 9 April. A week later, on 15 April, some 60 of those most inclined to support the Directors withdrew to form a separate assembly of their own at the Louvre, to which assembly a total of 207 electors eventually rallied. Both assemblies then elected their own deputies, those from the Oratoire being broadly the more sympathetic to Jacobinism and those from the Louvre being evidently subservient to the Directory. The extent and nature of the great Jacobin conspiracy which the Directors had so assiduously denounced is nevertheless apparent in the fact that only 3 of the 16 deputies elected at the Oratoire were Parisian democrats; while some men like Robert Lindet and Prieur of the Marne represented the older Jacobin tradition, many were eminently respectable republicans. This prospective delegation indeed included Cambacérès, the future Second Consul, and no less than three future Directors—Roger Ducos,

---

justification; but it is nonetheless significant that it was made when the last third of the men of the Convention had to retire. In the event, 85 retiring deputies, of whom 22 were men of the Convention, were re-elected (Meynier, op. cit., p. 90).

[1] See: The Constitution of the Year III, Titles III and IV, articles 23 and 40 respectively (J. Hall Stewart, *A Documentary Survey*, pp. 577, 579); Meynier, op. cit., pp. 82–4; Woloch, op. cit., p. 297; and Lefebvre, op. cit., p. 131.

Gohier and General Moulin. After investigating this dispute early in May, a five-man commission of the Legislative Body divided in its turn: the majority advised that both sets of elections ought to be annulled, but the minority recommended that the elections made at the Louvre should alone be declared valid. The minority report, which was undoubtedly made on the Directors' instructions, was then adopted—a decision which effectively ended all investigation of particular controversies and cleared the way for the presentation of a collective list of admissions and exclusions.[1]

This general list, nominally proposed by yet another commission of five, was in fact certainly drawn up by the Directors with the collusion of the members of the commission, notably Bailleul—though the latter explicitly denied this in debate.[2] Being approved both by the Five Hundred and the Elders, it became law on 22 Floréal An VI (11 May 1798); and being a revision of the results of the elections (as Bailleul put it, to make the application of principles more rational), it is commonly called the *coup d'état* of 22 Floréal. On this occasion the elections in approximately half (47 out of 96) of the departments were accepted without qualification. In eight departments, however, they were annulled outright, and in 19 others the men chosen by seceding minorities of the electors were preferred to those named by the majorities. Elsewhere, particular elections alone were invalidated. In sum, this meant that of the 347 seats that were due to be filled, 53 were left vacant, 106 were filled by men selected by the Directors in preference to others, and the remainder went to men of whose election the Directors approved. Politically this purge was imperfect, for some 60 of those who took their seats proved unreliable, so that the probability is that about one third of the reconstituted Councils remained hostile to the Directors' rule. The trend of development is nevertheless apparent in the fact that approximately half of those who were admitted to the Councils had previously been fairly prominent local officials.[3] In effect, the parliament of the

[1] I follow here the figures and the account given by Woloch, op. cit., chapter 11 ('Electors and Elections in Paris'), pp. 311–43. The assembly which met in the Louvre is often referred to as that at the Institute, since those concerned actually withdrew to the Institut de France in the Louvre.

[2] Barras, *Memoirs*, III, p. 275.

[3] See Lefebvre, *The Directory*, pp. 133–4, and Meynier, op. cit., pp. 90–3. It may be added here that, as in Fructidor, the parliamentary purge was accompanied by a corresponding rejection of newly-elected local officers and judges, some 60 of whom were dismissed or invalidated—whereas 68 of those who became deputies had previously been Commissioners of the Directory. Conclusions about this should, perhaps, be treated with some reserve, since the

Republic was becoming both a co-optive oligarchy and a body increasingly composed of placemen, nominated by and dependent upon the Directors.

Although it is now fashionable for historians to pay less attention to political crises than to other developments, the *coup d'état* of 22 Floréal is much too instructive to be lightly set aside as (to quote one authority on the Revolutionary period) 'a harmless manoeuvre'.[1] There was, of course, neither bloodshed nor proscription nor any display of force on this occasion, which at first sight may seem sufficiently sordid to be better forgotten. In reality, however, the Legislative Body's acceptance of the Law of 22 Floréal was undoubtedly an event of high significance. In the first place, it fully vindicated those who had seen the previous *coup d'état*, that of 18–19 Fructidor, as inflicting a mortal wound upon the Constitution of 1795—which was, of course, the first effective constitution of the first French Republic.[2] The Directors, who had in 1797 violated that Constitution by physical force, now in 1798 violated it again by political manipulation, their second purge being, indeed, worse than the first since it was still more deliberate and far more consciously selective of particular men and particular elections. If anything, too, it had even less justification, for although one may suspect that the Right-wing opponents to the Directory in 1797 were generally as willing to work within the Constitution as were the Jacobins in 1798, the Directors, much-vaunted 'royalist' conspiracy was certainly far more real than the 'anarchical' one they invented in 1798. In both instances, no doubt, the Directors to some extent shared the fear, born of vivid recollections of the recent past, which made the most fantastic allegations credible; but, as certainly, they exploited that fear to the full for their own purpose. After 22 Floréal there can be little room for doubt that that purpose was the consolidation by revolutionary means of a régime that was in reality as politically reactionary as it was socially conservative. To the men at the Luxembourg Palace and their minions in the Councils, the Revolution had become synonymous with the situation of 1795 and the status

---

parliaments of France throughout the Revolution were invariably composed of men of the same judicial-administrative class. Nevertheless, as the Directory had since 1795 been dismissing some local officials and nominating others in their stead, serving members of the official class who secured parliamentary seats may be increasingly considered as being government nominees.

[1] C. Brinton, *A Decade of Revolution, 1789–99* (New York, 1963), pp. 214, 217.

[2] Barras, the Director most sympathetic towards Jacobinism, subsequently described the *coup* of 22 Floréal as fatal to the Republic: *Memoirs*, III, p. 466.

they had then attained, and in striving to perpetuate this position they extinguished all its initial light of liberalism.

To condemn the Directors' intolerance of all opposition is not, however, to exonerate others. If the Directors were determined to subordinate the Legislative to the Executive and to make it at most an advisory body, the resistance of the deputies can only be described as slight. True, General Jourdan, once the hero of Fleurus, dared to demand more specific evidence about the supposed conspiracy; and François Lamarque,[1] one of the principal pro-Jacobin spokesmen, pointing to the perils of the precedent which was being set, prophetically remarked that if the establishment of the Republic—by which he meant at least the observance of the Constitution—was to be perpetually deferred, the day would come when the assembly would be wholly composed of nonentities. Such protests as these are, however, less remarkable than the apathy and acquiesence which prevailed in the parliament, the great majority of the deputies apparently being so self-interested or so fearful as to be astonishingly subservient.[2] Further, the electorate itself was also either apathetic or doctrinaire: despite the vigour of the Jacobins' campaign, no more voters seem to have participated in the elections of 1798 than in those of 1797, and the exclusiveness of the Directorials was fully matched by that of their opponents. Differences of interpretation apart, both sides seem to have been convinced that, while they alone were 'pure and virtuous' citizens, those who opposed them were 'enemies of the republic'. That conviction, comprehensible enough in the great crisis of 1792–4, had in fact been one characteristic of the Revolutionary outlook, and where it predominated neither majority rule nor representative parliamentary government was possible. The most fatal aspect of the Directory's *coup d'état* of 1797 and 1798 was that they inevitably revived the antagonisms and intransigence of the past. Each in turn stifled a movement towards compromise within the Constitution, so weakening the whole concept of government by consent within a free and lawful Republic. As Dherbelot, a deputy who said that he had never previously spoken in public, courageously told the Council of Five Hundred on 7 March, the freedom of the people depended upon that of their parliament, and the acceptance of the purge meant nothing less than the transference of sovereignty from the people to the government.[3]

---

[1] *Biog. Notes:* LAMARQUE.
[2] The debate is well-summarised in Meynier, op. cit., pp. 73–81.
[3] Ibid., p. 80.

Part Three
Authority Triumphant, 1798-1802

'*My defect is to be unable to bear injuries.*'

Napoléon Bonaparte: Roederer, P. L., *Mémoires sur la Révolution, le Consulat et l'Empire* (ed. O. Aubry, Paris, 1942, p. 170).

12 The Battle of the Pyramids

13 '18 brumaire': Napoleon before the Council of Five Hundred in the
Orangerie at St Cloud, 19 brumaire (10 November 1799)
François Bouchot

7. The Advent of Bonaparte, May 1798-November 1799

By what may well be thought something more than a mere coincidence, both Bonaparte and Sieyès left France immediately after the *coup d'état* of 22 Floréal (11 May 1798). On 19 May, whilst Nelson's reconnaissance force of three battleships and five frigates was approaching Toulon, Bonaparte's massive armada sailed from that harbour towards Genoa. Next day a strong gale arose, which carried the French swiftly down the eastern coast of Corsica and Sardinia; but the British ships were dispersed and driven well to the west of those islands. Not until 22 June—by which time Bonaparte had seized Malta and sailed on to Alexandria— could Nelson obtain any information about where the French might be; and then, being strongly reinforced in ships of battle but wholly without frigates, his pursuing fleet actually passed its quarry in the darkness of the night. Meanwhile in France it had been announced that Sieyès (who could probably have become a Director had he so wished) had accepted an important diplomatic mission to Prussia.[1] There the new king, Frederick William III, had to be prevented from abandoning his father's policy of neutrality and joining the alliance which the powers of Europe were gradually forming against France. Sieyès, who stood very much on his dignity as the accredited representative of the Great Republic, in fact played some part in keeping Prussia neutral; but though he remained in Berlin until May 1799, neither by threats nor by promises could he fulfil his great dream of inducing Frederick to join France in a sort of European union against Britain and Russia.

Striking as it is, the simultaneous absence from France of Sieyès and Bonaparte is unlikely to have been preconcerted. More probably, both had independently come to believe that there was as yet nothing to be

[1] Sieyès, who was offered this appointment on 30 April, accepted it on 7 May; he made a speech in the Five Hundred resigning his seat on 15 May and arrived in Berlin on 20 June. Bonaparte left Paris on 3 May, arriving in Toulon on the 8th.

gained by direct intervention in the affairs of the Directory, but that much could be achieved for France abroad. If this was so, both were deluded, their ambitions and their arrogance blinding them to the hostility France had aroused everywhere by her apparently endless aggrandisement. The subsequent failure of both men's grandiose enterprises may even be seen as symbolic of the year 1798–9, in which the Republic, discredited at home and defeated abroad, sank to the nadir of its fortunes.

After 22 Floréal the position of the Directory seemed unassailable; but its decline can confidently be dated from that *coup d'état*. Even the renewal of its membership for 1798 simply served to emphasise its isolation, for *ad hoc* legislation, closely related to that concerning the verification of the deputies' credentials, had been approved in the previous February to ensure that this election would be held before any new deputies entered the Councils. Thus after the ballot for retirement had eliminated François de Neufchâteau—who promptly resumed his previous place as Minister of the Interior—a prominent lawyer, Jean-Baptiste Treilhard,[1] was elected a Director on 16 May. This choice, too, reflects the static and exclusive character the Directory had acquired, for Treilhard, an arrogant man of minor importance, had been a vindictive opponent of Catholicism in the National Assembly in 1790 and a regicide member of the Convention in 1793. In the circumstances it is significant, if scarcely surprising, that a banquet in Paris in June should have been disrupted by the refusal of some of the deputies present to drink the health of the new Directory.[2]

The plain fact is that in the year following 22 Floréal the Directory, which had practically dictatorial power over France and much of western Europe, had scarcely any positive support. Alleging 'conspiracy', either on the Right or on the Left, it had twice within eight months repudiated substantial electoral movements in favour of greater flexibility in government. Further, as if to demonstrate their isolation, the Directors followed up their rejection of the Jacobins in Floréal by rounding on the Right and intensifying the search for those who had escaped arrest in Fructidor. In the latter half of 1798, too, the drive to enforce the cult of the *décadi* was more fully developed, the use of the Revolutionary Calendar being made compulsory and a new series of national festivals being inaugurated by François de Neufchâteau. All this inevitably involved the authorties in incessant conflicts with the clergy and with all who disliked having to work on Sundays—to say nothing of being bound by law to

[1] *Biog. Notes:* TREILHARD.
[2] Lefebvre, *The Directory*, p. 135.

wear the national cockade and to address others only by the title of 'citizen'.[1]

It would, however, be wrong to think of this renewed attack upon the Right as illustrative of the 'see-saw' policy so often ascribed to the Directory. On the contrary, the Directors were evidently striving to suppress all opposition, from whichever quarter it might come. With the notable exception of Barras, they did all they could to curb the development of democracy throughout the area occupied by French troops. In Switzerland and in the Cisalpine Republic, this was one major cause of their recurrent clashes with their own agents and generals; in the Dutch Republic, it led to a further purge of the government by French forces on 12 June 1798. At home, too, the alienation of the Jacobins in Floréal was aggravated thereafter by such severe surveillance that it is permissible to describe the atmosphere in some cities as that of a police state.[2] More sensitive than ever to criticism, the Directory extended indefinitely the power it had obtained in Fructidor to suppress publications it considered seditious, and by denying the Jacobins as well as the Right any real freedom of expression it naturally fomented in fact the conspiracies which had long loomed large in its imagination.

Even within the narrower limits of the Legislative Councils themselves the government could not secure the solid support that it expected to reward its ruthless rearrangement of the election results. In retrospect, LaRevellière-Lépeaux believed that this was above all the fault of two new deputies, the brothers of Bonaparte, Joseph and Lucien;[3] these, he was sure, deliberately did all they could to discredit the Directory and excite discontent so that the situation would remain fluid until Napoleon could return.[4] Although the exaggeration here is evident, the presence in parliament of these two men was undoubtedly embarrassing, particularly as Lucien quickly emerged as an unusually able orator. Impetuous and impassioned, he was soon foremost in denouncing the intolerance of the régime and avowing that the men who had been deported in 1797 had had good reasons for opposing the Directors.

The gradual growth of hostility to the government in parliament nevertheless involved much more than matters of personality. As Barras

---

[1] Legislation of 3 April (regarding the calendar), and of 4 August and 9 September 1798.

[2] Woloch, *Jacobin Legacy*, p. 363. See also R. Cobb, 'Note sur la répression contre le personnel sans-culotte de 1795 à 1801', *Annales Historiques de la Révolution française*, XXVI (1954) and *The Police and the People: French Popular Protest, 1789–1820* (Oxford, 1970), pp. 165–8.

[3] *Biog. Notes:* JOSEPH BONAPARTE; LUCIEN BONAPARTE.

[4] Lépeaux, *Mémoires*, II, p. 358; see also Barras, *Memoirs*, III, p. 320.

had always said, it was highly dangerous for the Directory to attempt to establish a republic while excluding republicans from it; and, as he had foreseen, the Directors' extravagant and indiscriminate denunciation of everyone on the Left as anarchical led to the alienation of some of their own supporters.[1] Moreover, the all too obvious purging and packing of parliament in Fructidor and Floréal, together with the Directors' cavalier attitude towards the Councils thereafter, eventually aroused resentment and a real desire for greater parliamentary independence. Consequently in 1798–9 more and more men of the centre made common cause with the existing Jacobin minority, and controversy increased correspondingly.[2] In the administration of France and the occupied territories, in the scale of governmental expenditure and in the scandals associated with the attempt to meet all military needs by bargaining with contractors, this new opposition found perpetual causes for complaint; and the Directors, for their part, held the Councils and the Treasury responsible, even to the point of treason, for the permanent penury of the government.[3] In these circumstances even the more stalwart supporters of the Directory grew disaffected, some contemplating the possibility of re-establishing stability by making a complete change in the personnel of the executive, and others going further and favouring a more or less drastic revision of the constitution itself. Amongst these last, it may be said, were Daunou, who had been one of the principal authors of that constitution, and Boulay of the Meurthe, the henchman of Sieyès.

Being thus isolated from the legislative, which was itself severed from its electorate—and still more from the disenfranchised or disenchanted mass of the population—the Directory of 1798–9 appears almost infinitely remote from the realities of French life. Success alone, it may be thought, might have made the Directors' virtual dictatorship more tolerable and given it some sanction of popularity: but although the period was in fact one of remarkable administrative achievement, the beneficial effects of this were at first far less apparent than the immediate disadvantages. Long before the executive's best endeavours could become productive, its members had to encounter the consequences of their

[1] Barras, *Memoirs*, III, p. 414.

[2] Lefebvre, *The Directory*, p. 135; A. Meynier, *Les Coups d'états du Directoire: Le Vingt-deux Floréal An VI et le Trente Prairial An VI* (Paris, 1928), pp. 187–8.

[3] Lefebvre, op. cit., p. 142; Meynier, op. cit., pp. 173–6; Lépeaux, *Mémoires*, II, pp. 184–5. The expedition to Ireland, the classic case of the starvation of a military expedition by the financial authority, is described in: T. Pakenham, 'Humbert's raid in Ireland, 1798', *History Today* (October, 1969).

prolonged political intransigence and of the inflation of French power in Europe.

The men most associated with the Directory's reforms were the Minister of Finance, Ramel,[1] and the Minister of the Interior, François de Neufchâteau.

As has been remarked here,[2] the Directory's first *coup d'état*, the real seizure of power on 18–19 Fructidor, was accompanied by the partial liquidation of the National Debt.[3] By the Law of 30 September 1797, which was probably the most drastic financial measure of the whole Revolutionary period, one third of the debt was consolidated and registered as a sacred charge upon the nation: but the other two-thirds were converted into bearer bonds of equivalent value and re-issued to the stockholders as securities which would be accepted as part of any payment for the purchase of national property. The benefit of this measure to the State may be seen from the fact that it at once reduced the annual interest on the debt from about 240 million francs (which was approximately one quarter of all governmental expenditure) to about 80 million francs. Conversely, of course, it struck a shattering blow at the incomes of the stockholders, and their situation was soon made even worse by the rapid depreciation of the new bonds, which represented the bulk of their original capital. Consequently the 'Ramel liquidation', which was not technically a repudiation of the National Debt, was tantamount to that for the greater part of the obligation; and although it may be regarded in retrospect as an inevitable consequence of the financial follies of those earlier revolutionaries who had tried to meet all expenses by manufacturing paper money, it did immense harm to innumerable small investors, to the credit of the state and to the reputation of the Directory.

To Ramel this bankruptcy was but part of a larger endeavour to limit expenditure while increasing revenue. By reducing the payment of interest on the debt, and by slashing the military estimates as soon as the war with Austria ended, he fairly soon succeeded in reducing the expenditure of the state from 1,000 million to 616 million francs, and so produced a balanced budget for the first time in the history of the

---

[1] *Biog. Notes:* RAMEL.

[2] See above, chapter 6.

[3] Lefebvre, op. cit., chapter 11, particularly pp. 139–40; Godechot, *Les Institutions de la France*, pp. 435–6; and Goodwin, 'The French Executive Directory—A Revaluation', *History* (December, 1937), pp. 208–9. For the continuation of the process of liquidation by Bonaparte, see chapter 8 below.

Revolution.[1] His accompanying attempt to increase revenue by reorganising taxation and improving the methods by which it was assessed and collected necessarily took much longer, particularly as every major proposal had to be approved by the Legislative Councils—which were deeply averse to any return to the indirect taxation characteristic of the Old Order, and profoundly suspicious of any reform likely to increase the independence of the Directors. Between 1797 and 1799, and particularly in the autumn of 1798, Ramel nevertheless established four basic forms of direct taxation: a tax on trading licences (*contribution des patentes*); one on land (*contribution foncière*); one on moveable property and personal servants (*contribution mobilière et personelle*); and one, an innovation approximating to an income tax, on doors and windows.[2] The assessment and collection of direct taxation was simultaneously removed from the control of locally elected bodies and entrusted instead to officials working in each department under the direction of a commissioner of the central government.[3]

These major financial measures were undoubtedly a very considerable achievement. In securing them, Ramel was indeed building even better than he knew, for these taxes, which laid the foundation for the recovery of state finance when Bonaparte became Consul, remained basic to the French fiscal system until the beginning of the Great War in 1914. Initially, however, these important innovations were unpopular, as were other minor taxes which were introduced or reorganised at this time, like the stamp duty on journals and the toll on the use of the main roads;[4] and the improvement in the system of tax collection was long offset by the inexperience of the first overburdened commissioners. In this whole matter, everything depended upon the durability of the peace in Europe, which in fact lasted only until the spring of 1799, and upon the stability and reliability of political authority, which did not exist in the days of the Directory. Despite all Ramel could do, the government he served was still compelled to live financially from day to day, dependent in part

---

[1] Goodwin, op. cit., p. 209. The war with Britain was financed in part by means of a loan and in part by the sums seized in Switzerland and the Papal States.

[2] These were approved by the Laws of 22 October, 23 and 24 November and 23 December 1798.

[3] Legislation of 13 November 1798.

[4] There was also a slight but significant development of indirect taxation, including a small increase in the tobacco tax and the restoration of the *octroi*, the tariff imposed on goods brought into towns from the countryside as a means of financing some municipal services.

upon the vast sums it extracted from the satellite states,[1] and perpetually involved in controversy with the Councils.

Ramel's reforms were matched by the enlightened endeavours of François de Neufchâteau to stimulate agricultural and industrial production, both of which were being transformed in Britain at this time. A man of intelligence and imagination who was well aware that the state could indirectly do a great deal to promote social and economic welfare, he sought amongst other things to develop technical information services, to establish agricultural societies, to improve communications, to advance education and to assist the poor. In all this, it should be said, his support of the *décadi* played an important part, for the national festivals associated with the cult were intended to promote economic progress as well as cultural unity. One of them, that held on 18–21 September 1798 to commemorate the establishment of the Republic, was in fact the first Industrial Exhibition: organised on the Champ-de-Mars, it was so successful that it was repeated in 1799.

Ultimately, however, the work of both Ramel and François de Neufchâteau was frustrated by the economic and political difficulties of the day. In sharp contrast to the earlier part of the decade, when paper money was plentiful but practically worthless, the years that ended the century were a time of deflation and depression. Due in part to the Directory's enforced abandonment of the paper money of the Revolution in 1797, and in part to the fundamental fact that the harvests of 1796–8 were exceptionally good, this deflation was beneficial to men of small means, who now at last found food cheap and plentiful. Their situation is traditionally symbolised by what they called the 'three eights': wine at eight *sous* per pint, meat at eight *sous* per pound, and bread at eight *sous* for the quartern loaf.[2] On the other hand, the more substantial farmers and landowners were hard-hit by the persistent fall in prices and land-values, and so were the merchants, manufactorers and businessmen whose prosperity in a predominantly rural country depended directly upon that of the agriculturalists. In these circumstances, which were aggravated by the traditionalism of a multitude of small proprietors and by the complete stagnation of overseas trade in wartime, it would have been surprising if even a strong and popular government had been able to stimulate long-term economic development.

[1] In the two years 1797–9 these amounted to at least 158 million francs. Godechot, *Les Institutions de la France*, p. 439.

[2] Lefebvre, op. cit., p. 145. On the economic situation of France at this time, see also Godechot, op. cit., pp. 441–50.

Here again, however, the root of the trouble was that the men who might have promoted French prosperity had no confidence in the rulers of France. If money only came back into circulation very slowly, if credit was only obtainable with difficulty and at a high rate of interest, this was certainly very largely due to the fact that the Directory was economically and politically discredited. To the propertied classes, on whom the Directors and the Republic itself ultimately depended, the period was indeed to be one of bitter memory, in which the burden of depression was made the more grievous by the government's most necessary measures—the cancellation of interest payments on most of the National Debt, the increase in taxation, and Ramel's rigorous (but surprisingly successful) drive to collect all arrears of tax payments. In the event, then, the determination of the two most remarkable ministers of the Executive Directory in its most dictatorial days availed little, save that they established a structure for Bonaparte to complete when confidence and prosperity returned. In the meanwhile, the Directory was soon to be reduced to the point of being unable to pay even its own commissioners.[1]

Onerous in themselves, the great fiscal laws of the autumn of 1798 were the more unpopular because they were evidently part and parcel of the Directory's preparations for further wars, and were indeed coincident with the reintroduction of conscription. The need for this had long been apparent, for the French forces were still in 1798 those organised after the great national levy of August 1793. The revolutionary expansion of France, together with Britain's stubborn determination to continue the conflict until a new continental coalition could reduce France to her original limits, now made more military strength imperative. As early as January 1798—less than three months after the Treaty of Campo-Formio with Austria, and before Bonaparte had even proposed the Egyptian expedition to the Directors—General Jourdan had brought forward a plan for the formation of an additional army of 100,000 men. This the Councils had found unsatisfactory, but his revised proposals, generally known as the Jourdan Law, were approved on 5 September. These established compulsory military service for all single men between the ages of 20 and 25, who were to be called to the colours, as need arose, according to their annual classes; and an initial levy of the first 200,000 men was demanded within the month.

Eventually, and particularly in times of emergency, this conscription may have restored some degree of national character to an army which

---

[1] Godechot, op. cit., p. 139. On the return of economic prosperity in the time of the Consulate, see Soboul, *La Ire République*, p. 263.

was becoming increasingly professional.[1] Its most immediate effect was, however, to make the Directory seem detestable to many of those who might have been rallied to its rule by the reduction in the cost of living. To introduce conscription was in fact to make a positive demand upon the mass of the population, a grave risk for an unpopular government in a country that wanted peace almost above all else; and, as in the spring of 1793, the result was resistance. In Belgium, in particular, much of the countryside rose in revolt in November 1798, occasioning a 'peasants' war' which took two months to suppress and led to the wholesale deportation of the priests who were held responsible; and although the Directors, having learnt by bitter experience, did not attempt to apply the law to Brittany and the Vendée, the *chouan* bands there were soon strengthened by a new influx of evaders and deserters. The nation-wide hostility towards both conscription and war is sufficiently indicated by the figures themselves. Of the first class of 203,000 conscripts, 60,000 were declared unfit by local medical boards which were often scandalously lenient; of the remaining 143,000, only 97,000 presented themselves for service; and of these, thanks to desertion, only 74,000 finally reached the armies. The law was then amended in April 1799 to restore the bad old practice by which a conscript could escape service by finding someone to take his place; but despite this, and despite the fact that war had been declared on Austria that March, only 71,000 of the next 200,000 presented themselves, and only 57,000 of these reached their units.[2]

Everything in short, indicates that in the year which followed the *coup d'état* of 22 Floréal the Directory's apparent power was an illusion. Although many of its measures were well-meant and necessary, its evident illegitimacy and isolation deprived it of the moral authority and the public confidence it required to effect them. Existing, as it seems, simply on sufferance, this government had in 1799 to encounter the shocks and strains of another widespread European war.

Enough has already been written here to show that this new conflict was very much of the Directory's own making.[3] It is nevertheless evident that the Egyptian expedition occasioned the renewal of hostilities in Europe, for while Bonaparte's triumphs added to the number of France's foes, his absence and misfortunes stimulated them to action.

[1] Soboul suggests that this was 'in part' its effect (*La Ire République*, pp. 268 and 269); but the case seems far from strong.

[2] Lefebvre, op. cit., pp. 172–3.

[3] A view also held with some slight difference of emphasis by Lefebvre (*La Révolution française*, 3rd ed., Paris, 1963), p. 517) and Meynier, op. cit., p. 163.

Having reached Alexandria on 1 July 1798, the general's forces inflicted a crushing defeat upon the superb (but ill-armed) cavalry of the Mamelukes at the battle of the Pyramids on 21 July. Ten days later, however, Nelson's battlefleet found that of France lying securely at anchor in Aboukir Bay, with its van and rear close inshore and all its main armament shifted to seawards. In the brilliant and decisive engagement which ensued, the British ships divided, some keeping a constant course and others nudging the sandbanks to enter the bay behind the French, so that each French ship in succession was subjected to a cross-fire of shattering broadsides. This battle, in which only two of the French fleet of 13 ships of the line escaped destruction, transformed the whole strategic situation in the Mediterranean. Bonaparte and his army being now isolated in Egypt, Turkey declared war on France on 9 September; the Kingdom of Naples, which had long lived in expectation of a French attack, seized the opportunity to invade the Roman Republic, capturing the city of Rome itself on 26 November; and Russia, whose half-crazed Tsar had set himself up as the protector of the Knights of Malta,[1] entered the war in alliance with Turkey on 23 December. By the end of the year a further treaty between Britain, Russia and Naples had consolidated these alliances, with which Austria was secretly associated.[2] Perhaps the most remarkable feature of the formation of this second coalition was the extent to which the powers were prepared to set their own antagonisms aside in order to subdue France: the Sultan allowed the Tsar's fleet to pass freely from the Black Sea into the Mediterranean, and it was Austria's decision to allow Russian forces to cross her territory that caused the French to declare war on her on 12 March 1799.[3]

In point of fact, this new war began well for France, for the Court of Naples, urged on by Nelson,[4] had moved prematurely. As soon as it became clear that no immediate Austrian assault was to follow the

[1] The Tsar had also been alarmed by the French occupation of the Ionian Islands, one of the stipulations made by Bonaparte at Campo-Formio, and the expulsion of their forces by the Russians occurred early in 1799. Malta itself was recaptured by a British force in 1800.

[2] Austria was allied to Naples, and the Neapolitan army which invaded the Roman Republic was commanded by the Austrian general Mack.

[3] Fighting had previously been begun in the passes of the Grisons in Switzerland.

[4] And by Emma, Lady Hamilton, the wife of the British Ambassador and the close friend of the Queen of Naples. Professor Palmer's description of Nelson himself as 'a pronounced anti-Jacobin' (*The Age of the Democratic Revolution*, II, p. 380) is pleasingly indicative of the difference of emphasis between his interpretation and my own.

Neapolitan attack, the French armies calmly completed their conquest of all that remained independent in Italy. Acting on the assumption that the King of Sardinia was associated with Naples, General Joubert seized control of Piedmont in November 1798. Rapidly rallying his forces in the Roman Republic, General Championnet, the successor of Berthier there, regained Rome in mid-December and then in his turn invaded Naples, where a new 'Parthenopean' Republic was proclaimed in January 1799. Finally, the pacific Dukedom of Tuscany was also occupied in March, as a consequence of which the unfortunate Pope Pius VI was dragged from his refuge in Florence and taken to France, where he died ignominiously at Valence in August at the age of 81.[1] Thus before the renewal of European war had led to any major clash of arms, the armies of France had gained control of all Italy save Venetia.

This period of triumph, in which the republicanism of the Revolution reached its furthest extent, passed so swiftly that it is easily forgotten. It is nevertheless of interest, if only because it occasioned a direct confrontation between the civil government and the generals. To the latter, and to the locust armies of France, the occupation of new lands in Italy meant not only loot, but almost life itself; but in Paris the Directory was anxious to ensure that the process of exploitation should at least be systematic and beneficial to the state.[2] This difference, explosive in itself since it involved by implication a vast deal of accumulated bitterness about fraudulent contractors, incompetent politicians and rapacious generals, was further complicated by a deeper distinction of policy: in general the soldiers, as ardent republicans, were willing and even eager to work with local revolutionaries, whereas the Directors were concerned to curb nationalist and democratic developments and to keep conquests for eventual barter. Complicated almost beyond belief by particular local issues and personal antipathies, this problem had long plagued the Directory in its endeavour to coordinate and control the states associated with France; and to make matters worse, developments in the Cisalpine Republic in 1798 had shown all too clearly that Barras and his henchmen

---

[1] Almost literally *dragged*, since he was paralysed in the legs. Before crossing the Alps he had begged to be allowed to die at Rome, but he had been told: 'one can die anywhere'. E. E. Y. Hales, *Napoleon and the Pope* (London, 1962), p. 13.

[2] François de Neufchâteau's festival in commemoration of the fall of Robespierre, held in Paris on 27 July 1798, had been marked by a procession displaying, *inter alia*, the Apollo Belvedere and the bronze horses of Venice. Doubts were, however, beginning to arise, and Daunou wrote to Lépeaux that the proposal to dismantle Trajan's Column for shipment from Rome was going too far: '*Il faut un terme à tout*'. Meynier, op. cit., p. 179.

were acting independently, supporting extremism and lining their pockets in the process.

This situation, which had already led to the transfer of one commander, General Brune, from Italy to Holland, caused the Directors to revive the practice of attaching representatives of the civil government to particular military commands. Of the three such appointments which were made on 26 November 1798, two were simply unsuccessful: in Switzerland, the commissioner was ignored by the general (Masséna) and soon asked to be recalled; and in Milan the general (Joubert) himself resigned his command. The third appointment, however, precipitated a crisis. Faipoult, the commissioner attached to General Championnet[1] in the Roman Republic, accompanied the latter's forces when they invaded Naples; but Championnet disregarded him, proclaimed the Parthenopean Republic in direct defiance of his orders from Paris, and seized every scrap of treasure he could acquire. Faipoult, going to the other extreme, then intervened, attempting to confiscate the plunder for the benefit of government and to institute more systematic taxation.[2] Championnet, who seems to have seen himself as a new Bonaparte, responded by threatening Faipoult with the firing squad and expelling him from Naples; and to the fury of the armies, the Directory ordered Championnet to be arrested.[3]

By now, however, mightier men and more powerful armies were in motion, augmenting the maladies of France. According to the plans concerted by the Coalition, France and her satellites were to be subjected in 1799 to a triple assault: an Anglo–Russian army was to effect a landing in Holland; and two other Russian armies, commanded by Korsakov and the far-famed Marshal Suvorov,[4] were to assault the French in Switzerland and Italy respectively. In fact, the French tried to anticipate this attack by declaring war upon Austria also and at once taking the offensive against her; but this merely multiplied the strength of their enemies. General Jourdan, entrusted with command of the army of the Danube, repeated his performance of 1796: after advancing to Lake Constance, he was defeated by the Archduke Charles of Austria at

[1] *Biog. Notes:* CHAMPIONNET.

[2] Plunder apart, Championnet proposed to levy a tax of 60 million francs; but the Directory considered that direct military government might raise 200 millions.

[3] The order being dated 25 February 1799, Championnet travelled in some style to Turin, whence he was transferred to Grenoble and imprisoned. See J. Godechot, *Les commissionaires aux armées sous le Directoire* (Paris, 1937), II, p. 277.

[4] In Byron's words, 'half demon and half dirt'.

the battle of Stockach on 25 March, 1799, and promptly fell back to the Rhine and resigned his command. In Italy, too, it was the Austrians who were victorious. There General Schérer—previously a much detested Minister of War—was unsuccessful in his attack on Verona and in a battle at Magnano on 5 April, and he also retreated, retiring to the River Adda and resigning his command to Moreau, whom Lépeaux had attached to the army as an 'Inspector'.[1]

At this point the arrival of the Russian armies shattered the whole façade of French republican power. Advancing across Lombardy, Suvorov forced the passage of the Adda at Cassano on 27 April and entered Milan in triumph next day. By 27 May he was in Turin, whilst Moreau at Coni was practically back in Provence. Everything in Italy now depended on Championnet's successor, Macdonald,[2] who brought the Army of Naples northwards to take the Austro-Russian forces in the flank: but after Suvorov had held him at bay in a three-day battle on the banks of the River Trebbia (17–19 June),[3] he was forced to take refuge in Genoa, where Moreau managed to join him. Meanwhile Masséna[4] in Switzerland, the bastion of the defence of France, had withdrawn before the armies of the Archduke Charles: but he turned to win the (first) battle of Zurich on 4 June. By holding a position between the enemy and the valley of the Rhine, he then at least stayed the tide of invasion; and as it happened, the allies afforded France some respite during the summer. Of all Italy, however, France now held nothing but the small republic of Genoa.

These events, which might have enabled a government of some stature to rally the nation in support of the common cause, coincided with the decline and disintegration of the Second Directory, to which the news of defeat after defeat contributed very considerably. Although the elections of 1799, which began as usual on 21 March, took place before the magnitude of the military *débâcle* became apparent, the Directory was then

[1] According to Lépeaux, the appointment of General Schérer (whom Bonaparte had superseded in 1796) was partly due to Barras and partly to the fact that he was one of the few generals willing to work with a civil commissioner; but Lépeaux had pressed for the appointment of Moreau, whom others distrusted on account of his delay in exposing Pichegru in 1797. Lépeaux, *Mémoires*, II, pp. 379–80.

[2] Jacques Etienne Macdonald (1765–1840), an officer of Scots origin who had been aide-de-camp to Dumouriez and who was subsequently to become a Marshal and the Duke of Taranto.

[3] Given in the English translation of Lefebvre, *The Directory*, p. 175 as 17–19 July.

[4] *Biog. Notes:* MASSÉNA.

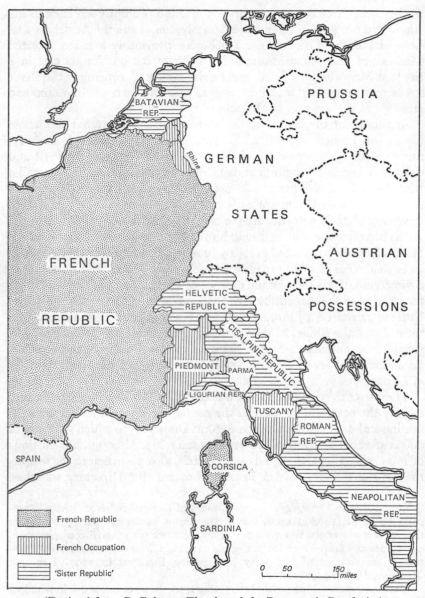

(Derived from R. Palmer, *The Age of the Democratic Revolution*)

The French Republican System, March 1799

held responsible for the war, for the evil state of the armies, and for all the accumulated troubles of the time. As in 1798, the Directory itself strove to organise and influence the electorate through its commissioners and through additional agents, encouraging secessions in the electoral assemblies of hostile areas and reiterating its warnings against what Lépeaux called the 'two horrible factions' of anarchy and royalism.[1] Yet, as in every previous election, the voters returned men who opposed the government: indeed, it would seem that the more a man was thought to be supported by any or all of the Directors, the more certain it was that the electors would prefer another candidate.[2] What is more, when the Legislative Councils came to consider the alternative candidates presented by the 27 electoral assemblies in which schisms had occurred, they systematically selected those of the original assemblies—a procedure which in all but five of the 25 cases which were controversial was favourable to the opponents of the government. Thus the men who had ruled France since Fructidor were repudiated on all sides, and about 50 deputies of Jacobin sympathy, as well as many more orthodox dissidents, took their seats in the Councils.[3]

That the Directors should have lost the elections of 1799 in this way is not, of course, remarkable, the defeat being an annual event. What is far more striking is that they should have accepted the result so passively, a thing they had never done before. This was probably due in part to the antagonisms which had arisen amongst the Directors themselves, particularly about the problem of appointing and controlling the generals; but it also seems likely that, as Lépeaux's correspondence suggests, these men had become pedantically convinced that parliamentary affairs were relatively unimportant, and that the executive, the true representative of the nation, was beyond any sort of censure.[4]

[1] This in his speech in commemoration of the execution of Louis XVI on 21 January. The only apparent changes in the Directory's attitude would seem to be that the two factions were no longer identified, and the 'anarchists' were equated with those who were spoiling the State by fraud and peculation. Meynier, op. cit., p. 194.

[2] Ibid., pp. 199–200. Meynier estimates here that of 187 candidates promoted by the Directors, only 66 were returned by the electors.

[3] On the schisms, see Woloch, *Jacobin Legacy*, pp. 364–5.

[4] On this point, Lefebvre suggests that 'the Directory or its officials were aware of a hostility they could not hope to overcome' in the management of the elections (*The Directory*, p. 178); and it is usual to remark that in this matter François de Neufchâteau was more scrupulous than Merlin de Douai had been in 1798. Compare Barras (*Memoirs*, III, p. 419): 'Serious dissensions were now apparent in the Directory'; and for Lépeaux's letter *On the Significance of the*

Since such a government could not be brought down by legitimate means, and was most unlikely to resign, the Councils had recourse to something like conspiracy. In this, they were much favoured by fortune, for on 9 May the lot for the annual retirement of one Director was drawn by Reubell, the strongest and ablest of the five. Thus, as in 1797, an absurd constitutional device deprived the Directory of a key figure at a crucial hour. In wider perspective, indeed, the elimination of Reubell may be said to have been fateful for France; for although little enough has appeared in these pages to suggest that the rule of the Directory was beneficial, he at least had sufficient insight to perceive the folly and futility of foreign conquest,[1] and it is at least possible that he might have been better able than his successors to keep Bonaparte under control.[2] As it was, he retired, and in his place the Councils on 16 May elected Sieyès, who was well known to be dedicated to some drastic revision of the Constitution of 1795.[3]

The speed with which events then developed suggests that there had been a good deal of previous collaboration[4] between Sieyès in Berlin and his friends in the Councils, who were also probably in touch with the Jacobins through Lucien Bonaparte, and with some of the generals, particularly Joubert.[5] Certainly by the time Sieyès returned to Paris and took his place as a Director the first steps towards assuring him ascendancy had been taken. On 25 May a cry was raised in the Councils for the punishment of the men responsible for the financial deficit and for the deplorable condition of the armies;[6] and by 5 June further news of

---

Name 'Representative of the People', see his Mémoires (III, p. 58ff.) and Meynier, op. cit., pp. 188–92.

[1] Of the loss of Italy he remarked: 'Repeated triumphs have puffed our pride and perhaps corrupted our heads . . .': G. D. Homan, 'Jean-François Reubell, Director', French Historical Studies, No. 1 (1960), p. 434.

[2] Ibid., pp. 434–5, where Reubell is described as a statesman of the first rank; compare Barras (Mémoires, III, p. 432), who says that he was 'the very soul of the Directory'.

[3] Woloch suggests that this was not yet clear (Jacobin Legacy, p. 368); but I do not have the impression that it was any great secret.

[4] Lefebvre regards this previous collaboration as probable (The Directory, p. 181); Paul Bastid (Sieyès et Sa Pensée (Paris, 1939), pp. 213, 219) speaks of it as certain.

[5] Biog. Notes: JOUBERT.

[6] The reader will appreciate that here and in what follows the proceedings in two separate chambers were really involved. Broadly, however, the Elders, where the Sieyès group was strong, consistently sanctioned the moves initiated in the Five Hundred by Boulay of the Meurthe and others. I have therefore kept to the simpler collective.

military disaster, of renewed royalist activity and of apparent republican disintegration, enabled Sieyès' spokesman, Boulay of the Meurthe, to obtain a resolution requiring the Directory to make a full report upon the military situation within the next ten days. Then, after Sieyès had assumed office on 9 June, two more of his associates suddenly forced matters to a crisis on 16 June: one, Poullain-Grandpré, won a decision that, as no reply had come to the demand for a report, the Councils should remain in emergency session; and a second, Bergasse, suddenly challenged the technical validity of Treilhard's position as a Director, securing a vote for his immediate expulsion.[1]

The significance of this last move followed from the fact that Treilhard, who was personally the least important of the five Directors, happened to be the one who now held the balance amongst them. According to the memoirs of Lépeaux, who was of course a highly prejudiced witness, Sieyès had from the moment of his arrival declined to cooperate with his new colleagues in any way;[2] but Barras, perfidious in peril, had quickly associated himself with him in opposing Lépeaux, Merlin and Treilhard. The elimination of the latter would consequently leave Lépeaux and Merlin isolated in the face of the hostile Councils, and Lépeaux was apparently prepared to defy the deputies by supporting Treilhard, and even to seek military aid. Treilhard, however, settled the matter by picking up his umbrella and walking out; and next day, 17 June, the election of Louis Gohier,[3] a prominent judge of Jacobin sympathies, gave Sieyès and Barras the majority.

After this the only remaining problem was that of forcing Lépeaux and Merlin out as well, and as they declined Sieyès' invitation of 17 June that they should resign, a major offensive was launched against them in the Councils next day. On 18 June 1799, the day of 30 Prairial, Bertrand du Calvados, another of Sieyès' men, openly accused Lépeaux and Merlin of treason, denouncing them as responsible for the loss of public money and for the mutilation of the national parliament in the *coup*

[1] Treilhard had been a deputy until May 1797, and his election as a Director in May 1798 took place four days before the elapse of the complete year required by article 136 of the Constitution as an interval between these two functions. The exploitation of this regulation on this occasion is evident from the fact that the same disqualification was applicable to Sieyès himself.

[2] Lépeaux asserts that Sieyès constantly commented: 'Things are not done this way in Prussia', and rejected all requests for his guidance by saying: 'You would not understand me: do it your own way' (*Mémoires*, III, p. 384). Although this sounds likely enough, Bastid discounts it as a hostile legend (op. cit., p. 218).

[3] *Biog. Notes:* GOHIER.

d'état of the previous year (i.e., 22 Floréal). Boulay then took up the tale with a savage personal assault upon Lépeaux as a religious crank and upon Merlin as a small-minded Machiavelli; and blithely disregarding his own participation in the *coup d'état* of 18–19 Fructidor, he assailed them also for the continuous subjection of the legislature since that date. In sum, these attacks amounted to a skilful if unscrupulous appeal to the various resentments of the chambers, and their consequence was that the two Directors had either to resign or risk indictment and trial for treason. Prolonged and painful scenes ensued as Barras, and deputation after deputation from the Councils, strove to browbeat or persuade Lépeaux, on whom all depended, to retire, while in the wings Joubert and Bernadotte growled that they could soon conclude the affair with 20 grenadiers, or even a corporal's guard.[1] Eventually, however, Lépeaux succumbed, writing a letter of resignation (which Merlin copied verbatim) in which he re-asserted his ardent love for the republic and his belief that his conduct had been beyond reproach; and he then withdrew from public life entirely.[2]

To Lépeaux, 30 Prairial seemed a fatal day for the Republic, and he had no doubt that the principal responsibility for it was that of 'the proud faction of the generals, never able to endure civil authority'.[3] To accept this would be to over-simplify a complex situation; but the day, a successful one for some of the soldiers, is certainly indicative of the increasing participation and importance of military men in politics. Generals like Joubert and—despite his defeats—Jourdan had been prominent in the attack on the Directors, who were of course convenient scapegoats in disaster; and although no troops were used on this occasion, the fear of force appears to have been a factor of considerable importance on both sides. Moreover, although in Lefebvre's view the government which had allowed the armies of France to decline into destitution was guilty of at least criminal negligence, the Second Directory, and Lépeaux in particular, had made a major effort to subordinate its generals to civil control—which was now promptly repudiated. Appointed Minister of War, Bernadotte quickly released Championnet from prison, and his rehabilitation was soon completed by appointment to the command of the Army of the Alps, which was intended for the destruction of Suvorov. As for the civil commissioners,

[1] Barras, needless to say: *Mémoires*, III, pp. 456–7.
[2] For detailed accounts of these scenes, see Lépeaux, *Mémoires*, II, pp. 389–407, and G. Robison, *Revellière-Lépeaux, Citizen Director*, pp. 223–5.
[3] Lépeaux, *Mémoires*, II, pp. 235, 333, and *passim*.

the last of them was sent home as soon as Joubert, who became the new commander in Italy, reached his headquarters.[1]

On the other hand, Lépeaux's identification of his own downfall with that of the Republic can be discounted, indicative though it is of the conviction the Directors had always had that republican righteousness was theirs alone. The day of 30 Prairial was indeed both constitutionally and politically one of retaliation for the *coups d'état* of 1797 and 1798, it being an occasion on which the executive was overwhelmed by an alliance of the democratic Left, eager to avenge 22 Floréal and assert its right to influence affairs, with the conservative majority which resented the subordination to which it had been reduced since 18–19 Fructidor. But if, as Lucien Bonaparte asserted, the Directors had abused their authority, the circumstances of their fall do little to substantiate his claim that 'The Legislative Body has rightfully resumed its foremost place in the state.'[2] Rather does the unfolding of the conspiracy suggest that one clique had skilfully exploited the general discontent in order to supersede another. Immediately, too, the essential change effected on 30 Prairial was one of personalities: Lépeaux and Merlin were replaced by two relatively insignificant men, the magistrate Roger Ducos[3] and a minor general, Moulin;[4] but the powers of the Directory remained unaltered. If to all this it be added that the real head of the new government was Sieyès,[5] a man whom some at least knew to be determined to fortify the executive by a revision of the Constitution, little is left of any parliamentary victory.[6]

[1] The increasing importance of the military is often said to be reflected in the Councils' selection of successors for Merlin and Lépeaux, for 5 of the 7 candidates proposed by the Five Hundred were either generals or admirals. I have however preferred to think that this is more indicative of the feeling that the military reverses made the presence of some soldier other than Barras desirable in the executive.

[2] Meynier, op. cit., p. 228. Lucien in fact referred to 'the majority of the Directors' (presumably excluding Sieyès and Barras) and to the authority 'entrusted to it' (presumably in furtherance of the fictitious but convenient assumption that the Councils had willingly offered the Directors power in Fructidor).

[3] *Biog. Notes:* ROGER DUCOS.

[4] *Biog. Notes:* GENERAL MOULIN.

[5] P. Bastid, *Sieyès et sa pensée*, 821. This is, however, not to say that the new government should be thought of as a united force under his control.

[6] On this point, Lefebvre comments: 'the event involved an interpretation of the Constitution which . . . tended towards a parliamentary system'. Interesting as it would be, I have not attempted here to assess the strength of that tendency in the Councils. In general, see Lefebvre, *The Directory*, p. 182; Meynier, op. cit., p. 228; and Woloch, op. cit., p. 367: but all are here somewhat disappointing.

As this implies, the rule of law, restricted in 1795 and set aside in 1797, was not restored on 30 Prairial. That day, indeed, is far better understood as a first than as a final step. With the connivance of Barras, Sieyès and his associates had expelled an entrenched government and ended the veto it had imposed upon all political change in France. The process, coinciding as it did with the great national crisis arising from Austro-Russian advance, necessarily entailed some concessions to the Jacobins and some re-animation of political life: but to Sieyès and the men of the majority, these were in all probability no more than transient and incidental consequences of the fall of the Second Directory. Their real objective, the establishment of a more stable political system— which meant, above all, the abolition in 1799 of the recurrent crises caused by annual elections—still remained to be achieved. In the mean-while the government retained the emergency powers derived from earlier 'exceptional' legislation.

For a short period it nevertheless appeared as if there was to be a real resurgence of democracy in French politics. Of the four new Directors, three—Roger Ducos, Gohier and Moulin—had been amongst those excluded from the Councils as Jacobins in Floréal, and although Ducos soon seemed Sieyès' shadow, Gohier and Moulin remained of that per-suasion.[1] The Jacobins were also strongly represented in the general replacement of ministers and other officers of the old Directory, the appointments of Bernadotte as Minister of War, of Robert Lindet as Minister of Finance and of General Marbot as Commander of the Army of the Interior being particularly significant. More freedom was afforded to the Press,[2] the principal Jacobin paper, the *Journal des hommes libres*, was again published openly; and with the tacit approval of authority, political clubs rapidly reappeared in Paris and many provincial towns.[3] Moreover, as the focal point of this revival, a new Jacobin Club was established within the precincts of parliament itself. Modelled on its

---

[1] The new Directory of course consisted of Sieyès, Barras, Roger Ducos, Gohier and Moulin. Although it is sometimes referred to as the Third Direc-tory, I have avoided the use of that name.

[2] On 27 June a resolution of the Five Hundred abrogated that Article 35 of the Law of 19 Fructidor which suspended the freedom of the press, and this the Elders ratified on 1 August. This, however, by no means deprived the government of its powers of control, either under Article 145 of the Constitution or under the Law of 27 Germinal IV. See Aulard, *A Political History of the French Revolution*, IV, p. 391 and, for the 'relatively meager' results of the new 'freedom', Woloch, op. cit., pp. 376–9.

[3] Woloch, op. cit., p. 379 (particularly note 23); and, for the Paris Club, pp. 379–86.

once mighty predecessor, this new 'Society of the Friends of Liberty and Equality' attracted about 250 deputies and up to 3,000 members, who met, symbolically enough, in the Manège—the old Riding School of the Tuileries which had housed all the National Assemblies of the Revolution.[1]

Yet if the summer of 1799 provided these progressives with their long-awaited opportunity to influence the conduct of affairs, it also imposed the severest of tests upon them. While the people of France, alienated and apathetic, had remained unmoved by the events of 30 Prairial,[2] the general fear of Jacobinism was still a most potent force. In the elections of 1798 and 1799 that fear had of course been shamelessly exploited by the Second Directory and its supporters, who had constantly asserted that bleeding heads would roll if ever the 'anarchists' returned to power;[3] but those who thus evoked men's memories of the Terror did so in the certain knowledge that they were appealing to deep-seated anxieties.[4] The new Jacobins' only prospect of success consequently lay in moderation in speech and action alike. The circumstances of the summer, however, were wholly adverse to the exercise of any such restraint. Not only were the Jacobins, who had been ostracised for so long, excited and exalted by their own apparent recovery, they were also immediately involved in a great endeavour to rally and organise the nation against the advancing Russians. Nor was military effort alone involved, for within France itself the royalist Institutes, re-formed since

[1] Occupied by the National Constituent Assembly on its removal to Paris from Versailles in October 1789, the Riding School was in continuous use as a parliament house until the Convention was able to occupy new quarters in the Palace itself on 9 May 1793. When in 1795 a bicameral legislature was established, the Council of Five Hundred reoccupied the same building until accommodation at the Palais Bourbon became available.

[2] 'Our reverses or our successes occasion neither anxiety nor joy . . . Internal change excites no more emotion. Questions are asked by curiosity, answered without interest, heard with indifference . . .'; police report on Paris for Prairial, quoted by A. Meynier, *Le 18 brumaire an VIII* (Paris, 1928), p. 10.

[3] Examples of this sort of language abound. The extract from one of François de Neufchâteau's circulars of 1799 cited by Lefebvre (*The Directory*, p. 178) is perhaps particularly striking as obvious propaganda by a relatively moderate man: 'No more brigands in office . . . Would you like to see the law of the *maximum* reimposed? Would you like to see Féraud's murderers reappear carrying his bleeding head on a pike?'

[4] Apart from the inherent probability of this, I am strongly influenced here by the duration of the fears of our own time—particularly, perhaps, that of the massive unemployment of the great Depression. In 1799 only five years had elapsed since 1794.

1797, were busily organising a new insurrection, and by the middle of June 1799 counter-revolutionary terrorism was rampant in some southern departments, particularly the Haute-Garonne.[1] What is more, in April an unaccountable incident, apparently indicative of royalist savagery, had horrified France: on leaving the Congress at Rastadt, the three French plenipotentiaries had been attacked by Austrian hussars, who had killed two of them outright and left the third for dead. Thus, as the death of these deputies was daily commemorated in the Council of Five Hundred,[2] 1793 seemed to have come again, and the Jacobins naturally responded to the challenge by making militant speeches and demanding revolutionary measures.

Since this defiant attitude tallied with the national need, the Jacobins were for a time able to take the lead in legislation: but since their strength was superficial, their success depended on the acceptability of their proposals in the Councils. In the circumstances, the majority of the deputies were at first ready enough to welcome emergency measures, and three of these were approved in rapid succession in the month which followed 30 Prairial. On 27 June General Jourdan himself proposed what he called a new *levée en masse:* all five classes of conscripts specified in his earlier law were to be called up simultaneously, and the recent concession regarding substitutions was abruptly withdrawn. At the same time it was agreed to raise 100 million francs by a forced loan.[3] As finally approved in detail on 6 August, this imposed such severe taxation upon the rich that a man of considerable wealth might be required to hand over three-quarters of his income. Finally, on 12 July, the notorious 'Law of Hostages' made the unfortunate relatives of *émigrés* (and the nobles, who were already deprived of all civic rights) answerable for political disorder: in any department declared to be 'disturbed', these people were to be arrested; four of them were to be deported for every 'patriot' who was murdered, and all were to be collectively responsible for paying fines and compensating the victims of royalist attacks. Further, an accompanying offer of an amnesty to rebels was offset by the warning

[1] J. Godechot, *La Contre-Révolution, 1789–1804*, pp. 361–5.

[2] The seats of the two dead deputies were swathed in black and their names were read aloud at the opening of each session of the Chamber. The survivor, Jean Debry, was given a standing ovation on his return, becoming President of the Five Hundred for Prairial. A. Meynier, *Le Vingt-deux Floréal an VI et le Trente Prairial an VII* (Paris, 1928), p. 205.

[3] General Jourdan in fact proposed both these measures of conscription and taxation on the same day, 27 June; the latter was accepted in principle on that date, the former becoming law next day.

that the recalcitrant would be executed on identification by a military commission.

To the country, these laws were of course repugnant. At worst, they renewed all the old fears and hatreds of the Revolution, particularly amongst the well-to-do, and at best they were met everywhere by evasion and resistance sufficient to deprive them of much beneficial effect. The mass conscription, which was expected to lead to the enlistment of 223,000 men, in fact raised only 116,000; and the forced loan eventually produced only about one third of the expected sum. As for the Law of Hostages, that seems hardly ever to have been applied: although some areas were subsequently declared to be 'disturbed', the law remained primarily a trumpet blast against the royalists. It may indeed be that all three laws were more revolutionary in tone than in actual substance;[1] and harsh and discriminatory as two of them were, they seemed to the Councils appropriate and necessary at a time when invasion and civil war were thought to be imminent.

The Jacobins, however, were not concerned with national defence alone. Convinced that corruption and inertia were the real evils of the day, they were sure that republican morale would only be restored if those responsible for the repudiation and repression of democracy in 1798 were publicly punished. Urged on by the Press and by a spate of petitions, the Jacobin deputies repeatedly demanded this, and on 12 July —the day on which the Law of Hostages was passed—the Council of Five Hundred accepted a report in favour of indicting all four of the fallen Directors[2] and General Schérer, the hated ex-Minister of War. This, however, proved to be the height of the Jacobin revival. According to the relevant articles of the Constitution,[3] which had been carefully drafted to prevent any repetition of the recurrent proscriptions of deputies characteristic of 1793–4, 33 days had to elapse before such an indictment could even be referred to the Council of the Elders, and in this interval the issue shattered the coalition which had overthrown the old Directory. However great the national emergency, the conservative deputies who had sanctioned and supported the exclusion of the Jacobins in 1798 could not repudiate the past completely; rather, indeed, did the proposed indictment convince them that the Jacobins were still a danger-

---

[1] Professor Palmer suggests that although the language of popular revolution was used in these measures, they in fact authorised the developing state to conscript men methodically and to establish a form of progressive income tax. See *The Age of the Democratic Revolution*, II, p. 364.

[2] I.e., Reubell, Treilhard, Merlin and Lépeaux.

[3] Articles 158, 117–21 and 77.

ously inquisitorial party.[1] As for the new Directors, their personal interests clearly coincided with considerations of policy: although Barras, as the sole survivor of the Second Directory, was evidently in peril, and although ignoble personal motives can also be imputed to Sieyès,[2] there can be no doubt that they were right to refuse to countenance legal proceedings which would open the road to endless recrimination and so undermine the security of all future government.

Thus within three weeks of their apparent triumph on 30 Prairial the Jacobins' ominous conduct and extravagant language made many fear that a new Terror was about to begin, and Sieyès was able to take advantage of this to further his own plans. By this time he was, indeed, already preparing the ground for a final *coup d'état*. Since the Constitution could not legally be altered, and since the Council of Five Hundred would certainly oppose any attempt to employ parliamentary methods in order to strengthen the executive, the revision which Sieyès was determined to effect demanded the use of military force by a reliable general. In the early summer of 1799 Sieyès fully expected that this man would be General Joubert. Certainly every effort was made to build up his reputation by publicity, and before he left Paris on 16 July to assume his new command in Italy he was expediently married to a lady of good family, Mlle de Montholon, who was probably expected to attract the support of exiled Feuillant leaders like La Fayette.[3] On this side, it only remained for Joubert to assume the offensive and win a spectacular victory for France—and for Sieyès.

In the interim, it was Sieyès' own task to remain in office and to restrict the power of the Jacobins, and this he did with considerable courage and skill.[4] As President of the Directory, he first took advantage of the anniversary of 14 July to assail the members of the clubs, who: 'in an earlier time of calamity . . . had sought to represent the nation to the exclusion of its duly elected deputies'. Aided by the reckless attitude of the Jacobins in the Manège, he was then able to arrange for one of his friends in the Elders to denounce that Club for preparing 'the resurrection of the Terror'. On that same day, 26 July, the Elders ruled that no political society should be permitted to meet within the precincts of

---

[1] As Lépeaux bluntly put it in his published reply to the allegations against him: 'I maintain that it was with good reason that the Directory recognised the existence of an anarchist party'. *Mémoires*, III, pp. 157–8. Compare Woloch, op. cit., pp. 371–4.

[2] As they are, for example, by Lefebvre, *The Directory*, p. 188.

[3] Bastid, *Sieyès et sa pensée*, pp. 229–31.

[4] Ibid., pp. 222–3; Meynier, *Le 18 brumaire An VIII et la fin de la République* (Paris, 1928), pp. 16, 21, 25. See also Woloch, op. cit., pp. 379–86.

their Council, and the Club had to retire to a church in the rue du Bac, where it became more irresponsible than ever. Sieyès was then able to repeat the pattern of his first manoeuvre. Twice more, on the anniversaries of the fall of Robespierre and of the overthrow of the monarchy (i.e., 27 July and 10 August), he denounced the 'monstrous power' that the Jacobins had had in the past and swore that he would never allow it to return. Bitterly abused in reply, he contrived to dismiss first the Minister of Police and then Marbot, the Jacobin military commander in Paris, replacing the one by Fouché and the other by General Lefebvre, a staunch but harmless republican.[1] Thus reinforced, he acted rapidly: on 13 August, when the Council of Five Hundred was opening its final debate on the indictment question, he persuaded the Directory to approve an order presented by Fouché for the closure of the Club as a source of public dissension. Put into immediate effect by Fouché's police and Lefebvre's soldiers, this was a substantial victory, the result of which was apparent on 18 August, when the Five Hundred finally rejected the indictment of the ex-Directors by the narrow margin of 217 to 214 votes.[2]

Now, however, the counter-revolutionaries and the allied armies renewed their assault, thwarting Sieyès' plans and all but overwhelming France. Hardly had the Jacobin Club been closed than evil tidings began to reach Paris. First, it was belatedly learnt on 13 August that the royalists of the Haute-Garonne had risen in force on the 5th, investing and isolating the Jacobin stronghold of Toulouse.[3] Then on 23 August came the news that the French offensive in Italy had failed miserably and that General Joubert was dead. Possibly because he was unduly hurried by political considerations, Joubert had hastened northwards from Genoa without waiting for Championnet's army to join him through Piedmont. After he had been killed in a preliminary skirmish, his forces had been utterly defeated by those of Suvorov in a great battle at Novi, and the unfortunate Moreau, who was again attached to the army as an adviser,

[1] Appointed on 20 July, Fouché assumed office on his return from The Hague on the 29th, and Marbot was dismissed on 11 August. General Marbot (Antoine, 1750–1800) was the father of the more famous Jean-Baptiste Marbot (1782–1854); François Joseph Lefebvre, subsequently Marshal (1804) and duc de Dantzig (1808) was an Alsatian of humble origin who had risen from the rank of sergeant since 1789.

[2] Meynier, op. cit., pp. 49–50.

[3] Toulouse was of course a city in which the forces of counter-revolution were strong and the democrats correspondingly militant. It was for this reason, as well as on account of the importance of the city throughout southern France, that its control was vital to both sides.

had had to assume command and take the survivors back to Genoa. Yet even this disastrous news was soon overshadowed by that of graver peril, for on 27 August 10,000 British were landed successfully in Holland some four miles south of Helder. Captured at anchor in the Zuider Zee, the few remaining ships of the Dutch fleet had promptly hoisted the colours of the House of Orange, and as both British and Russian troops reinforced the landing it seemed that the Dutch army might also surrender and leave rebellious Belgium open to the invader. Strategically, indeed, the whole axis of the allied attack had shifted: so that the Austrians might have a free hand in Italy, Suvorov's forces were now directed towards Switzerland, and the Archduke Charles similarly moved northwards towards the Rhine and the Low Countries, leaving another Russian army under Korsakov in Zurich.

So far as France itself was concerned, it soon became apparent that the royalist threat was less serious than it seemed at first. Acting with great vigour, the republicans of Toulouse defended their city until the arrival of reinforcements from adjacent departments enabled them to take the offensive and eventually to rout the royalists at Montréjeau on 20 August. Moreover, whereas this rising had occurred prematurely, a great insurrection in Brittany and Normandy, which was meant to co-incide with it, only began two months later, when it could be checked without undue difficulty.[1] On 2 September Sieyès nevertheless struck hard at the Right-wing Press, ordering the deportation of the staff of 34 journals still affected by the Law of 19 Fructidor.

More remarkably, the sudden intensification of the national crisis did *not* incline Sieyès towards the compromise with the Jacobins which was almost customary in such circumstances. On the contrary, on 3 September the Directory issued a second order, by which the staff of 16 other papers, including the two principal Jacobin journals, were to be arrested for conspiracy under Article 145 of the Constitution.[2] This bold departure from precedent, which may well be taken as representative of Sieyès' whole policy, merits more consideration than it is commonly afforded, for it is not to be explained by his reliance on the army. As we have seen, the generals had participated in and profited by the destruction of the Second Directory on 30 Prairial; but they were far from being

---

[1] On both insurrections, see Godechot, *La Contre-Révolution, 1789–1804*, pp. 368–75.

[2] It should not, of course, be supposed that in either case the orders were fully effected; the two Jacobin journals, indeed, soon reappeared under different names. See Woloch, *Jacobin Legacy*, p. 379 and, for the orders, Lefebvre, *The Directory*, p. 191.

an independent third force in politics. Apart, perhaps, from having some common contempt for civilian politicians, they were as sharply divided as the deputies, and by substantially the same issues. If some, like Moreau, were 'moderate' and conservative republicans, others, like Jourdan, were fervent Jacobins. Indeed, since Joubert was dead, and since men like Jourdan and Bernadotte, the Minister of War, seemed dominant in Paris, Sieyès' sustained hostility to the Jacobins at this time looks very like a courageous re-assertion of civil authority.

On the other hand, the situation undoubtedly illustrates the appalling disunity of the leaders of France in an hour of peril. Apparently some of the Jacobins, including Jourdan, even tried to persuade Bernadotte to arrest Sieyès and his associates,[1] but were unable to overcome the general's irresolution. For their part, the Jacobins had good reason to suspect that Sieyès was preparing a *coup d'état*; and some even alleged, and probably believed, that he and the other Directors were ready to betray the Republic and collaborate with the invader in order to destroy democracy. As one Jacobin succinctly said: 'The Directors have a new constitution in one pocket and a treaty in the other'.[2] The latter part of this allegation can be confidently dismissed: like Lépeaux and others before him, Sieyès hated and feared the Jacobins, and was fully prepared to use force against them; unlike Lépeaux, he was also prepared to alter the Constitution in order to consolidate the social and political power of the conservatives; but he was nevertheless a firm French republican.[3]

A less improbable explanation of Sieyès' conduct, cast in terms of acute class-consciousness and half-hearted patriotism, is, however, still current. Professor Lefebvre, for example, cites (amongst other telling texts) the bitter comment of Lamarque: 'Some people want the people to be used to repel the barbarians; others are afraid of using that omnipotent force, in other words they dread the mass of Republicans more than the hordes from the north'.[4] Whatever truth there may be in this suggestion that conservatives like Sieyès were so dominated by social fear that they were only secondarily concerned with winning the war, the

[1] This is accepted by Vandal: A. Vandal, *L'Avènement de Bonaparte* (Nelson ed., London, 1910), I, pp. 161–2.
[2] Ibid., p. 160.
[3] In a brief reference to the neo-Jacobinism of 1799, Professor Palmer (*The Age of the Democratic Revolution*, II, pp. 565–6) refers to this as 'the excited reaction of an abortive democracy' and comments tellingly upon the strength of social fears and antagonisms in France; but neither the scale of his work nor the sharpness of the distinctions he draws between democracy and counter-revolution permit him to develop the difficulty of Sieyès' position at this time.
[4] Lefebvre, *The Directory*, p. 187.

credibility of the charge is of considerable significance. In 1799, as in 1793[1]—and, sadly, in more recent times—some Frenchmen were fully prepared to believe that others, quite apart from the royalists, placed their own social and political interests above the safety and even the independence of the nation; and since to all concerned their opponents then seemed far fouler than foreign enemies, domestic divisions transcended matters of national defence.

It was this attitude, quite as much as the impending allied invasion, which caused General Jourdan to demand on 13 September that the Council of Five Hundred should declare the country to be in danger. To all who heard them, these words at once recalled the most tremendous and terrible times of the Revolution: symbolic in themselves of popular patriotism and Jacobin power, they also implied the immediate suspension of the Constitution and the assumption of emergency powers by extraordinary committees—and the displacement of the existing Directory. Furious conflict followed. Amidst clamour from the public galleries, deputies came to blows, and Boulay of the Meurthe, who happened to be presiding, was threatened with death. Significantly, however, several prominent deputies, particularly Daunou and Lucien Bonaparte—who now separated himself from the Jacobins—condemned the once dynamic formula as dangerous rhetoric, unlikely to lead to anything but a renewal of violence and terrorism;[2] Lucien, indeed, explicitly asserted that it would be far better to take constitutional measures to strengthen the power of the existing executive. Eventually the exhaustion of the assembly allowed Boulay to adjourn the debate, and Sieyès, convening the Directory at midnight, got Roger Ducos and Barras to agree to dismiss Bernadotte, energetic War Minister though he was.[3] When Bernadotte accepted his dismissal, and when it became clear that there was not going to be any significant popular support for the Jacobins, the crisis was almost over. Though tumultuous controversy continued next day, Jourdan's motion was eventually rejected by 245 votes to 171.[4]

---

[1] The situation and attitudes of 1799 are very close to those of the spring of 1793, before the Revolution of 2 June gave the Montagnards control, though there also are vital differences. See my own *French Revolution*, chapter 6, including, for example, Carnot's note in March 1793: 'We need expect no peace from our enemies, and those at home are worse than those abroad'.

[2] Compare Barras' description of it as 'worn out . . . no longer productive of any results': *Mémoires*, III, pp. 569–72, and Woloch, *Jacobin Legacy*, p. 371.

[3] The Directors in fact notified Bernadotte that they had decided to accept an offer made previously that he should return to active service.

[4] According to Vandal, op. cit., I, p. 168, all the efforts of the Jacobins only attracted some 8–900 people to the approaches to the Councils, which were

This defeat was decisive, for the Jacobins had failed in the most favourable circumstances to revive the militant radicalism of the Revolution. If this was in part because some particular measures had alienated all whose attitudes and interests were conservative, it was also because the policies of the Jacobins seemed sterile and their temper terrifyingly reminiscent of 'the reign of Robespierre'. One last success was indeed obtained on 24 September, when the Five Hundred were brought to unanimous agreement that the death penalty should be imposed upon anyone who countenanced any proposals for peace which involved either constitutional change or territorial sacrifice: but this proved an empty gesture, which was conveniently forgotten until the Elders quietly rejected it in October. Yet in their few remaining weeks of ineffectual opposition to the Directory, the Jacobins showed that for all their rhetoric they still represented something fundamental to freedom: in resisting oligarchy, they sought to the last to establish laws to guarantee more freedom to the Press and more security to political societies.[1] Any opportunity even to influence events was, however, removed from them by the sudden transformation of the military situation of France.

Of this the hero was Masséna, 'the cherished child of Victory'. As soon as the Archduke Charles had moved off to the Rhine with the main Austrian army, Masséna fell upon Korsakov's Russians, crushing them completely at the second Battle of Zurich (25–7 September 1799). At the same time General Lecourbe, perhaps the most famous mountain general of the day, had defended the St Gothard Pass against Suvorov, and although the latter finally fought his way through to Altdorf, the news of Korsakov's defeat forced him to take his army along the Alps into Austria.[2] The whole of Switzerland being thus in French hands, Masséna was able to move to Constance, so threatening the flank of the Austrian advance on the Rhine and compelling the Archduke Charles's army, which had just taken Mannheim, to retire hurriedly to the Danube. These events also proved fatal to the allied invasion of Holland. Although the British eventually landed 40,000 men, including 12,000

---

under strong military guard. The Jacobins pressed the final vote to an indvidual vote by nominal roll, in the old revolutionary tradition; ibid., p. 169.

[1] For a more detailed consideration of this, see Woloch, *Jacobin Legacy*, chapter 13 (pp. 369–99, particularly p. 395). The reader should, however, appreciate that Professor Woloch's Jacobins are rather the men of the clubs than those of the Legislative Councils in Paris.

[2] An epic march, which cost the Russians 13,000 men as well as all their guns and baggage.

Russians, their advance down the peninsula proved painfully slow,[1] and the French commander, General Brune, twice repulsed attacks by throwing in his reserves. Although not decisive in themselves, these reverses (at Bergen on 19 September and at Castricum on 6 October) caused the invaders to halt; and the rapid development of disease, together with the news that no help was to be expected from Austria, then led to the decision to withdraw. By the Convention of Alkmaar, which was signed on 18 October, Brune—whose own situation was far more difficult than the British supposed—agreed that the allies could evacuate Holland provided they repatriated all French prisoners, and this they did by the beginning of November.

The French victory was not, of course, complete. In Brittany and Normandy, the *chouans'* uprising began in mid-October; Britain remained supreme at sea; and when Championnet led the Army of the Alps into Italy, he was defeated by the Austrians at Grenola (4 November) and thrust back into France. The French had nevertheless freed themselves from all danger of invasion, consolidated their control of the Dutch Republic, Switzerland and the right bank of the Rhine, and—much to the relief of the Austrians—driven the Russian armies out of western Europe.[2] They had, therefore, good reason to rejoice: but the elation of the Councils reached a climax of enthusiasm when on 13 October the Directors announced that Bonaparte had landed near Fréjus in Provence four days previously.

This reaction, like the rapturous welcome the general received as he made his way to Paris, was scarcely affected by the fact that he came back with only two frigates and a carefully selected staff of officers.[3] Nor, indeed, was it then apparent that the Egyptian enterprise had been a spectacular failure. After the destruction of his fleet at the battle of the

[1] The naval advantages of landing on a peninsula being, of course, counter-balanced by the military difficulties of advancing along it. In this instance, heavy surf also made it difficult to maintain supplies; and as Sheridan caustically remarked in the Commons, the British discovered that Holland was a country intersected by dykes, and that the weather was not so good in October as it was in June. For the Helder campaign, see Sir A. Bryant, *The Years of Endurance*, pp. 278–94.

[2] Some of the Russians remained for a time in the Channel Islands, a base from which the British government had some hopes of sending forces to support the *chouans* in western France.

[3] In September the Directors had written to Bonaparte authorising him to return *with* his army, but (practical difficulties apart) he did not see this letter before reaching Paris. Individual proposals that he should be arrested, made, for example, by Bernadotte, were abandoned as soon as public enthusiasm for Bonaparte became apparent.

Nile on 31 July–1 August 1798, Bonaparte had long remained completely isolated from France. Acting as an independent ruler, he had devoted his endless energy to an attempt to establish Egypt as a permanent colony of France. In this remarkable endeavour he had, amongst other things, instituted local and national consultative assemblies of Egyptian notabilities; insisted that the Mohammedan faith be respected; and initiated innumerable projects for the modernisation and improvement of Egyptian life. He had also suppressed a major revolt in Cairo in October 1798, carried the war against Turkey into the enemy's country by advancing into Syria in the spring of 1799,[1] and hurried back to Egypt in time to annihilate at Aboukir the great expeditionary force which the Turks had sent against him (25 July 1799). Then, on learning from newspapers (sent to him by the British) of the loss of Italy and the danger to France itself, he had handed over his command to General Kléber and returned to France past the British blockade. This, however, was by no means an admission of failure: on the contrary, Bonaparte clearly had every intention of reinforcing and re-equipping the garrison of Egypt as soon as possible; and in France itself, his victory over the Turks at Aboukir—which had been announced amidst thunderous applause on 5 October—was equated with those of Brune and Masséna in Holland and Switzerland.

But even if it had been realised that most of Bonaparte's achievements in Egypt were simply writings in the sand, the warmth of his welcome would not have been diminished. Nor was it of any consequence that the tide of defeat in Europe had been stayed before his arrival. To a country long conscious of its lack of his ability in battle, he came—as it so happened—at a time of splendid success, and public rejoicing, an almost forgotten feeling in France, accompanied his advent. Still more important, since his name alone was associated with the settlement with Austria in 1797, a people wearied of war were confident that his coming presaged permanent peace.

Yet more even than victory and the pacification of Europe was expected of Bonaparte. As much as anything, men hoped that he would revive and restore the Republic itself. That at the end of 1799 its condition was deplorable is indisputable. Although economic prosperity was gradually returning, and although Ramel's reforms had laid the foundations for financial stability, the government itself was desperately short

---

[1] I here follow Felix Markham (*Napoleon*, London, 1964, p. 51) in treating the Syrian campaign as something which was to Bonaparte a side-show at the time; and I consequently omit to refer in the text to the defence of Acre by the Turks and by Sir Sidney Smith's naval squadron.

of money. As income from conquest had been abruptly cut off, and as the advances made by distrustful bankers in anticipation of revenue from the forced loan had been swiftly spent, there was so huge a deficit that a new bankruptcy was imminent.[1] Since no money was available to pay public servants, the administration of the state was practically in abeyance,[2] and brigandage, the product of persecution, war and weakness, was still rife throughout large parts of the land.[3] Moreover, as the Jacobin resurgence had been halted, a further restriction of republican freedom seemed certain, while the oppression of the Church and the Right was apparently perpetual.

Of all these evils, which are of course described at considerable length in the works of Bonapartist historians, the common cause was the complete lack of public confidence in the government and the future. While there can now be little doubt that the administrative achievements of the Directory between 1795 and 1799 were considerable, insecurity made them inoperative, and there seems no adequate reason to suppose that matters would have improved without some fundamental change.[4] Although, as we have seen, Sieyès had successfully checked the Jacobins' revival, their revolutionary language and far-reaching legislation had reawakened widespread social anxiety and profound political fears. Moreover, although the conservatives in the Councils had begun to modify the forced loan and the Law of Hostages as soon as the military crisis was over, the approach of new elections in 1800 made the future as unpredictable as ever. To restore confidence and make good government possible, constitutional change was clearly imperative, and Bonaparte, resolute, popular and politically detached, was as clearly the man

[1] Godechot, *Les Institutions*, p. 440.

[2] Lefebvre, *The Directory*, p. 195.

[3] See the Report on the Situation of the Republic submitted by Fouché to the Directory in October 1799: Aulard, *L'Etat de la France en l'an VIII et en l'an IX* (Paris, 1897). See also the synopsis of the incidence of White Terrorism given by R. Cobb, *The Police and the People*, p. 109; and chapter 8 below.

[4] In the concluding pages of his admirable revaluation of the work of the Directory ('The French Executive Directory—A Revaluation', *History* (Dec. 1937), pp. 201–18), Professor Goodwin suggests that the Directors had solved their main constitutional difficulties, the problem of the annual elections having proved susceptible to treatment by systematic corruption and occasional *coups d'état*. Probably more stimulating than serious, this suggestion should be set aside for 1799, a year in which the annual elections led directly to the fall of the Directors and to all the alarms associated with the revival of Jacobinism. That, as Meynier asserts (*Le 18 brumaire*, p. 9), the Jacobin laws may well have been inspired by the government, and that Sieyès eventually overcame the Jacobin thrust, are relevant, but not in my view material points.

14 The installation of the Council of State at the Petit Luxembourg,
25 December 1799

15 Moreau
engraved by Pannier

16 Georges Cadoudal
lithograph by Delpech

to effect it. As the story has it, Sieyès was actually sounding out Moreau as a possible successor to Joubert when the news of Bonaparte's return arrived, and Moreau, as politically indecisive as ever, promptly said: 'There is your man. He will make your *coup d'état* far better than I'.[1]

As for Bonaparte himself, he clearly came to France with every intention of obtaining a decisive voice in French affairs. Few formalities marked his return to Paris, which he entered unobtrusively on 16 October, and for the most part he remained quietly at his house in the rue de la Victoire, apparently taking pleasure only in addressing the Institute on Egypt and its antiquities. Being besieged by callers, he was nevertheless soon in contact with everyone of importance, and it is evident that he was assiduously assessing the situation and evaluating both people and parties. Of Sieyès he seems at first to have been suspicious: but whether this attitude was real or assumed,[2] he certainly realised quickly enough that Sieyès alone had substantial support in the Councils and amongst the conservative classes of France—on whom, as he saw, any new order would have to depend. The common interest of the two men drew them inexorably together, and from the end of October their occasional public meetings were supplemented by clandestine conferences between Sieyès and Talleyrand, who acted as Bonaparte's principal go-between. Since the general was in fact entering a conspiracy already partially prepared, an early date, that of 9 November, was fixed for action.

In the interim,[3] it was Bonaparte's particular task to win the widest possible range of support, particularly from those generals who were either, like Lefebvre, loyal to the existing order, or, like Jourdan and Bernadotte, far more inclined to favour a Jacobin *coup*. Since in this Bonaparte—who had no regard for truth—had of necessity to be all things to all men, it is by no means easy to discern his true intentions. It would, however, seem that he really meant to rid the state of corruption and incompetence, and that he was unreserved in avowing his determination to maintain the republican form of government. Further, since

---

[1] The story was apparently derived by Vandal from the family tradition of the deputy Baudin of the Ardennes, who was present at the interview and who is reputed to have died of joy immediately afterwards.

[2] Earlier contacts between Sieyès and Napoleon through Lucien are considered briefly by Bastid, op. cit., p. 232 and Meynier, op. cit., p. 98.

[3] The summary of the events which culminated in the *coup d'état* of 18–19 brumaire which follows is generally derived from A. Vandal, *L'Avènement de Bonaparte* (2 vols, Paris, 1907–8; Nelson, London, 1910); from Meynier, *Le 18 brumaire et la fin de la République* (Paris, 1928); and from J. Thiry, *Le Coup d'état du 18 brumaire* (Paris, 1947).

he was also resolved to end national disunity and to silence all party controversy, it was of the first importance to him that the *coup* should not seem to be the work of any particular political party or section of the nation, not excluding the army. He therefore strove not to extend a conspiracy but to inspire men to participate in a manifestation of national purpose, as much civilian as military in character, and as far removed from illegality as possible. This general position is well illustrated by his attitude towards Fouché, the Minister of Police, who had been recommended to him by Réal as an indispensable man and one who knew everything. Such a man Bonaparte found the ex-Terrorist to be: but he was nevertheless careful to keep him on the fringe of the preparations for the disruption of the Directory, and when the day of action came he was to rebuke him angrily for his initiative in closing the gates of Paris: 'We are acting with the nation and by its strength alone. Let no one be disturbed, and the triumph of opinion will have nothing in common with the uprisings of minorities.'[1]

Whatever the truth of this may be, all concerned were agreed that the existing Constitution, with its five Directors, its independent Legislative and Treasury and its annual elections, was incompatible with firm and consistent government. Their general objective was therefore that of creating a new and stronger executive authority,[2] and for this it was necessary to destroy the Directory and to persuade the Councils to appoint both a provisional government and a commission charged with the task of proposing permanent constitutional reforms. More immediately, since the Jacobins were still strong enough to offer resistance in the Council of Five Hundred, and might even yet secure support from Paris, it was thought essential to arrange the removal of the Councils from the capital. For this preliminary stage every possible preparation was made; but the problem of managing the Councils once they were out of Paris was apparently left largely to chance. As for the constitutional changes themselves, the probability is that no more discussion took place than was necessary to establish the existence of general agreement about some broad principles—which can be determined without

---

[1] Thiry, op. cit., pp. 61, 116.

[2] Significantly, the apparently obvious alternative solution, that of subordinating the executive to the legislative to a greater extent, does not seem to have been thought worthy of consideration. This may be explained in part by the power of the Jacobins in the Five Hundred in 1799 and by the identification of legislative supremacy with Jacobinism and Terror in 1793–4; essentially, however, men thought in terms of making government enlightened and efficient, not in terms of its responsibility to parliament.

difficulty from the course of events in France and in the associated republics since 1795.[1]

The day of 9 November 1799, immortal as that of 18 Brumaire, was in fact one of public pageantry and private sharp practice. Before daylight, messages were sent out calling the members of the Council of Elders to an emergency meeting at 7 a.m.; but good care was taken to ensure that all those unsympathetic to Sieyès received these notices too late. When the Council met, Sieyès' associates at once reported the discovery of a formidable Jacobin plot, and so succeeded in obtaining a decree by which the Elders, in accordance with their constitutional powers,[2] transferred the entire Legislative Body to St Cloud, where both Councils were required to meet at noon next day. At the same time Bonaparte was made responsible for their security and appointed to the command of all military forces in the area save the guards of the Councils and of the Directory—a reservation which he subsequently deleted personally. This appointment of a military commander by the Elders alone was one of doubtful legality, but as all deliberation in Paris was now illegal, opposition was easily stifled. Moreover, as a military review had been arranged for the occasion, troops were already lining the streets, and all that remained was for Bonaparte to take control. Having assembled a multitude of officers at his house on the pretext of a sudden journey, he was able to answer the Elders' call by immediately leading a brilliant cavalcade to the Tuileries. By mid-morning he had somewhat ambiguously sworn to defend a Republic founded upon true freedom, and was free to review the troops in the sunshine.

The old government, however, was not yet quite defunct. At an early hour Gohier and Moulin, whose conduct throughout seems to have been as irreproachable as it was unrealistic,[3] attempted to convene a meeting of the Directors at the Luxembourg. They found, however, that Sieyès and Roger Ducos were unaccountably absent, and Barras—whose pres-

---

[1] See chapter 8 below.

[2] The Constitution of the Year III (1795), Articles 102, 103. These authorised the Council of Elders to change the place of residence of the Legislative Body by specifying the place and time of a new meeting; such a decree was to be irrevocable, and no further deliberation by either Council in the town where they normally resided was from that time onwards to be valid.

[3] Gohier's indignation about the duplicity surrounding him—he had been invited at midnight to join Josephine for breakfast at 8 a.m., but was suspicious enough to send his wife instead—permeates his own account of events: Lescure *Bibliothèque des Mémoires, Nouv. sér.*, t. XXX, no. 2: *Mémoires sur les Journées révolutionaires* (Paris, 1875). Vandal, op. cit., I, p. 301, however suggests that he was at least partially privy to what he regarded as a move to eliminate Barras.

ence would at least have given them majority standing—was long at his toilet. Barras was in fact awaiting a summons from Bonaparte, whose ally he supposed himself to be: but when Talleyrand and Admiral Bruix called upon him, they came with a letter of resignation ready for his signature: 'Convinced that the perils of liberty are now surmounted . . . I joyfully resume the simple rank of citizen'. Rejoicing or sorrowing, Barras probably accepted at least the promise of something substantial, and so allowed himself to be persuaded to depart for his country house, suitably escorted by a strong guard of dragoons. Gohier, having bitterly upbraided Fouché for his disloyalty, next accompanied Moulin to the Tuileries, where they discovered their two missing colleagues in conference with Bonaparte and nearly all the ministers.[1] Only then did they become fully aware of what was in progress; but although they were pressed to resign, as Sieyès and Ducos said they had done themselves, they refused to do so, and returned instead to the Luxembourg—where Moreau neutralised them (and himself) by keeping them in close protective custody. Not until next day, when it had become obvious that no one was prepared to lift a finger for the Directory, did they consent to resign.

Thus far all had been successful, Paris seeming delighted by developments and more elated than over-awed by the activities of the army. What is more, at the Bourse the price of government stock had already risen sharply. The Councils, however, had still to be encountered at St Cloud, and to the astonishment of Cambacérès, at this time Minister of Justice, an evening meeting of all the principals with Bonaparte failed to reach any positive decisions about how the next step should be taken. It seems, indeed, that both Bonaparte and Sieyès were relying on each other to control the Councils, and as Bonaparte refused outright to arrest the leading Jacobin deputies, no one knew quite what to do.[2]

Probably on this account, the day of 19 Brumaire (10 November) was to prove one of protracted uncertainty. During the morning deputies, officials, military detachments and spectators converged on St Cloud; but like Madame de Staël, who had returned to Paris from Switzerland the previous day and was now ready to remain or depart as things developed, a good many people kept their carriages close at hand. To make matters worse, accommodation for the Councils was not ready until well into the afternoon, and as the deputies waited on the terraces

[1] Robert Lindet, then Minister of Finance, had only arrived belatedly; Dubois-Crancé, the ex-Montagnard Minister of War, did not attend at all, and the *coup* marked the conclusion of his political career.

[2] Vandal, op. cit., I, p. 321.

of the palace they became aware that the alleged terrorist plot was merely a myth meant to excuse and facilitate a conservative stroke against the existing system. Consequently when the Councils at last met, the fury of the Five Hundred, whose members all took an oath to maintain the Constitution of 1795, was reflected in the uneasy protests and indecisive proceedings of the Elders; and soon the re-appearance of the Jacobin generals, Jourdan and Augereau, signified that the success of the *coup* was swaying in the balance.

It was in these circumstances that Bonaparte reluctantly agreed to attempt to win the day by addressing both the Councils personally. This proceeding, one utterly unnatural to him, was completely unsuccessful. In the Elders he was, to say the least, unconvincing and unimpressive,[1] and his entry into the Five Hundred occasioned a scene which was subsequently made symbolic of the criminal character of Jacobinism and of the futility of parliamentary tumult. Greeted as soon as he was seen by angry cries of 'Down with the tyrant!' and 'Outlawry, outlawry!', Bonaparte was surrounded, jostled, and apparently even seized by the shoulder by one particularly powerful deputy, Destrem.[2] Helpless and genuinely shaken, the general had to be rescued by Murat and other officers from outside.

This shocking situation at least had the effect of precipitating action, in the initiation of which the salient figure was not Bonaparte but his brother Lucien. As President of the Five Hundred, Lucien kept the deputies from taking any firm decisions for as long as he could, and then contrived to join his brother outside the building. There, he appealed to the soldiers to disperse a factious minority of men who had sought to slay, and were now about to proscribe, the general. Momentarily, however, all was again in doubt, for as the men of the regular army had been deliberately kept well to the rear, the troops addressed were the guards of the Councils, and these were clearly loath to betray their trust. Only Lucien's promise to stab Bonaparte with his own hand if he should ever harm liberty, and the bold example of Murat in advancing towards the hall, made these men move. Once begun, however, all was quickly over: entering the Orangerie with bayonets fixed and drums beating, the guards swiftly cleared the room, many of the deputies shedding their distinctive Roman robes and following the spectators ignominiously through the windows. Thus—unexpectedly—the Legislative Councils

---

[1] It was on this occasion that Bonaparte so far lost composure that he spoke of appealing to his 'companions in arms': 'Remember that I march accompanied by the god of Victory and the god of fortune'.

[2] See also the note at the beginning of chapter 8 below.

as well as the Directory perished in the *coup d'état* of 18–19 Brumaire. While this dramatic event ended all effective opposition to the completion of the *coup*, its immediate sequel may be thought equally indicative of the situation at the time. In the first place, the Elders accepted the proposal that, in place of the Directory, there should be a provisional Consulate composed of Sieyès, Roger Ducos and Bonaparte, and that their own Council should adjourn for six weeks while a committee of 25 of its members prepared new constitutional laws. Since the Council of Five Hundred was no longer in session, this 'decree' was, of course illegal. Matters, however, were not left there. Later that night a sufficient number of the Five Hundred were brought together again and persuaded to accept the same proposals—save that there were now to be two constitutional commissions instead of one, and that 62 deputies of the Five Hundred were named as being excluded from their seats. The Elders, having withdrawn their initial 'decree', then reconsidered and approved the revised resolutions, which became the Law of 19 Brumaire.[1] 'Legality' was thus preserved and some provision made for the re-establishment of constitutional rule, and at two o'clock in the morning of 11 November (20 Brumaire) the three provisional Consuls took an oath of loyalty to 'the Republic, one and indivisible', as well as to 'Liberty, equality and the representative system'.

Since Bonaparte now had power within his grasp, the *coup d'état* of 18 Brumaire (as the events of both days are commonly called) cannot reasonably be isolated from its consequences—and, as we have seen, the words 'representative government' had for him a singularly literal meaning. It may nevertheless be said here that neither the causes nor the course of the *coup* seem in themselves to support the view that these events mark the destruction of constitutional government and the advent of military dictatorship in France. Rather would it seem that the Constitution of 1795 had long since lost all validity; as Bonaparte told the Elders when he appeared before them at St Cloud: 'You yourselves destroyed it on 18 Fructidor, on 22 Floréal, on 30 Prairial: nobody has any respect for it now'. Far from being on the point of attaining stability, the Directorial régime seems to have been irretrievably committed to recurrent violence. Certainly the 'conspiracy' which led to the *coup* was one in which almost everybody of any prominence participated, and a good many of these people were high-minded men who had become convinced that drastic change was fully justifiable. To them, the purpose

---

[1] *L'Ancien Moniteur*, XXIX, pp. 893–4. It may be remarked that the Moniteur specially refers to the evening session of the Five Hundred as beginning at 9 p.m., 'the majority of the Council having returned'.

of that change was not to destroy, but to re-establish, the Republic; and although experience showed that for this the executive had to be made more powerful, their objective, as Cabanis told the rump of the Five Hundred on the night of 19 Brumaire, was not to create, but to prevent, dictatorship.[1]

How far Bonaparte himself shared these opinions still remained to be seen: but at least he seemed to do so. If in private his masterful attitude had already caused Sieyès some alarm, in public his presence had been far more important than his actions; and as his avowed concern was for the general interest, so all his influence had been directed against pro-scriptions and the use of military force. In fact, of course, the army's strength was displayed throughout the crisis, and—when all else failed —soldiers were used to disperse the deputies of the Council of Five Hundred. This, however, does not necessarily mean that Bonaparte's success was founded solely, or even primarily, upon military power. Rather would it seem that the *coup* was mostly a matter of civilian chicanery; that the display of arms was really superfluous, important though it was in re-associating civil and military opinion; and that the great majority of civilians and soldiers were at one in wishing to silence the Jacobin deputies—who were nothing if not intransigent. All were conscious that a past of prolonged stagnation might now at last be giving way to a more progressive and flexible future; but none could yet tell what balance would be struck between freedom and tyranny.

---

[1] Vandal, op. cit., I, pp. 394–6; Thiry, op. cit., p. 169. *Biog Notes:* CABANIS.

8. The Year of Achievement, November 1799-October 1800

Immediately after the *coup d'état* of 18–19 Brumaire, a grenadier, Thomas Thomé, was presented with a valuable diamond; and a little later the same man was publicly honoured, embraced by Josephine, and raised to the rank of captain. According to the story, he and three others had protected Bonaparte when the latter had been assailed in the Orangerie at St Cloud, and he had personally saved the general's life by thrusting himself forward to receive a dagger stroke aimed at Bonaparte by one of the deputies.

Apart, however, from this one piece of wild exaggeration,[1] the new government deliberately discouraged all attempts to dramatise the days of Brumaire. Far from being either royalist or revolutionary, these were presumed to have been essentially national and moderate, and the 24 delegates who were sent out to the provinces to explain what had occurred had explicit instructions to behave mildly and to emphasise that the cause of moderation had at last triumphed in France.

It should be said at once that this official interpretation of the days of Brumaire as what Cabanis called 'the *coup d'état* of the moderates' is far from being generally accepted. According to one view, the simple truth is that the power of the army, a political force ever since the soldiers were first called in to control Paris in the spring of 1795, had at last prevailed. A more mature argument, and one that bears the stamp of Lefebvre's great authority, is that as the revolutionaries were constantly confronted by counter-revolutionary conspiracy, by civil war and by allied coali-

[1] The story derives from Bonaparte's own proclamation of 19 Brumaire, according to which: 'Twenty assassins rushed upon me, and aimed at my breast. The grenadiers, whom I had left at the door, ran forward and placed themselves between me and the assassins. One of these brave men had his clothes pierced by a stiletto. They bore me off.' (*Ancien Moniteur*, XXIX, p. 900). The truth would seem to be that one of the deputies concerned in the scuffle, the Corsican Aréna, had been paring his nails when Bonaparte entered the Orangerie, that he still had his penknife in his hand when he was gesticulating at the general, and that the grenadier's collar was torn in the course of the affair.

tions, all their experiments with liberalism were bound to fail. Some sort of dictatorship was thus imperative; but since civil coercion, the Terror, had become anathema, the advent of military government was inevitable. By this view, Bonaparte's power was of this type from the very beginning: as Lefebvre put it, 'Regardless of what he and his apologists may have said, his rule was from its origins an absolute military dictatorship'.[1]

While some writers of this school are more inclined than Lefebvre to see gradual change in the extent and character of Bonaparte's power,[2] this is because they are also even more concerned than he to identify the *coup d'état* of Brumaire with the triumph of a particular social class. The Revolution, it is said, had in effect destroyed the bourgeoisie of the old order, and in its place there had appeared a new class of men whose wealth was founded upon speculation. First as Thermidorians and then as Directorials, these men, together with the minor merchants and the greater peasant proprietors who supported them, had sought both to exploit and to consolidate their position; but when in 1799 the threat of counter-revolution seemed likely to lead to a revival of the Terror—which was to these new 'notables' was synonymous with social democracy and economic regulation—they became Brumairians and brought Bonaparte to power in order to preserve their own social and economic supremacy. The *coup d'état* being thus essentially anti-democratic and anti-national, the general's subsequent success in suppressing political freedom occasions no surprise.

These recent restatements of the view that Brumaire was both the triumph of a class and the advent of a dictatorship of course contribute much to an understanding of the period. As we have seen, Bonaparte had indeed attained high office through the support of a particular group of politicians, and it would be more than naive not to recognise that some of those men, and many more who hastened to join them, had their own material interests well in mind. Moreover, even apart from the pressures exerted by the counter-revolution, the republicans' acceptance of some form of strong government had become an ever-present possibility; having failed in so much, and having become in the process so isolated a minority in the nation, their faith in their ability to enlighten their own generation was undoubtedly wearing thin. Yet while some characteristics

[1] G. Lefebvre, *Napoléon* (Paris, 1965), p. 65: '. . . *son pouvoir, de par son origine, fut une dictature militaire, donc absolue*'. I have followed the translation of Henry F. Stockhold (*Napoleon, From 18 Brumaire to Tilsit*, London, 1969, p. 63).

[2] See, for example, A. Soboul, *La Iʳᵉ République*, p. 291: '*Le 18 brumaire . . . ouvrit la porte au pouvoir personnel: mais l'évolution ne vint à terme qu'en 1804 . . .*'—although this is admittedly contradicted a few lines later.

of the time appear in high relief in these longer perspectives of history, others are apt to be veiled in shadows. That Bonaparte became Emperor of the French in 1804 is irrefutable: but to assume that he and all Frenchmen had perforce to travel a predetermined road from Brumaire onwards, and that neither he nor the Brumairians meant what they said about moderation and national unity, is not an approach likely to lead to a proper appreciation either of the men or of the issues of the day.

That the dominant spirit of the new government was that of Bonaparte is not in doubt. When its three members held their first official meeting in the Luxembourg on 11 November, Roger Ducos apparently surprised Sieyès by inviting Bonaparte to preside; and although they in fact agreed to officiate in daily rotation, it was at once evident that the general was not going to limit himself to military matters. Cross-questioning everyone in an endless succession of interviews, and daily rising from breakfast to say to his secretary 'Come, let us get to work!', Bonaparte was soon to justify the remark about him which is attributed to Sieyès; 'Gentlemen, you have a master—a man who knows everything, wants everything, and can do everything'.[1] He was nonetheless technically but one of three members of a provisional government; and the powers of that government were simply those of the old Directory, with the additional right of proposing laws for the approval of the two commissions appointed by the Elders and the Five Hundred. If in the circumstances this position can be considered equivalent to a dictatorship, it is only the more remarkable that throughout its brief life the Provisional Consulate in fact acted with the utmost circumspection.

At this time one of Bonaparte's first concerns was simply that of investigation. Thus the delegates who were sent to the provinces were not expected to act as pro-consuls, but to assess public opinion and return as soon as possible. Although similar enquiries were begun in all directions, the state of the nation's finances was subjected to particularly searching review. Indeed, it is said that Gaudin, who now accepted the Ministry of Finance which he had refused in 1795 and which he was to hold until 1814, was given but two hours to establish himself in office and begin work.[2] The appointment of General Berthier to the Ministry of War[3] similarly reflects Bonaparte's anxieties about the condition of the armies and the military situation in western France.

---

[1] Bourrienne, *Memoirs of Napoleon Bonaparte*, p. 104; Las Cases, cited J. M. Thompson, *Napoleon Bonaparte*, p. 145.

[2] J. Thiry, *Le Coup d'état du 18 brumaire*, pp. 183–4.

[3] Berthier was replaced by Carnot at the time of the Marengo campaign, and in 1800 Mollien as Minister of the Treasury supplemented Gaudin as Minister

While the results of these first enquiries were reassuring so far as news of the nation's reception of the *coup d'état* was concerned, Bonaparte was certainly appalled by the destitution of the Treasury and by the general stagnation of public administration. According to his secretary, Bourrienne, he spent most of his time at the Luxembourg in planning ways and means of raising money, and after visiting a prison he exclaimed: 'What fools these Directors were! To what a state have they reduced our public establishments! But wait a little: I will put all in order.'[1] Although initially the government had to live from day to day, relying heavily upon loans from bankers, its first important measures were financial ones. On 19 November the savagely selective taxation of the previous August, the 'forced loan', was abolished in favour of a comparatively small all-round increase, and on 24 November the earlier legislation of Ramel was reinforced by a law which made still more precise provision for the assessment and collection of taxation by officers of the central government. At the same time some of the traditional practices of the old order were boldly adapted and applied. In each department men of wealth were appointed as Receivers-General of Taxation and were compelled to make advances to the government in anticipation of revenue. Further, on 27 November a Security Bank was established and endowed with certain monopolies in order to support these promissory notes and other bonds issued by the government.[2]

The state's desperate need for money of course compelled Bonaparte to seek the cooperation and support of men of means and to promise them stability. As he told one delegation of bankers and notabilities, the government was to be one of 'social defence, friendly to order, respectful of all forms of property, and pacific in foreign affairs'.[3] This, however, should not suggest that his interest was limited to their well-being alone, for from the beginning he repudiated party and sought to unify the nation by calling all men to its service. Speaking always of a new order of things, his watchwords were those of reconciliation and reconstruction. Retaining the ex-Terrorist Fouché as Minister of Police, he

---

of Finance, The other Ministries, with their principal holders during the Consulate were: Marine (Forfait, to Decrès); Foreign Affairs (Talleyrand); Interior (Lucien, to Chaptal); Justice (Abrial); Police (Fouché) and Military Affairs (Dejean).

[1] Bourrienne, op. cit., pp. 104, 126.
[2] Lefebvre, G., *Napoléon* (Paris, 1965), pp. 83–4; Ponteil, F., *Napoléon Ier et l'organisation authoritaire de la France* (Paris, 1965), pp. 55–7; Godechot, *Les Institutions*, pp. 544–6.
[3] Calvet, H., *Napoléon* (Paris, 1966), p. 51.

remarked that the evil of the past must be forgotten; appointing Talleyrand to the Ministry of Foreign Affairs a few days later, he told him that all his concern must be for the future; and having both men as ministers, he asked: 'What revolutionary will not have confidence in an order of things in which Fouché is a minister? What gentleman may not hope to make a life in a country where a Talleyrand de Périgord has power? Guarded to left and right, I open a great road for all to follow.'[1] In the same spirit, as the Law of Hostages was abrogated on 13 November, so an order for the deportation of 37 Jacobins, drawn up and published by Fouché (probably at Sieyès' instigation)[2] was first disavowed and then revoked by Bonaparte on 25 November. Whatever his motives may have been, and however rigorous his rule was to prove, his advent at least offered France the novel experience of a *coup d'état* which was not accompanied by immediate purges and prompt proscriptions.

Nor is it a matter of small significance that the great work of the Provisional Consulate was the preparation of a new constitution. The horror that men had of any sort of arbitrary or illegal régime is well illustrated by the words of Boulay of the Meurthe when he raised the question of the constitution with Sieyès on the morrow of 19 Brumaire: 'So here we are in a provisional state of affairs . . . We must get out of it as soon as possible.'[3] It was, indeed, precisely because the Constitution of 1795 had made illegality unavoidable that so many men had accepted the *coup d'état*: Madame de Staël was not by any means alone in recognising that, as she wrote in 1798, 'in reality, the balance of powers in the present Constitution is redressed annually by revolution'.[4] On 19 Brumaire, too, the two Commissions of the old Legislative Councils had been specifically charged with the task of preparing fundamental changes in the old constitution, 'of which the defects and inconveniences have been made manifest by experience'.[5] If Bonaparte personally was not unduly concerned about constitutional niceties, his attitude and conduct certainly suggest that he, too, was anxious to legalise his position as rapidly as possible.

So obvious were the 'defects and inconveniences' of recent years that there was a wide measure of agreement about the nature as well as the

---

[1] Thiry, op. cit., pp. 185, 193; Soboul, *La Ire République*, p. 305.

[2] Bastid, *Sieyès et sa Pensée*, pp. 249–50. It seems probable that Fouché published the list in order to promote its disavowal.

[3] Thiry, op. cit., p. 181.

[4] *Des Circonstances actuelles qui peuvent terminer la Révolution*, Godechot, *La Pensée révolutionnaire 1780–1799*, p. 287.

[5] Godechot, *Les Institutions*, p. 473.

necessity of change. Generally, men attributed the evils of the time to what was regarded as the excessive power of their parliaments. This, it was felt, produced at best a great deal of legislation, but very little effective law. The experience of Revolution had, moreover, convinced many that the turbulence and irresponsibility of large elected assemblies was a direct cause of arbitrary government, particularly if such assemblies sat in permanent session and had sufficient control of legislation and finance to force the executive to have recourse to violence in self-defence. Beyond this, not only frequent elections but also the electoral process itself had become abhorrent to all but the ostracised Jacobin minority. Faith in democracy, so remarkable a feature of 1789, had been replaced by disillusionment and distrust. This was not, as some would say, simply a matter of the self-interest of the beneficiaries of the Revolution: as Madame de Staël very rightly, if perhaps somewhat optimistically, wrote: 'The Republic was established 50 years before opinion was ready for it', and in consequence 'free elections would be incompatible with its maintenance'.[1]

Essentially, therefore, the difficulty was that of reconciling the representation of the people in public affairs with the foundation of a system of government which should be strong and stable, but yet subject to the rule of law. Since the shock of Fructidor in 1797 a good many prominent people, including Bonaparte, Benjamin Constant, Madame de Staël and Daunou,[2] the principal architect of the Constitution of 1795, had written about this, and the Directors had drafted or amended many constitutions for the various satellite republics—work in which Daunou and Bonaparte had both had a considerable share. As Raymond Guyot pointed out some years ago,[3] these various plans and projects reflect certain broad developments in French constitutional ideas, including the growing belief that constitutions were best prepared and presented by a small group of men working together for a limited period. In general, the tendency was towards centralisation. Executive power was concentrated in fewer hands, and the power of representative assemblies was limited by making them smaller and allowing them to meet only at specified intervals and for the particular purpose of sanctioning the government's legislative and financial proposals. In general, too, the process of election was being abandoned in favour of some combination

---

[1] 'des élections abandonnées à elles-mêmes seraient très défavorables au maintien de la République . . .' Godechot, La Pensée révolutionnaire, p. 287.

[2] Biog. Notes: DAUNOU.

[3] R. Guyot, 'Du Directoire au Consulat: Les Transitions', Revue Historique, Vol. CXI (1912), pp. 1–31.

of co-option and nomination, and there was growing insistence upon 'graduality of function'—by which only those experienced at one political or administrative level would be eligible for appointment to the next. On the other hand, parliaments were being thought of as bi-cameral, or even tri-cameral, with upper chambers independent enough to check abuses either by government or by the more popular assemblies. That there should also have been a tendency to extend the franchise is more remarkable, for all else deprived the voters of effective power. If in this self-interest is evident, there was also some real belief that the principle of popular sovereignty should be maintained in this way until the electorate was better educated and more rational.

In the light of all this it is not surprising that Boulay of the Meurthe should have been astonished to discover on 11 November that Sieyès, the great constitutional authority who was commonly assumed to have perfected a plan for the better government of France, had nothing prepared in writing.[1] He was, however, ready enough to explain his ideas to Boulay, who took notes and prepared a draft constitution from them. Complex though this was, it accorded well with contemporary thought, for Sieyès proposed to limit the activity of the electorate to the preparation of lists of persons eligible for public office in each locality. These 'notables', in their turn, were to list those of their own number eligible to act at the departmental level; and in the same way the notables of the departments would name from amongst themselves those best suited to accept national responsibilities. After an initial period of co-option, it would be possible from this foundation to fill three parliamentary assemblies: a Tribunate, to deliberate upon legislation proposed by the government, and to watch over the interests of the people; a Legislative Body, to act as a jury and approve or reject legislation without discussion; and a Senate, to nominate the members of the other two chambers and to act as a supreme court with the authority to invalidate all unconstitutional actions. As for the executive, Sieyès proposed that there should be two Consuls, one for domestic and one for foreign affairs, each of whom would name his own ministers and so initiate a descending scale of appointments through the ranks of the eligible notabilities. To crown this edifice there was to be a 'Grand Elector', a representative of the Republic who would be without any personal power except that of appointing, and if necessary dismissing, the Consuls. Nominated by the

---

[1] Thiry, op. cit., p. 226. Since various versions of Sieyès' thoughts were prepared by different people—Boulay, Roederer and Daunou—it is by no means easy to determine what was his alone. Expressions like 'Sieyès' plan' in what follows should be read with this point in mind.

Senate, which was for Sieyès by far the most important body in the state, the Grand Elector would also be liable to 're-absorption' into it if he should exceed the bounds of his authority.

This carefully-contrived system of checks and balances was made known to Bonaparte through such intermediaries as Roederer[1] in the last week of November 1799. Up to a point he seems to have accepted it without much demur, as well he might; but Sieyès' proposals for the division of the executive power filled him with scorn. 'Such a government', he wrote, 'is a monstrosity, composed of heterogeneous ideas which offer nothing reasonable.'[2] More particularly, he rejected outright the idea of the Grand Elector—'a pig manured with millions'—as a device expressly designed to reduce him to impotence.[3] After further consultations, and even a stormy interview with Sieyès, had failed to break the deadlock, Bonaparte took matters much more into his own hands. At the beginning of December the members of the 'constitutional sections' of the two Commissions appointed on 19 Brumaire were assembled at the Luxembourg, where Daunou, one of their number, was charged with the task of drafting an alternative series of proposals. The result of this was that by 7 December Bonaparte was able to call to his apartments all 50 members of the two Commissions, and to set before them, in the presence of Sieyès, both the latter's proposals and those of Daunou, which were at once more realistic and more liberal.[4] A week of intensive effort then sufficed for him to secure approval of those features of each draft which came closest to meeting his own ideas about 'representative government', his success being due in no small measure to his ability and tirelessness.

On 13 December this process culminated in what really amounted to a second *coup d'état*. In the first place, the members of the two Commissions were abruptly called upon to sign as complete the Constitution as it then stood, no vote being taken. Since the Commissions ought strictly to have reported back to the old Legislative Councils, which were technically only adjourned until mid-February, this informality actually broke the strand of legal continuity which had been preserved in Brumaire. Further, although votes were cast for the election of new Consuls, Bonaparte suddenly set them aside uncounted and called upon

---

[1] *Biog. Notes:* ROEDERER.

[2] Thiry, op. cit., p. 231 citing *Corres.* XXX, 409.

[3] It is equally, if not more, likely that Sieyès was thinking that Bonaparte would be the Consul particularly charged with responsibility for diplomatic and military affairs, and that the Grand Elector would be Sieyès himself.

[4] Guyot, op. cit., pp. 30–1.

Sieyès to select the three he preferred. Sieyès, who seems to have lost most of his real interest in proceedings as soon as the unity of his original grand design had been shattered, responded by nominating Bonaparte, Cambacérès and Lebrun, names which were at once approved by acclamation. As Bonaparte had already given much thought to the selection of his colleagues, the probability is that all this was pre-arranged; and in the same way, it was understood that Sieyès himself would become president of the new Senate, the recruitment of which would then be in his hands.[3]

Despite these developments Sieyès' plan remained the foundation of the new Constitution. As he had proposed, lists of those who had the confidence of the electorate (which consisted of all adult citizens)[2] were to be drawn up in the year beginning in September 1800, and in the interim the representatives of the people were to be chosen from above. His tri-cameral parliament was also accepted: a Tribunate of 100 members and a Legislative Body of 300 were to be nominated by a Senate consisting initially of 60 selected members. Although Daunou had wanted the Tribunate as well as the Executive to have the right of proposing legislation, Sieyès plan prevailed here also: laws were to be drafted and proposed by a Council of State, debated by the Tribunate, and argued by representatives of both these bodies before the Legislative Body, which was to approve or reject them without either amendment or discussion. Similarly, although Bonaparte distrusted Sieyès' Senate and did all he could to weaken it, it was established as the guardian of the Constitution, and Daunou's alternative proposal of a separate High Court was set aside. On the other hand, Sieyès' Grand Elector and divided executive disappeared, and in accordance with Daunou's proposal executive power was entrusted to three Consuls, of whom one, the First Consul, was to have superior powers and greater responsibilities.

It was in this that Bonaparte's own impact upon the Constitution was most apparent, for he had succeeded in securing for the First Consul powers far greater than anything Daunou or anyone else had contemplated. Being appointed by name as First Consul for a term of ten years, Bonaparte was to have a monopoly of the power of appointing all officers of state, civil and military, local and national, excepting only judges of

---

[1] Godechot, *Institutions*, pp. 479–80.

[2] With minor exceptions, all resident Frenchmen over the age of 21 were citizens—the stipulation regarding residence of course excluding all *émigrés*. The Constitution of 1799 is available in English in J. Hall Stewart, *A Documentary Survey of the French Revolution*, pp. 767–79.

appeal and justices of the peace. Having, as has been said, the right to initiate legislation through the Council of State, he had also complete control of all proposals concerning taxation and expenditure, both of which were to be included in an annual financial law. Most important of all, the Consulate was not to be a deliberative body controlled by the will of its majority: the Second and Third Consuls were to be consultative officers, with the right of recording their opinions—but 'thereafter the decision of the First Consul shall suffice'.

In the view of Vandal, whose history of the advent of Bonaparte has become a classic, these few words determined the destiny of France.[1] Though that may be hyperbole, they certainly restored to government the unity of direction it had so largely lacked since 1789. The authority of the First Consul was also sanctified by massive popular support, for the Constitution of the Year VIII (1799) had a final article, apparently added at Bonaparte's own behest, to stipulate that it should be submitted to the people for acceptance. A plebiscite was consequently held in the month of Nivôse (mid-January–mid-February, 1800). This of course amounted to a vote of confidence in a régime which was already in existence and to which there was no alternative; and as the customary meetings of the primary assemblies were now replaced by a procedure for the formal registration of individual opinions, the part played by the people in establishing the new order was in reality no more than minimal. It is nevertheless clear that before Brumaire many men had regarded the complete collapse of government, if not an actual dissolution of society, as imminent and apparently inevitable,[2] and that the Constitution's promise of order and a more closely regulated freedom was correspondingly welcome. The general opinion may indeed be rightly represented by that of the woman who was reported to have said that it was enough for her to know that Bonaparte was in the Constitution.[3] Certainly the result of the plebiscite—which was given as 3,011,007 in favour, as

---

[1] Vandal, A., *L'Avènement de Bonaparte* (Nelson, 1910), II, p. 25.

[2] See, for example, the private letter of L.-J. de Roujoux, Prefect of Saône et Loire: 'by 18 Brumaire of Year VIII we were perishing, we had not six weeks existence left, the social order was falling into absolute dissolution' (M. Rebouillat, 'L'Etablissement de l'administration prefectorale dans le département de Saône et Loire', *Revue d'Histoire Moderne et Contemporaine*, t. XVII (1970), p. 867; or the *Souvenirs* of de Broglie (I., pp. 31–2): "Those who have not lived through the epoch of which I speak can form no idea of the profound misery into which France fell [between Fructidor and Brumaire]. We were plunging back under full sail into the abyss of the Terror without a gleam of consolation or of hope.'

[3] Calvet, op. cit., p. 53.

compared with 1,562 against[1]—was overwhelmingly positive; and since the Constitution, unlike all those that had preceded it, did not attempt to restrict the power of government by any definition of fundamental political rights, Bonaparte's position at the opening of the year 1800 was one of exceptional legal strength.

It was nevertheless by no means one of arbitrary power. If Bonaparte had become pre-eminent by participating in Sieyès *coup d'état*, his first care had been to make his authority legitimate; and since legislation had to be approved by the Legislative Body, and final constitutional decisions were reserved for the Senate, the Constitution seemed to impose real limits upon his freedom of action. It was, indeed, an abuse of power by the Tribunate that was then most commonly feared. Moreover, although the Constitution had been hurriedly completed to Bonaparte's own considerable advantage, this was probably due much more to his impatient desire to tackle practical problems than to any machiavellian project of self-aggrandizement. Rather would it seem that at this time his real wish was, as Cambacérès supposed, simply that of being the chief magistrate of a magnificently organised Republic.[2] To the liberal republicans, too, Bonaparte seemed at once one of themselves[3] and a man of sufficient stature to be above considerations of sordid self-interest. As Garat told the commissioners of the Elders on 14 December, the limitation of the power of the executive would be all the stronger for being enshrined not in a charter, but in the heart and even the passions of a really great man.[4] Although Sieyès took umbrage, declaring that he would not be a mere aide-de-camp and that he sought only to retire,[5] he was apparently consoled by the influence he had in the selection of senators and deputies, as well as by the gift of a substantial estate.

It was in this atmosphere, although of course considerably before the outcome of the plebiscite was known, that Bonaparte first caused the Constitution to be published on 15 December 1799 and then declared it to be in effect on 25 December. At the same time, and amid much

---

[1] Godechot, *Institutions*, p. 480—where the number of abstentions, something over 4 millions, is stressed. For the falsification of the figures by Bonaparte's staff see C. Langlois, 'Le plébiscite de l'an VIII ou le coup d'état du 18 pluviôse an VIII', *Annales historiques de la Révolution française*, XXIV, pp. 43–65, 231–46. Comparable figures for the Montagnard Constitution of 1793 and the Constitution of 1795 are: 1,801,918 to 11,610, and 1,057,390 to 49,938.

[2] Thiry, J., *L'Aube du Consulat* (Paris, 1948), p. 9.

[3] Carey, R. G., *The liberals of France and their relation to the development of Bonaparte's dictatorship, 1799–1804* (Chicago, 1947), p. 3.

[4] *Procès-verbal, Commission du Conseil des Anciens*, p. 223.

[5] Bastid, *Sieyès et sa Pensée*, p. 255.

soliciting for appointments, the processes of nomination were hurried forward. As has been said, Bonaparte had personally selected as the Second and the Third Consuls two respected moderates, Cambacérès and—as a man more representative of the old order—Lebrun,[1] both of whom had much administrative as well as political experience. Together these two assisted Sieyès and Roger Ducos, the two Provisional Consuls who had been named as Senators in the Constitution, to nominate a majority of the new Senate, which was then filled by co-option on 25 December.[2] This chamber, of which such eminent men of letters as Monge and Volney were typical members, then remained in session overnight to approve Sieyès' lists of the 300 members of the Legislative Body and the 100 members of the Tribunate. Inevitably, the majority of these assemblies consisted of men who had previously been deputies in one or another of the Councils of the Directory, there being little distinction in their somewhat colourless ranks save that the Tribunate included some notable liberal republicans like Daunou and Benjamin Constant. Thus those whom Vandal and others disparage as 'the beneficiaries of the Revolution'[3] were confirmed in their places without the embarrassment of election. Since Bonaparte had been even more prompt in appointing the members of his Council of State,[4] which was in fact to be for some time the real nerve-centre of the administration, he was able to inform the Senate on 27 December that his government was properly constituted and in operation.

The character claimed by this new order of things is at least indicated by the proclamations which accompanied each successive stage in its establishment. Of these the best known is that which marked the promulgation of the new Constitution on 15 December, a terse announcement which presaged the restoration of strength and stability to France both at home and abroad and ended with the bold assertion: 'Citizens, the Revolution is established upon its original principles: it is over'.[5] Here, reference to 'the sacred rights of property, equality and liberty'—

---

[1] *Biog. Notes:* CAMBACÉRÈS and LEBRUN.

[2] The two retiring and the two serving Consuls selected 29 Senators, a figure which raised the total—including Sieyès and Roger Ducos—to 31, a majority of the 60 members of which the Senate was initially to be composed. Membership was to be raised to 80 by the selection of the two new members annually, a process in which the First Consul and the two parliamentary chambers were to reach agreement.

[3] 'des révolutionnaires nantis': Vandal, op. cit., I, p. 13 and *passim*.

[4] This met for the first time on 22 December. Originally consisting of 16 members, it was rapidly increased to 29. See Thiry, op. cit., p. 29.

[5] J. Hall Stewart, *A Documentary Survey*, p. 780.

in that order—follows the significant statement: 'The Constitution is founded upon the true principles of representative government'. Somewhat more specifically, on 19 Brumaire Bonaparte had announced the advent of the Provisional Consulate with the words: 'Conservative, tutelary and liberal ideas have regained their former place';[1] and on 25 December, when the Constitution came into effect, he accepted the responsibility of making the Republic respected abroad, feared by its enemies, and loved by its own citizens—a love which would be fostered by government 'in the spirit of order, justice and moderation'.[2] According to Roederer, Bonaparte explicitly forbade him to include any specific promises in the drafts of these proclamations, remarking that his ten-year term of office would scarcely suffice to put things in order and that France had the right to judge him by his efforts over that period.[3] In general, however, the First Consul may be said to have promised to govern France in the public interest and in a way which would be socially and politically conservative, but neither illiberal nor unjust.

So far as France was concerned, Bonaparte's first major objective was the noble one of reconciliation. In a private letter dated 24 November he wrote: 'The simple title of French citizen is worth far more than that of Royalist, Clichien, Jacobin, Feuillant, or any of those thousand and one denominations which have sprung up during the past ten years from the spirit of faction, and which are hurling the nation into an abyss from which the time has at last come to rescue it, once and for all. That is the aim of all my efforts.'[4] Deeds appropriate to these remarkable words soon ensued. Unhampered by regard for any abstract idealism, and happily able to achieve much merely by relaxing the penal legislation of the past, Bonaparte began his Consulate by several significant measures of emancipation. On 24 December, most of those who had previously been proscribed—including men like La Fayette, Carnot and Barthélemy, Barère and Vadier—were granted amnesty and the opportunity of public service.[5] Next day the first steps were taken towards the abolition of legislation which penalised men by classes: the restrictions which had

---

[1] *Ancien Moniteur*, Vol. XXIX, p. 900; See also Aulard, *A Political History*, IV, p. 34, for comment upon the newness of the words 'conservative' and 'liberal'.

[2] Thiry, op. cit., p. 34.

[3] Roederer, P. L., *Mémoires sur la Révolution, le Consulat et l'Empire* (ed. O. Aubry, Paris, 1942), p. 120.

[4] *Napoleon's Letters*, ed. J. M. Thompson, pp. 80–1. The letter, written to Citizen Beytz, was intended as a reassurance and a justification of the *coup d'état*.

[5] The amnesty was not extended to Billaud-Varenne on the left nor to Pichegru on the right.

been imposed upon the relatives of *émigrés* were at last lifted; full civil rights were restored to those who, being of noble birth, had continued to reside in France; and since the Constitution precluded the making of any further exceptions to the laws about the *émigrés* themselves, the Council of State was instructed to prepare legislation to clarify and close the lists identifying these exiles.

At this same time similar measures marked the opening of a new era of toleration towards the Church. Sensitive as ever to changing conditions, the Police Minister Fouché sent out on 17 December a circular indicative of his desire that all consciences should be free and all cults equally respected; and before the end of the month he was instructed to investigate the position of all deported priests—some of whom were indeed immediately released from confinement on the Ile de Ré. Further, on 28 December an order allowed the Church to make use of all available buildings on any day save that of the *décadi*. That exception had little meaning, since the civic cult was now quietly abandoned, and in the interest of national unity Bonaparte abolished as contentious all the festival days of the Revolution save those commemorating the Fall of the Bastille on 14 July and the establishment of the Republic on 22 September. Still more significantly, on 30 December orders were issued to afford full funeral honours to the body of Pope Pius VI, which had remained in a coffin in the *Hôtel du Gouvernement* at Valence since that unfortunate man had died in August.[1]

In his dealings with the royalists Bonaparte struck a sterner note. At the time of the *coup d'état* of 18 Brumaire the Directory's commander in Western France, General Hédouville, had begun secret negotiations with the *chouan* leaders, whose recent successes in repeated raids on the towns and cities of Normandy and Brittany concealed the real exhaustion of their forces. By 12 December these negotiations had led to the opening of a conference at Pouancé, a village near Châteaubriant, and it then appeared that in return for such concessions as freedom of religion and the restitution of confiscated property, the royalists were prepared to lay down, but not to surrender, their arms. To Bonaparte, however, an agreement of this sort, akin to the one which had been concluded at La Prévalaye in 1795, was profoundly unsatisfactory: for although he certainly wanted to pacify the west, over which an army of some 40,000 men was dispersed, he saw submission, and ultimately the acceptance of

---

[1] Bonaparte had realised this situation when he passed through Valence on his way to Paris when he returned from Egypt. See E. E. Y. Hales, *Napoleon and the Pope* (London, 1962), pp. 12–14. The Pope's body was later returned to Rome for final burial.

the new oath of fidelity to the Constitution, as the prerequisites of permanent peace. Essentially, therefore, the question was not one of agreeing upon terms, but whether or not the royalists could accept Bonaparte's authority, and this problem was complicated by their hope that he might be persuaded to rule France for the King until a restoration could be openly effected. This issue was quickly clarified on 28 December when a personal interview took place at the Luxembourg between Bonaparte and two of the principal royalists, the guerilla 'general' d'Andigné and young Hyde de Neuville, the debonair and elusive head of the royalist organisation in Paris. To these men Bonaparte offered all that they asked, and he invited them, for their part, to abandon the lost cause of the Bourbons and enlist beneath his flag; but though he won their admiration, their allegiance remained beyond his reach.[1] The complete failure of the meeting was quickly followed by the disruption of the conference at Pouancé and by the publication of a proclamation in which the First Consul offered amnesty to all who would lay down their arms —and war and execution to all who would not. Soon afterwards Generals Brune and Lefebvre were sent to the west, to which strong reinforcements were transferred from the republican army in Holland.

Whatever may be thought of the beginning of the First Consul's period of power, his policies were evidently new and different. If he and the Brumairians together held a monopoly of political and social power, some of those who had previously been oppressed could now look to a brighter future, and few Frenchmen could have remained long unaware that strong hands had begun to direct affairs of state. Not all of this, however, was universally welcome. Although such *chouan* leaders as Bourmont and d'Autichamp capitulated early in 1800, others like Count Louis de Frotté and Georges Cadoudal remained irreconcilable, as did the more determined democrats; and even 'enlightened' liberals like Cabanis, who had welcomed the new régime, began to remember their conviction that government ought to be in accordance with the law, and to look askance at a Consul who not only rescinded revolutionary legislation, but did so by simple decree.[2]

---

[1] Hyde de Neuville, who describes Bonaparte on this occasion as: 'the marvellous man, the giant, a new Hercules', records: 'I would gladly have saluted the High Constable'. *Memoirs of Baron Hyde de Neuville* (trans. F. Jackman, 2 vols., London, 1913), p. 125ff. See also H. Gaubert, *Conspirateurs au temps de Napoléon* (Paris, 1962), pp. 14–16, and for the negotiations in general, Lefebvre, *Napoléon*, p. 91; Godechot, *La Contre-Révolution*, pp. 375–6; Thiry, *L'Aube du Consulat*, pp. 44–55.

[2] Carey, *The Liberals of France*, p. 5. Bonaparte made early and frequent use of administrative orders as distinct from major proposals requiring legislation.

Some feeling of this sort may have contributed to the tension which marred the first meetings of the legislature, which began its session on 1 January 1800. Since the Constitution confined the role of the larger assembly, the Legislative Body, to that of a jury, voting to accept or reject legislative proposals but not debating these itself, controversy was naturally concentrated in the smaller chamber, the Tribunate, which met in the Palais Royal.[1] Although in comparison with the great Convention, or even with the Council of Five Hundred, this hand-picked house was extraordinarily sober and sedate, two episodes in its earliest meetings antagonised Bonaparte and alarmed public opinion. The first of these may be dismissed as merely unfortunate. On 3 January, when the tribunes were considering the plight of tradesmen displaced by their own occupation of the palace, one of their number, Duveynier, recalled that its gardens had been the centre of the rising which had led to the fall of the Bastille and the end of royal absolutism; but he was also foolish enough to point the moral: '. . . if anyone should dare to speak here of an idol fifteen days old, we will remember that we have seen the destruction of one founded for fifteen centuries'. This untimely comment, which seemed to confirm the common fear that the Tribunate would be another centre of turbulence and dissent, was nowhere well-received, and matters were made worse two days later, when another tribune, in apology, exhausted everyone's patience by his repeated praises of the First Consul, 'he whom the whole universe admires'.[2]

The second episode was similar to the first in that a particular speech, this time by Benjamin Constant, gave great offence to Bonaparte. On this occasion, however, an important issue was involved. As it happened, the first bill to be put before the parliament was one to define in detail the legislative procedure outlined in the new Constitution. According to this, legislation drafted by the Council of State was to be presented to the Legislative Body by three of the Councillors, who would also explain its purpose and nature; and, after that, a copy of the proposed law—but not of the explanatory statement—would be sent to the Tribunate, together with notice of the date on which its representatives would be required to report and defend its decision before the Legislative Body and the Councillors. Not surprisingly, the tribunes were far from enthusiastic about this plan, their principal objections being that they would have no means of knowing what considerations had influenced

---

[1] The Senate, which met in private, would only be concerned with legislation if a constitutional issue arose.

[2] *Archives Parlementaires* (Paris, 1862), t. I, pp. 17, 35–6; Thiry, op. cit., pp. 115, 119.

the Councillors in framing the law, and that their own discussions might well be unduly hurried if they had constantly to conform to predetermined deadlines. It was in this context that Constant spoke on 5 January; but he broadened the debate by indicating that the tribunes' role would inevitably be one of endless opposition, which must appear factious since it could not be other than ill-informed. The assembly, he suggested, was being deliberately placed in an impossible position: regarded with suspicion, it was being treated as if it were an enemy army, and one which could be out-manoeuvred if it were presented with proposals in such rapid succession that none of them could ever be mastered or modified. Constant consequently urged his colleagues to reject the plan, and he appealed to the government to have more confidence in a house which was already far too weak to be dangerous to anyone.[1]

Neither result followed. On the contrary, Bonaparte reacted very sharply to this first indication of open criticism, permitting himself an outburst in which, according to one of the commissioners of the Tribunate, he exclaimed: 'My enemies deserve nothing from me save steel!'[2] Although no blow fell, this anger became common knowledge, and that night Madame de Staël's recently re-established salon was almost deserted. At the request of Fouché, moreover, Madame de Staël herself left Paris for a period of residence in the country; and Sieyès, too, found this an appropriate time to withdraw to the estate he had been given near Versailles—an acquisition awarded in recognition of his services, and one universally regarded as the price of his acceptance of the new order of things in France. Nor was the public, weary of rhetoric and contemptuous of assemblies of nominated placemen, impressed even by Constant's prescient appeal to authority: 'Do not grudge us the power of language!' The law on procedure was consequently accepted in the Tribunate by 54 votes to 26, and it was then approved by the Legislative Body by 203 votes to 23. Thus a potentially critical occasion passed without disaster, the Councillors of State being indeed sufficiently impressed by the seriousness of the tribunes' arguments to give them some reassurance about the duration of debates and to agree that

[1] *Archives Parlementaires*, t. I, pp. 12ff., with Constant's speech 30–4.

[2] Miot de Melito, *Memoirs*, p. 160. Although Bonaparte's anger was no doubt calculated, it may be explained without any assumption that he deliberately desired to discredit the Tribunate. If, as seems likely, he wished to limit their freedom of speech, Constant's comments would have been uncomfortably accurate, and his irritation may well have been increased by the recollection that Constant had but recently sought his favour with protestations of loyalty.

in future a copy of explanatory statements about legislation would be communicated to them. The tribunes' prospects of making constructive criticism effective through responsible debate had nevertheless been seriously compromised by the events of this first week of their proceedings.

Some five weeks later the results of the plebiscite were publicly proclaimed in Paris; and then, on 19 February 1800, the First Consul changed his residence and the seat of government from the Luxembourg to the Tuileries. The move, symbolic of the advent of an order which was meant to be as strong and durable as the old monarchy, was made a state occasion, for Bonaparte was well aware that a government must have charisma if it is to merit consideration.[1] In fact, many of the officials were hard-pressed to find formal attire, and the Treasury was so depleted that much of the procession was made up of carriages which commonly plied for hire, but which now had their licences overlaid with paper numerals. Bonaparte, however, rode with his colleagues in a coach drawn by six splendid white horses, and mounted men and martial music accompanied the Consuls to the Palace, where the Guards were reviewed for the first time on the newly-prepared parade ground. The efficacy of the spectacle in imparting a sense of the power and purpose now present in government was reflected in an appreciable rise in the funds; and a reception given next day for the diplomats of the states associated with France indicated that respectability had been restored to French affairs.[2]

Although to the First Consul none of this was unimportant, these beginnings of popular pageantry and official ceremonial were merely one aspect of the work of national reorganisation, a task to which he devoted concentrated effort for 18 hours each day. The figure is, perhaps, less revealing than an episode which occurred in the Council of State at a somewhat later date: the Councillors being exhausted by a particularly prolonged discussion, Bonaparte exhorted them to further efforts with the words: 'Wake up, gentlemen! It is only two in the morning—we must earn the money the people gives us!'[3] In the hands of such a man as this government inevitably acquired an ever more personal character. Thanks to his powers of work, his attention to detail, his remarkable memory, and the highly organised secretariat—an expansion of that of

[1] *'Cela m'ennuie, mais il faut parler aux yeux'* (cited in Thiry, op. cit., p. 95).

[2] Thiry, loc. cit. It is generally agreed that Bonaparte's court was from the beginning a moral one, and that both he and Josephine were quick to reprove dress or conduct inappropriate to the dignity of France and the challenge of the times.

[3] Roederer, *Mémoires*, p. 177.

the Directory—which grew up outside his study to record the innumerable reports which reached him and the instructions which he continually dictated, he soon became far more fully informed about the whole situation of France than anyone else could possibly be. Moreover, although Bonaparte invariably sought information and opinion from all whom he encountered, his constitutional position as the one who had the final voice in all administrative matters naturally led him to regard even his most trusted colleagues and councillors as advisers, just as the ministers were separately his subordinates. Thus although the government became in one way more formalised as a regular routine of meetings of the various sections of the Council became established, its structure remained essentially flexible: Bonaparte could call anyone he wished to any meeting for consultation, or he could simply summon an individual official to his study, the room in which the final decision would be taken and from which it would be put into effect.

Military considerations apart—and it is appropriate to recall that the First Consul was constantly preoccupied with the problem of mustering enough men to inflict a final defeat upon the armies of Austria—the situation of France in the early months of 1800 was certainly one which demanded immense and sustained endeavour in the exercise of firm authority. Contemporary reports[1] indeed indicate that the worst period of civil violence, the 'crime, devastation, discouragement and despair' which Fouché had reported in the west as recently as October 1799, was already a thing of the past. Although bands of brigands, 'the scum of revolution and of war',[1] still terrorised some parts of the west and the south-east, their depredations—the highway robberies, the raids on towns, the murders of local officials and of those who had purchased 'national' land—were gradually becoming less frequent and less widespread. But if the greater part of the country could be called tranquil, maladministration remained a major evil, for over a period of years decentralisation, political instability and the chronic impoverishment of

---

[1] I.e., those given in F. A. Aulard, *L'Etat de la France en l'an VIII et en l'an IX* (Paris, 1893), and in F. Rocquain, *L'Etat de la France au 18 Brumaire* (Paris, 1874). The former contains the reports compiled by Fouché dated 4 October, 22 October and 15 December 1799, and one built up by the Ministry of the Interior from information furnished by deputies in the autumn of 1800; the latter, reports to Bonaparte from various Councillors of State charged with investigating the condition of the various military areas in Year IX. Thus the greater part of the returns relates to late 1800–early 1801, when the general position had presumably improved.

[2] Rocquain, op. cit., p. 146: report of Fourcroy from the Vendée, December 1800.

the state had caused apathy, incompetence and downright dishonesty to flourish in the conduct of public affairs. In financial matters, the fact that there was a deficit of 400 million francs on the budget for 1799 may be matched with the malversations practised in Western France by General Tilly, whose accounts showed office expenses and 'extraordinary secret expenses' amounting to 121,294 francs in nine months,[1] or with the situation of the hospitals in the area of the Bouches-du-Rhône, which were in debt to an amount almost twice that of their normal annual income. In still more human terms, this last deficit meant that only 7lb of meat a day was available for 80 patients in one hospital in Toulon, and that in a single year only 18 out of 618 orphans survived in the hospitals of Marseilles.[2] Similarly, to say that the roads, bridges and public buildings of France, as well as its canals, rivers and harbours, were generally so sadly neglected that many of them were fast becoming unusable, is but to make a material statement: more significance may be seen in the report that in one area the theft of timber from a national forest had become such an established custom that whole communities would arrive to load their wagons in broad daylight, and even if the police made arrests the courts could not enforce convictions.[3] No multiplication of such examples is required to show that, as Fouché had pointed out in October 1799, the nation's ills were not to be met by any one law, but by a sufficiency of both funds and competent officials.[4]

The former need was not met easily, particularly as Bonaparte had of course to ensure that the army which was to defeat Austria was as well supplied as it could be. Throughout the year 1800 the government indeed lived from day to day, relying heavily upon bankers' loans, public lotteries and the caution money which had to be deposited by financial officers great and small. Despite the improved system of tax-collection and the gradual revision of the assessment rolls, no budget could be presented for 1800. Indeed, despite the final repudiation of most of the old National Debt in March 1801—when the 'Bonds of the Two-thirds' issued to stockholders in September 1797 were converted into annuities at the rate of $\frac{1}{4}\%$ of their capital value—in that year the expenditure of 526 million francs was still 32 millions more than income; only in the Year X (1801–2) was the first small credit balance achieved. Bold measures, like the arrest of the financier Ouvrard and the foundation of the Bank of France in February 1800, nevertheless enabled Bonaparte

---

[1] Ibid., p. 77: report of Barbé-Marbois from Brittany, January 1801.
[2] Ibid., pp. 29–34: report of François de Nantes from the Midi, January 1801.
[3] Ibid., p. 63; also François de Nantes.
[4] Aulard, op. cit., Fouché's report of 4 October 1799.

to take one decisive step: in the summer of 1800 the government paid the current salaries of its own officials in hard cash.[1]

By that time, too, the whole structure of local government had been reorganised and new officials had been appointed. The Law of 28 Pluviôse (17 February 1800), which was to prove one of the foundation deeds of modern France, was in part a simplification of the administrative areas established by the Constitution of 1795. The departments were now divided into *arrondissements*, each somewhat larger than the 'district' of the Revolutionary period; and since the attempt of 1795 to group many small communities into imaginary 'municipalities' was now believed to have made local government unnecessarily circuitous and complex, the commune was re-established as the third unit in a three-tier structure. The Law further made a single official answerable for each of the three levels: the department had its prefect, who was explicitly charged with responsibility for the administration of the whole area, and he had as his subordinates in each *arrondissement* a sub-prefect and in each commune a mayor. Save for the mayors of towns or villages with less than 5,000 inhabitants, who were to be appointed by the prefect, all these officials were to be the nominees of the First Consul. Similarly, at each level there was to be a local council, the general council of the department being supplemented by a smaller but more permanent prefectoral council; and all the members of all these councils were also to be nominated either by the First Consul or, at the municipal level, by the Prefects. The councils, it may be added, were generally to meet only for two weeks in each year, and they were to have no more than advisory functions, their principal business being that of the assessment of taxation.[2]

A month later the complementary law of 18 March made corresponding changes in the organisation of the judicial system. At the lowest level the local justice (*juge de paix*) remained as an arbitrator in civil disputes and a magistrate in simple police matters. The number of these justices, whose abilities were often limited, was, however, drastically reduced in favour of development at the second level, the court of the *arrondissement*. Apart from the division of these tribunals into sections in the larger towns, there were to be slightly more than 400 of them,

---

[1] Ouvrard was forced to disgorge some 14 million francs: Lefebvre, *Napoléon*, p. 94. For the financial measures taken at this time, see also A. Goodwin, 'The French Executive Directory, A Revaluation', *History*, XXII (1937), p. 209; Ponteil, op. cit., pp. 58–9; and Godechot, *Institutions*, p. 544ff.

[2] Lefebvre, op. cit., p. 85; Ponteil, op. cit., pp. 42–7; Godechot, op. cit., p. 508ff.

each having at least three judges and both civil and criminal jurisdiction. At the level of the department the existing criminal court was retained; but the new law established a fourth tier of 29 courts of civil appeal, whose areas of jurisdiction were loosely derived from those of the *parlements* of the old monarchy; and there was also to be a new Supreme Court consisting of 48 judges. A further important feature of the Law, and one which may even be considered indicative of a fundamentally repressive purpose in it, was a considerable increase in the powers of the representative of the central government who acted as the public prosecutor in criminal cases.[1] This reorganisation of the administration of justice was generally welcomed as one which made the lower courts more accessible to the public and yet provided for the possibility of appeal to a more distant and detached judicial body. As in the new system of local government, however, a major innovation was that appointment from above now replaced election from below: with the single exception of the justices of the peace, all the new judges—of whom there were to be a great many—were to be nominated, and all save those of the Supreme Court, who were to be selected by the Senate, were to be named by the First Consul.

Thus in local, as in national, affairs, the nomination of almost every public official by the central government appears as a fundamental feature of the Bonapartist system. This was not quite such a radical departure from precedent as was once supposed: as we have seen, in the days of the Directory the coincidence of electoral apathy and recurrent political crises had provided many opportunities for the Directors to replace one set of commissioners by another, and for those commissioners to rid themselves of locally-elected councillors. Bonaparte, however, carried the process considerably further, both by ensuring that his Prefects were complete strangers to their administrative areas and by eliminating popular election altogether. If this was in large measure a recognition of reality, it was also a far cry not only from the democratic ideal of 1789, but also from the aspirations of those republicans who still hoped that representative government, as they understood it, could gradually be expanded with the passing years. In fact, in 1800 and for many years to come local autonomy and local democracy were simultaneously stifled in France, and to some at least this seemed in retrospect to mark the real destruction of the republican system.[2] That the Tribunate both accepted the new laws and recommended them to the

---

[1] Lefebvre, op. cit., pp. 88, 129. On the reorganisation of the judicial system, see also Godechot, op. cit., p. 522ff., and Ponteil, op. cit., pp. 49–54.

[2] Miot de Melito, op. cit., p. 162.

Legislative Body should not, however, suggest that the tribunes were already completely cowed: brief as their debates had to be, they clearly show that the speakers had grave doubts about developments. The general feeling of the house was nevertheless that of Daunou, who urged his colleagues to approve the Law of 28 Pluviôse as one which the state of the country made a matter of the most urgent necessity: imperfect though it was, it would, he believed, be dangerous to delay its implementation by attempting to improve it.[1]

In terms of efficiency the merits of the new system were of course those of unity, strength and speed in administration. As the Legislative Body was told on 16 February, 'the orders of the government will be transmitted to the uttermost limits of the body politic with the swiftness of an electric current'; and this was no mean consideration at a time when a tribune could say: 'for ten years we have seen men deliberate when action was imperative!'[2] Nor were the Prefects themselves—of whom Thibaudeau was one—left in any doubt about the nature of their responsibility. Carefully selected by Bonaparte on the advice of his brother Lucien (who had been Minister of the Interior since December) and on that of others like Cambacérès, Lebrun and Talleyrand, all of whom were well informed about the personalities of their time, the first Prefects were most commonly men who had been moderates during the Revolution. Some of them, like Mounier, Jeanbon St-André and Letourneur, once a Director, had indeed then obtained eminence and well-merited renown. To those first presented to him before they left Paris to take up their appointments, Bonaparte nevertheless gave the explicit instruction: 'Never be men of the Revolution, but men of government'. That note was to be echoed repeatedly in the circulars subsequently sent out by Lucien. Officially the Revolution was over, and 'a profound gulf perpetually separates what is from what has been'; the Prefects had therefore to be oblivious of all party alignments and to strive to rally all citizens to the service of the country. Above all, they were to appreciate that independent judgment about matters of government was not required of them in their essentially local capacity: 'general ideas must come from the centre . . . it is from there alone that uniformity of action can emanate'.[3]

[1] *Archives Parlementaires*, I, pp. 179–86. The Law was accepted by the Tribunate by 71 votes to 25 and by the Legislative Body by 217 votes to 63; the re-organisation of the judiciary, the Law of 27 Ventôse, was similarly accepted in the Tribunate by 59 votes to 23 and in the Legislative Body by 232 votes to 41.

[2] *Archives Parlementaires*, I, p. 188. See also Ponteil, op. cit., p. 47.

[3] Rebouillat, M., 'L'Etablissement de l'administration prefectorale . . . Saône

None of this is to say that a highly efficient method of government was established in France overnight. For one thing, a centralised structure is not necessarily monolithic. In creating a particular Prefecture of Police for Paris, as Bonaparte did by the Law of 28 Pluviôse, he to some extent duplicated the function of Fouché as Minister of Police; and elsewhere the Prefects had responsibilities in police matters to the First Consul but not to the Minister. If that situation was one which tended to increase Bonaparte's personal power, it was also one ambiguous enough to enable Fouché to build up an administrative empire of his own. Moreover, by no means all the Prefects were as zealous and efficient as they were expected to be. As Bonaparte himself recognised, their immediate duty of stimulating recruitment and the payment of taxation was one that required a great deal of energy;[1] and there soon developed also the serious problem of maintaining the peace while returning *émigrés* lived alongside those who had acquired their lands.[2] But although the First Consul's correspondence was soon to be interspersed with expressions of his dissatisfaction with this Prefect or with that, at the beginning of March in the year 1800 he could write with confidence: 'Here everything goes from good to better. The Prefects are going to their posts, and I hope that within a month France will at last be an organised State.'[3]

Addressed to General Brune, then the principal republican commander in the campaign against the *chouans*, these words also reflect Bonaparte's growing conviction that the situation in Western France was at last being brought under control. The offer of an amnesty which was made at the end of December 1799 had in fact been followed by the resumption of military operations as soon as seven days of grace had expired; and in accordance with Bonaparte's explicit instructions, the war was to be waged without mercy until the *chouans* were genuinely and totally disarmed.[4] Under this pressure, the less bellicose leaders

---

et Loire', *Revue d'Histoire Moderne*, t. XVII (1970), p. 860, 863; Ponteil, op. cit., p. 101–2; and Savant, J., *Les Préfets de Napoléon* (Paris, 1958), pp. 28–30.

[1] Thiry, op. cit., p. 131.

[2] This is strongly reflected in the report compiled by the Ministry of the Interior and included by Aulard, *L'Etat de la France*. There is there the reference to the Prefect in Deux Sèvres who invited both those who had lost their estates and those who had acquired them to a reconciliation banquet . . . an experiment which 'has not produced the desired effect'.

[3] Markham, *Napoleon*, p. 68.

[4] 'The disarmament must be real and total . . . It would be a good example to burn two or three large communes chosen from those which do the most

soon yielded to the persuasions of the abbé Bernier,[1] an influential priest whose ardent royalism had recently changed to enthusiasm for the Consulate, and agreed to submit separately. Such surrenders as those of d'Autichamp and Châtillon, respectively (and nominally) the principal *chouans* south of the Loire and in the area of Maine and Anjou, left the more obdurate isolated, and one by one these were compelled to cease hostilities. Consequently as February ended Bonaparte was able to begin transferring troops from Western France to the eastern front, and on 21 April, after Brune's command had been passed to Bernadotte, the Constitution was declared to be in effect in the West as in the rest of France.

This successful repression of the guerilla resistance did not, however, mean that Bonaparte's war with the royalists was at an end. If organised rebellion was broken, brigandage inevitably continued. Moreover, amongst those who had fought the Revolution for so long there were still many who would never accept defeat. In Paris, the royalists' realisation in December 1799 that Bonaparte was not interested in acting on behalf of the King had led first to a hostile outburst against his régime in the Press, and then to a bold demonstration by Hyde de Neuville and his friends, who on 21 January commemorated the anniversary of the execution of Louis XVI by publicly distributing copies of his will and by contriving to drape the portico of the Church of the Madeleine with black cloth embellished with fleurs de lys. The First Consul, for his part, seized the opportunity to suppress all but 13 of the 73 journals then published in Paris. More deplorably, he chose to regard the royalists' escapade as a declaration of war, and ordered the immediate execution of Henri de Toustain, a young nobleman recently arrested in Paris while purchasing arms for the *chouans* in Maine. Further executions followed, and as more captives were shot the royalists grew the more determined to kill Bonaparte himself, an enterprise to which they easily attracted many desperate men as the *chouan* bands were broken and dispersed. Of the three most famous and obdurate leaders of the western rebellion, only one, Bourmont, who submitted on 4 February, came to terms with Bonaparte and lived in apparent peace in Paris. A second, Count Louis de Frotté, who remained longest under arms in Normandy, gave himself up under promise of safe conduct only to be arrested on the night of 15 February; he was shot, together with his six companions, three nights

---

harm . . . Weakness alone is inhumanity': to d'Hedouville, 5 January 1800 (*Corres.* VI, 4499) cited Thiry, op. cit., pp. 154–5.

[1] *Biog. Notes:* BERNIER.

17 A contemporary impression of the attempt to assassinate Bonaparte on 24 December 1800

18 Costume of the Tribunes, 1803

later when a sudden court-martial interrupted their journey to Paris. Whether or not this notorious episode was something Bonaparte deliberately designed,[1] it undoubtedly hardened the hostility of the third and greatest of the *chouan* leaders, the herculean peasant Georges Cadoudal,[2] whom Bonaparte had described to Brune as 'the most dangerous of enemies'. Although Cadoudal made a nominal submission on 14 February, he remained irreconcilable, and even two personal interviews with Bonaparte and the offer of high military command failed to move him. On the contrary, he promptly threw in his lot with his friend Hyde de Neuville, to whom he exclaimed as he left the Tuileries: 'What a mind I had to stifle the man with these arms!'[3] After this, open civil war and the possibility of an agreed peace gave way to a new *chouannerie* of conspiracy.

The First Consul was nevertheless now sufficiently sure of the situation in France to abandon the pretence of negotiation with the enemy abroad which had been maintained since December 1799.[4] Since the Russians had withdrawn from the war and the British were beyond Bonaparte's reach, his immediate objective was the defeat of the Austrians, and to this end he had on 25 January given secret orders for the formation of an additional army of at least 40,000 men at Dijon. In the circumstances the assembling and equipping of such a force was a

[1] The detachment escorting the Count to Paris was intercepted by a courier bearing orders for his immediate court-martial, and since he had not agreed to any surrender of arms his condemnation followed. It is not, however, clear whether Bonaparte knew that he had been afforded safe conduct, and Bonaparte's inclination towards striking examples has to be balanced against the freedom he afforded others to visit him in Paris. What is certain is that general policy of being ruthless to suppress the rebellion speedily was Bonaparte's, and that the pressure on the military to clean up quickly and be ready to move to the eastern frontier was perpetual.

[2] *Biog. Notes:* CADOUDAL.

[3] Gaubert, *Conspirateurs*, pp. 19–22, and Hyde de Neuville, *Mémoires*, p. 144, the two interviews taking place on 5 and 29 March. On the subject more generally, see: Lefebvre, *Napoléon*, p. 91; Godechot, *La Contre-Révolution*, pp. 376, 387; and Thiry, op. cit., pp. 154–74.

[4] When the Constitution was declared to be in effect, Bonaparte had sent personal letters to the King of Great Britain and the Emperor of Austria offering the possibility of peace. These were, in effect, rejected, primarily because neither power was convinced that the new régime in France offered a sufficiently secure basis for negotiation. In consequence, as perhaps in Bonaparte's intention, the sincerity of all concerned is open to question. All that can be said with confidence is that it is unlikely that Bonaparte would have been prepared to accept anything like the limitation of French power which the allies then felt to be essential to their own security.

matter of desperate improvisation, both financial and military,[1] and at its best the so-called Reserve Army was a stop-gap force. Intermingled with raw conscripts and a variety of garrison troops, the veterans of the west formed the core of an army which had few cavalry and even fewer guns. At the beginning of April, when Carnot took over the War Office and Berthier assumed its command, the Reserve Army nevertheless stood ready to move either into southern Germany or into Italy.

In the event General Melas, who had 100,000 Austrians under his command in northern Italy, moved forward first, falling with 60,000 men upon the remnants of the Army of Italy in Piedmont (6 April). Masséna was then besieged in Genoa, and Suchet and some 10,000 French were driven back to defend their own territory along the line of the River Var. Bonaparte, however, had no intention of meeting the enemy on the Mediterranean coast and breaking through the Maritime Alps into Piedmont and Lombardy as he had done so brilliantly in 1796. For the new campaign he had a still bolder plan: while Moreau, the commander of the Army of the Danube, was to cross the Rhine and advance through the Black Forest to the Danube, the Reserve Army was to march round Lake Geneva, cross the Alpine passes, and descend into the Lombardy plain from the north to assail the Austrians from the rear. For the success of this plan it was imperative that Masséna should maintain the defence of Genoa, for the longer the siege there lasted the more deeply the Austrians would be drawn into the trap which Bonaparte was preparing for them.

The French campaign began at the end of April, when Moreau's men crossed the Rhine and started a steady but successful advance eastwards; but to Moreau's chagrin the last important order which the First Consul gave before he himself left Paris on 6 May was one by which 25,000 men of the Army of the Danube were to be detached to reinforce the attack upon Italy. That operation also developed successfully, the main body of the French effecting the crossing of the Great St Bernard Pass between 15 and 23 May. Despite the famous picture by David, Bonaparte did not lead this advance in person, for the First Consul could not constitutionally hold military command. But although in fact Bonaparte unromantically followed in the rear of the army, David's representation of the march symbolises the strategic brilliance, the meticulous organisation and the driving energy responsible for this major feat of arms, and these were indisputably Bonaparte's alone. By 4 June, when Masséna's men, scarcely able to stand, finally yielded Genoa, Bonaparte—who had rejected the possibility of relieving them—

[1] See Lefebvre, *Napoléon*, pp. 93–4.

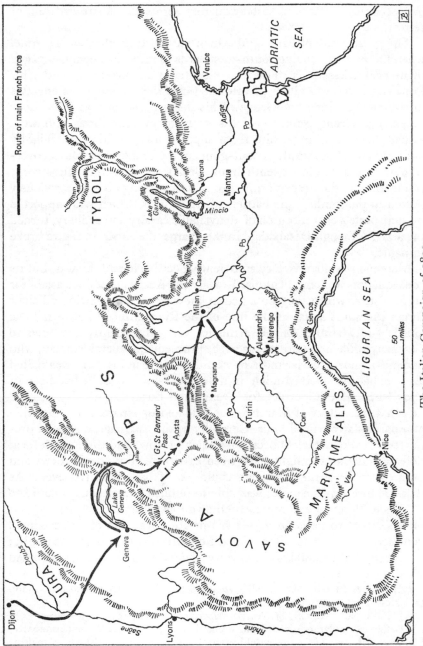

The Italian Campaign of 1800

Route of main French force

Dijon

JURA

Doubs

Saône

Lyons

Rhône

Geneva

Lake Geneva

SAVOY

A L P S

Gt St Bernard Pass

Aosta

Magnano

Turin

Po

Coni

Var

MARITIME ALPS

Nice

LIGURIAN SEA

Genoa

Alessandria

Marengo

Trebbia

Milan

Cassano

Po

Mincio

Mantua

Lake Garda

Verona

Adige

Po

TYROL

Venice

ADRIATIC SEA

0   50 miles

had occupied Milan and stood squarely across the Austrians' line of retreat.

The great battle of Marengo[1] which ensued took place on 14 June, when the French, moving south-westwards to meet the enemy, engaged them near Alessandria. This was essentially an encounter battle, for Bonaparte, who was either ill-informed or deceived about the enemy's intentions, had little knowledge of his dispositions, and at a late hour despatched strong elements of his army to prevent those who were actually advancing upon him from slipping away to his rear. Slightly outnumbered, but completely out-gunned, the French were almost overwhelmed: but at the eleventh hour Desaix, perhaps the ablest corps commander in the French army, brought in a strong division previously posted to the south of the battlefield. Its assault, which was supported by Bonaparte's concentration of all available cavalry and artillery, turned the scale. Although Desaix died in the charge, the Austrian centre broke in panic.

Marengo was not a victory sufficiently decisive to end the war, but its consequences were momentous. In Italy the Austrians at once asked for an armistice, which they obtained at the cost of withdrawing all their forces eastwards as far as the line of the River Mincio, between Lake Garda and Mantua. As this armistice was subsequently extended to Germany while negotiations for peace proceeded, General Moreau, who had out-manoeuvred far more powerful forces than his own, was halted after he had occupied Munich, in much the same way as he had been in 1797.[2] Far more important for France and Europe, however, was the fact that the victory of Marengo consolidated Bonaparte's own position at a particularly crucial hour. Carefully as the campaign had been prepared, it had nonetheless been a gambler's throw: had the French been defeated, the army might have been extricated, but the financial and political credit of the Consulate could hardly have been retrieved.[3] As it was, however, Bonaparte was able to publish a misleading manifesto in which Marengo was represented as a most magnificent victory, and on his return to Paris on 2 July his position was that of an acclaimed conqueror. Nor did he fail to seize the opportunity to impress the public: the return to the capital of the cavalry of the Consular Guard, which had

---

[1] Sir James Marshall-Cornwall, *Napoleon as Military Commander* (London and New York, 1967), pp. 94–113.

[2] J. Philippart, *Memoirs of General Moreau* (London, 1814), pp. 174–5.

[3] Lefebvre's judgment is still more positive on this point: 'If he (Bonaparte) had been defeated, his career would undoubtedly have been finished'. *Napoléon*, p. 99.

participated gloriously in the last charge of the battle, was carefully timed to occur on the anniversary of 14 July, a day which was now celebrated more enthusiastically than ever.

None of this blinded Bonaparte to the fact that his absence had revealed the terrible precariousness of his régime and of the new-found stability of France. Inevitably, his departure had opened the possibility of his defeat or death, so that even those loyal to him were compelled to consider to which man or system they might have to have recourse. Although little is known of these intrigues, it would seem that both Joseph and Lucien Bonaparte, who had their own reasons for feeling disgruntled, were involved in them, and that the names of men like La Fayette, Moreau, Bernadotte and Carnot were canvassed as those of possible successors to the consulship. The more intellectual associates of Sieyès and Madame de Staël, both of whom were again in Paris, probably even speculated about the possibility of restoring the Directory and the Constitution of 1795;[1] and outside the pale of political respectability, the hopes of both the jacobin and the royalist conspirators were revived by this time of transient opportunity.[2] The impression that such dissidence was probably inevitable in a system constitutionally so close to despotism is confirmed by the sequel: for although the First Consul's triumph in Italy eased the immediate tension, the permanency it imparted to his power rather aggravated than ended the deepest causes of political conflict. The liberal republicans generally believed,[3] or affected to believe, that the conclusion of the military crisis would be followed by the restoration of more freedom to the legislature; but Bonaparte's awareness of the unrest in Paris during his absence almost certainly deepened his distrust of them as intriguing 'ideologues'.

Thus when he seemed, as many contemporaries later concluded,[4] most free to choose between increasing and decreasing his authority, Bonaparte was, by his own avowal, somehow 'aged in heart'[5] and inclined to share the anxieties of those who feared that his sudden death

---

[1] Bastid, *Sieyès et sa Pensée*, p. 268, considers that Sieyès was not directly involved on this occasion. He seldom was.

[2] For the activities of the Jacobins, such as they were, see Gaubert, *Conspirateurs*, pp. 37–9. Cadoudal, who had earlier escaped from France to London with Hyde de Neuville, landed in Normandy secretly on 3 June.

[3] Though not, apparently, Madame de Staël, who later affirmed that she had wished for Bonaparte's defeat in the field as the only means of checking the growth of tyranny. Soboul, *La Iʳᵉ République*, p. 314.

[4] E. g. Miot, *Memoirs*, p. 175; Fouché, *Memoirs* (ed. Chas. Knight, London, 1892), p. 109; Hyde de Neuville, *Memoirs*, p. 152.

[5] Soboul, loc. cit.

would cause further years of dissension and disorder. From this time onwards the idea that he should establish an hereditary régime, even if that meant divorcing Josephine, was in many minds, and was particularly attractive to those who were, like Talleyrand, more inclined to a form of monarchy than to republicanism. By the end of July, however, Bonaparte seems to have set such thoughts aside. According to Miot, he then told Cabanis that there ought always to be a Consul-elect; and Roederer reports him as saying: 'Only I can govern France. I am persuaded that no one save myself, were he Louis XVIII or Louis XIV, could govern France at this time.'[1] Perhaps he may have been sincere in concluding that same conversation by saying that his true heir was the people of France—whose sovereignty he had, indeed, personally toasted at the banquet given at the Tuileries on 14 July.

Whatever the truth about this, Bonaparte at this time certainly continued his general policy of reconciliation and reconstruction without making any concessions to the 'metaphysicians' of parliamentary liberalism. In March and April, indeed, freedom of opinion had been further restricted by Lucien's action in increasing the control of the theatres in Paris and by the suppression of three more journals—so that only nine police-regulated papers, all more or less technical or official, remained in circulation in the capital.[2] On the other hand, the Councillors of State were spurred to new endeavours, five of them being particularly charged with the enormous task of consolidating into a single Civil Code the complex mass of legislation the Consulate had inherited from the old order and the Revolution. Others again wrestled with the labyrinth of laws and the lists of names involved in the problem of the emigration. On 3 March an act had been passed to define the *émigrés*, whose return was forbidden by the Constitution, as those listed as having left France before 25 December 1799; but so many came back with the Consulate that a commission had to be appointed to find some middle way between Fouché's inclination to abandon any attempt at discrimination and Bonaparte's desire to examine each case individually.

Beyond laying these foundations of the future, Bonaparte was also beginning to prepare the way for an agreement with Rome and the restoration of the Catholic faith in France. On 5 June, when he was in Milan, he had given a remarkable address to an assembly of the clergy in the cathedral. Deploring earlier interference with religion and the ill-treatment of the unfortunate Pius VI, he had ascribed these in part to 'the cruel policy of the Directory' and announced that it was his own

[1] Miot, *Memoirs*, p. 181; Roederer, *Mémoires*, p. 127.
[2] Hauterive, E., *Napoléon et sa Police* (Paris, 1943), pp. 155–7.

intention to ensure that Catholicism was preserved in its entirety. Nor did these words apply to Italy alone, for he also said that he hoped soon 'to have the happiness of removing every obstacle which might hinder complete reconciliation between France and the head of the Church'.[1] A fortnight later, when Marengo had been won and the First Consul was making his way back to France, he had in fact initiated negotiations in conversation with Bishop Martiniana of Vercelli, by which point the Concordat of the following year was already sketched in outline.[2] To such an agreement after a decade of conflict and persecution there were naturally many objections on both sides; but a conversation reported by Roederer on 18 August shows that Bonaparte had begun the process of converting his councillors considerably before the first representatives of the Papacy arrived in Paris in November. To Roederer, Bonaparte indeed said substantially what he had also said at Milan: 'No society can exist without morality: there is no good morality without religion; it is religion alone that gives to the State a firm and durable support . . .'[3]

Yet although after Marengo Bonaparte resumed the work of reconstruction and showed himself ready to welcome all who were prepared to accept and serve the new France, he now repudiated the royalists more firmly than ever. To the Count of Provence, the Pretender, who had written to him twice since Brumaire (20 February and 4 June) to offer him high honours if the monarchy were restored, he finally replied decisively on 7 September. The letter, courteous but brief, included one salient sentence: 'You must give up any hope of returning to France: you would have to pass over a hundred thousand dead bodies'.[4]

In the judgment of Thibaudeau, now Prefect of the Gironde and on 22 September to be appointed a Councillor of State, the first year of Bonaparte's rule had:

produced an extraordinary metamorphosis. Before 18 Brumaire, everything pointed to something like an actual dissolution of society, and now within a few months all was life and prosperity . . . The enthusiasm for the destruction of old landmarks which had marked the early days of the Revolution was now succeeded by enthusiasm for the reconstruction and regeneration of France. There was, however, one great distinction between the two epochs. In the early days,

[1] F. Markham, *Napoleon*, p. 79; M. Hutt, *Napoleon: Great Lives Observed* (N.J., 1972), p. 28.
[2] H. H. Walsh, *The Concordat of 1801* (N.Y., 1967), pp. 32–9.
[3] Roederer, *Mémoires*, pp. 147–8, with Markham and Hutt as cited above.
[4] *Napoleon's Letters*, ed. J. M. Thompson, p. 90 (*Corres.* VI., 5090).

all was tumult and disorder: now a firm hand guided and directed every movement.[1]

Speaking to Roederer on 1 October, Bonaparte himself described his achievements after his own fashion: 'Soon I shall have been governing for a complete year. I have closed the Manège, repulsed our enemies, put our finances and administration in order, and I have not shed a drop of blood.'[2] If, as the royalists had reason to know, this was not wholly true, it may nonetheless be thought a reasonable assessment of a year remarkable in retrospect and full of hope for the future.

[1] Thibaudeau, A. C., *Bonaparte and the Consulate* (ed. and trans. G. K. Fortescue, London, 1908), p. 6.

[2] Roederer, *Mémoires*, p. 137. The reference to the Manège might perhaps be given as: 'I have silenced the Jacobins' (either the Club or the Assembly being implied).

9. The End of the Republic, October 1800-August 1802

On 22 November 1800 the second four-month parliamentary session of the Consulate was begun by the reading of a review by Bonaparte of the situation of the Republic. After recalling 1799 as a time of general confusion and uncertainty, the First Consul summarised the considerable achivements of his administration and indicated its immediate intenttions, particularly emphasising his determination to codify the laws, to suppress brigandage and to secure the position of all who had purchased national property. His report, however, was avowedly an interim one: recognising that the condition of the country was still alarming and that many hopes remained unfulfilled, he justified his government more by its continuing resolution and activity than by its initial accomplishments.[1]

Such stern caution seems singularly appropriate to the time, for in retrospect it is clear that the ending of the year 1800 and the beginning of 1801 was a period of great consequence in the history of the Consulate and of freedom in France. Superficially somewhat episodic, the events of the autumn and winter show that political tensions within France became acute at a time of crucial importance to the development of the First Consul's plans for reorganisation at home and triumphant victory abroad. In this situation Bonaparte was for the first time forced to choose between the observance of the letter and of the spirit of the Constitution, and both the manner of his reaction to the crisis and the means he adopted to overcome it were to prove fatal for the Republic.

At this time Bonaparte was deeply involved in various momentous negotiations. One of these, the endeavour to effect a reconciliation between France and the Papacy, was long kept highly confidential, for Bonaparte was well aware that the restoration of Catholicism in France would be regarded as so appallingly retrogressive by most of the men of the Revolution that its achievement would strain their loyalty to the

[1] 'Exposé de la situation de la République, 1er Frimaire An IX', *Bulletin des Lois* (3 sér., Paris, An IX) II, p. 112.

Consulate to the limit. For this reason, quite apart from any other, the terms of an agreement had to be very favourable to France, and the Papal representative, Cardinal Spina, had no sooner arrived in Paris on 6 November than he was confronted with stringent preliminary demands. The Papacy, it appeared, was required to accept the fact that the confiscated lands of the Church were lost for ever; and Bernier, Bonaparte's agent in the negotiations, insisted that all the orthodox French bishops, the very men who had remained most loyal to Rome, would have to resign their dioceses so that new men, acceptable to both sides, could be appointed in their places.[1] Although these initial conditions at first seemed wholly unacceptable to the Papacy, which was in any case inclined to await the outcome of the renewal of the war between France and Austria, the French government tended rather to increase than to diminish the pressure of its demands. Success in this attitude, however, naturally depended upon Bonaparte's ability to maintain an impression of impregnable strength.

While directing these negotiations, Bonaparte was also assiduously courting the friendship of Russia. Utterly unstable by nature, the Tsar Paul I had ceased to support the Second Coalition against France after his armies had experienced disaster in 1799; and in September 1800 Britain's capture of Malta, of which island Paul held himself to be the protector,[2] increased his hostility to that country. In these circumstances Bonaparte had little difficulty in persuading him to come forward as the natural champion of the neutral states. In mid-December Russia led the other Baltic powers—Denmark, Sweden and Prussia—in a re-establishment of the League of Armed Neutrality, which implied the exclusion of British trade from the Baltic and Germany—and the possibility of combined naval action against Britain.[3] Beyond this, however, Bonaparte wrote repeatedly to Paul in the expectation that Russia could be attracted into an open alliance with France. This, he hoped, would unite Europe against Britain and enable the French to consolidate their position in Egypt, and it might even open the way to a combined Franco-Russian

---

[1] Lefebvre, *Napoléon*, p. 130–1.

[2] Paul had accepted the title of Grand Master of the Knights of St John after the members of that order had been expelled from Malta by Bonaparte in 1798.

[3] Established on 16 December 1800, the League was joined by Prussia on 18 December. Its formation was facilitated by Bonaparte's earlier adoption of a more liberal policy towards neutral shipping: he now accepted the view that the flag of a neutral ship protected its complete cargo—a concession he could afford to make since French naval forces were in no position to intercept cargoes bound for Britain. It was on this basis that peace was made between France and the United States in September 1800.

assault on India.[1] In the event, this grandiose scheme proved to be a house of cards: but in December 1800 Bonaparte's repatriation of Russian prisoners of war, and the Tsar's decision to despatch the diplomat Kolytchev to Paris as his personal representative,[2] certainly seemed to foreshadow some settlement and combination between them.

Still more important, the desultory negotiations which had been taking place between France and Austria since Marengo now approached their climax. Although the new Austrian chancellor, Louis de Cobenzl, arrived at Lunéville in Lorraine on 5 November to negotiate a treaty, his talks with Joseph Bonaparte remained inconclusive until the armistice made after Marengo expired on 28 November. By that time Napoleon had two armies, those of Brune on the River Mincio and of Macdonald in the Grisons, poised for action in Italy, while a third, that of Murat, was also available in Piedmont; and in all probability he expected to lead these forces to victory in person. As it happened, however, the decisive blow was struck by Moreau in Bavaria almost as soon as hostilities began. On 3 December Moreau utterly defeated the Austrians at Hohenlinden, capturing all their baggage and artillery as well as more than 12,000 men of their army. By brilliant pursuit, moreover, Moreau also captured 25,000 more prisoners, advanced to within reach of Vienna and, on 25 December, compelled the Austrians to accept at Steyer a new armistice and to agree that they would make peace apart from Great Britain. To this achievement the operations in Italy proved only ancillary, even though by mid-January the successes won by Brune and Macdonald[3] compelled the Austrians there also to accept an armistice at Treviso and to retire behind the Tagliamento River. It need hardly be added that Bonaparte's demands upon Cobenzl mounted as his armies

[1] On 12 January 1801 the Ataman of the Don Cossacks, General Orlov-Denisov, was in fact ordered to march with some 22,000 men against India. This operation, which ended disastrously in mud and ice north of the Aral Sea, would seem to be the outcome of an independent decision by the Tsar, not directly connected with the more speculative plans projected in conjunction with Bonaparte. See: J. W. Strong, 'Russia's Plans for an Invasion of India in 1801', *Canadian Slavonic Papers*, VII (1965), pp. 114–26.

[2] Bonaparte met General Sprengtporten, the Russian officer who was sent to conduct the prisoners (now re-armed and clad in new uniforms) back to Russia, in Paris on 10 December; the Tsar's letter to Bonaparte announcing his despatch of Kolytchev to Paris was written on 18 December. It was at this time, too, that Paul expelled the unfortunate Louis XVIII from his territories.

[3] Particularly the advance by Macdonald through the mountains of the Tyrol in the depths of winter, an advance which turned the flank of the Austrian forces on the Mincio and the Adige rivers. For these campaigns in general, see Lefebvre, *Napoléon*, pp. 100–1.

advanced, for now indeed there was opening before him a splendid prospect of French domination in Italy and French hegemony in Europe.

The realisation of this prospect nevertheless depended to a considerable extent upon the position of Bonaparte in France, for the harder he pressed the Papacy and the princes of Europe, the quicker they would be to take advantage of any indication of French domestic division. This is not to say that there was any question of the increasingly successful First Consul being repudiated either by the people of France or by the men who had helped him to acquire office 12 months previously. As we have seen, however, Bonaparte's successes naturally tended to stimulate the belief that he could and should liberalise his régime, and since Marengo there had been frequent signs that France was ill at ease. On the one hand, a revival of the activities of the *chouans* was signalled by the kidnapping of the Senator Clément de Ris in September and by the murder on 19 November of Audrein, a regicide member of the Convention who had become the Constitutional Bishop of Finistère—a crime Bonaparte countered by the execution on 18 December of the Chevalier de Margadel, who had been his prisoner since May.[1] On the other hand, real and imaginary Jacobin plots to assassinate the First Consul proliferated;[2] and at the centre of affairs, Lucien Bonaparte, the Minister of the Interior, was packed off to Madrid as an ambassador after his officers had distributed a pamphlet in praise of Napoleon which ended by advocating the adoption of an hereditary monarchical system.[3] More significantly still, the parliament had no sooner reassembled than it rejected as unconstitutional the first of three measures proposed to it by the government. The other two, which related to the powers of police and magistrates, were then promptly withdrawn, ostensibly so that they could be better correlated to a more important and controversial bill to create emergency courts to check brigandage.[4]

[1] The kidnapping of Clément de Ris, who was first held for ransom and then released on the open highway, was commonly believed to have been arranged by Fouché so that he could secure possession of incriminating papers about the intrigues afoot against Bonaparte at the time of Marengo. It was, however, organised by Cadoudal. See Godechot, *The Counter-Revolution*, p. 389.

[2] See below.

[3] The 'Parallèle entre César, Cromwell et Bonaparte', which was distributed on November 1st. The greater part of this work was written by Fontanes, the obsequious essayist who was the lover of Bonaparte's sister Eliza and who became in 1808 the Grand Master of the University. The authorship of the final pages is sometimes ascribed to Lucien and sometimes to Napoleon himself.

[4] The rejected measure, which concerned the organisation of the National Archives, was defeated in the Tribune by 85 votes to 5 and in the Legislative Body by 209 to 58. *Archives Parlementaires*, I, p. 273.

According to Miot de Melito, who was at this time a member of the Council of State, the First Consul was still determined not to abandon his policy of reconciliation. On 20 October an important Order-in-Council had extended amnesty to all those *émigrés* who had not actually borne arms against the Republic, and despite the discontent in the Tribunate and the recent crimes committed by the *chouans*, Bonaparte repudiated any intention of renewing the proscription of men by classes. As soon as parliamentary opposition became apparent, Bonaparte nevertheless made it plain to his councillors that he regarded the Tribunate and the Legislative Body as hostile: 'public opinion must pronounce between them and us . . . if it is for them, we must renounce our rule'. Seeing the Government as the true representative of the people, he regarded parliament as being, 'as it were, its mouthpiece . . . the principal and easiest mode of addressing the public and leading opinion in the desired direction'. Seeing no present possibility of proposing any further laws with any certainty of success, he voiced the thought that it would be most practical simply to do without them until the membership of the Legislature could be changed 'by renewals to be made at intervals by the Senate . . . We cannot fight the English, the Russians, the Austrians, the Legislative Body and the Tribunate at the same time.'[1]

It was in these circumstances, and on the eve of the anniversary of the establishment of the Constitution in 1799, that there occurred on 24 December 1800 (3 Nivôse, an IX) one of the most dramatic events of the period, the attempt to assassinate the First Consul by the use of an 'infernal machine'.[2] As it so happened, that Christmas Eve—which many Catholics could now celebrate by quietly attending midnight mass—was also the occasion of the first presentation in Paris of a new oratorio by Handel, *The Creation of the World*, a piece which was of particular interest since the recent development of the music of Germany was still almost unknown in France. Bonaparte, it appears, was weary and reluctant to attend the performance at the Opera House in the Rue de la Loi (the present Rue Richelieu); but once his decision was taken, he left the Tuileries so hastily that his escort had to follow instead of preceding

[1] Miot de Melito, *Memoirs*, pp. 199–202.

[2] For a more fully annotated account of this the reader may be referred to my essay, 'The Crime of 3 Nivôse' in *French Government and Society, 1500–1800* (London, 1972), and to the references given there. Alternatively, see the appropriate sections of H. Gaubert, *Conspirateurs au temps de Napoléon Ier* (Paris, 1962) or J. Thiry, *La Machine Infernale* (Paris, 1952). Quotations not otherwise identified in the present text derive from the *Mémoires* of Miot, Thibaudeau and, on occasion, Fouché.

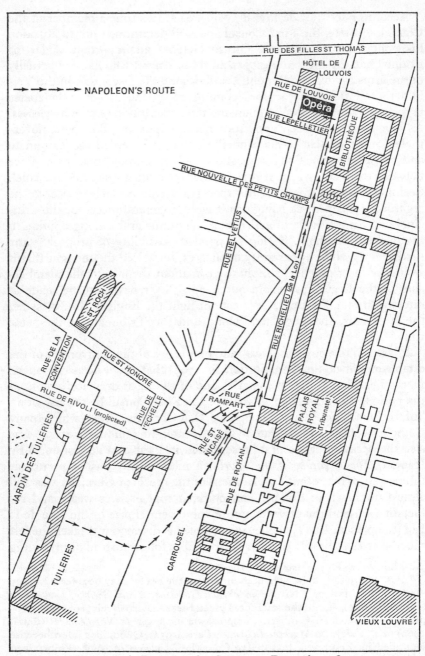

Bonaparte's Route to the Opéra, 24 December 1800

his carriage, and the ladies of the party—Josephine, Bonaparte's sister Caroline Murat and his step-daughter Hortense de Beauharnais—were left at the doors of the palace. Preceded only by a single horseman, the First Consul's carriage raced across the new parade ground on the Place du Carrousel and swung into the narrow Rue Niçaise, which led north-wards to the Rue de la Loi (see map p. 256). Just beyond the corner, however, a brief check occurred: finding the way partially blocked by what seemed to be a water-cart, the leading guardsman beat back its horse with the flat of his sabre, and as soon as he had done so the Consul's carriage went hell-for-leather through the gap. But the cart in fact carried a large iron-bound barrel tightly packed with gunpowder and scrap-metal, and its fuse was already ignited as Bonaparte passed. The violence of the explosion which followed was such that some 15 houses were gutted and at least 60 people were killed or injured in the vicinity.[1]

Although the blast of the explosion shattered his carriage-windows and hurled one of his escort from the saddle, Bonaparte remained un-injured. Outwardly calm and unconcerned, he went on at once to the Opera, where appropriately enough the introductory 'Representation of Chaos' was just being played. Soon afterwards he was joined in the consular box by Josephine, in evident distress: the ladies' carriage, caught by the explosion whilst crossing the Place du Carrousel towards the Rue Niçaise, had been showered with broken glass from the win-dows of the Tuileries and borne hard against the iron railings by its bolting horses. Repeated acclamations long delayed the resumption of the oratorio, and even after the Bonapartes had retired the excitement was such that the performance had eventually to be abandoned.

Coming as it did at a time of considerable national and international tension, this outrage proved to be of far greater consequence than is generally recognised.[2] By no means the least of its results was the fact that Bonaparte benefited by the general indignation it aroused. On 25 December the Legislative Body and the Tribunate went as assemblies to congratulate him on his escape, and their addresses, like many others

---

[1] Statements of the casualties of course vary. Lefebvre, op. cit., p. 121, gives the commonest estimate, that of 22 killed and 56 injured. An editorial footnote to the *Memoirs* of Fouché, p. 127, gives a detailed statement of the allocation of 77,601 francs by the government to 57 injured or bereaved individuals.

[2] Lefebvre, op. cit., pp. 121-2 and Soboul, *La Ire République*, p. 135, both indicate the significance of the affair succinctly, though neither attaches as much importance to it as is suggested here. Generally, however, historians have tended to treat the matter as a mere episode.

from lesser bodies, reflected real appreciation of the extent to which the achievements of the past year, and the present security of France both at home and abroad, depended upon his survival.

As one journalist put it: 'Had the attempt succeeded we should have been thrust back into an abyss of evils'.[1] This reaction naturally reinforced the position of those men in Bonaparte's court who were seeking to persuade him to become an hereditary ruler.

Talleyrand, who can be considered one of the principal exponents of this policy, was at first particularly exultant, for his great rival Fouché, who had become the chief opponent of any move towards monarchy, could of course be held responsible as Minister of Police for all that had happened. Fouché, moreover, was generally regarded as a terrorist and a protector of terrorists, and almost everyone was convinced that the explosion in the Rue Niçaise was essentially a jacobin crime. Bonaparte personally probably shared this belief; he certainly impressed it immediately upon the crowd of courtiers and officials who hurried to join him at the Tuileries as soon as he returned from the Opera. Striding furiously to and fro before them, and pausing only to confront the immobile and isolated Fouché, he inveighed at length against the 'agitators' whom he held responsible for every outrage that had occurred since 1789. 'These', he cried, 'are the jacobins, the terrorists, wretches in perpetual revolt against every form of government . . . These are the assassins of 3 September, the authors of 31 May, the conspirators of *prairial*.'[2]

Although Fouché subsequently described this tirade of 24 December as 'an orgy of blind and furious passion',[3] Bonaparte's conviction was by no means ill-founded. The combination of revolution and repression *had* produced men who lived for conspiracy, and since 1799 their numbers had been swelled by their association with a few of the many officers whom Bonaparte had discharged in the process of re-organising the army. Moreover, as Bonaparte knew well, in recent months these men's perpetual talk of insurrection and tyrannicide *had* led to a number of plots against his life. On 14 July the First Consul was to have been shot on the Champ de Mars by a disaffected company of grenadiers; in August, he was going to be ambushed on his way to Malmaison, or perhaps the château there would be fired and a killing arranged in the confusion; and in September there was one plan to penetrate the Tuileries by way of its sewers, and yet another to shoot the 'tyrant' down with a

---

[1] Cited by Gaubert, op. cit., p. 91.
[2] Thibaudeau, *Bonaparte and the Consulate*, p. 50.
[3] Fouché, *Memoirs*, p. 129.

powerful air-gun as he laid the foundation stone of a monument to Generals Desaix and Kléber[1] on the Place des Victoires.

Much of all this was, of course, mere tavern-talk, which the police noted and ignored, and some of it was certainly deliberately worked-up by one or other of the various police forces of Paris for their own and Bonaparte's benefit. A residue, however, was real enough. The original 'Conspiracy of the Opera', a plot by a number of French and Italian jacobins[2] to stab Bonaparte when he attended the first performance of *The Horatii* on 10 October, was certainly encouraged by an *agent provocateur* who was employed with the assent of the First Consul and with the connivance of Dubois, the Prefect of Police for Paris; but although it was encouraged and led to a convenient sensation, it was a plot which was revealed to the police, not one which was invented by them. Still more sensational, and considerably less artificial, was the explosion which shook Paris on the night of 17 October and which led to the arrest on 7 November of a certain Chevalier, whom Fouché apprehended as 'a man of atrocious mind and delirious reputation'. In his room the police discovered[3] the original 'infernal machine'—a large barrel crammed with powder and grape-shot, and so devised that it could be detonated from a distance by a tug on the trigger of a musket attached to it. It appeared that it was a first model of this primitive bomb that had been exploded on 17 October and had all but killed the seven people concerned in the experiment. Small wonder that on the night of 24 December the in-

[1] Desaix, who saved the day at Marengo, had died in the hour of victory. Kléber, to whom Bonaparte had confided the command of the Army of the Orient when he returned to France in 1799, was assassinated by a young Syrian on the same day as Marengo was fought, 14 June 1800.

[2] This term is not now used in a precise sense, but simply, as it was at the time, as a convenient label for those who were, or were believed to be, revolutionary democrats.

[3] Since the government published its accounts of all these various plots *after* the explosion in the Rue Niçaise, when their value in influencing public opinion was greatest, it is far from easy to determine how much truth they contain. The Opera Plot of 10 October, which Richard Cobb describes as being of 'doubtful odour', was certainly deliberately developed by the police of the Paris prefecture, whose officers were eager to steal a march upon the men of Fouché's Ministry of Police. This is not, however, to say that all the evidence was fabricated by the police, and Cobb would seem to me to go somewhat too far in assuming that the infernal machine found in Chevalier's room was probably planted there by the police. See R. Cobb, 'Note sur la répression contre le personnel sans-culotte de 1795 à 1801', *Annales historiques de la Révolution française* (1954), pp. 26, 43; and compare *Recueil des décrets . . . de Napoléon Bonaparte 1799–1812, extraits du Moniteur par Lewis Goldsmith* (London, 1813), pp. 112 and 118–20, where the examination of the machine by Monge is cited in full.

furiated First Consul should have exclaimed: 'The proof that the jacobins are guilty is that the infernal machine of the Rue Niçaise is the duplicate of that of Chevalier!'

In all probability, too, Bonaparte's anger sprang in part from justifiable indignation. Even in our own more callous age the explosion of a powerful bomb in a confined and densely-populated city street is seen as an atrocious act; and those who were maimed or bereaved on this occasion were almost all humble men and women who lived and worked in the maze of small streets between the Tuileries and the Rue St Honoré. In demanding some means of effective action, as he did when his Council of State met the next day (25 December), Bonaparte was not acting discreditably. 'I do not think of myself', he said, 'but of the social order which it is my duty to re-establish.' Equally, however, it was certainly to his advantage to act swiftly to demonstrate to all the world that his power and authority were undiminished—and the opportunity now presented to him to rid himself once and for all of the jacobins was as certainly one which he thought too good to miss. Thus his demand became the very different one of general retribution. To him the question of the guilt or innocence of the jacobins in this particular instance ceased to matter, and what he called 'the more or less tedious forms of justice'[1] paled before the political desirability of ridding the Republic of undesirables: 'Blood must flow ('*il faut du sang*'). There must be as many shot as there were victims, say 15 or 20, and 200 more must be transported . . . We must finish with these wretches by condemning them for their accumulated mass of crime.'

As Bonaparte spoke, his horrified Councillors gradually realised that the period of proscriptions was by no means over. In the words of Thibaudeau: 'This speech entirely altered the question: it was no longer a matter of legal judgment, but of transporting or shooting men wholesale as a measure of public safety'.[2] What is more, when one of the Councillors, Admiral Truguet, bluntly asked whether similar steps would be taken to deal with the men of the counter-revolution, the *émigrés* and the priests, Bonaparte rounded upon him in rage, angrily asking whether the Council wanted him to proscribe whole classes of people. That, nevertheless, was what was happening, for what the Council was witnessing was the abandonment of the policy of general reconciliation in favour of one which would destroy the extreme republicans.[3]

[1] Miot de Melito, op. cit., p. 205.
[2] Thibaudeau, op. cit., p. 55.
[3] J. Holland Rose, the great English historian of the Napoleonic period, goes further. Rightly remarking that 'Bonaparte's policy with respect to plots de-

Although the Council of State was abruptly dismissed as soon as Truguet had been silenced, Bonaparte eventually got his way. In practice, this meant that Fouché as Minister of Police was required to prepare a list of 130 men who 'were not actually taken red-handed, but were known to be capable of preparing and committing the crime of assassination'.[1] He had also to denounce these jacobins as 'a class of men who have covered themselves with crime for the past ten years'; and Bonaparte himself silenced the last doubts of his Councillors by reiterating the point that the crime of 3 Nivôse was only the occasion for his action: 'We banish these men . . . for all that they have done and all that they still might do'.[2] Consequently on 5 January 1801 the first convoy of those who were 'to be kept under special surveillance beyond the European territories of the Republic' left Paris for Nantes, en route for the Seychelles Islands; and others followed later. Very few of these men were of even as much prominence as Rossignol or Fournier l'Américain, who had acquired some notoriety in the great days of the Revolution; and once the first furore had died down some of them were quietly forgotten on the Ile de Ré or the Ile d'Oléron. Nevertheless, 68 men were sent without trial to the Seychelles in 1801, and 26 others were despatched to Guiana in 1804; and more than half of these died in exile.[3] Further, the more important of the conspirators whom the police had arrested earlier in the autumn now paid with their lives for a crime which they at least could not possibly have committed. The four men seized for their participation in the 'Conspiracy of the Opera' on 10 October were publicly tried and guillotined on the Place de Grève on 30 January 1801, and Chevalier and his principal associate, the inventors of the 'infernal machine', were less ostentatiously tried by a military commission before being shot on the plain of Grenelle on 11 January. Thus did Bonaparte complete the annihilation of the Left.[4]

In all this Fouché acquiesced, so preserving his place, his influence, and possibly even his life. If, as he later claimed, he personally saved

---

serves close attention', he concludes that 'he now quietly but firmly exchanged the policy of balancing parties for one which crushed the extreme republicans and enhanced the importance of all who were likely to approve or condone the establishment of personal rule'. J. H. Rose, *The Life of Napoleon I* (London, 1916), p. 307.

[1] *'N'ont pas été pris le poignard à la main; mais connus . . . pour être capables de l'aiguiser et de le prendre.'*

[2] Thibaudeau, op. cit., p. 66.

[3] The exact figures being, as always, indeterminate, I here follow Lefebvre, *Napoléon*, p. 121. See also R. Cobb, op. cit., p. 35.

[4] Lefebvre, op. cit., pp. 121–2.

many lives by reducing the length of the proscription list, he seems also to have seized the opportunity to ensure that some of those who knew too much about his own past were sent into exile.[1] From the moment that he was berated by Bonaparte at the Tuileries on 24 December, he had nevertheless steadily maintained that the jacobins were *not* responsible for the crime in the Rue Niçaise; and on 18 January 1801, while the process of proscribing them was still continuing, he finally presented Bonaparte with incontrovertible proof that the real criminals were the royalists. Starting from his certain knowledge that a number of prominent *chouans* had come to Paris in November and December, and had then disappeared from view, he succeeded by systematic detection in tracing the paraphernalia of the crime—particularly the remnants of the mare which had drawn the cart—back to three of these 'agents of Georges' (Cadoudal). When on 18 January the first of these, a subordinate called Carbon, was arrested and found to be ready to talk freely, the truth was revealed. It then appeared that the trio—Carbon, Limoëlan (a Breton gentleman resident in Paris and apparently reconciled to Bonaparte's rule) and Robinet de Saint-Régent (an ex-naval officer who was the chief of the *chouans* of Ille et Vilaine and Cadoudal's personal emissary to Paris)—had resolved to employ against Bonaparte a duplicate of Chevalier's 'infernal machine', the potency of which had become common knowledge in Paris. Their plan, by which Limoëlan was to signal the First Consul's approach from the corner of the Place du Carrousel so that Saint-Régent could ignite a carefully-timed fuse, miscarried because Limoëlan was disconcerted by Bonaparte's unorthodox procession, and so failed to give the signal. Though Limoëlan escaped uninjured from both the explosion and the police, Saint-Régent was badly battered by the blast, and he was easily overcome when he was discovered in hiding on 27 January.

The first effect of this revelation was that Fouché was vindicated and the reaction towards an aristocratic and hereditary system was temporarily checked. As Bonaparte admitted: 'Fouché judged better than most; he is right; it is necessary to keep an eye upon the returned *émigrés*, upon the *chouans* and upon all of that party'.[2] But here again it was really Bonaparte's position which had grown the greater. Apart from Saint-Régent and Carbon, who were (quite rightly) executed on the Place de Grève on 20 April after a much-publicised trial, nearly a hundred sus-

---

[1] Cobb, op. cit., p. 42, refers to notes in Fouché's hand: '*Eloigner de Paris les réfugiés lyonnais*'.

[2] M. A. Thiers, *History of the Consulate and Empire of France under Napoleon* (Edinburgh, 1879), p. 201.

pected royalists were rounded-up and either imprisoned or interned without formality. Nor did this mean that there was any question of exonerating the proscribed jacobins: Berlier,[1] a councillor who had the courage to speak to Bonaparte about this, was once again calmly told that the jacobins had been deported for their sustained opposition to all orderly government. Thus the failure of the *chouans* enabled Bonaparte to strike down his enemies, real or supposed, on both sides simultaneously.

Fully as significant is the fact that in proscribing the jacobins Bonaparte for the first time employed the Senate as a means by which he could evade and distort the Constitution whenever he wished. Initially, on 25 December, he had required his councillors to suggest some legal means of action against the 'anarchists', and they had responded by proposing that the bill then before them concerning the creation of extraordinary tribunals to check brigandage should be extended to encompass crimes aimed at any of the three Consuls. Bonaparte, however, had immediately and furiously rejected this proposition as inadequate, and this was certainly partly because it would have compelled him to win the support of the Tribunate.

After a series of further meetings between selected councillors and ministers had been arranged by Cambacérès, the Council was reassembled to approve—with only three dissident votes—a second solution, by which it was recommended that the government, having already sufficient authority to take action, should do so on its own responsibility. The First Consul nevertheless rejected this proposal also, no doubt perceiving that the Council was in fact refusing to lend the sanction of its own authority to extra-judicial action. It was at this point that Bonaparte had personally insisted that the Council should present a report against the 'agitators' to the Senate, together with a resolution that some extraordinary measure, other than a law, was necessary.[2] Four days later, on 5 January, the Senate, the body charged by the Constitution with the duty of 'sustaining or annulling all acts referred to it as unconstitutional by the Tribunate or the Government', gave its decision: the laws and the constitution being silent on the means of ending the daily dangers to the safety of the state, the will of the people could only be expressed by the Senate as the 'natural judge' of the measure proposed by the Government; and the Senate considered this

---

[1] *Biog. Notes:* BERLIER.

[2] Developments in the Council of State are fully described by Thibaudeau, op. cit., pp. 51–75.

proposed 'Act of Government' to be in accordance with the preservation of the constitution.[1]

This was not, of course, surprising, since Bonaparte had taken the precaution of ascertaining the opinion of the Senate as early as 29 December. It is more remarkable that there was apparently some dissent from a few of the Senators, Lanjuinais in particular being said to have called out: 'No *coups d'états*! *Coups d'états* destroy states!'[2] The result can nevertheless confidently be considered a foregone conclusion, for the Senate was a small body which met in private; and although the Senators were irremovable, they were carefully selected men, greatly interested in stability—to say nothing of the rewards which were in Bonaparte's gift. Hitherto the Senate had indeed been an unimportant body, appointment to which was little more than an honour; as Bonaparte had said to Roederer, 'It is a tomb, fit only for men who have finished their careers'.[3] But as Talleyrand, who probably spoke for Bonaparte, said in December 1800: 'What is the good of having a Senate if we do not make use of it?'[4] In consulting the Senate about the proscription of the jacobins, Bonaparte had in fact made use of it as a means of silencing all constitutional opposition to a wholly unwarrantable perversion of the rule of law; and, having succeeded once, he had within his grasp a weapon capable of giving some semblance of legality to any arbitrary act. Nor was he unaware of the significance of what he was doing, one reason for his flat refusal to revoke the banishment of the jacobins being his determination to preserve the sanctity of a decision by the Senate.

Nor is it altogether fanciful to suggest that the man thus armed became more dictatorial in nature as a result of the attempt to assassinate him and the difficulties he encountered when he demanded retribution. Certainly his fury at the Tuileries on the night of 24 December seems unbounded, and the opposition of his councillors next day engendered a paroxysm of rage. Even Roederer noted that the First Consul's very voice then seemed to become unrecognisable, and Thibaudeau wrote that when the Council was dismissed all its members were saddened, this being 'the first occasion on which the freedom of each man's opinion had been silenced by such a tirade'.[5] The family atmosphere previously

[1] The preamble of the *senatus-consultum* is cited in full in translation in Aulard, *The French Revolution*, IV, p. 186.

[2] Oral tradition reported in Aulard, op. cit., p. 187.

[3] Roederer, *Mémoires* (ed. Aubry, Paris, 1942), p. 115. It should be added that at this time Senators were debarred by the Constitution from holding any other public office.

[4] Miot de Melito, *Memoirs*, p. 209.

[5] Roederer, op. cit., p. 166; Thibaudeau, op. cit., p. 57.

characteristic of the Council of State, an assembly of Bonaparte's chosen and trusted advisers, was indeed never fully recovered, and after this the First Consul tended increasingly to consult selected men individually or in private councils when important decisions were in question.[1]

His attitude towards parliamentary opposition, too, now became even more obviously contemptuous. The Tribunate, which had approved all but two minor bills in its first session and which was to approve all but three[2] in that of 1800–1, cannot really be considered intemperate. Many, if not most, of its members believed that as they and the government had the same objective, that of re-establishing the greatness of France, it was their duty as well as their right to point out the defects in legislative proposals. To Bonaparte, however, all public criticism was fast becoming intolerable disloyalty: instead of 'declaiming in the Tribune', these people ought to come and talk to him in his study.[3] Although by 28 January 1801 the legislature had accepted the government's revised proposals about the police and the magistrates,[4] this smouldering anger was enflamed anew by the hostility of the Tribunate to the most important measure of the session, that concerning the creation of emergency courts to curb brigandage.

By this measure, which in fact became law on 7 February (18 Pluviôse an IX), Bonaparte was empowered to establish special tribunals wherever, and for as long as, he thought it necessary. These courts, each composed of a presiding officer, two judges from the criminal courts, and five persons (including two soldiers) nominated by the First Consul personally, were authorised to pronounce judgment, without a jury and without appeal, on habitual criminals and crimes of violence. To Bonaparte the adoption of this system, which was a reversion to a practice not

---

[1] This is not to say that the Council of State, and its various sections, did not still retain a central place in Bonaparte's government, the process by which it became formalised being a gradual one. On Bonaparte's private councils, more particularly apparent in the imperial period, see: C. Durand, 'Conseils privés . . . de 1800 à 1814', *Revue d'histoire moderne et contemporaine*, Vol. XVII (1970), p. 814.

[2] Godechot, *Les Institutions*, p. 489. The most important of these was the annual Finance Law, which was rejected on technical grounds on 29 March by 56 votes to 30. It was, however, subsequently accepted by the Legislative Body by 227 votes to 58.

[3] Thibaudeau, op. cit., p. 29.

[4] The two laws about the police and the justices of the peace, the principal effect of which was to reduce the number of the latter from 6,000 to 2,600, were approved by the Tribune by 63–25 and 59–32 and by the Legislative Body by 226–48 and 218–41 votes.

uncommon in the days of the old monarchy, seemed imperative both to expedite the punishment of crime and to prevent the intimidation of witnesses and jurymen; and in fact the courts, which were initially established in as many as 32 departments of France, did contribute considerably to the restoration of law and order without becoming instruments of political repression.[1] The Republicans in the legislature, however, were understandably alarmed by the implications of such a measure as this, coming as it did immediately after the ruthless elimination of the jacobins. Presented with the proposal early in January, the Tribunes debated it heatedly for two weeks at the end of the month, Benjamin Constant and Daunou in particular deploring the disappearance of the jury and the fearful risks implicit in giving the government so much discretionary power. Another tribune, Ginguené, was still more forthright: condemning as tyrannical the power vested in the commissioner who would decide whether accused persons were to be sent before a regular court or a special tribunal, he asserted that the Constitution of 1799 had established a representative system, and that the Revolution had been made to sustain representative government against excessive personal power.[2]

These criticisms evoked a further furious outburst from the First Consul. Addressing some of the Senators on 29 January, he exclaimed that there were in the Tribunate 'a dozen or so metaphysicians who ought to be thrown into a pond. Like vermin, they infest my clothes; but I will shake them off. I am a soldier, a son of the Revolution, and I will not tolerate being insulted as if I were a king. I am not the man to stand that sort of treatment!'[3] The fact that the law was eventually accepted both by the Tribunate (by 49 votes to 41) and by the Legislative Body (by 192 votes to 88) did nothing to placate him, for such figures in such assemblies were tantamount to votes of no-confidence. In effect, the parliamentary opposition was to be given but one more opportunity to cooperate before the authority of the Senate was again invoked to silence it.

Intolerant of his own Tribunate, Bonaparte was still more intransigent in his dealings with other countries: being by now involved in imposing his will upon much of Europe, he could not countenance opposition anywhere. The Treaty of Lunéville, which ended the war with Austria on 9 February 1801, was essentially a dictated peace, the product of

[1] Lefebvre, *Napoléon*, p. 124.
[2] Soboul, *La Ire République*, p. 318, and *Archives Parlementaires*, p. 70ff. (particularly pp. 178 and 232 for Daunou).
[3] Lefebvre, op. cit., p. 125, and Thibaudeau, op. cit., p. 31.

French power and the alarming possibility of a Franco-Russian alliance, and Bonaparte did not hesitate to announce that if it were broken by Austria the armies of France would soon stand in Prague, Venice and Vienna.[1] The terms, which Cobenzl considered frightful, were substantially those of Campo-Formio. Austria, allowed to retain Venetia, was again compelled to recognise the cession of Belgium, the expansion of France to the Rhine frontier, and the re-establishment of a Cisalpine Republic possessing all northern Italy west of the Adige River as well as the two Papal Legations of Bologna and Ferrara. More important, perhaps, French power was predominant throughout Italy, and, as in 1797, the problem of providing compensation for the dispossessed princes of the Rhineland gave France an entry into the affairs of the German states. No more than before could such a peace really be anything more than temporary truce.

The treaty, it may be added, also guaranteed the independence of the 'sister republics' of France—the Dutch, the Swiss, the Cisalpine and the Genoese (Ligurian) Republics. But the Republic of Bonaparte was still essentially as revolutionary as ever in its identification of might and right, and events swiftly showed that its ruler cared little for either the independence or the republicanism of small states. By the beginning of 1802 the Dutch had been compelled to accept a revised constitution; the Swiss had begun to find that Bonaparte was less interested in the previously sacrosanct 'unitary constitution' than in finding men who would work with France; the Cisalpine Republic had been reorganised as the Italian Republic, with Bonaparte as its president and its legislative council as his nominees; and Genoa was for all practical purposes a French military area. Nor is it without interest that all four republics had been informed that it would be in order for them to recognise the Kingdom of Etruria. This, the first of the vassal kingdoms of the future, was created from the Grand Duchy of Tuscany as a gift to the royal family of Spain (in return, fantastic as it may seem, for Spain's restoration of Louisiana to France).[2]

Since after Lunéville only Britain remained actively at war with France, much of the re-organisation of the countries under Bonaparte's control was directed towards the destruction of her trade. It was to this end, although with only partial success, that Spain was persuaded to

[1] L. Madelin, *Histoire du Consulat et de l'Empire* (Paris, 1939), IV, pp. 71–2.
[2] Spain restored Louisiana—then almost all territory west of the Mississippi—to France on 1 October 1800, the arrangement regarding Tuscany being confirmed by the Treaty of Aranjuez on 21 March 1801. Talleyrand's instruction to the associated republics was dated 17 June 1801.

attack Portugal in the so-called 'War of the Oranges' (May–June 1801);[1] and a treaty made with the King of Naples on 28 March bound that ruler to exclude British ships from his harbours and to accept French garrisons in the ports of Otranto and Brindisi. Bonaparte's hope that the whole continental coastline could be closed to the British was, however, frustrated by the initiative of Nelson in continuing the bombardment of the Danish fleet at the battle of Copenhagen (2 April 1801), an action which re-opened the Baltic to British shipping and effectively broke up the League of Armed Neutrality. Nor, as it proved, were the Italian ports to be used to reinforce the French army in Egypt, for a British force commanded by Sir Ralph Abercrombie landed at Aboukir Bay on 8 March 1801, and inflicted a crushing defeat upon the French at the battle of Alexandria (21 March). Although Abercrombie himself died of the wounds he received in this action, the subsequent fall to his successor of the cities of Cairo (28 June) and Alexandria (30 August) led on 2 September to a convention by which the French commanders in Egypt agreed to evacuate the country in return for repatriation in British ships.

These reverses were aggravated by the assassination on the night of 23 March of the Tsar Paul, potentially Bonaparte's most powerful ally. His successor, the Tsar Alexander I, promptly sought and soon reached agreement with Britain (17 June). Bonaparte, however, was able to turn even his failures to good account. Having no alternative, he too made terms with Alexander; and although this peace (8 October) amounted to a recognition of Russian rights in the Middle East which Bonaparte had previously persuaded Paul to forgo, he was able to represent it as another positive step towards the general pacification of Europe. Still more important, the First Consul was able to offset defeat in Egypt by exploiting Britain's desire for peace. At the beginning of the year William Pitt, the minister whose resistance to the Revolution had for so long been the rock on which the British war effort rested, had resigned in consequence of his inability to honour his promise of emancipation to Catholics in Ireland, and his successor, Addington, had almost at once offered to open negotiations for peace with France (21 February).[2] Bonaparte's

---

[1] By both attacking and making peace with Portugal before the French expeditionary force of 22,000 men under General Leclerc, Bonaparte's brother-in-law, could come into action, Spain secured a province and a massive indemnity, while Lucien Bonaparte and Talleyrand secured substantial fortunes. Napoleon, however, got only a nominal assurance that British ships would be excluded from Portuguese harbours.

[2] Within two weeks of the conclusion of peace between France and Austria at Lunéville on 9 February. Pitt's resignation occurred on 5 February.

immediate assumption that it was the final terms of peace which were in question, and that neither party could possibly be expected to surrender any of its own conquests from the other, promptly prejudiced the outcome of the ensuing talks, since this implied that the British were prepared to purchase peace by giving up the naval bases and colonial possessions they had taken from France's allies. The British nevertheless persevered in their approach, for behind it lay not only much weariness with war and anxiety about the economy, but also a widespread conviction that the Revolution had ended with the Directory and that the experiment of living in peace with Bonaparte ought at least to be attempted. As he became aware of the strength of this feeling, and of the sheer feebleness of Addington's government, Bonaparte naturally took full advantage of his ability to make and maintain his own terms for a settlement. In particular, having learnt before the British of the imminent surrender of his men in Alexandria, he threatened to break off the negotiations unless they could be concluded immediately; and in consequence of this a Preliminary Peace of London was signed between the two powers on the night of 1 October 1801.

Although six months more were given to negotiation before this peace was made definitive at the Treaty of Amiens on 27 March 1802, the basis of the settlement changed so little that it can appropriately be indicated here. In brief, Bonaparte agreed to withdraw his garrisons from the Kingdom of Naples and the Papal States; but Britain, whose ships controlled the sea-routes of the world, retained of all her acquisitions only the islands of Ceylon and Trinidad, which had been taken from Holland and Spain. This meant that Egypt was restored to Turkey, the Cape of Good Hope to Holland, and even Martinique to France; and since the treaty was not accompanied by any agreement concerning commerce, one of the most vital issues between the two nations, France was again afforded the opportunity to become a considerable maritime and colonial power. Bonaparte's despatch of General Leclerc[1] and an army of 20,000 men to San Domingo in December 1801, an expedition sent to suppress the slave revolt led by Toussaint L'Ouverture, is sufficient indication that the opportunity would not be neglected. In all this, on the other hand, the French hegemony in Europe remained unchallenged, as did the essential Revolutionary concept that he who speaks

[1] One of the more attractive of the French generals, Charles Leclerc (born in Pontoise in 1772) had been a senior staff-officer at the siege of Toulon in 1793. He subsequently served Bonaparte with distinction in the Italian campaign and married Pauline Bonaparte, his general's sister. He died of yellow fever in San Domingo in 1802.

in the name of the nation need not acknowledge any higher law in international affairs. Thus after eight years of war the British, despite their recent victories, accepted a peace which depended upon the good faith of Bonaparte, only holding back Malta, the key to the control of the Mediterranean, until it could safely be given to a Neapolitan garrison to keep for the Knights of the Order of St John.

Bonaparte's success in these negotiations in 1801 was matched by his achievement in reaching agreement with Rome for the restoration of Catholicism in France. As has been said, this reconciliation was bound to be obnoxious to all those who clung to the ideology of the Enlightenment and the passionate anti-clericalism of the Revolution; but Bonaparte was of course much more concerned with immediate political and social realities than with remote abstractions. Believing that only the hope of immortality could reconcile the poor to the inevitable hardship of their lot in this world, he regarded religion as the foundation of social stability; and knowing that the majority of the people, particularly in the countryside, had remained firmly attached to Catholicism, he thought it folly not to associate his government with their faith. As he had said in August 1800: 'My policy is to govern men as the greatest number of them wish to be governed'.[1]

The numerical strength and political influence of the minority of unbelievers were nevertheless of considerable importance, for just as Bonaparte had to have a settlement obviously favourable to the French state in order to placate them, so the new Pope, the gentle and saintly Pius VII, was anxious to re-establish religion in order to check the growth of apathy and indifference in the cities. The Concordat which was signed on 16 July 1801 was consequently based upon a series of concessions by the Papacy. By the terms of the agreement, Catholicism was to be recognised as 'the religion of the majority of Frenchmen', a formula which made religious toleration legitimate; and the Papacy also agreed to accept the loss of the lands of the Church and the replacement of the existing bishops by men acceptable to Bonaparte. In practice this last condition meant that Bonaparte nominated 32 new Bishops as well as re-appointing 16 of those who had remained loyal to Rome and 12 of those who had become leaders of the 'Constitutional Church'.[2] Further,

[1] J. C. Herold, *The Mind of Napoleon* (Columbia U.P., 1955–1965), p. 79 (citing Roederer, *Journal* (ed. M. Vitrac, Paris 1909), p. 16).

[2] The bishops whom Bonaparte nominated were to receive canonical investiture from the Pope. The Constitutional Church now ceased to exist except in so far as some Catholics continued to support a number of Constitutional bishops who refused to accept the Concordat and succeeded in keeping an independent denomination, the 'Petite Eglise', alive.

by the Concordat bishops and clergy alike were required to take an oath of fidelity to the Constitution and to ensure that prayers were offered for the Republic at the conclusion of divine services. In return for these concessions, and for the Papacy's acceptance of a redrawing of the boundaries of dioceses to coincide with those of the new courts of appeal, Bonaparte agreed that France would afford Catholics freedom of public worship 'subject to essential police regulations', and would pay the salaries of all bishops and clergy. Finally, it was a feature of the new system that the parish priests were to be appointed by the bishops, on whom they were now far more dependent than in the days of the monarchy.

Reached in Paris in July 1801, these arrangements were ratified by the Pope in August and by Bonaparte in September. They had, however, still to be sanctioned by the French legislature, and—to anticipate the course of events once again—on 8 April 1802 Bonaparte took the drastic step of publishing a long list of additional Organic Articles, which had been drawn up without the knowledge of the Papacy in order to strengthen the position of the State still further. In brief, these reaffirmed, and ordered the teaching of, the Gallican principles of 1682, forbidding the Pope from issuing any bull or calling any general council of the Church in France without the express authorisation of the government; and they imposed the strictest of regulations upon every public form of religious activity, down to the very dress of the priest. This measure may be seen as symbolic of the nature, and perhaps even of the ultimate fate, of the Concordat as a whole. In the short term, it was indisputably immensely beneficial both to Bonaparte and to France; for the support of the Church gave some sanctity to his authority, and his re-establishment of Catholicism ended the schisms and persecutions which had been both the boast and the bane of the Revolution. In a longer perspective, however, Bonaparte's subordination of the bishops to the State served to stimulate unrest amongst the lower clergy, who tended increasingly to look to Rome for spiritual leadership. Thus as religious life revived ultramontanism developed apace beneath the shield of the Concordat, foreshadowing a further century of dissension.[1]

The unilateral act by which the Organic Articles were imposed upon the Church may also be considered symbolic of the way in which the Papacy was treated throughout the negotiation of the Concordat.

---

[1] On the Concordat and the Organic Articles, see Lefebvre, *Napoléon*, pp. 127–34; H. H. Walsh, *The Concordat of 1801* (N.Y. 1933/1967), particularly pp. 50–60; and Jean Godel, 'The Church under Napoleon', *Revue d'histoire moderne*, t. XVII (juillet–septembre 1970), pp. 837–45.

Although in this instance, unlike that of the talks which led to the Treaty of Amiens, both sides were hard bargainers, Bonaparte's success was again obtained—and ultimately compromised—by his persistent identification of diplomacy with domination. In the middle of May 1801, when the Pope considered it impossible to make more concessions without imperilling the purity of the Catholic faith, his negotiators in Paris and at the Vatican were informed that France could not modify her demands and that Bonaparte would regard any further procrastination as a personal affront, which he would answer by an immediate occupation of all the Papal States. This, and other similar ultimata, were accompanied by the repeated threat that unless a conclusion was reached with a set term of days Bonaparte would abandon the talks and Catholicism together and establish some form of 'natural religion' instead.[1] Even at the last moment, when Cardinal Consalvi (who had arrived in Paris on 2 June to avert imminent disaster) was presented with an eighth, and apparently final, text of the agreement, he discovered that it had been modified without his knowledge, and 19 hours of exhausting debate were necessary to secure the ninth version which he signed at two o'clock in the morning of 16 July.[2] As Spina wrote, these methods so cut across established diplomatic practice that even the most experienced diplomats were often completely at a loss;[3] and in the final result the Church was, in the words of one modern authority, 'mercilessly subjected to the will of the French government'.[4]

At the end of the year 1801 Bonaparte could nevertheless fairly claim that he had won a fine position for France, and the opening of the third session of parliament on 22 November was marked by Thibaudeau's reading of an impressive review of what had been accomplished in suppressing brigandage, ending religious strife and establishing a general European peace.[5] Now, these treaties had to be approved, as had the first articles of the new Civil Code, to the preparation of which the First Consul and his councillors had already devoted more than a hundred meetings; and beyond this there lay ambitious proposals for the development of secondary education, and of course the controversial Concordat itself. It was, however, soon apparent that the deputies, so consistently slighted in the past, were no longer willing to assemble simply in order to ratify treaties and to endorse decisions taken by the Council of State.

---

[1] J. Thiry, *Le Concordat et le Consulat à vie* (Paris, 1956), pp. 63–8, 78, 81–2.
[2] Walsh, op. cit., p. 52.
[3] Thiry, op. cit., p. 68.
[4] Walsh, op. cit., p. 60.
[5] *Archives Parlementaires*, II, p. 728.

The first sign of this increased hostility to the government was the election on 22 November of Dupuis, a well-known opponent of Catholicism, to the presidency of the Legislative Body. Shortly afterwards the tribunes made their presence felt by taking exception to a sentence in the treaty which Bonaparte had concluded with the Tsar. In this, the two rulers had made reference to 'their subjects', and although the Tribunate in fact ratified the treaty, as well as four others, within a few days, the phraseology occasioned a lively debate[1] in which Chenier asserted that five million Frenchmen had died to secure the title of 'citizen' for their countrymen. More important, the chambers rejected most of the first legislative proposals of the session. Not surprisingly, perhaps, they accepted the adjournment of the abolition of capital punishment, which the Convention had said should come into effect when peace was attained; but they showed considerable hostility to the government's attempt to reintroduce the branding of hardened criminals, a practice which the National Assembly had abolished in 1791. As to the Civil Code, the first article to be brought forward was decisively rejected in both houses as ill-defined and incoherent, terms which reflected the deputies' well-founded suspicion that the whole Code would be more inclined to the autocratic than to the revolutionary tradition.[2]

What is more, at this same time the deputies, and even many of the Senators, sought to assert their independence by their selection of new members of the Senate. As it happened, there were three vacancies to be filled in that assembly, one arising from the death of a Senator and two being the new places that were to be created each year until there were 80 Senators in all. According to the Constitution, the Senate was to select its new members from candidates proposed by the Tribunate, the Legislative Body and the First Consul, and if the situation had been harmonious it should have been possible to make at least one appointment pleasing to each of these. Both the Tribunate and the Legislative Body nevertheless rejected the first government candidate: the tribunes chose a moderate, Demeunier, and the deputies of the Legislative Body selected Grégoire—the most illustrious champion of the Constitutional Church. Bonaparte promptly responded by naming three further official candidates, all of whom were generals—Lamartillière, Jourdan and Berruyer. Influenced to some extent by Sieyès, who significantly reappeared in Paris at this juncture, the senators selected Grégoire for the first of the three vacancies; and the opposition, not content with this

---

[1] Ibid., III, p. 48.
[2] Ibid., p. 373. See also Thibaudeau, op. cit., pp. 33–5.

success, at once proceeded to secure, in both the Tribunate and the Legislative Body, the nomination for the second seat of Daunou, who was perhaps Bonaparte's principal opponent in parliament.[1]

The First Consul's reaction to this sudden surge of hostility was characteristically uncompromising. The tribunes he described as dogs, as enemies, as people who had prejudged every issue; half of them, he asserted, were trying to re-establish the Terror, while the others were working to restore the monarchy.[2] Though this may well be thought grossly unfair, there is of course much to be said for the more restrained view, expressed by several of Bonaparte's councillors, that the government had to be able to count on the support of a majority of deputies if all the arduous work done in the Council of State was not to be wasted. But if the opposition had begun to become factious and irresponsible, this was certainly largely because Bonaparte himself had always prevented it from fulfilling any constructive role. As Cambacérès remarked at the time, he had lost the majority support he had once enjoyed simply because he had no idea of how to manage large assemblies.[3]

Bonaparte's actions at this point seem in fact to be far more premeditated than those of the deputies. On 23 December, as soon as the first article of the Civil Code had been rejected in the legislature, he told the Council of State that some way must be found to end futile debate; and he himself suggested that the Tribunate might be split into five small sections, each of which might be allowed to discuss legislation in private with the corresponding sections of the Council—a solution substantially the same as that ultimately adopted in 1802. More immediately, he accepted a councillor's suggestion that they should wait a little longer, saying in military vein that he would risk two more engagements and then go into winter quarters if things went against him.[4] The first of these encounters, the Tribunate's consideration of the second article of the Civil Code, was, to continue the metaphor, a victory, since the article was accepted by a vote of 64 to 26; but the second was a defeat, for on 1 January 1802 the Tribunate rejected the third article of the Code by 61 votes to 31, Chenier making no bones about saying that while everyone wanted a Civil Code, they wanted one free from the gothic prejudices that the Revolution had reversed. In immediate reaction, Bonaparte sent a message to inform the Legislative Body that all

---

[1] J. Thiry, *Le Sénat de Napoléon* (Paris, 1932), pp. 80–5.

[2] Thibaudeau, op. cit., pp. 40–3; Thiry, *Le Concordat et le Consulat à vie*, pp. 155, 158.

[3] Thibaudeau, op. cit., p. 41.

[4] Ibid.

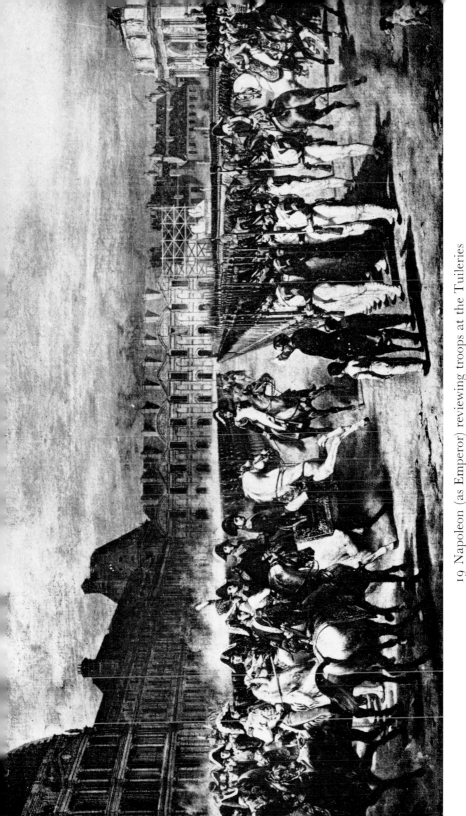

19 Napoleon (as Emperor) reviewing troops at the Tuileries
Horace Vernet

The coronation of the Emperor Napoleon I

the government's proposed legislation was to be withdrawn.[1] On the same day (2 January) he also browbeat the Senators into submission, telling many of them at an audience that they owed the peace to the generals whom they were reluctant to accept in their ranks. Asserting that certain people were thinking of establishing an Orléanist monarchy, he so disconcerted Sieyès that the poor man had to retire from the room; and he ended by saying explicitly that if the Senators chose Daunou to fill their second vacancy, he would regard that as a personal affront, a thing they knew he never accepted.[2]

The sequel to all this may be considered almost a foregone conclusion. In the first place, on 4 January the Senate hastily selected General Lamartillière to fill its second seat, feebly pretending that the nomination of Daunou was not officially available. Secondly, as the result of a meeting of the Council of State on 7 January, it was decided that the session of the legislature, which was now occupied only with formalities and local matters, could legitimately be considered at an end, and that in consequence the Senate could be asked to resolve the constitutional situation. More specifically, the Senate was required to decide whether the constitutional rule which called for the renewal of one fifth of the membership of both the Tribunate and the Legislative Body in the course of the current calendar year could now be brought into effect, and, if so, what means should be adopted to make the changes. As was fully expected, the Senate, now once again reduced to something like subservience, for a second time consented to twist the constitution to silence opposition. In the middle of January, 1802, the issue, and indeed the fate of parliament, was determined by the Senate's decision that it would be constitutionally valid to proceed with the renewal of the membership of the two chambers, and that this could be done most quietly and expeditiously if a commission of the Senate itself were to select those who should retire and name others to replace them. The result of this was the elimination—by selection, not by lot—of 60 members of the Legislative Body and 20 of the Tribunate, and it need hardly be said that those who were excluded were men like Benjamin Constant, Chenier, Daunou and Ginguené, the opponents of Bonaparte.[3] Of the incoming placemen,

---

[1] *Archives Parlementaires*, III, pp. 373, 376: 'It is with pain that the government finds itself obliged to withdraw until a later date, laws which the nation has awaited with so much interest', *etc.*

[2] Thiry, *Le Sénat de Napoléon*, pp. 80–5.

[3] Thiry, *Le Concordat et le Consulat à vie*, pp. 161–5, according to whom the method adopted was first recommended by Cambacérès. Since Bonaparte left for Lyons on 8 January (to reorganise the Cisalpine or Italian Republic, of which he became the president), it fell to Cambacérès to effect the scheme; but

Lucien Bonaparte was by far the most notable, and it was he who presented the purged chambers with the measure of 1 April 1802 by which the Tribunate was divided into three sections which would consider legislative proposals in private before the full assembly met in public. Even this was not enough for Bonaparte, who soon modified the procedure by a decree to ensure that there would be five sections, the leaders of which would first consider legislation alongside appropriate members of the Council of State and under his own personal presidency. Thus, as Thibaudeau wrote, there vanished the last shadow of representative government.[1]

The way was thus cleared for the approval, in an extraordinary session of the so-called legislature, of as many measures as the First Consul was prepared to put forward. This session opened on 5 April, a week after the protracted period of European wars was officially ended by the conclusion of the Peace of Amiens between Britain and France. Bonaparte then left the deputies in no doubt about what was expected of them: in replying to the Legislative Body's compliments, he wrote: 'You will be unanimous, as is the nation, in the result of your deliberations'.[2] In this he referred particularly to the conclusion of religious peace, and the Concordat, accompanied by the Organic Articles and by corresponding Articles providing similar status for the Protestant churches, was in fact quietly accepted by the Legislative Body on 8 April. Although discussion of the Civil Code was not to be resumed for a further year, the controversial law to reimpose the branding of criminals was also duly approved on 13 May, and a week later similar sanction was given to the re-establishment of slavery in the French colonies.

Even so, Bonaparte found it expedient to avoid re-opening in the Legislative Body the old problem of the émigrés. Although many, perhaps even the majority, of these had already returned to France, this

---

Bonaparte wrote repeatedly to urge the importance of eliminating his enemies from the two assemblies. In the event, the Senate simply published the list of those members *retaining* their seats: *Archives Parlementaires*, III, pp. 403–6.

[1] Thibaudeau, op. cit., p. 47. Thibaudeau of course used the term 'representative government' in its usual sense, not in that of Bonaparte. Strictly, his comment might be thought more applicable to the regulation in the Constitution of Year XII (18 May, 1804) by which, when the Empire was established, the Tribunate was forbidden to hold any general session for the discussion of laws, which were to go directly from the section to the Legislative Body. Thibaudeau was nonetheless right in his contention that from 1802 the public were deprived of any real knowledge of impending legislation, all that mattered being done in private.

[2] Thiry, op. cit., p. 189.

had happened in defiance of the ban maintained in the Constitution of 1799, and the matter was singularly appropriate for another intervention by the Senate. It was therefore by a third *senatus-consultum*, that of 26 April 1802, that the First Consul extended a general amnesty to all the *émigrés* who were not notoriously hostile to the Republic. While the number of those still proscribed was not to exceed 1,000, the others had to return, and take the oath of fidelity to the Constitution, before the end of the year (23 September 1802); and they had also to remain under the supervision of the police for the next ten years.[1]

In this same session, too, other laws, equally indicative of Bonaparte's concept of how society should be organised, were passed to establish a new educational system and to reward service to the State. On 1 May the 'central schools' which had been established in 1795 to provide secondary education, not only in the sciences but also in the liberal arts and the republican tradition,[2] were swept aside, provision being made for the creation instead of *lycées*, schools to which selected students would be sent with state scholarships for a higher education, under military discipline, which should fit them for office either in the army or the civil service. Still more important at the time was the creation on 19 May of the Legion of Honour, a measure which Bonaparte described as: 'a first step towards the organisation of the nation'. Membership of the Order, which would be a reward for meritorious service to the State in either military or civilian life, carried with it both an appropriate rank ('Grand Officer', 'Commander' or 'Knight') and a small life-pension: but it would also depend upon selection by a Grand Council nominated and presided over by Bonaparte. To this measure alone was there any serious resistance, for it was rightly seen as an infringement of the fundamental republican belief in the equality of all citizens. As Berlier said in the Council of State: 'The proposed Order leads directly to an aristocracy'.[3] The law was nonetheless accepted—by 14 votes to 10 in the Council, by 50 to 38 in the Tribunate and by 116 to 110 in the Legislative Body. In the circumstances this was equivalent to a vote of censure, which one contemporary described as: 'the last effort of the national representation against the encroachments of an arbitrary and absolute power'.[4]

Thus in the early summer of 1802 Bonaparte's power to rule and re-

[1] Lefebvre, op. cit., p. 157; see also Greer, *The Incidence of the Emigration*.

[2] See J. Hall Stewart, *A Documentary Survey of the French Revolution*, p. 619.

[3] Thibaudeau, op. cit., p. 142. On the measure in general, see also Markham, *Napoleon*, pp. 80–1, or R. B. Holtman, *The Napoleonic Revolution* (Philadelphia, 1967), pp. 196–7.

[4] C. Fauviel, *The Last Days of the Consulate* (ed. L. Lalanne, N.Y., 1886), p. 37.

organise France as he thought fit increased considerably and obviously. Although it was still possible for men of repute to record their reservations about his actions and to hope that his increasingly autocratic rule might yet be liberalised, active opposition to it had of necessity to become clandestine. Consequently even at this time, when the First Consul enjoyed great prestige as the man who had brought peace to France and to Europe, conspiracies against him continued. Elusive as are the details of these, it seems likely that there was some collusion between some political figures, including some Senators, and some high officers in the army, without whose intervention effective action against Bonaparte had by now become impossible.[1] Disgruntled generals of course abounded, for the peace which brought him popularity thwarted others' hopes of advancement, and the reconciliation with Rome was a hard pill for the soldiers of the Republic to swallow. The ceremony held in Notre Dame on Easter Day (18 April) to mark the inauguration of the Concordat was indeed somewhat disturbed by the evident displeasure of the generals who were ordered to attend, and it is said that General Delmas, a regular rough diamond, told Bonaparte bluntly that evening that the occasion had been 'a fine monkish show, lacking only the presence of the hundred thousand men who gave their lives to end the whole business'.[2]

While only one sadly mismanaged plot, the 'Conspiracy of Rennes', emerged from much loose talk amongst the soldiers, that affair at least reveals something of the situation. Essentially, towards the end of May many copies of two seditious broadsheets came to light in Paris and the various garrison towns of north-western France. One of these, an 'Appeal to the Armies of France by their Comrades', was singularly forthright: 'Soldiers! You no longer have a fatherland, the Republic has ceased to exist. A tyrant has seized power . . . The émigrés return from every hand, hypocritical priests are paid by the tyrant . . . All your conquests have been in vain!' This appeal, which amounted to a call to the garrisons to be ready to rise as soon as their generals gave the word, was traced back without much difficulty to a General Simon, who was arrested with a few of his subordinates. The significance of the affair lies, however, in the fact that Simon was chief-of-staff to General Bernadotte, who as commander of the armies in the west then had at his disposition not only his own forces, but also a considerable number of men who were being assembled for embarkation to the West Indies. Many of

---

[1] H. Calvet, *Napoléon*, p. 65; see also Soboul, *Le Ire République*, p. 330, and Lefebvre, op. cit., pp. 142–3.

[2] Thibaudeau, op. cit., p. 162.

the latter, moreover, were men of General Moreau's Army of the Rhine, which was traditionally hostile to Bonaparte; and Bernadotte was believed to have been associating with Moreau in Paris.[1]

How far the ramifications of this plot really extended remains a matter of speculation, particularly as it was thought expedient to hush it up. In the event Simon and his associates remained untried in prison; the troops were dispersed, the most disaffected regiment, the 82nd of the line, being sent to San Domingo and Martinique in perpetuity; and Bernadotte's exclamations of astonished innocence were accepted. At Fouché's suggestion, however, various politicians were advised to leave Paris, not the least amongst them being Madame de Staël. As for Bonaparte, who seems to have been convinced that Moreau had had some hand in the affair, he remained distrustful, insistent upon the pre-eminence of civil authority[2]—and triumphant.

Contemporaries and historians alike have indeed often suggested that the period immediately after the conclusion of the Treaty of Amiens was the time of greatest opportunity in Bonaparte's career. Having the world at his feet, it is said, he was then freer even than after Marengo to choose between republican authority and despotic power. As Thibaudeau, the man of the Revolution who had become a valued Councillor of State, wrote in his *Memoirs*, the ruler of France now stood at the parting of the ways: for though the men of the Revolution had long since abandoned all hope of establishing the republic of their dreams, they still believed that it might yet be possible to found one 'worthy of the dignity, advancement and destiny of the human race . . . such a Republic being by no means incompatible with the existence of a head of the State'. But Thibaudeau also remarks that it had long been apparent that Bonaparte was 'tending steadily towards concentrating the authority of the State in his own hands and shaping the fortunes of France into absolute dependence on himself alone'.[3] By the time European peace was attained in 1802, Bonaparte's course was determined, his 'choice'—if indeed a choice was possible for a nature such as his—having in all probability been made some 18 months beforehand, at the turn of the year 1800–1. As Carnot, now the only Revolutionary of stature to be a member of the Tribunate, said in a great speech on 3 May 1804,[4] the conclusion of the

---

[1] Gaubert, *Conspirateurs au temps de Napoléon Ier*, pp. 137–54; Baron de Marbot, *Memoirs* (trans. A. J. Butler, London, 1892), I, pp. 114–20.

[2] Lefebvre, op. cit., p. 143, where it is suggested that Bonaparte's denials that he ruled France as a general were particularly emphatic at this time.

[3] Thibaudeau, op. cit., pp. 216–17.

[4] A point made by Soboul, op. cit., p. 318.

Treaty of Amiens was in fact followed by a series of measures—the assembling of a purged parliament, the promulgation of the Concordat, the formation of the Legion of Honour, the reorganisation of education and the rehabilitation of the *émigrés*—which were evidently of a monarchical and aristocratic character.

Aided and abetted by such men as Cambacérès, Talleyrand, Roederer and Lucien Bonaparte, whose influence increased as the fortunes of Fouché fell, the First Consul now proceeded to make his régime permanent and still more autocratic. Even if all did not occur precisely as was planned, the Life Consulate, which was for all practical purposes a monarchy, was indisputably established by design.[1] In the first place, on 6 May the legislature was officially notified of the conclusion of the Treaty of Amiens; and at the instigation of Bonaparte, who acted through Cambacérès and a number of selected senators, the Tribunate was moved to invite the Senate to determine how best to afford the First Consul some striking sign of the nation's appreciation of his services. Two days later, on 8 May, the Senate debated its own commissioners' proposal to extend the powers of the First Consul for ten years (this period being additional to the decade of authority already given to him by the Constitution of 1799). At this point, however, the arrangements went astray, perhaps because the propaganda prepared by Roederer, which called upon the Senate to grant Bonaparte all the time he would need to ensure the welfare of France,[2] did not reach the chamber soon enough to be distributed. A motion by a subservient Senator to offer the First Consul authority for life aroused antagonism, and Lanjuinais, true to a lifetime of independence, even cried out that the ten-year extension would be 'a flagrant usurpation, placing the Republic in jeopardy'.[3] The Senate consequently determined by secret ballot simply to re-elect Napoleon Bonaparte to the consulship for the additional period of ten years. This, it should be added, was the first occasion on which the name Napoleon occurred in an official document.

Displeased, Bonaparte replied on 9 May that he could not accept this 'new sacrifice' of service to the people unless the invitation were formally confirmed by the will of the people. A plebiscite had therefore to be arranged, and Bonaparte, retiring to Malmaison, left Cambacérès to see that this was duly authorised. The form of the question, framed by Roederer and adopted by a few selected councillors in private assembly,

[1] See particularly Thiry, *Le Sénat de Napoléon*, p. 100.
[2] 'Give him the century which has begun with him'. Thiry, *Le Concordat et le Consulat à vie*, p. 204.
[3] Ibid., p. 205.

was nevertheless submitted to Bonaparte, who at once struck out a section by which the people would have been asked to authorise him to name his own successor. The proposal that 'The will of the people be taken on the question: Shall Napoleon Bonaparte be Consul for life?' was then sanctioned by the Council of State, though five councillors, of whom Thibaudeau was one, expressed dissent by abstention.[1] Finally, by another manoeuvre, the proposal was sent for endorsement to the Legislative Body and the Tribunate although neither body (unlike the Senate) had any constitutional authority in the matter. There then followed an interval of three months for the registration of the popular vote, and on 2 August the Senate, relegated to the role of a tally-clerk, announced the expected result: the French people having manifested its will by 3,568,885 votes in favour of the proposal, with only 8,574 against it, Napoleon Bonaparte was proclaimed Consul for life.

Although in the course of these proceedings the Tribunate praised Napoleon's readiness to defer to the sovereignty of the people, no such sincerity should be attributed to him. As Thibaudeau remarks, in this whole matter the initiative was his alone;[2] and he certainly knew the practical value of what he was doing. His recourse to the plebiscite not only secured for him the life appointment which the Senate had withheld, but also enabled him to re-assert the claim that his authority, derived from the people alone, was independent of, and superior to, that of the Senate or any other body. His appreciation of the more theoretical political potentialities of the doctrine of popular sovereignty is moreover unquestionable. That idea, it will be remembered, was the one which he had identified in September 1797 as France's only positive contribution to political thinking for 50 years; and once it was firmly wedded to his own conception of a representative government, whose whole authority emanated directly from the nation, both despotism and opposition naturally became unthinkable. As he had explained to his councillors in the crucial meetings of 7–8 January 1802, 'the French government represented the sovereign people, and there can be no opposition to the sovereign'.[3] He was, nevertheless, careful not to allow the matter of the succession to be included in the plebiscite, for that would have implied that he was not free to act without explicit public sanction.

---

[1] Thibaudeau, op. cit., pp. 224–5. The names of the other four may also be recorded: they were Bérenger, Berlier, Dessole and Emmery. By contrast, Regnault de St-Jean d'Angély pressed for prompt action: 'We should not lose any time if we are to prevent public opinion from going astray'.

[2] Ibid., p. 228.

[3] Ibid., pp. 43–5; see also Thiry, Le Concordat et le Consulat à vie, p. 163.

In those same meetings of the Council in January Bonaparte had also made it clear that his respect for the Constitution of 1799 counted for nothing in comparison with his understanding of the immediate needs of the State and his right to rule as he thought best. Constitutions, he had said, were always subordinate to the exigencies of men and circumstances. 'A constitution which hampers the action of Government must be altered . . . It is high time to reorganise the Constitution in such a way that the Executive may be given a free hand.'[1] This re-organisation Napoleon effected immediately he became Consul for life, dictating the new instrument of government personally.

The Constitution of 1802 (Year X), if such it can be called, was given nominal approval by the Council of State and promulgated on 4 August in the form (needless to say) of yet another *senatus-consultum*. Superficially, this remarkable document[2] greatly increased the authority of the Senate, just as Napoleon had anticipated on 8 January, when he had described that body as one insufficiently employed but well-fitted to exercise extraordinary powers in periods of emergency. Now it received the right to issue both 'organic' and 'regular' *senatus-consulta*. By the former, it could interpret the constitution. By the latter, it could annul the decisions of the law-courts; suspend the jury system, and even the constitution, wherever this seemed necessary; determine the duration of periods of imprisonment before trial; and dissolve the Legislative Body and the Tribunate. All these powers, as well as others like that of appointing judges of appeal, were however illusory, for the real right of exercising them rested with the First Consul. In practice, no *senatus-consultum* could arise save on the initiative of the government, which was to consider it first in a small private council, the members of which were to be nominated by Napoleon. Further, the First Consul, who was to preside over the meetings of the Senate, also awarded himself the exclusive right of presenting candidates to its vacant seats—and while at least 14 places were to be filled within the year to raise the membership to 80, the addition of 40 more places now remained in the First Consul's discretion. If it be added that the new constitution also authorised senators to hold remunerative appointments in the public service, and that when Napoleon first increased the number of the senators, on 4 January 1803, he also endowed the senators with substantial residential

---

[1] Thiry, loc. cit.
[2] L. Duguit, H. Morrier, R. Bonnard, *Les Constitutions et les principals lois politiques de la France depuis 1789* (7th ed., Paris, 1952), pp. 120–8; see also Lefebvre, op. cit., pp. 137–41.

estates (*sénatories*), it is apparent that the chamber was simply a tool in his hand.

For the rest, the powers that remained to other bodies were reduced correspondingly. The recognition that ministers were *ex officio* members of a Council of State that was not to number more than 50 indicates that that body had become formalised, the centre of political power being in whatever private councils Napoleon chose to employ. The Legislative Body, deprived of fixed terms for its sessions, could be called or dismissed as the government willed; and there were to be now no more than 50 tribunes, meeting separately in their various sections. Even Sieyès' elaborate scheme for the graduated election of 'notables' was now eliminated in favour of the creation of electoral colleges, which would be still more conservative and easily controlled. Well might Joseph Bonaparte remark, as he did in January 1803 when he watched the senators calculating their incomes under the new dispensation: 'I have no more illusions about republicanism in France—it no longer exists'.[1]

There was indeed astonishingly little resistance either to the Life Consulate or to the Constitution of 1802. Some men, like the President of the Tribunate, simply expressed what was really a hope as if it were a conviction: 'Napoleon . . . will respect the nation and consolidate its freedom . . . he will surround himself with those men of goodwill who, having made the Revolution, are concerned to sustain it'.[2] Others, stronger in spirit, protested obliquely, as Camille Jourdan did in publishing the pamphlet entitled: 'The True Meaning of the National Vote'. Ostensibly written in warning that Napoleon might be succeeded by one who would abuse his great authority, this was in reality a plea for some guarantees of freedom in a rapidly developing dictatorship: 'We desire deliverance from the vague and indefinite power of the police, the principal resource of all despotic governments'.[3] Few men, however, were as bold as Carnot or La Fayette, who continued to oppose the Life Consulate to the end because it was not accompanied by any firm safeguards for law and liberty.[4] In general, the men of the Revolution and the Republic recognised that resistance had become impossible. As even Lanjuinais said: 'Nothing now remains save to keep silent, and that is what I shall do'.[5]

[1] Miot de Melito, *Memoirs*, p. 260.
[2] Thiry, *Le Concordat et le Consulat à vie*, p. 214.
[3] Thibaudeau, op. cit., p. 243. See also R. G. Carey, *The Liberals of France and their relation to the development of Bonaparte's dictatorship, 1799–1804* (University of Chicago, 1947), p. 11.
[4] Thiry, op. cit., p. 215.
[5] Ibid., p. 204.

In this unhappy story, a last word may remain with Thibaudeau. He tells us that when Napoleon had the Life Consulate within his grasp, and was considering the ways in which he would modify the Constitution of 1799, he remarked: 'At this moment I am on a level with foreign sovereigns'.[1] In reality, however, that objective had still to be attained. As Napoleon knew well, and as those about him were constantly reminding him,[2] all that he had achieved still depended upon his own survival. Not surprisingly, men of all shades of opinion sought some more permanent guarantee of stability, both for themselves and for France; and just as some looked to the elimination of Josephine and the foundation of an hereditary monarchy, so others, including Thibaudeau, still continued to hope that Napoleon could be convinced that the strongest government was really one based upon an effective parliamentary system. When constitutional change was being discussed, Thibaudeau pressed this point so much that Napoleon suggested he should state his case in writing. This Thibaudeau did, and to his recommendations he added a warning: 'It is no light thing to give the death blow to a Republic. You will kill the Revolution at the same time. All the feudal institutions will surround your throme. Probably you will not wish it so; they will come in spite of you, and you will end by submitting to them.'[3] No reply was received; but at the end of July 1802, a few days before he was presented in the Council of State with a Constitution of a very different kind, Thibaudeau was assured by Josephine herself that Napoleon had no thoughts of founding an empire. To this the great republican replied: 'Madame, the First Consul deceives you; he deceives us all'.[4]

---

[1] Thibaudeau, op. cit., p. 232.

[2] E.g., the remark of Cambacérès to Thibaudeau on the evening of 3 August 1802: 'The whole system at present rests upon the life of one single man'. Thibaudeau, op. cit., p. 249.

[3] Markham, *Napoleon*, p. 88, and Thibaudeau, op. cit., pp. 234–41, 265–7.

[4] Thibaudeau, op. cit., p. 245.

Conclusion: The Empire and the Republic 1802-1804

In April 1804, just before the Empire was inaugurated, Napoleon told his brother Joseph that he had always intended to end the Revolution by establishing an hereditary system; and he added: 'I thought such a step could not be taken before five years had elapsed ... I see now, by the eagerness of those about me, that I was mistaken.'[1] Since Napoleon commonly assumed that he had anticipated all eventualities, his comment upon his past intention must be regarded with reserve: but the renewal of war with Britain in 1803 and the exposure early in 1804 of yet another royalist conspiracy against Napoleon's life certainly facilitated the creation of the Empire by intensifying men's anxieties about the future. Uneasiness was indeed implicit in a system in which all apparently depended more and more upon the survival of a man who had no obvious and legitimate heir.[2]

Welcome though it was to the great majority of people in both Britain and France, the Peace of Amiens was essentially an experiment in co-existence. To the British, the question was whether it would now be possible to resume normal economic and political relationships with a France which was stabilised and ready to recognise the reality of an international law not of her own dictation. More specifically, the British regarded the Peace of Amiens, almost regardless of what it actually said, as an agreement that the existing European situation would be maintained; in their view it meant at the least that any further changes would be both effected by agreement and accompanied by adjustments or 'compensations' designed to preserve the same general distribution of power amongst the rulers of Europe. To Napoleon, however, the treaty had no such symbolic significance. Regarding it simply as a specific

[1] Miot de Melito, *Memoirs*, p. 323.
[2] The problem of course continued to perplex men's minds after the Empire was established. In November 1804, for example, Roederer reports Napoleon as exclaiming: 'My death! It is always a matter of my death!' Roederer, *Mémoires*, p. 208.

agreement, he held himself bound at most only to honour its clauses according to their letter and in approximate conformity to the corresponding actions of the British. Since to him France's other activities were of no concern to Britain, he saw the question simply as that of how far Britain was prepared to accept the natural development of his power in Europe and overseas without protest or interference.

Events soon demonstrated the incompatibility of these opposing points of view. Although the British eventually restored the Cape of Good Hope to the Dutch, they were most reluctant to do so before the French had withdrawn their troops from the Dutch Republic itself; but Napoleon correctly maintained that he had made no specific agreement with Britain about evacuating Holland, and he kept that country firmly under his own control. Nor was Switzerland liberated for long. Although the French forces there were withdrawn soon after the agreements at Lunéville and Amiens,[1] the rapid development of a revolt in the cantons against the men and the constitution hitherto upheld by France speedily led to renewed French intervention: in October 1802 an army commanded by Ney defeated the rebels and re-occupied the republic. Since by that time Napoleon had also reinforced his position as President of the Italian Republic by the annexation of Elba and Piedmont, as well as by the occupation of Parma, the British government protested strongly against all these actions even before Lord Whitworth, the newly-appointed ambassador to France, left London. To this protest, Napoleon replied by demanding 'the whole Treaty of Amiens and nothing but that Treaty'; but Britain replied in turn by demanding 'the state of the Continent at the period of the Treaty of Amiens, and nothing but that state'.[2]

Beyond this fundamental difference of view about the future of Europe (a difference which was to be hardened early in 1803 by the increase of French influence in Germany)[3] there stood the equally insoluble prob-

---

[1] Swiss independence was guaranteed by the Treaty of Lunéville, and the withdrawal of French troops in 1802 was preceded by Swiss acceptance of Napoleon's 'Malmaison Constitution' of May 1801. The revolt of 1802 arose in part from 'patriotic' resistance to the continuation of the new constitution, which made only half-hearted concessions to federalism, and in part from resistance to the continuation of French control of the strategically vital Valais.

[2] J. H. Rose, *The Life of Napoleon I* (6th ed., 1913), p. 405. Compare Lefebvre, *Napoléon*, p. 165, where the two quotations are given in reverse order.

[3] On 25 February 1803 the Imperial Diet of the Holy Roman Empire accepted arrangements for the reconstruction of the German states which were founded upon agreements reached privately in Paris. Amongst other consequences, the settlement considerably increased the influence of France upon the states of southern Germany. See Lefebvre, op. cit., p. 174.

lems that arose from Napoleon's commercial and colonial ambitions. Despite Britain's hopes that peace would lead to freer trade with France and its satellites, the First Consul did not depart from a policy of strict protection, in which particularly high tariff barriers were raised against the entry of British goods. Being convinced that France ought to be self-sufficient, and that the French monetary crisis would only be finally resolved when more gold and silver came into the country than was allowed to leave it, he also equated British trade with British commercial exploitation and held that he had to guard the continent against it. Further, he seems to have seen the Peace of Amiens primarily as an opportunity to re-establish a strong French colonial empire. Initially his principal interest was in the New World, but the disasters which overtook the expedition to San Domingo, together with the unexpected strength of America's reaction to the possibility of French activity in Louisiana,[1] compelled him to think increasingly of enterprises in the Middle East and in India—to which a small French expeditionary force was indeed despatched early in March 1803. When Britain, which was at this time particularly alarmed by the accumulation of evidence of French designs on Egypt, once more protested, Napoleon calmly proposed that the two powers should divide the globe between them. As Lord Whitworth reported in February 1803: ' "Finally", he asked, "why should not the mistress of the seas and the mistress of the land come to an arrangement and govern the world?" '[2]

To that unanswered question the British might well have replied that by the spring of 1803 Napoleon's actions were as menacing to her own security as they were to the general peace of Europe; and although Britain placed herself technically in the wrong by retaining possession of Malta, she had sound moral as well as military reasons for doing so. If in the event it was also Britain which first broke the peace, Lord Whitworth being ordered to return home if he received no satisfactory answer to the ultimatum he presented on 26 April 1803,[3] the real responsibility for the renewal of the war was indisputably Napoleon's. By his own admission the First Consul regarded the peace merely as one of momentary advantage, which he was naturally bound to exploit to the

---

[1] Although the expedition to San Domingo was initially successful in restoring French power there, disease and a new negro revolt against a premature attempt to reimpose slavery ultimately wrecked the enterprise. The Louisiana Purchase, by which France sold Louisiana to the United States for 80 million francs, was signed in Paris on 3 May 1803.

[2] Lord Whitworth's despatch of 21 February 1803, cited by J. H. Rose, op. cit., p. 416.

[3] The ambassador finally left Paris on 12 May.

full. While his talk of 'goading John Bull into war' was probably intended to conceal the fact that the relative rapidity of the British reaction had exceeded his expectations, there seems no reason to doubt the deliberation of his remark to Thibaudeau that military success was even more necessary than internal peace and useful institutions to dazzle and content the French people. A First Consul's actions, he explained, 'must be dramatic, and for this, war is indispensable . . . Hated by our neighbours, obliged to deal at home with large classes of enemies, we need to impose on friends and foes alike by the deeds of glory which are won only by war.'[1] In this respect, as in others, Napoleonic imperialism was a reality long before the Empire was officially established.[2]

Before the war which now began finally ended in 1815, that imperialism was to extend from Lisbon to Moscow; but in the last days of the Consulate no one gained much glory. Initially, the British seized every French vessel within their reach, and Napoleon retaliated not only by impounding British ships but also by ordering the arrest and internment of every Englishman of military age who could be found in France. This action, which Napoleon justified on the ground that these people would be bound to serve in the militia if they returned to Britain, struck at many who had hastened to visit France when the peace began, and it was then generally regarded as a singularly severe and uncivilised measure. The First Consul also ordered General Mortier and an army of 25,000 men to occupy Hanover; and, despite the protests of the King of Prussia, the embargo on British trade was then extended to the mouths of the Elbe and the Weser. At the same time forces commanded by St Cyr moved into the Kingdom of Naples and reoccupied the ports of southern Italy, Napoleon's pretext being that his treaty with Naples was dependent upon the British evacuation of Malta. All these measures, together with the exaction of inordinately heavy tribute from every state within the French orbit, were however subordinate to the First Consul's

---

[1] Thibaudeau, *Bonaparte and the Consulate*, pp. 118–21; see also Lefebvre, op. cit., pp. 159, 165.

[2] Compare Lefebvre (op. cit., p. 167), where it is remarked that the conflict between Bonaparte and England was in reality one between two imperialisms. That comment might well be tempered by the reflection that the British mercantilist empire of the eighteenth century was more commonly one of 'salutary neglect' than of close control; and if on the one hand its regulations were more strictly enforced after the American Revolution, the wars with France which began in 1793 effectively silenced a strong movement in Britain for the adoption of freer trade. There was, moreover, a world of difference between Bonaparte's personal despotism and the British system of parliamentary and constitutional government.

main endeavour, the mustering on the Channel coast of a great expeditionary force for the invasion and destruction of Britain herself. The assembling of the ships and barges, the perpetual training of the troops, and Napoleon's frequent personal inspections of his forces were to remain the principal features of the war for the next two years. Apparently invincible, the 'Army of England' became in due course the core of the Grand Army which was to dominate Europe for a decade.

It was in this essentially stagnant situation that the Count of Artois in Britain, and even, in all probability, some subordinate ministers in the British government,[1] renewed their support of the *chouans*, the much-dreaded Georges Cadoudal being landed in France with a number of resolute royalists on 21 August 1803. The avowed object of these men, who soon found friends to shelter them in Paris, was to kidnap the First Consul; but it is virtually certain that they intended to kill him, in some ambuscade if not by simple assassination. Cadoudal, however, was understandably reluctant to act until the next step had been determined: either there should be a prince of the royal house available in France to step forward immediately Napoleon fell, or some man of stature should be found and persuaded to assume authority for an interim period. The royalists thus became involved, amongst other projects, in an attempt to secure the support of General Moreau, the victor of Hohenlinden and Napoleon's most respected republican rival. In December 1803 General Pichegru, who had remained an exile ever since he had been banished as a 'royalist' in 1797, was consequently sent clandestinely to Paris to reach some understanding with his old friend Moreau.[2]

This approach inevitably jeopardised the success of the conspiracy. The delay was dangerous in itself; and as the plot widened, more and more intermediaries were necessarily involved. Moreau, moreover, was notoriously cautious, not to say indecisive, in political matters, and he was far too honourable a man to mingle easily with would-be murderers. It appears, indeed, that he broke off a first encounter with Pichegru in the open street as soon as he suspected that Cadoudal was in the vicinity, and two further meetings had to be arranged early in February 1804 before he would commit himself at all. Even then he only advanced— or so it was alleged—as far as a general statement of what amounted to

[1] J. H. Rose, *The Life of Napoleon I*, pp. 450–2.
[2] The reader will recall that Moreau had served under Pichegru during the latter's victorious campaign in Holland in 1794, that he had succeeded him as commander of the Army of the Rhine, and that he had incurred grave suspicion in 1797 by his hesitancy in revealing his discovery of Pichegru's previous contacts with the agents of the royalists.

benevolence towards a successful stroke by Pichegru and 'his people'.[1]

As that expression suggests, these meetings may have been more concerned with the situation of the Republic if Napoleon were overthrown than with the possibility of a Bourbon restoration. Certainly some royalists seem to have been convinced that their own cause was being betrayed, and to have been correspondingly ready to talk freely to the police when they were arrested.[2] It is also, however, evident that the police subjected their prisoners to both moral intimidation and even physical torture.[3] Napoleon, moreover, knew at least some part of what was afoot from Fouché. Deprived of his position as Minister of Police when the Life Consulate was established, the latter had kept his organisation at work in the hope of regaining Napoleon's favour, and he undoubtedly had at least one *agent provocateur*, Mehée de la Touche, deeply involved in a different, but not unrelated, royalist conspiracy. Certainly Napoleon was, by one means or another, sufficiently well-informed to order the arrest of Moreau on 15 February, and to initiate an intensive search for Pichegru and Cadoudal. The incredulity with

[1] Dubious in itself, the evidence against Moreau is further complicated by the interpretation of it by histories written after Napoleon's downfall. There thus occurs a striking illustration of a republican reputation suffering from both Bonapartist and royalist assault. The case against Moreau rested in part upon the evidence of one Rolland, who stated that he had in all innocence sheltered Pichegru in Paris and had eventually been sent to obtain a final statement from Moreau. In this, which follows, the words italicised were commonly cut out after 1814: 'I cannot put myself at the head of any movement *for the Bourbons; they are all so ill-conducted, such an attempt would not succeed.* If Pichegru acts in another way, and, in that case, I have told him that it would be necessary that the consuls and the governor of Paris (Murat) should disappear, I believe I have a strong enough party in the Senate to obtain authority: I should use it at once to put all his people in safety, and afterwards to act as public opinion dictated; but I shall not engage myself in anything in writing.' See *Interrogatoires subis par le Général Moreau* (Paris, An XII), and cp. Fauriel, *Last Days of the Consulate* (Paris, 1886), p. 132, A. H. Lapierre de Châteauneuf, *Histoire du Général Moreau* (Paris, 1814), p. 107. Miot de Melito, who was one of those made responsible for the examination of Moreau's papers in 1803, concluded that he took no active part in the plot, but that 'it seemed beyond doubt that he had agreed with Pichegru what was to ensue upon the event': *Mémoires*, p. 305.

[2] Compare the declaration of Bouvet de Losier: 'Sent to sustain the cause of the Bourbons, I was obliged to fight for that of General Moreau'. Châteauneuf, *Histoire du Général Moreau*, p. 106.

[3] There is no lack of evidence of this, e.g. Berthier's order for the questioning of the *chouan* Desol: 'If you find him hesitant, you may even squeeze his thumbs under the hammer of a musket'. E. d'Hauterive, *Napoléon et sa Police* (Paris, 1943), p. 55.

which the news of the arrest was received in Paris was somewhat modi-fied when Pichegru was also taken on 27 February, and the effect was still greater when Cadoudal himself was discovered and overpowered on 9 March (after a struggle in which one officer was killed and another seriously injured). Consternation and anxiety nevertheless remained, particularly as the barriers at the gates of Paris were closed for several days during the search, just as they had been during the most critical days of the Revolution.

Although it is uncertain how much of the conspiracy was known to, or even promoted by, Napoleon and his police,[1] he seems to have sus-pected still greater dangers and to have been seriously alarmed. Certainly particular attention was paid to statements made just before Moreau's arrest by a minor *chouan* called Querelle, who was broken down by being confronted by a firing squad.[2] In addition to stating that Cadoudal was in Paris, this man revealed details of the royalists' landing-place on the Normandy coast and indicated that the arrival of a royal prince was imminent. The commander of the *gendarmerie d'élite*, General Savary, a man always ready to do the dirtier work of depotism, was consequently despatched post-haste to Normandy, where he and his men, together with a prisoner who knew the necessary signals, waited in vain for almost four weeks. By the end of that time Napoleon had become con-vinced, principally from information furnished by the disreputable Mehée de la Touche, that the expected prince was not the Count of Artois from Britain at all, but the young duc d'Enghien, the grandson of Condé, who was then living at Ettenheim near Strasbourg, in the territory of the Margrave of Baden.

There followed an episode which was immediately seen, and which has ever since been recognised, as one of the darkest stains upon Napoleon's record. On 10 March 1804, the day after the arrest of Cadoudal, the First Consul gave orders for the kidnapping of d'Enghien. Under the general command of the former marquis de Caulincourt, one

---

[1] Opinion on this point varies from Lefebvre's comment that 'The First Consul was in fact surrounded by treachery, of which he knew but a fraction' (*Napoléon*, p. 169) through to the view of Moreau's apologists that the whole conspiracy, from start to finish, was contrived by the police to discredit him. My own somewhat confused impression is that he knew much about, and was actively prompting, the nebulous scheme of Mehée de la Touche to fuse and expose both the royalist and the jacobin opposition to the Consulate, but that he was less well-informed about the much more menacing activities of Cadoudal. It may also be taken as certain that much of the information that reached him was highly exaggerated and most misleading, if not wholly fictitious.

[2] Pasquier, *Memoirs*, I, p. 179.

detachment of troops was to cross the frontier and arrest certain *émigré* leaders who were believed to be at Offenburg; and a second detachment, led by General Ordener, was to go to Ettenheim and seize the Duke, together with the renegade General Dumouriez[1] and others who were supposed to be with him. Caulincourt found nobody, and Ordener found only d'Enghien; but the latter was at once arrested and taken in secrecy to the forbidding fortress of Vincennes. There, during the night of 20 March, he was summarily court-martialled and shot, his body being deposited in an open grave prepared beforehand on orders from Paris.

Although it had soon become evident that the Duke knew nothing of either Pichegru's or Cadoudal's activities, he was by his own admission in regular receipt of a small allowance from Britain; and he did not hesitate to say that he had once borne arms against the Republic, and hoped to do so again. Had he been taken on French soil he would therefore have been liable to the death penalty as an *émigré* in foreign pay; but the fact that he was kidnapped on neutral ground meant that his execution amounted to murder. Even the court which condemned him did so only in the expectation that its formal sentence would be followed by a prompt reprieve—and because Savary himself stood behind the president's chair to keep things moving swiftly.

Despite some obscurities, notably that of the relative importance of the advice of Fouché and Talleyrand, both of whom were present at the Council meeting held immediately before the seizure of d'Enghien was ordered, the personal responsibility of Napoleon for the murder can hardly be in doubt. As Pasquier, who was subsequently Prefect of Police and in a position to examine the evidence, concluded: 'No doubt can exist that (Savary) received a peremptory order to hasten the final issue. He certainly did not act on his own responsibility.'[2] Nor is Napoleon's purpose difficult to discern. Always inclined to impress potential enemies by some spectacular demonstration of the strength of his arm, he could on this occasion rally the regicide element in France by shedding royal blood, and simultaneously show the men of the Right that their future would depend on him, not on some monarch whom he might

[1] Victor of Valmy in September 1792. Dumouriez' defection to the Austrians in the spring of 1793 had equated his name with treachery to the Republic.

[2] The suggestion that Savary acted on his own initiative derives from the story that Réal, then a Councillor of State with particular responsibilities in matters of police, was on his way to Vincennes with a fresh despatch from Napoleon when he met Savary and learnt that the duke was already dead. See Pasquier, Memoirs, pp. 202–4; *Indiscretions of a Prefect of Police . . . from the papers of Count Réal* (ed. A. L. Hayward, London, 1929), p. 75ff.; and J. H. Rose, *Life of Napoleon I*, p. 462, n. 1.

still be expected to restore. According to Miot de Melito, he indeed said as much on 24 March: 'I ordered the prompt trial and execution of the duc d'Enghien so that the returned *émigrés* should not be led into temptation'.[1]

If the consequences of this crime were indeed calculated in advance as coldly as Napoleon's later comments imply, his cynicism would seem to be well-founded. On the one hand, the tribune Curée exulted in the death of the Duke, exclaiming that Napoleon had shown himself to be of the same substance as the Convention; and on the other hand, only one man of note, Chateaubriand, who had recently been appointed an envoy, was sufficiently high-principled to resign his post in protest. It would nevertheless be wrong to suggest that all was correctly anticipated, for the murder left an indelible stain upon the honour even of those who had been most innocently and indirectly connected with it.[2] As has well been said, it 'did immense moral harm to the reputation which Napoleon had enjoyed during the Consulate as the hero-statesman'.[3] In all probability a good many young men of standing abruptly broke off their plans to enter his service: Pasquier, the future Chancellor, certainly did so, and so did Mathieu Molé, the heir to many generations of illustrious magistrates.[4] The murder, moreover, seems commonly to have aggravated anxiety and stimulated fear. As in 1794, apparently, men avoided asking questions and discussing events openly;[5] and when it was learned that on 6 April Pichegru had been found strangled in his cell, many believed that he too had been murdered, either by accident or by design.[6]

[1] Miot de Melito, *Memoirs*, pp. 313–14, where it is also reported that Napoleon remarked: 'Those who plan assassination cannot claim the (protection of) the law of nations . . . they put themselves beyond the pale'.

[2] Such as Caulincourt, who fainted when he heard the upshot of his raid into Baden, and who never wholly freed himself from suspicion despite the respect he won as Napoleon's emissary to the allies in 1814; or Hulin, who had long been honoured for his brave and upright behaviour during the attack upon the Bastille in 1789, but who had had to act as president of the court-martial on this occasion.

[3] F. Markham, *Napoleon*, p. 98.

[4] Faced with the prospect of wasting his life, Pasquier chose to enter Napoleon's service two years later, in 1806, when Molé also did so. Pasquier, *Memoirs*, I, pp. 223, 235–8; Count Molé, *Life and Memoirs* (ed. Marquis de Noailles, London, 1923), pp. 47–57.

[5] Miot de Melito, *Memoirs*, p. 310.

[6] Rumour had it that Pichegru had been strangled by four of Napoleon's Mamelukes, who were themselves shot the same night. The medical evidence indicated that Pichegru could have killed himself by the application of a

It was in this atmosphere, which can hardly have been much relieved by the fact that the new Civil Code was finally promulgated as a single law on 21 March, the very morning after d'Enghien's death, that Napoleon's well-drilled assemblies initiated the proceedings which led to the inauguration of the Empire. On 27 March[1] the Senate presented the First Consul with an address which called for the establishment of a High Court empowered to try crimes of conspiracy, and which also advocated the adoption of still more permanent institutions: 'You are establishing a new age, but you must ensure that it will be eternal'. Shortly afterwards, Cambacérès requested the Councillors of State to give their opinions, as private citizens, on the question of the desirability of hereditary government. Two promptly spoke in favour of this. Then, after a lengthy silence, Berlier explained that he would have to oppose it as a matter of conscience, no new developments having occurred since the establishment of the Life Consulate to make a further change imperative. If hereditary government were adopted, he said, 'no trace will remain of that Republic for the establishment and preservation of which France has sacrificed untold treasure and innumerable lives'. Of the 27 men thus informally consulted, however, only seven opposed the proposition.[2] Napoleon then told the Senate on 25 April that its advice that the supreme office should be hereditary[3] had been constantly in his thoughts, and that he would like to know his Senators' thoughts more fully.

After these preliminaries, arrangements were made for the next step to be taken by the Tribunate; the Legislative Body, which was not in session, was not even asked to reassemble. Initially, the obscure Curée was put up to propose the adoption of the hereditary principle;[4] a

---

tourniquet to his cravat; and most contemporary writers and later historians have concluded that since it would have been more beneficial than detrimental to Napoleon's interests to have placed him on public trial, the greater probability is that he committed suicide as one whose career, begun splendidly, had led only to disaster.

[1] I.e., 6 Germinal an XII. This is given in Lefebvre, *Napoléon*, p. 170, as 23 March.

[2] Thibaudeau, *Bonaparte and the Consulate*, pp. 310–14.

[3] Lefebvre (*Napoléon*, p. 170) and Godechot (*Les Institutions*, p. 500) insist that the Senate had said nothing of the sort. While it is true that its fulsome address to Napoleon was simply an address, and that it did not explicitly mention the hereditary principle, it would appear to me that it would be almost impossible to read its meaning in any other sense. See J. Thiry, *Le Sénat de Napoléon*, pp. 136–7.

[4] Most authorities give the date of Curée's proposition as 23 April, and so imply that Napoleon's reply to the Senate on 25 April was a sequel and perhaps

commission was then appointed to study the motion, and on 3 May the commission recommended, and the Tribunate approved, the wish that Napoleon be proclaimed 'the hereditary Emperor of the French'. The next day the Senate followed suit, adding—in vain—certain proposals for constitutional change intended to make its own chamber an hereditary one with an ultimate right of veto. The consequence of all this was that on 18 May 1804 a new constitution, that of Year XII, was promulgated as a *senatus consultum*. This began by stating: 'THE GOVERNMENT OF THE REPUBLIC is entrusted to an EMPEROR, who will take the title of EMPEROR OF THE FRENCH . . . NAPOLEON BONAPARTE, presently First Consul of the Republic, is EMPEROR OF THE FRENCH.' Consulted by plebiscite on the question of the adoption of the hereditary principle as specified in the second part of this constitution—though *not* on the acceptability of the imperial title itself—the electorate was subsequently said to have pronounced in favour of it by 3,572,329 votes to 2,579.[1] It may be added that this establishment of the Empire was openly opposed by only one member of the Tribunate, the great Carnot, and by only three members of the Senate, Grégoire, Garat and Lambrechts.[2] As Miot de Melito wrote: 'The friends of liberty and philosophical ideas had lost even hope; their long cherished dream of a Republican Government had faded . . . wearied with useless efforts, they sought only to avoid a return of the Bourbons or a revival of the Terror when Napoleon should die'.[3]

Six months were to elapse before Napoleon, duly anointed by Pope Pius VII with holy oil, took the imperial crown from the pontiff and placed it himself on his own head. The first major event of the new era was, however, the greatest state trial which had taken place in France since the days of the Revolutionary Tribunal, that of Georges Cadoudal, Jean Victor Moreau and 45 other alleged conspirators. This trial, which began on 25 May and ended on 9 June 1804, took place before 12 judges; but there was no jury, since the Senate had previously ruled that the use of juries in cases concerning attempts to assassinate the consuls should be suspended for a two-year period. The proceedings established clearly enough that Cadoudal—who avowed his purpose, but refused to implicate any one else—and a number of other royalists, including several

---

a consequence of it. So far as I have been able to determine, however, the Tribunate opened its proceedings on 30 April.

[1] Abstentions being taken as votes in favour: see L. Villat, *La Révolution et l'Empire*, II, p. 41.

[2] Lanjuinais being absent: Thiry, *Le Sénat de Napoléon*, p. 151.

[3] Miot de Melito, *Memoirs*, pp. 319–20.

prominent nobles, had indeed conspired to overthrow Napoleon and restore the Bourbons to the throne of France. The judges consequently had little difficulty in condemning Cadoudal and 19 others to death; and although Napoleon, yielding to the pleas of relatives, eventually pardoned eight of these,[1] all highly born, Cadoudal and 11 of his companions died by the guillotine in the Place de Grève on 28 June. All were defiant to the last: but the death of Cadoudal, 'the bravest of the Bretons and the last man of action of the royalists,'[2] effectively ended the sequence of attempts to kill Napoleon.

Of the others who had been accused of some form of complicity in the conspiracy, 17 were nominally acquitted,[3] five were placed under surveillance, and five were sentenced to imprisonment for a term of two years. Amongst these last was General Moreau, and the fact that he was neither acquitted nor condemned to death is a sufficient indication both of the political pressure on the judges and of the failure of the trial to achieve its primary purpose of discrediting him and the Republic of which he had become the representative. That purpose had indeed become all too evident as one improbable witness had succeeded another, and when they came to consider their verdict the judges were at first divided, a majority of seven to five favouring acquittal. Had that decision been accepted, it is not improbable that the sympathy of the public for Moreau, always clearly apparent, would have made the occasion one of triumphant demonstration.[4] As it was, the sentence followed a verdict of 'guilty with extenuating circumstances', the most that the time-servers on the bench could coerce their colleagues into accepting; and even that compromise was only obtained by a majority of eight to four, and that at four o'clock in the morning.[5] Deprived of

---

[1] The scenes which preceded these pardons are sketched in H. Gaubert, *Conspirateurs au temps de Napoléon I*ᵉʳ, pp. 252–3.

[2] J. H. Rose, *Life of Napoleon*, p. 472. Hyde de Neuville, Cadoudal's earlier companion, apparently abandoned his active opposition to Bonaparte about 1801, though he claims that he remained a fugitive in France throughout the period: *Memoirs*, pp. 176–8.

[3] They nevertheless remained prisoners of state for the duration of the Empire.

[4] Thuriot, one of the judges most determined to obtain the death penalty, maintained that to release Moreau would be to initiate a civil war. It may be remarked that Thuriot, himself one of the regicides of 1793, had been particularly responsible for preparing the case for the state against Moreau.

[5] These details are indirectly derived from the account subsequently published by Lecourbe, the judge who was most reluctant to return a verdict of guilty. He was subsequently discharged from office; and his brother, General Lecourbe, was also disgraced.

the opportunity of granting Moreau a reprieve, as it seems he intended to do, Napoleon allowed him to leave France for the United States;[1] and there Moreau remained for the next nine years, the idol and the last hope of Republican France.

In his later years, and particularly once the tides of fortune had turned against him, Napoleon was apt to speak more and more frequently of what he called 'my institutions' and 'my system'. Although it has been suggested in these pages that his determination to emancipate himself from all constitutional restrictions was one which evolved during the period of the Consulate, rather than one which had been reached before he first acquired office in 1799, many of the institutions characteristic of the Empire had certainly been firmly established before that régime was inaugurated in 1804. The 'system' was not, of course, complete; indeed, in 1812 Napoleon was to speak of it as something still to be consolidated, and to assert that for at least ten more years France would still be likely to revert to chaos if he should chance to die.[2] Nonetheless, the more closely developments during the Consulate are examined, the more evidently that period appears as a transitional one. Despite the undoubted brilliance of the achievements of those years, the advent of the Empire was implicit in them. The renewal of the war with Britain and the revival of the royalists' conspiracies may well have hastened the march of events, but they were the occasions, not the causes, of change.

The central feature of Napoleon's system was his own unceasing endeavour to supervise personally and meticulously every aspect of French affairs. While there is no need for us to examine here all that this implied,[3] it is instructive to review the general character of those institutions to which Napoleon himself seems to have attached particular importance. Amongst these, pride of place can confidently be assigned

---

[1] Madame de Staël tells us that as Moreau's ship passed those of the English fleet he was saluted as if he were the commander of an allied army. *Dix années d'exil: Mémoires de Mme de Staël* (ed. de Broglie & de Staël, Paris, 1818/61), p. 294.

[2] *Memoirs of General de Caulincourt* (ed. J. Hanoteux, Paris, 1933), II, pp. 224, 340. These remarks, and others quoted here, derive from Caulincourt's account of the conversation of Napoleon as the two men returned to France from Lithuania immediately after the retreat from Moscow.

[3] Admirable studies of Napoleon's administrative policies and achievements abound. Apart from the appropriate parts of Lefebvre's *Napoléon* and Geoffery Bruun's more general study, *Europe and the French Imperium, 1799–1814*, reference may be made to the stimulating study by R. B. Holtman, *The Napoleonic Revolution* (Philadelphia, 1967).

to his efficient and highly-centralised administration, which he thought should be advised and assisted by various bodies whose primary function was really that of winning the support of public opinion. Apparent in the time of the Directory, the trend towards the formation of an executive of this sort was clearly greatly accelerated by Napoleon's assertion of his own authority over that of his fellow consuls, as well as by his far-reaching reorganisation of both local and judicial administration early in 1800. Later he was also successful in silencing the Tribunate, in formalising the Council of State and in creating (in 1803) the new office of *auditeur* as a means of training young men for the highest administrative responsibilities. Consequently by 1804 France had a system of government which led directly to autocracy and required only elaboration as the Empire itself grew greater and more complex. Since the story of the Consulate indicates all too convincingly that a powerful and pervasive Ministry of Police was always an integral part of Napoleon's system, it need only be added here that the foundation of the Empire was very soon followed by the restoration of Fouché to that office (10 July 1804).

This, however, is not to say that either the Consulate or the Empire should be thought of as no more than a police state. Constructive, even noble in conception, much of Napoleon's work was manifestly necessary and earnestly desired by public opinion. Seeing France as he did as a country whose government had collapsed, and whose people were not so much freed from tyranny as fragmented by faction and infected by excessively individualistic ideas, he was constantly concerned not only to exalt his own authority but also to rebuild society and reunify the nation. As he explained matters to Thibaudeau in May 1802, 'The Revolution is over, the time for reconstruction has arrived . . . We now have a government, a source of authority, but all the rest of the nation is as so many grains of sand.'[1] As this suggests, he regarded good government as a prerequisite of progress: 'With a good administration all individuals will forget the factions of which they have been made members and will be permitted to be French'.[2] This, however, was by no means sufficient in itself, for Napoleon did not see society simply as millions of men united only in their common subordination to bureaucracy. He believed that if reconstruction was to be effective and enduring, the work of the administration must be supplemented by the re-establishment of other centres of social activity and more local

---

[1] Thibaudeau, *Bonaparte and the Consulate*, pp. 144–5.
[2] A quotation I owe to Holtman, *The Napoleonic Revolution*, p. 85.

'clusters of loyalties'.[1] In his words to Thibaudeau, he had to 'plant some masses of granite on the soil of France . . . In short, we must found Institutions'.[2]

As the men of the Revolution had done their utmost to destroy all the corporate bodies of old France, Napoleon was commonly confronted with the necessity of creating things anew. The greatest institution in the old order, the Church, was however disrupted, not destroyed, and here Napoleon's work was that of reconstruction. This, of course, rested upon the Concordat of 1801, perhaps the boldest and the most moment-ous of the achievements of the Consulate. As we have seen, the terms of that agreement were, to say the least, somewhat inequitable, and al-though Portalis, who was charged with the supervision of religion, often championed the cause of the Church most courageously, the conflict of authority that eventually led Napoleon to sanction the imprisonment of the Pope in 1809 was never far below the surface. There are, indeed, some indications that as soon as the Concordat was signed Napoleon began to toy with the possibility of attaining the spiritual as well as the temporal dominion of the world:[3] but whatever the truth of that, his restoration of religion was certainly a long step towards the magnificent ceremony which marked his consecration as Emperor in Notre Dame. If, by contrast, the Imperial University, Napoleon's other great instru-ment for influencing opinion and casting a whole generation into the same mould,[4] was not established as an Institution until 1808, its foundations were also based on the work of the Consulate. Having created the *lycées* in 1802, Napoleon further regulated their development in 1803; and in that year he also saw to it that the National Institute was reorganised, the School of Moral and Political Sciences being—significantly—suppressed.

The social changes that were initiated during the years of the Con-sulate similarly presaged a return to aristocracy and some form of monarchy. Throughout the period the Court steadily grew more formal and more splendid, and the Senate acquired prestige even as it lost

[1] A singularly appropriate phrase used by H. F. Stockhold in translating Lefebvre's *'faisceaux d'intérêts'*; *Napoleon, From Brumaire to Tilsit*, p. 142.

[2] *Bonaparte and the Consulate*, loc. cit.

[3] See H. H. Walsh, *The Concordat of 1801*, chapter 8 and particularly pp. 180ff.

[4] 'Above all we must secure unity: we must be able to cast a whole generation in the same mould . . . Let us have a body of doctrine which does not vary and a body of teachers which does not die.' Count Molé, *Life and Memoirs*, p. 61. Molé is reporting Napoleon's comments on public education at the first meeting of the Council of State at which he was present as an *auditeur* in 1806.

political power. In 1802 the foundation of the Legion of Honour, which Napoleon was later to call 'the finest of my Institutions',[1] was immediately recognised (and, so far as was possible, resisted) as marking a distinct departure from the revolutionaries' fervent faith in complete civic equality. Later in that year, too, the replacement of Sieyès' complicated 'Lists of Notabilities' by Electoral Colleges advanced the process further. These colleges provided a pool from which vacancies in the Senate, the Legislative Body and the Tribunate could be filled without public election; and as they were composed in the first instance of men recently chosen locally as 'Notabilities', who were to hold their seats for life, the whole process of public election was effectively evaded. As Lucien Bonaparte frankly explained, this meant that the 'electoral privilege' had become the 'exclusive prerogative' of the wealthy, whose possession of property necessarily interested them in the preservation of order and entitled them to be called 'the most enlightened class' of society.[2] Equally important, the change provided Napoleon with conservative corporate bodies in every part of France. These, without being entrenched hereditary bodies, were in many other respects similar to those which were characteristic of the old order throughout Europe. Well might Napoleon tell his Council of State: 'We have succeeded for the first time in forming intermediate bodies on the basis of equality'.[3] In 1802, in short, France had advanced so far towards an aristocratic system that the appearance of the Marshals and Dignitaries of the Empire in 1804, and even the eventual emergence of a new imperial nobility, occasions small surprise.

Finally, the codification of French law may well be considered

---

[1] Caulincourt, *Memoirs*, II, p. 311.

[2] Lefebvre, *Napoléon*, pp. 140-1.

[3] Thibaudeau, *Bonaparte and the Consulate*, p. 254. The reader should appreciate that (as I understand the matter) Napoleon was using the word 'equality' as if it were synonymous with 'the new order' as distinct from the pre-Revolutionary 'aristocratic' order. The latter had strong corporate bodies, which were able to challenge the central authority because they were largely composed of men who held their positions as inherited property. These had been destroyed by the Revolution, and Napoleon wished to replace them by others *of his own creation* in which men would hold their positions by nomination (with some appearance of election) and not by hereditary right. The new aristocracy, being one of service, would also be one more open to ability than that of the Old Order; but, despite his later claims, it is probable that Napoleon was at this time less concerned with fostering equality of opportunity than he was with finding a way of re-establishing rank in society without infringing either his own authority or revolutionary sentiment.

Napoleon's most enduring achievement; and here again the fundamental work, the completion of the Civil Code, was accomplished during the Consulate.[1] As is well known, the Code was adopted either wholly or in part in a great many other countries, where its emphasis upon the secular character of the state and the equality of all men before the law contributed very considerably to the gradual disappearance of the older 'feudal' order. In the history of France itself, the Code is in the first instance remarkable as the culmination of a decade of attempts to apply the principles of the Revolution to the conglomeration of old local codes and new national legislation, and so to evolve a single statement of civil law applicable to all Frenchmen. That this was achieved was very largely due to Napoleon, who personally participated in many of the meetings of the legal committee of the Council of State, and who ever expected of it a stupendous amount of work—as Pasquier put it, 'enough to frighten the imagination'.[2] Clear, succinct and generally enlightened, the Code was a compromise between the tried and tested maxims of the past and what was now regarded as the excessively abstract individualism of the Revolution. There was therefore some reversion to the tenets of Roman Law, traditionally strong in southern France—and conveniently favourable to the interests of the state. More particularly, Napoleon ensured that the Code favoured the family as the basic body in society, and enhanced the authority of the father in the family; but he also ensured that the state ultimately controlled the family by its determination of the laws of inheritance.[3]

As this suggests, the Civil Code had much in common with Napoleon's other 'institutions', for the very act of creation and regulation ensured that no part of the new order—with the significant exception of the ownership of property—existed in its own right. If the new corporate bodies supplemented the work of the administration by providing focal points for national unity, they were also designed to reinforce Napoleon's own authority. To Napoleon himself, however, these were but two sides

[1] Under the Empire, the Civil Code was renamed the *Code Napoléon*, and it was followed by the appearance of the Commercial Code in 1807 and the Penal Code in 1810. Codes of Civil and Criminal Procedure were also approved in 1806 and 1808 respectively.

[2] Pasquier, *Memoirs*, I, p. 249.

[3] The Code established the practice by which a man's property had to be divided amongst his children at his death—varying according to the size of the family, but neither more than half nor less than a quarter of the whole estate—only a proportion being left for him to bequeath at his discretion. Napoleon was personally opposed to this particular compromise, which indeed had profound social consequences.

of the same coin: as he said to Thibaudeau in 1802: 'I have thought it necessary to centralise and increase the authority of the Government in order to weld the nation more firmly together'.[1]

The pyramid of political power was, moreover, closely matched with that of the social structure of France. As Lefebvre has emphasised, Napoleon founded his authority squarely on the support of men of property, the sanctity of which was enshrined in the Civil Code. Although in the conditions of the time land, and the ownership of land, were particularly important, the commercial middle class was also appropriately favoured. From December 1802, for example, the formation of Chambers of Commerce was encouraged; but the Law of 12 April 1803 once again forbade working men to form associations of their own, and that of 1 December 1803 renewed the obligation for them to carry a written record of their employment, the long-detested *livret*, without which a worker was held to be no more than a vagrant. Nevertheless, increasing prosperity, itself in part the product of stability and public confidence, as well as good harvests and good government—particularly Napoleon's extensive programme of public works and the great care he took to see that the cities always had adequate reserves of grain—ensured that popular unrest was minimal during the later years of the Consulate. Nor should it be forgotten that Napoleon's evolving aristocracy was primarily one of service: though he may have been more suspicious of rootless talent than he later asserted, neither in his rewards nor in his rage was he any respecter of persons. In unifying the nation, he sought, as he said, 'to open a great road for all to follow'.[2] While conscription, the power of the police, the re-establishment of rank and the conservative influence of the new corporate bodies played their part in curbing discontent, in 1804 the French people generally were satisfied and proud of their leader, whom they still saw as a national hero.[3] In all, it was not without a good deal of justification that Napoleon claimed at St Helena:

---

[1] Thibaudeau, *Bonaparte and the Consulate*, pp. 266–7.

[2] See above, chapter 8, on the appointment of Fouché and Talleyrand. The reader may note that at this point I depart both from Napoleon's own emphatic assertions at St Helena that he had been almost above all else representative of 'the career open to talents'—a phrase that seems to derive from O'Meara's reports of his conversation in 1816–17—and from Lefebvre's argument that Napoleon only disliked 'feudal' privileges, but buttressed those of the bourgeoisie. See Hutt, *Napoleon*, pp. 33–6 and Lefebvre, *Napoléon*, p. 151.

[3] Lefebvre, op. cit., p. 159. Lefebvre adds that Napoleon had in reality already turned his back upon both the true cause of the nation and the principle of equality.

'In this gigantic struggle between the present and the past, I am the natural arbiter and mediator'.[1]

His arbitration, however, had no place for the Republic. True, in 1804 the tattered remnants of its raiment still concealed something of the nakedness of Napoleonic power. Technically, Napoleon, Emperor of the French, had been entrusted with the government of the Republic: as Joubert had said in the Tribunate on 2 May 1804: 'The nation is not resurrecting a feudal throne . . . The Revolution remains rooted in its original principles'.[2] Coins, stamped on one side with Napoleon's effigy and the words '*Napoléon, Empereur*', still carried on the other the inscription '*République française*', and until 1 January 1806 the Revolutionary Calendar, that supreme symbol of the advent of the age of reason, still survived to confuse contemporaries and confound historians. The true atmosphere of the times is, however, much more vividly reflected in the fact that in October 1803 Napoleon finally signed and enforced a formal order forbidding his arch-enemy, Madame de Staël, to reside within 40 leagues of Paris; as Lebrun had written in reply to one of her earlier appeals: 'Although the First Consul is not afraid of society gossip, he does not care to be thought so weak and imprudent as to allow his administration to become the butt of sarcasms'.[3] Considerable significance, too, may be found in the contrast between the new exaltation of Napoleon's birthday, 15 August, which was from 1802 celebrated as the festival of a newly-discovered 'St Napoleon', and the abandonment after September 1803 of the annual anniversary of the foundation of the Republic.

Established in emergency, when the Prussian army was expected at the gates of Paris and when great Danton's defiance of the foe seemed still to be ringing in men's ears, the name of that Republic was from its

---

[1] Las Cases, *Mémorial*, 18 April 1816, quoted in J. C. Herold, *The Mind of Napoleon*, p. 72. Napoleon of course referred not only to events in France, but to the whole range of the European conflict.

[2] Soboul, *La Première République*, p. 341.

[3] It was in consequence of this order that Madame de Staël left France for Germany. Considerable space would be required to correlate her movements with the main course of events and to do adequate justice to her writings and social–political activities. Suffice it to say that two of her greatest books, *De la littérature* (April 1800) and *Delphine* (December 1802), were fundamentally arguments in favour of the widest possible emancipation of the human spirit, and that Bonaparte rightly regarded these as refutations of the moral validity of the type of régime which he was in the process of establishing. *Delphine* was, indeed, prefaced by dedication to 'the silent but enlightened France'. See J. C. Herold, *Mistress to an Age*, pp. 231, 247, 253–5.

foundation synonymous with national survival through military victory. Three times—at Valmy in 1792, at Valenciennes in 1793[1] and at Zurich in 1799—apparently invincible armies of invaders had been held at bay; and at Jemappes and Fleurus, as at Marengo and Hohenlinden, each of these three major campaigns—to say nothing of Napoleon's Italian triumphs of 1796–7—had culminated in conquest by France. Throughout the decade,[2] too, foreign assault had marched hand-in-hand with counter-revolutionary conspiracy and actual or incipient civil war; and here again, from Toulon, Lyons and Savenay to Quibéron and Montréjeau, republican arms had eventually triumphed. To this extent, if to no other, the republican vision of 1792 had in time become a reality.

On the other hand, the republicans must be said to have failed in their intermittent endeavours to end the war in an enduring general peace. For all their pugnacious patriotism and their complete confidence in the universal applicability of their principles, the men of 1792 certainly did not identify the Republic with perpetual war; but in fact France was not to be at peace with all her neighbours until Napoleon signed the short-lived Treaty of Amiens, and consolidated his personal power by so doing. The causes of this constant conflict are of course so complex that it would be manifestly unjust to hold the French republicans wholly responsible for it. One fundamental issue may nevertheless be isolated here: whether the policy of the Republic was directed by idealists or swayed by the calculations of self-interested men, it remained revolutionary. Devoted to the doctrine of the sovereignty of the nation, the republicans persistently refused to acknowledge the validity of international law or of their neighbours' rights.[3] Tragically, the very principle

[1] Valenciennes in fact fell to the Austrians; but its defence, which the Duke of York said had cost the allies a campaign, symbolised the strength of France's resistance to attack.

[2] For the reasons indicated in earlier pages I here presume that the Republic remained a reality after Napoleon's *coup d'état* in 1799. Also for reasons indicated earlier, I consider it to have lost that reality at the opening of the year 1802, and to have become a hollow shell thereafter.

[3] It may perhaps be objected here that it is inappropriate to exalt the importance of international law in this context, the eighteenth century being notoriously a period of dynastic wars, partitions, and the balance of power. It would nevertheless seem to me to be the fact that what was then called the 'law of nations' or 'the public law of Europe' was a reality both in the positive sense that the relationships of the multiplicity of states of which Europe was composed were regulated by an intricate network of treaties, and in the subjective sense that men felt that disputes should be settled in certain ways and in accordance with certain principles. These treaties, methods and principles were indeed frequently violated in practice: but it would also seem to me to be

which had become identified with national unity in France was one which made her power incompatible with the freedom of other states, and in retrospect it would seem that peace was impossible until that power had been appreciably diminished.

Seemingly inseparable from national survival, national unity was also a matter of supreme concern throughout the years of the Republic. As we have seen, Napoleon constantly sought 'to weld the nation together'; but that objective was by no means his alone: in 1792, indeed, the newly-assembled Convention had hardly abolished the monarchy before it proclaimed the Republic to be one and indivisible, and very soon afterwards it became a capital crime even to speak in favour of federalism (16 December 1792). On the other hand, much of the history of the Republic is a sad tale of civil strife, in which terror and counter-terror, class-conflict and individual racketeering, persecution, ostracism, brigandage and conspiracy seem to succeed each other endlessly, whilst the majority of Frenchmen become ever more apathetic and inert. As innumerable books indicate, it has never been difficult for the apologists of Napoleon to suggest that he, and he alone, saved France from chaos.

So generalised a picture as this is, of course, misleading, if only because the most desperate crisis of the Republic occurred in the time of its infancy. In scale, at least, conflict diminished thereafter. The White Terror, for example, was geographically more limited than that of the Year II, and the *chouannerie*, shocking as it was, was but a pale reflection of the great western rebellion in 1793. But even if it be admitted that conflict, in one form or another, was continual at this time, that is not to say that nothing was prevented nor anything achieved. Initially a relatively simple matter of enthusiasm for France and for the Republic, in 1793 the idea of the unity of the nation was defined in excessively narrow terms. Identified with the monopoly of power by the Jacobins and the *sans-culottes*, it was also equated with the virtuous patriotism of the former and the egalitarian patriotism of the latter, and before long the burden of both became intolerable. In the year 1794–5 both were consequently repudiated as essentially violent minority movements. This caused much immediate human misery; and as power soon became the monopoly of those who possessed either

---

the fact that the French revolutionaries introduced a new element into the situation by denying the validity of the ethical basis of the accepted standards of behaviour. They did not simply break international law: they repudiated it in favour of what they held to be the higher principle of the sovereignty of the nation, itself the criterion of right and wrong.

property or office,[1] both radical democracy and the urban working-class remained effectively stifled—a fact of terrible consequence to later generations. It would nonetheless seem that when the Republic became a constitutional one in 1795 the possibility of attaining a wider national unity, and one more realistically based upon the consent of a predominantly rural population, was greater than it had been before.

That possibility was not achieved in the days of the Directory. The Directors, it seems,[2] were indeed much more successful than has been supposed both in curbing local violence and in initiating administrative reforms—which Napoleon later continued. But although the break made in Brumaire may have been in some ways more apparent than real, the Directors seem also to have been primarily concerned with maintaining unaltered the particular political situation which they had themselves inherited. Given the Republic of 1795, they strove above all else to petrify it. In practice this meant that a narrow political segment of a restricted—though not necessarily a wholly unrepresentative—social class kept itself in power by force, excluding all who wished to broaden the basis of the régime by identifying them either with the royalists or with the Jacobins. The Directors' doctrinaire determination to impose an artificial rationalist cult upon the people of France added religious to political persecution, and as crisis succeeded crisis the political nation grew ever narrower and more remote from the real one.

However one may regard Napoleon, there is no denying that his advent transformed this scene. Where men had looked backward, he fixed their attention on the future: where they had allowed their hard-won principles to degenerate into dogmas, he compelled them to think in terms of present problems and practical solutions; and where their horizons had become bounded by difficulties, he inspired them with the conviction that nothing was impossible, so that, as Pasquier said, 'the

[1] The Constitution of 1795 was, and was avowed to be, one in which political power was confined to the possessors of property; but it should be remarked that the Two-Thirds Decree which accompanied it, and the series of *coups d'état* which followed it, meant that in practice the men of the Convention continued to dominate the scene, and these were (broadly) lawyers and local administrators, not men of wealth in either land or money—though some certainly acquired these. The point is illustrative of the important difference in the interpretation of the Revolution between those who see it as a class struggle, as a collision of feudalism and capitalism, and those who see it as 'the replacement of one set of officials by another' in a pre-industrial—and inadequately analysed—society. See: A. Cobban, *The Social Interpretation of the French Revolution* (C.U.P., 1964).

[2] Until developments during the years 1795–9 have been studied more thoroughly, even cautious comment upon them should be treated with reserve.

gigantic entered into our very habits of thought'.[1] His authority, and the confidence it engendered, enabled him to make previous reforms effective, to initiate new ones of his own, and at least to limit the activities of those who had for so long been systematically defrauding the state. By combining moderation with severity in a manner that contrasts very sharply with the weaker liberalism of 1795, he was also able to end all serious danger of civil war. Still more important, he sought to substitute reconciliation for proscription; refusing—at least initially—to persecute men by categories, he called upon all to set past antagonisms aside and to devote all their energies to the service of France.

In terms of national unity the results were remarkable. Although the factions fell silent and the *émigrés* returned in considerable numbers, many of the republicans' objectives of 1792 were either attained, or were close to being attained, before the Republic ceased to exist in any real sense in 1802. Bound together by an effective central government which enjoyed widespread support, the nation had a uniform system of local government and judicial administration, and it was well on the way to securing a single and thoroughly considered code of law. The re-establishment of Catholicism, too, re-united the majority of French men and women in a common religious faith, though this was of course not that of most of the men of the Revolution. Nor should it be supposed for a moment that these gains were imposed by armed force: although the army was used, and used ruthlessly, in the west, the whole atmosphere of Napoleon's government during the Consulate was civilian, as was that of the Directory before it.

The Republic must nonetheless be recognised as a failure. In the vision which was seen in 1792, the nation was not only a united and independent state. It was also a secular community in which free and equal citizens would be governed, by their own consent and in accordance with an established law, through representative[2] assemblies at both the local and the national levels; and each and every officer was to be answerable for his conduct to the electorate. If we set aside equality of opportunity and equality before the law, which can be regarded as positive gains of the Revolution despite the recurrence of abuses and the social and economic pressures which so often nullified equality for the poor, practically nothing of this vision had acquired reality in the decade of republican endeavour. Despite repeated efforts to stamp it out, the

[1] Pasquier, cited by J. H. Rose, *The Life of Napoleon I*, p. 267.
[2] The *sans-culottes*, of course, believed in direct democracy, while the Jacobin ideal was that of debate in public; here, however, I speak of the liberal republican mean rather than of the more extreme forms of democracy.

Roman religion was re-established and resurgent. Throughout the period the process of election had steadily been supplanted by that of nomination, so that by 1802 every official of importance was appointed by, and responsible to, Napoleon alone; and nomination also dictated the composition of his local and national advisory councils. Everywhere it was Napoleon's 'Representative Government' which prevailed, and this in practice meant that he was personally able to exercise unlimited power as the personification of the sovereign people, whose will he consulted to confirm his own whenever, and as far as, he found that convenient. Worst of all, constitutional law could be, and was, violated at the will of government by the increasingly simple process of manipulating the nominal authority of the Senate. Since Napoleon's first experiment in employing the Senate to legalise an arbitrary act was successful in December 1801—January 1802, it may be said that from that time onwards his government was essentially dictatorial. In April 1803, when this had become fully apparent, Thibaudeau—who had already seen his hopes shattered twice, on 2 June 1793 and at the *coup d'état* of Fructidor in 1797—gave up his place on the Council of State and became instead Prefect of the Bouches-du-Rhône. His dream of republican freedom, like that of France, had faded and died, and the country was left to encounter the future with bitter memories, but without further experience of parliamentary government.

Those who pause to wonder why these things should have happened will find that the Marxian historians have an explanation readily to hand. Politically, we are told, the perpetual war and the recurrent threat of royalist counter-revolution constantly made some dictatorial form of government imperative; the republican liberals proved unable to meet this need primarily because they were socially representative only of a small, exclusive and essentially self-interested class of monied men, alienated from and antagonistic to the nation at large; and that oligarchy inevitably abandoned the liberals and freedom in favour of Napoleon and security.

Even thus crudely stated, this explanation has sufficient validity to make a fuller understanding of it necessary for any proper appreciation of the period. It need not, however, be accepted either in its entirety or as an exclusive truth. The review of events attempted in this book may suggest that more importance ought to be attached to ideas and ideals, to political factors, and to the part played both by particular personalities and by accident alone. If it be agreed, for example, that the failure of the Republic to achieve stability between 1795 and 1799 was a major cause of its ultimate destruction, it might be suggested that its instability sprang in part from the republicans' devotion to the doctrine of the separation of powers and their involvement in the processes of partial annual elections. It might be added that the device by which the composition of the Directory was determined annually by lot had fatal effects upon the balance of forces on at least two crucial occasions, and that once at least it deprived the government of the one man who might have been capable of concluding the war and keeping Napoleon in check. More generally, too, particular importance might well be attached to the singularly narrow and uncompromising characters of the principal Directors, and their deliberate rejection of the opportunities that occurred on various occasions by which they might have broadened the basis of their support.

If such considerations as these, to whatever part of the republican period they be applied, seem to be substantial, it follows that the determinist thesis must be considerably modified. It may well then appear that the ultimate disaster republican France encountered was the fact that when at last an extraordinarily able and flexibly-minded man acquired the power to govern effectively, he proved to be one who was totally intolerant of any opposition or of any restriction upon his own limitless ambitions. The exaltation of spirit Frenchmen experienced under his leadership in 1800 is consequently the measure of the despondency of the republicans in their day of disillusionment. By 1804 everything save personal despotism had been tried, and tried in vain. Resistance was not only hopeless, it had become purposeless. Nothing therefore remained save voluntary withdrawal from political life, or some form of subordinate service which might somehow make things better. As Berlier, who had so often braved Napoleon's anger, subsequently wrote in explanation of his acceptance of the title of Count of the Empire:

Certainly I might have refused it; but I should at the same time have been obliged to resign my post as Councillor State and as President of the Council on Prizes of War. These offices bestowed upon myself and my family an honourable and honest means of existence. Why should I have thrown them up, and what would France have gained had I done so? Things would have gone on exactly as before, and I should have ruined myself for nothing.[1]

[1] G. K. Fortescue, Introduction to Thibaudeau, *Bonaparte and the Consulate*, p. xviii.

Chronology

The Revolutionary Calendar

After the monarchy was abolished in France on 21 September 1792, the year 1792–3 became known as Year I of the Republic. When the Revolutionary Calendar was adopted in October 1793, its effect was made retrospective to the first anniversary of the abolition of royalty, so that 22 September 1793 became the 1st day of the 1st month (Vendémiaire) of the Year II of the Republic. Thereafter each year ran from September to September in a sequence of 12 months of 30 days each, with the five additional days appearing as *sans-culottides* on 17–22 September.

Since this idyllic pattern was inevitably modified by Leap Years, serious students of the period require a table of concordance such as that given in full in J. Godechot, *Les Institutions de la France*, or that given in all essentials in R. Holtman, *The Napoleonic Revolution*. Here, years of the revolutionary calendar are identified as they occur in the table of events by SMALL CAPITALS, and the 12 months are identified only by name and for the dates valid until 21 September 1799 (save that one additional day should be added for all dates in the six months from 21 September 1795 to 20 March 1796).

Vendémiaire	(vintage)	1–50	=	22 September–21 October
Brumaire	(fog)	1–30	=	22 October –20 November
Frimaire	(frost)	1–30	=	21 November–20 December
Nivôse	(snow)	1–30	=	21 December –19 January
Pluviôse	(rain)	1–30	=	20 January –18 February
Ventôse	(wind)	1–30	=	19 February –20 March
Germinal	(budding)	1–30	=	21 March –19 April
Floréal	(flowers)	1–30	=	20 April –19 May
Prairial	(meadows)	1–30	=	20 May –18 June
Messidor	(harvest)	1–30	=	19 June –18 July
Thermidor	(heat)	1–30	=	19 July –17 August
Fructidor	(fruit)	1–30	=	18 August –16 September
Sans-culottides:		1–5	=	17–21 September

Chronological Guide

The sub-divisions of this table correspond to the chapters into which this book is divided; they are inserted here for the reader's convenience, although not all of them represent generally recognised times of decisive change. Italics are used to distinguish events in the course of the wars as well as for foreign words and phrases. Small capitals indicate the beginning of each new year in the revolutionary calendar.

I. *WAR AND TERROR.*

1792

August	10	THE REVOLUTION OF 10 AUGUST.
		Capture of the Tuileries, suspension of Louis XVI.
September	2	*Surrender of Verdun to the Prussians.*
	2–6	The prison massacres in Paris.
	20	*BATTLE OF VALMY: Prussian retreat begins.*
	21	THE CONVENTION ABOLISHES THE MONARCHY.
	22	BEGINNING OF THE YEAR I
November	6	*BATTLE OF JEMAPPES: French conquest of Belgium.*
	19	France offers aid to all striving to recover their liberty.
December	3	The Convention decides to place Louis XVI on trial.

1793

January	14–17	The Convention votes to decide the fate of Louis XVI.
	21	EXECUTION OF LOUIS XVI.
February	1	*Declaration of War upon Britain and Holland.*
	15	Condorcet's constitutional proposals.
March	7	*Declaration of War upon Spain.*
	10	Creation of the Revolutionary Tribunal.
	16	Beginning of the revolt in the Vendée.
	18	*BATTLE OF NEERWINDEN: French retreat from the Netherlands.*
April	5	*Defection of General Dumouriez.*
	6	Creation of the Committee of Public Safety.
May	31	Rising in Paris.
June	2	THE REVOLUTION OF 2 JUNE: Purge of the Convention.
	24	The Convention accepts the Constitution of 1793.

July	13	Assassination of Marat.
	23	*Fall of the fortress of Mayence.*
August	10	Festival of Unity in honour of the Constitution of 1793.
	23	*Levée en masse decreed.*
	27	*Surrender of Toulon to the British.*
September	5	'Hébertist' rising in Paris: Terror 'the order of the day'.
	17	The Law of Suspects.
	22	BEGINNING OF THE YEAR II
	29	The general *maximum* in restraint of wages and prices.
October	9	Republican forces recapture Lyons.
	10	REVOLUTIONARY GOVERNMENT until peace decreed.
	16	*BATTLE OF WATTIGNIES: the Republicans relieve Maubeuge.*
	31	Execution of the 'Girondins'.
November	10	Festival of Reason in Notre Dame.
December	4	14 Frimaire II: LAW OF REVOLUTIONARY GOVERNMENT. Massacres at Lyons.
	19	*Republican forces recapture Toulon*
	23	Defeat of the Vendéans at Savenay.

1794

March	24	Execution of the Hébertists.
April	5	Execution of the Dantonists.
May	18	*BATTLE OF TOURCOING: rout of the British in Belgium.*
June	1	*British naval victory, the 'Glorious First of June'.*
	8	Festival of the Supreme Being.
	10	Law of 22 Prairial expedites work of the Revolutionary Tribunal.
	26	*BATTLE OF FLEURUS: French reconquer Belgium.*
	27–28	THERMIDOR 9–10: Overthrow and execution of Robespierre.

2. THE REACTION AGAINST THE TERROR.

1794

| July | 30–31 | Reorganisation of the Committee of Public Safety. |

August	1	Repeal of the Law of 22 Prairial.
	10	Reorganisation of the Revolutionary Tribunal.
September	1	Billaud, Collot and Barère leave the Committee of Public Safety.
	8	Opening of the trial of the 'federalists' from Nantes.
	22	BEGINNING OF THE YEAR III
October	13	Opening of trial of the 'revolutionary committee' from Nantes.
November	12	Closure of the Jacobin Club in Paris.
	23	Carrier sent for trial by the Revolutionary Tribunal.
December	8	Recall of the deputies who protested against the Revolution of 2 June 1793.
	16	Conviction and execution of Carrier.
	24	Abolition of the *maximum*.

1795

January	20	*The French army enters Amsterdam.*
February	17	The 'Pacification' of the Vendéans at La Jaunaye.
	21	Compromise decree on freedom of worship in France.
March	8	Recall of the surviving 'Girondins'.
	22	Debate on the indictment of Billaud, Collot and Barère.
	27	Food rations in Paris reduced by half.
	28	Fouquier-Tinville sent for trial by the Revolutionary Tribunal.
April	1	THE PARISIAN RISING OF 12 GERMINAL. Deportation of Billaud, Collot and Barère ordered.
	5	*PEACE OF BASLE WITH PRUSSIA.*
	10	'Disarming' of the 'terrorists' begins in Paris.
	18	Committee of Eleven appointed to reconstruct the Constitution.
	20	Peace of La Prévalaye with the *chouans*. Famine conditions in Paris. The White Terror rages in the Rhône Valley.
May	6	Conviction and execution of Fouquier-Tinville.
	16	*PEACE WITH HOLLAND* (at The Hague).
	20–21	THE PARISIAN RISING OF 1–2 PRAIRIAL. Further repression of Montagnards and *sans-culottes*.
	31	Abolition of the Revolutionary Tribunal.

3. *THE ACHIEVEMENT OF THE CONSTITUTION.*

1795

June	8	Death of the Dauphin, 'Louis XVII'.
	24	The Convention asserts its authority over Lyons: 'Louis XVIII' issues the Verona Manifesto.
	27	MAIN ROYALIST LANDING AT QUIBERON.
July	4	Opening of debate on the new Constitution.
	14	The '*Marseillaise*' is played in the Convention.
	20–21	Hoche destroys the royalist forces at Quiberon.
	22	*PEACE WITH SPAIN* (at Basle).
August	22	The Convention approves the Constitution of the Year III and the Two-Thirds Decree, subject to a plebiscite.
September	1	Re-enfranchisement of 'the terrorists'.
	23	BEGINNING OF THE YEAR IV; THE CONSTITUTION OF THE YEAR III and the TWO-THIRDS DECREE PROCLAIMED VALID BY PLEBISCITE.
October	1	*Annexation of Belgium* (incorporated in the Constitution).
	3	Re-arming of 'terrorists' is authorised.
	5	THE REVOLT OF 13 VENDÉMIAIRE.
	10	Bonaparte becomes commander of the Army of the Interior.
	25	The LAW OF 3 BRUMAIRE restricting the relatives of *émigrés*.
	26	Dissolution of the Convention.

4–5. *THE REPUDIATION OF THE LEFT and THE LOSS OF 'THE MIDDLE WAY'.*

1795

October	26–27	Formation of the Councils of the Elders and the Five Hundred.
		French forces compelled to retire from Germany.
November	2	The Executive Directory in being.
	30	Second issue of Babeuf's *Tribune*.
December		William Wickham in Berne.

1796

February	19	Destruction of the plates for printing the *assignats*.

	22	Rejection of plan for a new bank.
	27	Closure of the 'Panthéon Club'.
March	11	Bonaparte leaves Paris to assume command in Italy.
	18	Issue of the *mandats territoriaux*.
April	11–14	*Bonaparte breaks through the Austrian front into Italy.*
	16	Law of 27 Germinal against conspiracy.
	28	*Bonaparte imposes Armistice of Cherasco upon Piedmont.*
May	10	*Battle of Lodi: Bonaparte forces a crossing of the R. Adda.*
		Arrest of Babeuf and 'the Equals' in Paris.
	30	*Bonaparte forces an Austrian retirement to the R. Adige.*
June		*Jourdan's offensive into Germany fails.*
	20	*Moreau crosses the Rhine into Germany.*
August	5	*Battle of Castiglione near Mantua.*
		Moreau approaches Munich; Jourdan renews the offensive; France concludes treaty of alliance with Spain at San Ildefonso.
September	4	*Battle of Roverto near Mantua.*
	9	The 'Massacre' at Grenelle.
	22	BEGINNING OF THE YEAR V.
		Jourdan's forces driven back to France.
October		Lord Malmesbury's first peace mission to France begins.
		Bonaparte creates the Cisalpine Republic in Italy.
		Moreau retreats to the Rhine.
November	15–18	*Battle of Arcole near Mantua.*
December		The Law of 3 Brumaire is slightly modified.
	19	Lord Malmesbury ordered out of France.
1797		
January	6	*Expedition to Ireland fails at Bantry Bay.*
	14	*Battle of Rivoli near Mantua.*
	30	Brottier's royalist conspiracy exposed in Paris.
February	2	*BONAPARTE ENTERS MANTUA.*
	14	*British naval victory at CAPE ST VINCENT.*
	19	*Bonaparte imposes the Treaty of Tolentino upon the Papacy.*
		The trial of the Babeuvists begins at Vendôme.

March	12	*Bonaparte renews his offensive in Italy.*
April	16–18	*Hoche and Moreau resume the offensive across the Rhine.*
	18	*Bonaparte agrees to the PRELIMINARIES OF PEACE AT LEOBEN.*
		PARTIAL ELECTIONS OF YEAR V: substantial 'moderate' gains.
May		*Bonaparte enlarges the Cisalpine, occupies the Venetian, Republics.*
	20	The 'new third' enters the Councils; Barthélemy a Director.
	27	Conviction and execution of Babeuf at Vendôme.
June	9	Repeal of the Law of 3 Brumaire.
	23	Dumolard denounces Bonaparte's conduct in Italy.
July		Hoche's army is moved across France; the armies send loyal addresses to the Directory; Lord Malmesbury's second peace mission begins.
	14	Reconstruction of the ministries by Barras, Reubell and Lépeaux.
	25	Closure of all political clubs.
August	8	Augereau assumes command in the Paris area.
	13	Thibaudeau's interview with Madame de Staël.
	24	The Elders accept the repeal of the laws against the clergy.
	27	Lépeaux condemns royalist intrigue.
September	4	THE COUP D'ÉTAT OF 18 FRUCTIDOR.

6. *THE ABANDONMENT OF LEGALITY.*

1797

September	4	THE COUP D'ÉTAT OF 18 FRUCTIDOR.
	5	THE LAW OF 19 FRUCTIDOR.
		Merlin de Douai and François de Neufchâteau become Directors.
	17	Lord Malmesbury abandons his peace mission.
	19	Bonaparte's letter on 'Representative Government'.
	22	BEGINNING OF THE YEAR VI.
October	11	*British naval victory at Camperdown.*
	18	*PEACE OF CAMPO-FORMIO WITH AUSTRIA.*
November		Opening of the Congress on German affairs at Rastadt.

December	5	Bonaparte returns to Paris: dines with Ochs and Reubell (8); Luxembourg speech (10).

1798

January	22	*Purge of the Dutch Convention.*
	31	The Law of 12 Pluviôse (on sanctioning election results).
February		*Establishment of the Roman Republic; alliance forced upon the Cisalpine (21); march on Canton of Berne.*
	21	Dismissal of Sotin, the 'jacobin' Minister of Police.
	25	Merlin de Douai becomes President of the Directory.
March	5	*The Directors approve the expedition to Egypt.*
	22	*The 'Helvetic Republic' established in Switzerland.*
April		PARTIAL ELECTIONS OF THE YEAR VI: substantial 'jacobin' gains.
May	11	COUP D'ÉTAT OF 22 FLORÉAL.

7. THE ADVENT OF BONAPARTE.

1798

May	11	COUP D'ÉTAT OF 22 FLORÉAL.
	16	Treilhard becomes a Director.
	19	*Bonaparte sails from Toulon for Egypt: takes Malta (10 June), Alexandria (1 July).*
July	21	*Battle of the Pyramids.*
	31	*BATTLE OF THE NILE: destruction of Bonaparte's fleet.*
August	4	Law enforcing observance of the *décadi*.
	22	*Humbert's expedition to Ireland reaches Killala Bay.*
September	5	Jourdan's Conscription Law.
	9	*Turkey declares war on France.*
	22	BEGINNING OF THE YEAR VII.
		Ramel's reforms of French finances and taxation.
November		*RENEWAL OF WAR IN ITALY: Neapolitan forces take Rome (25); French occupy Piedmont.*
	26	Civilian commissioners are attached to the French armies.
December	15	*French forces re-occupy Rome.*
	23–29	*Russia allies with Turkey and Britain.*

1799

January	23	*French forces establish a Republic in Naples. Bonaparte advances into Syria.*

February	25	Order for the arrest of General Championnet.
March	12	*RENEWAL OF WAR AGAINST AUSTRIA.*
	25	*Defeat of Jourdan at Stockach.*
April	5	*Defeat of Schérer at Magnano.*
		PARTIAL ELECTIONS OF THE YEAR VII: substantial 'jacobin' gains.
	28	*Suvoroff takes Milan*; assassination of French envoys at Rastadt.
May	9	Reubell leaves the Directory.
	27	*Suvoroff takes Turin.*
		Bonaparte in retreat from Acre.
June	4	*Masséna victorious at (First) Zurich*; (17–19); *Macdonald's repulse on R. Trebbia.*
	9	Sieyès takes his seat as a Director.
	16	The Councils force Treilhard to resign.
	18	30 PRAIRIAL VII: fall of Lépeaux and Merlin de Douai (Ducos, Gohier and Moulin become Directors).
	27	Emergency legislation: the forced loan, the *levée en masse.*
July	12	The 'law of hostages'.
	14	Sieyès' anti-jacobin speech.
	25	*Bonaparte defeats the Turks at Aboukir.*
August	5	Royalist insurrection in Toulouse (checked at Montréjeau on 20).
	13	The Directory closes the 'jacobin club' in the Manège.
	15	*Death of Joubert, defeat of French at Novi.*
	18	Proposed indictment of the ex-Directors is rejected by 217–214.
	22	Bonaparte leaves Egypt for France.
	27	*Anglo-Russian invasion of Holland begins.*
September	13	Jourdan's *'La patrie en danger'* motion rejected by 245–171.
	23	BEGINNING OF THE YEAR VIII.
	25–27	*Masséna victorious at the SECOND BATTLE OF ZURICH.*
October	9	Bonaparte lands in France—reaches Paris 16.
	18	*Convention of Alkmaar: British evacuation of Holland.*
November	9–10	THE COUP D'ÉTAT OF 18–19 BRUMAIRE.

8. *THE YEAR OF ACHIEVEMENT.*

1799

November	9–10	THE COUP D'ÉTAT OF 18–19 BRUMAIRE: Provisional Consulate founded.
	13	Repeal of the 'law of hostages'.
December	13	The Commissions of the Councils 'accept' the Constitution and 'elect' the Consuls.
	25	THE CONSTITUTION OF THE YEAR VIII in effect.
	26	Emancipation of the relatives of *émigrés*.
	28	Final offer of pardon made to the *chouans*.

1800

January	5	Benjamin Constant's speech in the Tribunate.
	13	Establishment of the Bank of France.
February	17	Law of 28 Pluviôse establishes the prefectoral system.
	19	Bonaparte moves to the Tuileries.
	18	Execution of Frotté.
March	5 & 29	Bonaparte's meetings with Cadoudal.
	18	Law of 27 Ventôse establishes a new judicial system.
April		*Masséna besieged in Genoa.*
		Publication of *De la littérature*.
	21	The Constitution in effect in Western France.
May		*Moreau advances into Germany.*
	6	Bonaparte leaves Paris; *crossing of the Gt St Bernard* (15–23).
June	4	*Surrender of Genoa to the Austrians.*
	5	Bonaparte's address to the clergy in Milan Cathedral.
	14	*BATTLE OF MARENGO.*
July	2	Bonaparte returns to Paris.

9. *THE END OF THE REPUBLIC.*

1800

September	23	BEGINNING OF THE YEAR IX.
		Malta falls to the British.
		Negotiations with Austria continue at Lunéville.
October	10	The 'Opera Plot'.
	20	Amnesty extended to non-combatant *émigrés*.

November	1	Fontanes' 'Parallèle'.
	6	Cardinal Spina in Paris.
	19	*Moreau resumes hostilities against Austria.*
December	3	*BATTLE OF HOHENLINDEN.*
	16	*Formation of the League of Armed Neutrality against Britain.*
	24	THE CRIME OF 3 NIVÔSE: attempted assassination of Bonaparte.

1801

January	5	The proscription of the 'jacobins' approved by the Senate.
February	7	The Tribunate accepts the Law on Extraordinary Tribunals.
	9	*THE TREATY OF LUNÉVILLE WITH AUSTRIA.*
	21	*Addington's offer of negotiation from Britain.*
March	21	*Battle of Alexandria: British defeat of the French in Egypt.*
	23	*Assassination of Tsar Paul.*
April	2	*Battle of Copenhagen: disruption of the League of Armed Neutrality.*
	29	*Bonaparte's Malmaison plan for Switzerland.*
July	16	THE CONCORDAT OF 1801 between France and the Papacy.
	23	The Council of State begins work on proposals for a Civil Code.
September	2	*Beginning of the French evacuation of Egypt.*
	23	BEGINNING OF THE YEAR X.
October	1	*The Preliminary Peace of London with Great Britain.*
	8	*Peace between France and Russia.*
November	24	The Tribunate rejects the first article of the Civil Code.

1802

January	1	The Tribunate rejects the third article of the Civil Code.
	2	All governmental legislative proposals withdrawn.
	7	The Senate is asked to resolve the problem of the Tribunate.
	11–31	Bonaparte goes to Lyons, becomes President of Italian Republic.

March	27	*TREATY OF AMIENS CONCLUDED WITH BRITAIN.*
April	1	PURGE OF THE TRIBUNATE AND LEGIS- LATIVE BODY BY THE SENATE.
	8	Bonaparte adds the Organic Articles to the Concordat.
	18	PROMULGATION OF THE CONCORDAT: Easter Mass at Notre Dame.
	23	Amnesty extended to remaining *émigrés* by *senatus consultum.*
May	1	Education Law begins development of *lycées.*
	12	The assemblies approve the Life Consulate.
	19	Establishment of the Legion of Honour.
	20	Arrest of General Simon ends the Rennes Conspiracy.
August	4	THE CONSTITUTION OF THE YEAR X: by plebiscite and by a *senatus consultum*, NAPOLEON BONAPARTE BECOMES CONSUL FOR LIFE.

10. **1802–1804**: *SOME SALIENT DATES.*

1802

September	23	BEGINNING OF THE YEAR XI.

1803

January	4	Endowment of senatorial estates.
	23	Reorganisation of the Institute of France.
February	19	*Act of Mediation for Switzerland.*
April	12	Law of 22 Germinal prohibits workers' associations.
	26	*Ultimatum to France from Britain.*
May	12	*The British ambassador leaves Paris.*
August	20	Cadoudal disembarks in France.
September	24	BEGINNING OF THE YEAR XII: last festival of the Republic.
October	19	Final expulsion of Madame de Staël.
December	1	The carrying of work-cards becomes compulsory.

1804

January	28	Initial meeting of Pichegru and Moreau.
February 15 & 27		Arrest of Moreau and of Pichegru.
March	9	Arrest of Cadoudal.

Biographical Notes

Supplementary biographical information on some of the people who are most significant in this book; these notes should not be taken as complete in themselves, for they are complementary to the text.

AMAR (Jean-Baptiste André) 1750–1816, a lawyer at the *parlement* of Grenoble before the Revolution, became an ardent Montagnard in the Convention, in which he was a member of the Committee of General Security and a notable opponent of the Girondins. He abandoned public life after being acquitted of complicity in the conspiracy of Babeuf.

D'ANDRÉ (Antoine J. B.), 1759–1825. A counsel to the *parlement* of Aix before the Revolution, d'André was elected to the Estates-General as one of the nobility of Provence. As a liberal noble he supported the formation of the National Assembly and helped draft the Constitution of 1791. Thrice president of the National Assembly, he was close to Mirabeau and La Fayette, and came in 1791 to favour a conservative revision of the Constitution. In 1792 he emigrated to London; reappearing in Switzerland in 1795, he became a principal figure in the constitutional-royalist movement in 1797. After the *coup d'état* of Fructidor he escaped to Switzerland and to Vienna, where he lived honourably until able to return to France in 1814 and to hold high offices under the restored monarchy.

ARTOIS (Charles Philippe de Bourbon, comte d'), b. 1757, the youngest brother of Louis XVI. Shallow but conceited, he opposed all the King's proposals for reform before the Revolution and emigrated immediately after the fall of the Bastille in 1789. Until the emigration of his elder brother, Louis, comte de Provence, in 1791, he was the leader of the *émigrés*, and he remained the arch-enemy of the revolutionaries, whose cause his intransigence and unreliability did much to foster. Returning to Paris as Lieutenant-General of the Kingdom in 1814, he succeeded Louis XVIII as Charles X in 1824, and reigned until he was forced to abdicate by the Revolution of 1830. He died an exile in 1836.

AUGEREAU (Pierre François), 1757–1816. The son of a poor mason in the Parisian Faubourg St Marcel, Augereau enlisted while still a youth in the Royal Cavalry and rapidly acquired notoriety as a quarrelsome swordsman. Before the Revolution a chequered career included desertion from the French

Army, service under Suvoroff in the Russian Army, and desertion from the Prussian Army. Having served as a volunteer for the Republic in the Vendée, he rose to be a General in the Army of Italy and distinguished himself under Bonaparte at Castiglione and Arcola. Although he opposed the *coup d'état* of Brumaire as a republican, he became a Marshal (1804) and Duke of Castiglione (1806). He nevertheless abandoned Bonaparte in 1814 and abused him as he travelled to Elba. His offer of his service to the Emperor in 1815 was refused.

BABEUF (François Noel, called Gracchus), 1760–1797. A man of humble origins, Babeuf was keeper of the manorial rolls in the town of Roye in Picardy until the Revolution. Thereafter he became an ardent revolutionary and a radical journalist, and although he held administrative offices in the Somme and in Paris, he was constantly in danger of prosecution. Being in prison throughout the greater part of the Terror, he at first welcomed Thermidor; but he soon came to condemn the reaction. Arrested in February 1795, he was imprisoned until the following September at Arras and then transferred to the Plessis prison in Paris, and it was in these prisons that the ideas and organisation of a final egalitarian revolution developed. Being released in October 1795, Babeuf prepared to proceed with this, but the betrayal of the plot by a government agent led to his arrest in May 1795, and after a trial in which he defended himself in a great three-day speech he was condemned and executed in May 1797.

BARÈRE (Bertrand Barère de Vieuzac), b. 1755. A lawyer at Toulouse, he was a deputy in the Estates-General and in the Convention; an excellent orator and an able committee-man but a notorious trimmer, he moved steadily to the left with the Revolution. Although he abandoned Robespierre at Thermidor, he was identified with the Committee of Public Safety, for which he had been the principal spokesman in the Convention, and he was condemned to deportation in 1795. Evading this, he remained in France until he was granted amnesty by Bonaparte, who employed him briefly as a source of information. Died 1841.

BARRAS (Paul Jean Nicolas, vicomte de), b. 1755 in Provence. An officer in the royal army before the Revolution, he was elected to the Convention, in which he was a regicide and a notorious terrorist, being particularly associated with the bloody repression of counter-revolution at Marseilles and Toulon— where he first encountered Bonaparte. Recalled to Paris, he was prominent in overthrowing Robespierre, and earned a reputation as a strong man by organising the defence of the Convention both at Thermidor and at Vendémiaire (July 1794/October 1795). After holding office as a Director from 1795 to 1799, he was thrust from power and public life at Brumaire 1799, and passed the years of the Consulate and Empire either in exile or in closely observed residence in Montpellier. After the Restoration he settled near Paris and lived until 1829. His name is a byword for corruption and immorality.

BARTHÉLEMY (François de), 1747–1830. A diplomat of the old order, Barthélemy continued to serve the Republic and was particularly successful in
negotiating the Treaty of Basle with Prussia in 1795. Elected a Director in
1797, he was at once branded as a royalist and at the *coup d'état* of Fructidor
he was deported to Guiana. One of the small party which succeeded in
escaping from there, he remained in exile until the coming of the Consulate,
when he returned to France and became a member of the Senate.

BERLIER (Théophile), b. 1761. An advocate at Dijon, he was elected to the
Convention, in which he voted for the death of the King; but he remained
moderate and inconspicuous during the Terror. Thereafter he spoke frequently on legal problems, and was one of those who helped to draft the
Constitution of 1795. He nevertheless avoided political controversy. Appointed by Bonaparte to the Council of State, he contributed much to the
formulation of the Civil Code, becoming a Count of the Empire and serving
Bonaparte until 1815, after which he was exiled to Belgium until 1830. By
no means blind to the increasingly arbitrary nature of Bonaparte's régime, he
seems to have sought to ameliorate despotism by serving it intelligently. He
died at Dijon in 1844.

BERNADOTTE (Jean-Baptiste), 1763–1844. A handsome Gascon, Bernadotte
enlisted at the age of 17 and rose from the ranks to become a General of the
Army of the Sambre-et-Meuse under Jourdan in 1793. Transferred with his
division to the Army of Italy in 1796 (where his well-disciplined soldiers soon
clashed with their new comrades), Bernadotte became in effect Bonaparte's
ambassador to Vienna; but soon, as Minister of War and a potential 'Jacobin'
general, he appeared as an ambitious rival to him. Although he acquiesced in
the *coup* of Brumaire, his promotion to Marshal in 1804 and to the Principality
of Ponte-Corvo (1806) took place despite known intrigues against Bonaparte,
and were probably due in part to his marriage to Desirée Clary, once Napoleon's fiancée and later sister-in-law to Joseph Bonaparte. The uneasy relationship culminated in Bernadotte's election by the Swedish Diet as Crown
Prince of Sweden in 1810, a consequence of his release of Swedish captives
in 1806. From this time he identified himself with his adopted country,
joining the alliance against Bonaparte in 1812 and fighting against him at
Leipzig. Unable, as he probably expected, to succeed Bonaparte in 1814, he
returned to Sweden, over which he reigned as Charles XIV from 1828 to
1844.

BERNIER (Étienne), b. in Anjou 1762. A *curé* before the Revolution, Bernier
became one of the most influential advisers of the *chouans* before rallying to
Bonaparte in 1800. Having played a major role in the pacification of western
France in Bonaparte's interest, he became a principal agent in the negotiation
of the Concordat with Rome, services for which he was rewarded with the
appointment of Bishop of Orléans. Died 1806.

BERTHIER (Alexandre), 1753–1815, Bonaparte's famed Chief of Staff, had served as a staff officer in the American War of Independence and was in 1789 Major-General of the National Guard—a position which enabled him to assist the King's aunts to escape from France. After service in the Vendée he became chief staff officer to the Armies of the Alps and Italy. His meeting with Bonaparte began a long and remarkable military partnership. Becoming successively Minister of War after Brumaire, a Marshal and prince de Neu-châtel (1806) and prince de Wagram (1809), Berthier only gradually became disillusioned. Hostile to the attack on Russia in 1812, he was one of the first to abandon Bonaparte in 1814, when Louis XVIII made him a peer of France. Retiring during the Hundred Days, he was killed by a fall from a window two weeks before Waterloo.

BILLAUD-VARENNE (Jean Nicolas), b. 1756: an unsuccessful lawyer, violently radical and anti-clerical, he became a member of the Commune of 10 August 1792 and was subsequently elected a member of the Convention. At the *journée* of 5 September 1793 he entered the Committee of Public Safety as an exponent of ruthlessness, and helped to promote the development of revolutionary government. One of those who helped to overthrow Robespierre, he nevertheless had to resign from the Committee shortly after Thermidor, and in 1795 he was exiled to Cayenne. There he settled, marrying a native girl and emigrating to Haiti after 1815; he died there in 1819.

BOISSY D'ANGLAS (François), 1756–1826, a moderate member of the Estates-General, the Convention (where he voted against the death of the King), and the Legislative under the Directory until he was proscribed as a 'royalist' at 18 Fructidor (4 September 1797). Reinstated after Brumaire, he was a member of both the Tribunate and the Senate.

BONAPARTE (Joseph), 1768–1844, elder brother to Napoleon. Entrusted with increasingly important missions as Napoleon's greatness grew, he subsequently became in succession King of Naples and King of Spain, in both of which capacities he proved benevolent, seeking so far as possible to shield his subjects from the demands of the Emperor.

BONAPARTE (Lucien), 1775–1840, younger brother to Napoleon. Rising as much by his own merits as by his relationship to the general, he was instrumental as President of the Five Hundred in effecting the *coup d'état* of 18 Brumaire. Thereafter he became Minister of the Interior to Napoleon until the autumn of 1800, when political differences ended in his transference to Madrid as Ambassador. His independence, particularly in his refusal to repudiate his marriage to a lady insufficiently exalted for Napoleon's dynastic desires, then led to his exclusion from the affairs of the Empire.

BOULAY OF THE MEURTHE (Antoine J. C. Joseph), 1761–1840, was the son of a farmer in the Vosges who was helped by an uncle to become a successful lawyer at Nancy and at Paris. Although he served as a volunteer at Valmy and afterwards rose to the rank of captain, he was known to disapprove of the execution of the King, and he had to remain in hiding throughout the Terror. After resuming his legal career he was elected to the Five Hundred and remained closely associated with Sieyès until the advent of Bonaparte, for whom he became a Councillor of State (particularly concerned with the development of the Civil Code) and whom he served faithfully until the end. Banished in 1815, he returned to France in 1819, but took no further part in political life.

BRUNE (Guillaume), 1763–1815, the son of a lawyer, abandoned his father's profession in order to make a name in journalism and letters in Paris. One of the Volunteers of 1791, he obtained a commission and eventually the rank of General through the patronage of his friend Danton. During the Terror he helped to defeat the 'Federalists' at Pacey-sur-Eure and in Bordeaux; but his leniency and his association with Danton made it necessary for him to go into hiding in 1794. Being associated with Bonaparte in the repression of the rising of Véndemiaire, he followed him to Italy, did well, and obtained independent command in Holland in 1799, where he defeated the British at Bergen. Although made a Marshal in 1804 despite his hostility to the growth of the Empire, he acquired a reputation for ineptitude in war and extortion at all times, and he remained unemployed after being disgraced in 1807. In 1815 he died miserably at the hands of a mob in Avignon which believed him partially responsible for the massacre of the princesse de Lamballe in September 1792.

BUONARROTI (Filippo Michele), 1761–1837. An Italian revolutionary of aristocratic origin whose descent is traced from Michelangelo, he came to Paris by way of Corsica and became a commissioner of the Jacobin Republic to the Maritime Alps. Recalled to Paris and imprisoned in the Plessis prison, he became associated with Babeuf, in whose conspiracy in 1796 he was a central figure. After conviction he was held on l'Ile d'Oléron until Bonaparte sanctioned his release: but he nevertheless refused to rally to the Empire, against which he attempted to lead an insurrection at Grenoble in 1812. After a lifetime of exile he returned to Paris at the time of the Revolution of 1830, being then revered as a father-figure of revolutionary action. Author of the *Conspiration pour l'égalité dite de Babeuf* (Brussels, 1828).

CABANIS (Pierre-Jean Georges), 1757–1808, is perhaps best known as the doctor who was the friend of Mirabeau, at whose death-bed he alone was permitted to be present. A noted philosopher and man of letters, he was elected to the Legislative as a deputy for the Seine in 1797, and as an associate of Sieyès he was an active supporter of the *coup* of Brumaire. Appointed a member of the Bonapartist Senate, he remained friendly with Bonaparte despite his own opposition to the proscription of the Jacobins after the affair of the 'infernal machine' (see chapter 9).

CADOUDAL (Georges), b. near Auray in Brittany in 1771, the son of a farmer. He soon became prominent in the revolt of the Vendée, and was by 1795 the recognised leader of the guerilla bands of Morbihan, whom he led against the Directory from 1797. After the failure of his interviews with Bonaparte in March 1800, he took refuge in England, whence he returned later in the year to plot the overthrow of the First Consul. While some consider him to have been directly concerned in the attempt to assassinate Bonaparte on 24 December 1800, more sympathetic writers believe that he knew nothing of that plot, being concerned only in plans to waylay Bonaparte and kill him in open combat. A second return to France from Britain in 1803 ended in the arrest, trial and execution of Cadoudal in 1804.

CAMBACÉRÈS (Jean-Jacques Régis de), 1753–1824. A prominent lawyer at Montpellier, Cambacérès became a deputy in the Convention, where he voted for the death of the King and for the proposal that Louis be reprieved. After being a deputy in the Five Hundred and, in 1799, Minister of Justice, he participated in the *coup d'état* of Brumaire and—being in some sense a representative of what might be called the Left-Centre—became Second Consul to Bonaparte and, under the Empire, his Arch-chancellor. Although he abandoned Bonaparte in 1814–15 he was reinstated during the Hundred Days and exiled thereafter.

CARNOT (Lazare Nicolas), b. 1753. A captain in the engineers at the time of the outbreak of the Revolution, Carnot was elected a deputy both to the Legislative Assembly and the Convention, and in August 1793 he became a member of the Committee of Public Safety, in which he was particularly responsible for the organisation and direction of the great new armies of the Republic. After Thermidor, in which he turned against Robespierre, he barely escaped proscription with other 'terrorists' in 1795. Becoming a Director later in that year, he was forced to fly from France in Fructidor 1797, but he returned after Brumaire to serve Bonaparte briefly as Minister of War, and then to oppose him as a member of the Tribunate. After voting against the Life Consulate he retired, only returning to public life to help in the defence of France in 1814. Appointed Minister of the Interior during the Hundred Days, he was exiled as a regicide in 1816 and became a wanderer in Eastern Europe until his death at Magdeburg in 1823.

CARRIER (Jean-Baptiste), b. 1756. *Procureur* of Aurillac before the Revolution, Carrier was elected deputy to the Convention and acquired a most sinister reputation for organising the drowning of prisoners during the repression of Nantes and its vicinity after the defeat of the main forces of the Vendéan revolt (February, 1794). Although he contributed to the overthrow of Robespierre, he was sent before the Revolutionary Tribunal in November 1794 and guillotined in December as a terrorist.

CHAMPIONNET (Jean Etienne), 1762–1800. Having become a general in 1793, Championnet was appointed to command the French forces in Rome when Berthier accompanied Bonaparte to Egypt in 1798. It thus fell to him to repel the attack on the Roman Republic by Naples and to invade Naples and establish the Neapolitan Republic. Arrested for disobedience in consequence of his treatment of the civil commissioner Faipoult, he was imprisoned until the *coup* of 30 Prairial (18 June 1799), when his rehabilitation symbolised the collapse of the Directory's endeavour to impose its will upon its armies. Appointed to command the Army of the Alps, he was defeated by the Austrians at Genola on 4 November 1799, and died of sickness shortly afterwards.

CHARETTE DE LA CONTRIE (François de), 1763–1796, was a Breton naval officer who had left the sea and become the leader of the Vendéean rebels in the area of Machecoul at the time when notorious massacres there marked the outbreak of their rising. Although he took some part in the major campaigns of the war, his fame derives from his later activities as a guerilla leader who maintained resistance to the Republican forces in Lower Poitou. In February 1795 he signed the Treaty of La Jaunay, being then at the height of his power; but after resuming the war at the time of the Quiberon landing he was relentlessly hunted down. After capture he was shot at Nantes in March 1796.

COLLOT D'HERBOIS (Jean-Marie), b. 1750. An actor and a playwright, he became an ardent revolutionary and was, like Billaud-Varenne, in turn a member of the Commune and the Convention, in which he advocated extreme terrorism. Becoming a member of the Committee of Public Safety in September 1793, he was particularly associated with the slaughter of 'rebels' at Lyons after that city had surrendered to the forces of the Convention. One of those most responsible for the fall of Robespierre, he was exiled by the Convention in 1795 to Cayenne, where he died in 1796.

CONDORCET (Jean Antoine Nicolas, marquis de Caritat), b. 1743. A liberal aristocrat and an illustrious mathematician and philosopher, he became sympathetic to republicanism after the Flight to Varennes in 1791, and was elected to both the Legislative Assembly and the Convention. As the principal author of the constitutional proposals which the Montagnards condemned as 'federalist' in 1793, he went into hiding in Paris when they triumphed, during which time he wrote his remarkable *Esquisse d'un tableau historique des progrès de l'esprit humain*. After flying from the capital in March 1794, he was arrested and killed himself (28 March 1794).

CONSTANT (Benjamin Constant de Rebecque), 1767–1830. A notable literary figure and the author of the novel *Adolphe*, Constant was long closely associated with his Swiss compatriot Madame de Staël (q.v.). Coming to Paris in 1796, he collaborated with her in the publication of a succession of pamphlets advocating the adoption of moderate liberal-republican policies and it would seem that he was largely responsible for the foundation of the pro-Directorial Constitutional Circle in Paris in 1797. Becoming a member of the Tribunate of Bonaparte in 1800, he soon incurred the First Consul's suspicions, and he was first eliminated from the Assembly in 1802, and then banished. Returning to France at the time of the first restoration of Louis XVIII, he was quick to denounce Bonaparte's return from Elba: but he nevertheless rallied to the Emperor, and he was entrusted with the responsibility of drafting the 'Additional Act' by which the Imperial Constitution was at least nominally liberalised in 1815. A famous, if a somewhat inconsistent and ineffectual liberal, he was again banished after Waterloo, but returned in 1817 to become a deputy and a prominent opponent of the ultra-royalists between 1819 and 1830. He died shortly after becoming President of the Council of State in the July Monarchy.

DARTHÉ (Augustin Alexandre), 1769–1797, was a Jacobin leader in the Pas de Calais who had been associated with the activities of Le Bon at Arras. A member of the secret directory of the 'Conspiracy of the Equals', he refused to admit the competence of the court at Vendôme and remained silent throughout the trial.

DAUNOU (Pierre Claude F.), b. 1761. A member of the Oratorian order who became one of the constitutional clergy, Daunou was elected a deputy to the Convention and voted for the imprisonment of the King. He was later imprisoned until Thermidor as one of those who protested against the proscription of the deputies of the Gironde, so that he is sometimes called a Girondin. After Thermidor he was influential in planning the reorganisation of education and the Institut. Prominent in drafting both the constitution of 1795 and that of 1799, which he sought to make as liberal as possible, he became one of the most notable members of the Tribunate, from which he was excluded in 1802 as an opponent of Bonaparte. He died in Paris in 1840.

DUCOS (Pierre Roger), b. 1747. Once a magistrate in the Landes, Roger Ducos was an undistinguished but respected regicide member of the Convention and the Council of Elders, of which assembly he was on occasion president. Excluded in Floréal (after being re-elected at the end of his first term), he was appointed Director in 1799; and as he seems to have been convinced that it was imperative to eliminate Barras if a Restoration were to be avoided, this appointment presaged the *coup d'état* of Brumaire. After acting as Third Consul with Bonaparte and Sieyès in the Provisional Consulate of 1799, he became a Senator and served Bonaparte throughout the period of the Empire. Although he voted for the Emperor's deposition in 1814, he was exiled as a regicide in 1815, and died the next year.

DUMAS (Mathieu, comte), 1753–1837. Born of the *noblesse* in Montpellier, Dumas had a distinguished military career before the Revolution. Having acted as an aide-de-camp to Rochambeau in the American War, he was entrusted with various responsible missions in Europe before taking the place of Guibert on the *conseil de guerre*. In the initial years of the Revolution he was closely associated with La Fayette, whom he subsequently supported strongly in the Legislative Assembly. From the dissolution of that Assembly until the fall of Robespierre he remained in concealment or in exile, and after being elected to the Council of Elders in 1795 he was again forced to flee the country as a 'royalist' in 1797. Returning to France after Brumaire, he resumed his career as a senior staff officer in Bonaparte's service, being present, for example, at Austerlitz, Wagram and Moscow. His capture by the allies in 1815 no doubt facilitated his admission to the service of Louis XVIII, as his opposition to Charles X enabled him to become a peer in the Orléanist period. Having served Bonaparte, Louis XVIII and Louis Philippe as a Councillor of State, he died in 1837 after a long period of illness.

DUSAULX (Jean), b. 1728, a soldier who had fought in the Seven Years War (1756–63). He was that rare being, a deputy to the Convention for Paris who was not a Montagnard. He was also an elderly man in a youthful assembly, and he was struck off the list of those to be expelled from the Convention on 2 June 1793 after Marat had contemptuously dismissed him as an old dotard. He had been imprisoned at the Port Libre from 3 October 1793 as one of those who signed the Protest of the Seventy-five against the events of 2 June. Died 1799.

FOUCHÉ (Joseph, duc d'Otrante), b. near Nantes 1759, the son of a merchant captain. Educated by the Oratorians, he became one of their teachers in minor orders and was in 1789 the principal of their college at Nantes. Renouncing his orders, he then became a Jacobin and was elected in 1792 as a deputy to the Convention, in which he soon passed from the right to the left. In a notorious mission he encouraged attacks on Christianity, and he was associated with Collot d'Herbois both in the savage repression of Lyons and in the plot to overthrow Robespierre in Thermidor. Impeached in 1795, he lived in poverty and obscurity until after the *coup d'état* of Fructidor 1797, when Barras entrusted him with diplomatic missions to Italy and Holland and eventually appointed him Minister of Police in 1799. In this capacity he welcomed and served Bonaparte until the Ministry was suppressed in 1802. Re-appointed in 1804, he seemed indispensable until Napoleon learnt in 1810 that he was in secret contact with Great Britain, and banished him to Aix. The Duke of Otranto, as he had become in 1809, was made Governor of the Illyrian Provinces in 1813; returning to Paris after the fall of the Empire, he was instrumental in arranging the Restoration, but he was nevertheless banished as a terrorist and a regicide in 1816. He died a naturalised Austrian at Trieste in 1820.

FRÉRON (Louis), b. 1754. An ardent revolutionary, the author of the violent journal *l'Orateur du peuple* was elected to the Convention and was associated with Barras in the murderous enforcement of the Terror in the Midi. After participating in the overthrow of Robespierre he became notorious as a reactionary, striking at the Jacobins through organised gangs known as *la jeunesse dorée* and subsequently encouraging the White Terror in south-eastern France.

GOHIER (Louis Jérôme), b. 1746, was a Breton magistrate who became a deputy to the Legislative Assembly without distinguishing himself sufficiently to be re-elected to the Convention. Described by Madame Roland as an ambitious mediocrity, he succeeded her friend Garat as Minister of Justice in March 1793 and held that post until the autumn of 1795—though the authority of all ministers was much reduced during the Terror. As a Director in 1799 he was in some measure a rallying point for the Jacobin revival, but he was outmanoeuvred without difficulty by Sieyès and Bonaparte and re-tired from public life after Brumaire. Becoming Consul in Holland two years later, he finally retired when that country was annexed outright by Napoleon in 1810. Died 1830.

GRÉGOIRE (Henri), 1750–1831. As a deputy for the clergy to the Estates-General, Grégoire welcomed the Civil Constitution of the Clergy and became Bishop of Blois. Being also an early enthusiast for republicanism, he was elected deputy to the Convention and to the Council of Five Hundred, and as the recognised head of the Constitutional Church he was selected to serve in Bonaparte's Legislative Body and Senate. As sincere and courageous a Catholic as he was persistent in his endeavours to re-establish an effective Gallican Church in France, he upheld his cause through the Revolution despite repudiation from Rome and rebuffs by the rationalists in France; but Bonaparte's Concordat of 1802 shattered his hopes. Resigning his bishopric, he remained a quiescent opponent of the Emperor, for whose deposition he voted in 1814.

HOCHE (Louis Lazare), 1750–1797. During the Revolution Hoche rose from being a sergeant of the National Guard in Paris to become one of the foremost generals of the Republic. As commander of the Army of the Moselle in 1793 he forced the Austro-Prussian forces to evacuate Alsace; but he was then denounced and imprisoned as a suspect. After contributing very considerably to the pacification of the West after Thermidor, a process which included the defeating of the Quiberon expedition, he led an ill-fated expedition to Ireland in 1796. Victorious in Germany as commander of the Army of the Sambre and Meuse, he appeared a potential counter-weight to Bonaparte; and Barras in fact made use of his army and his republican reputation in July 1797; but he returned at once to Germany, where he died suddenly at the age of 47.

JEANBON SAINT-ANDRÉ, 1749–1813, a Protestant pastor and an ardent democrat, became deputy to the Convention, in which he voted for the death of the King and opposed the 'Girondins'. As a member of the Committee of Public Safety he was particularly responsible for naval matters and was frequently absent from Paris, as he was at Thermidor. Like Lindet he is usually thought of as primarily a great administrator. Imprisoned until the amnesty which marked the closure of the Convention, he subsequently became a consul at Algiers and Smyrna, and then returned to France to serve Bonaparte as a prefect.

JOUBERT (Barthélemy), b. 1769. An able subordinate commander of Bonaparte's in the Italian campaign of 1796–7, Joubert later became commander of French forces in Holland and, in 1798, Italy. Having resigned his command over differences with the civil commissioner of the Directory, he returned to Paris and participated in the *coup* of 30 Prairial by which Lépeaux and Merlin were removed from the executive. His reappointment to command of the Army of Italy, intended by Sieyès to be the prelude to victory and to a more far-reaching reconstruction of the Directory, led in fact to his death at the battle of Novi in 1799.

JOURDAN (Jean-Baptiste), b. Limoges 1762. After serving with the French forces in the American War of Independence, Jourdan settled down as a haberdasher in Limoges. Re-entering the army in 1792, he rose to command the Army of the North: victor of Wattignies in 1793, he won still greater fame in 1794 as commander of the Army of the Sambre-et-Meuse at the battle of Fleurus. After reverses on the Rhine in 1796, he resigned and returned again to his trade, but he was elected to the Council of Five Hundred, where he moved the conscription law of 1798 which remained in force throughout the period of the Empire. Hostile to Bonaparte in 1799, he was created a Marshal in 1804 but held only minor commands until Joseph Bonaparte, with whom he was more closely associated, secured greater responsibilities for him in Spain. Defeated by Wellington at Vittoria (1813), he returned to France with Joseph, and accepted the deposition of Napoleon and the Restoration. He died in Paris in 1833.

LAMARQUE (François), 1755–1839. A man of the Dordogne, Lamarque became an advocate to the *parlement* of Paris and a deputy in the Legislative Assembly and the Convention. An opponent of the clergy and the *émigrés*, he was also a regicide; but his career in the Revolution was broken when he was one of those sent to investigate the affairs of Dumouriez' Army of the North in 1793, and was arrested and handed over to the Austrians. Imprisoned until December 1795, he became a member of the Five Hundred and an ardent supporter of the Directory against the Right. Excluded from the Council in Floréal as a Jacobin, he accepted minor diplomatic appointments until he re-entered the house in 1799 and again supported the Jacobin cause. After Brumaire he was not one of those nominated to the new legislature, but became first a prefect and then *procureur* to the Court of Appeal, an office he held throughout the Napoleonic period. After living in Geneva and Austria from 1816 to 1819, he remained in retirement in France until his death.

LANJUINAIS (Jean Denis), b. 1753 d. 1827, was a prominent Breton lawyer who became a deputy to the Estates-General and one of the founders of the Breton Club, from which the Jacobin Club probably derived. A stalwart opponent of privilege in 1789–91, when he was one of the chief architects of the Civil Constitution of the Clergy, he was also one of the most outspoken critics of the Mountain in the Convention. Although proscribed, he remained in concealment throughout the Terror, and subsequently became a member of the Council of Elders (1755–May 1797) and of the Senate of Bonaparte. Notably courageous throughout his life, he was one of the few who openly opposed the advent of the Empire; and he subsequently voted for the deposition of Bonaparte in 1814, and opposed the royalist reaction after 1815.

LAREVELLIÈRE-LÉPEAUX (Louis-Marie de), 1753–1824. A deputy for Angers to the Estates-General and for Maine-et-Loire to the Convention, he was an ardent republican who proposed the famous decree of 19 November 1792 by which France offered fraternity to oppressed peoples. Although a regicide, he withdrew from the Convention after 2 June 1793 as a form of protest against the domination of the assembly by the Mountain. Returning to the Convention after Thermidor, he helped to prepare the Constitution of 1795, and under this he became a Director from 1795 to 18 June 1799. Refusing loyalty to Bonaparte, he lived in retirement thereafter.

LE BON (Joseph), b. at Arras 1765. A priest who had renounced his calling, as a member of the Convention he served on the Committee of General Security and acquired notoriety by his pitiless enforcement of the Terror as a Commissioner of the Convention at Arras and Cambrai. Imprisoned after Thermidor, he was executed at Amiens on 9 October 1795.

LEBRUN (Charles François), b. 1739. An advocate, Lebrun became tutor to the son of Maupeou, and so became the latter's principal secretary and assistant in promoting royal reform. After Maupeou's disgrace in 1774, Lebrun retired, but he nevertheless was called upon to be deputy to the Estates-General. While still sympathetic to reform, he disassociated himself from violence, and was imprisoned during the Terror. A member of the Council of Elders from 1795, he took no active part in the *coup d'état* of Brumaire, but he was named as Third Consul, apparently on the advice of Cambacérès. Remaining particularly interested in financial reform, he became Arch-Treasurer of the Empire, and, in 1810, Governor of Holland. Although made a peer by Louis XVIII at the first Restoration, Lebrun had to surrender this rank after the Hundred Days, when he had re-entered Bonaparte's service as Grand Master of the University. Restored to the peerage in 1819, he died in 1824 aged 85.

LETOURNEUR (Louis François), 1715–1817, Officer of Engineers, deputy to the Legislative Assembly and the Convention, where he voted for the death of the King and for the referendum. He served for a time on the Committee of Public Safety, was a Director from 1795 to 1797 and became a Prefect during the Consulate.

LINDET (Jean-Baptiste Robert, usually known as Robert Lindet), 1743–1825, was a lawyer who became deputy for the Eure to the Legislative Assembly and the Convention. As a moderate member of the Committee of Public

Safety he was particularly responsible for the organisation of the Central Food Commission. Surviving Thermidor, he was imprisoned after the popular rising in Prairial (May 1795) and excluded from the Legislative Body which succeeded the Convention. He became Minister of Finance in 1799, but refused to recognise Bonaparte and resumed legal practice.

LOUVET (Jean-Baptiste Louvet de Couvrai), b. 1760, was a Parisian novelist and journalist who became closely associated with the Rolands and the deputies of the Gironde, whom he supported whole-heartedly in his paper. As a deputy in the Convention, he acquired fame by personally denouncing Robespierre in October 1792. Proscribed in 1793, he went into hiding and wrote highly emotional memoirs. He later became a member of the Council of Five Hundred, but died suddenly in 1797.

MASSÉNA (André), 1758–1817, subsequently Marshal, Duke of Rivoli and Prince of Essling. Known as '*L'enfant chéri de la Victoire*' for his part in the Italian campaign of 1796, and known throughout the period for his rapacity, Masséna's greatest achievements were the defence of Zurich against the Russians in 1799 and the defence of Genoa against the Austrians in 1800. His career was blighted by his failure to force the Lines of Torres Vedras during the Peninsula War, after which Bonaparte offered him little employment.

MENOU (Jacques François), born in Touraine 1750, an officer who became a deputy to the Estates-General and was subsequently unsuccessful in campaigning against the Vendéans; forced surrender of faubourg Saint-Antoine, Prairial 1795; disgraced after Vendémiaire; accompanied Napoleon to Egypt, where he became the laughing-stock of the army by adopting the faith and customs of Islam, even to the point of marriage; eventually, as Abd Allah Menou, capitulated to the British at Alexandria in 1801. After being a member of the Tribunate, he became governor of Tuscany and then of Venice, where he died in 1810.

MERLIN 'DE DOUAI' (Philippe Antoine), 1754–1838, an *avocat* to the *parlement* of Douai, became a deputy to the Estates-General and to the Convention, in which he acquired notoriety as the principal author of the Law of Suspects in September 1793. He was nevertheless one of those who overthrew Robespierre and brought about the closure of the Jacobin Club in 1794. A highly-skilled and formidable lawyer, he became Minister of Justice under the Directory, and then a Director after Fructidor (1797), a *coup* to which he personally contributed considerably. Being particularly responsible for the thwarting of the neo-Jacobin resurgence in the elections of 1798 (the *coup* of Floréal), he was himself overthrown with Lépeaux in Prairial (1799). Subsequently, however, he proved himself as indispensable to Bonaparte as he had been to the men of the Revolution, and he served as *procureur* to the Court of Appeal from 1801 to 1814, being also a Councillor of State and a Count of the Empire. The fall of the Empire ended his career, and he remained in exile throughout the period of the Restoration.

MOREAU (Jean Victor), 1763–1813. After serving under Pichegru in the conquest of Holland in 1793, Moreau succeeded him as commander of the Army of the Rhine and Moselle in 1796; but despite success in the field, including a famous fighting retreat through the Black Forest, he was deprived of his command soon after the *coup d'état* of Fructidor 1797, being suspected of royalist sympathies because he failed to reveal evidence of Pichegru's negotiations with Condé. In 1799, when the French were defeated at Novi, he again saved an army, and in 1800 he matched Bonaparte's victory at Marengo by defeating the Austrians at Hohenlinden (3 December). Although regarded as a truly republican rival to Bonaparte, he was politically too honourable, or too inept, to survive: having become involved in a further conspiracy of Pichegru's, he was sentenced to two years' imprisonment in 1804. When Bonaparte commuted this sentence to one of exile, Moreau retired to the United States. Eight years later he yielded to pleas to assist the allies to overthrow Bonaparte and entered the service of the Tsar as an adviser—only to be mortally wounded by a cannon-ball in a minor engagement.

MOULIN (Jean François A.), b. 1752. A minor official before the Revolution, Moulin volunteered for military service in 1791 and rose to the rank of general in the campaigns in Western France. Imprisoned briefly during the Terror for his leniency towards his prisoners, he showed more severity as commander of the Paris area after Fructidor: but he was always an administrative rather than a fighting soldier. As a Director in 1799 he represented the brief ascendancy of moderate Jacobinism: but his refusal to resign his position at the *coup* of Brumaire may not be unrelated to his later (vain) efforts to collect his gratuity. After a period of retirement he ended his life in 1810 as the garrison commander at Antwerp.

MURAT (Joachim), 1767–1815, the son of an innkeeper, became aide-de-camp to Bonaparte after Vendémiaire; after accompanying Bonaparte to Italy and Egypt, he became a general and married Caroline Bonaparte. Noted both for his spectacular uniforms and for his brilliance and bravery as a cavalry commander, he eventually succeeded Joseph Bonaparte as King of Naples; but he defected to the allies after Leipzig, only to be shot in the following year by the followers of Ferdinand IV.

FRANÇOIS DE NEUFCHÂTEAU (Nicolas), 1750–1828. Beginning his career by somewhat dubious writings, François became *procureur* to the Council of St Dominica, a deputy to the Legislative Assembly and—having refused to sit in the Convention—Minister of the Interior in 1797. After the *coup d'état* of Fructidor in that year he became one of the Directors, an office he held until he returned to the Interior after being displaced by lot in 1798. Excluded from the Ministry after the *coup* of Prairial (June 1799), he subsequently became a member of Bonaparte's Senate and a Count of the Empire. As Minister and Director he is particularly associated with both the administrative and economic reforms of the period and with the endeavour to establish the cult of the *décadi*.

ORLÉANS (Louis Philippe Joseph, duc d'), b. 1747. A direct descendant of the brother of Louis XIV, he was notable for both riotous living and for unscrupulous and self-centred 'liberal' opposition to Louis XVI's government before the Revolution, which he is suspected of promoting in hopes of becoming Regent if not King. Sent to England immediately after the events of October 1789, he returned to become, as Citizen Equality, a deputy for Paris in the Convention, in which he voted for the death of Louis XVI. Accused of complicity in the treason of Dumouriez in 1793, he was imprisoned at Marseilles and executed in Paris on 6 November 1795. His son, *Egalité fils*, who had fought at Valmy and Jemappes, followed Dumouriez into exile in 1793 and subsequently became King Louis-Philippe (1830–48).

PICHEGRU (Jean Charles), b. 1761. A sergeant-major in 1789, Pichegru accepted the Revolution and advanced rapidly in rank, becoming commander of the Army of the Rhine in 1793. Transferred to the Army of the North, he became known as the 'Conqueror of Holland' after his successes there in 1794–95. After restoring order in Paris in Germinal (April 1795) he returned to the Army of the Rhine, but entered into negotiations with the *émigrés*, soft-pedalled in military operations, and was dismissed in March 1796. Elected to the Council of 500, he became its president, but was deported to Guiana as a royalist after the *coup d'état* of Fructidor (1797). Escaping thence, he reached London and joined Cadoudal (q.v.). Arrested in Paris, he was found strangled in prison while awaiting trial (6 April 1804).

PRIEUR-DUVERNOIS (Claude Antoine, called Prieur of the Côte-d'Or), b. 1763. A military engineer, he was elected deputy for the Côte-d'Or to the Legislative Assembly and the Convention. Closely associated with Carnot, he became a member of the Committee of Public Safety, in which he contributed particularly to the development of munitions and supplies. In danger, but not proscribed, after Thermidor, he interested himself in education and the development of the Polytechnic. Elected to the Council of 500 in 1795, he retired from political life in 1798 to resume his career in military administration. Died 1832.

PROVENCE (Louis Stanislas Xavier, comte de), b. 1755, the eldest surviving brother of Louis XVI. An 'enlightened' prince, he accepted the initial stages of the Revolution but left France for Brussels at the time of the Flight to Varennes (June 1791). Styled 'Regent of the Kingdom' after the death of Louis XVI, and 'Louis XVIII' after that of the Dauphin 'Louis XVII' in 1795, he was restored to the throne in 1814 and 1815.

PUISAYE (Joseph, comte de), b. 1755. As commander of the National Guard at Evreux in 1793, Count Puisaye had attempted to rally the forces of Normandy against those of the Convention after 2 June. Frustrated at Pacey-sur-Eure on 13 July, he became the principal—and probably the most realistic—organiser of Anglo-royalist intervention in Western France. After the failure of the Quiberon expedition in 1795, of which he was one of the commanders, and of further efforts to organise effective rebellion in the West, he emigrated to Canada (1798–1801); thence he returned to England, becoming a naturalised Englishman and dying at Hammersmith in 1827.

RAMEL DE NOGARET (Jacques), 1760–1839. Originally an advocate at Carcassonne, Ramel was in turn deputy to the Estates-General, the Convention and the Five Hundred. Although a regicide, he spoke little in these assemblies, being principally interested in finance. Becoming Minister of Finance under the Directory, he served until he was replaced by Lindet in June 1799, and thereafter he held no office of importance until the Hundred Days, when he became a prefect—but only to be exiled to Brussels, where he died.

MADAME RECAMIER (1777–1849), a celebrated beauty, was the wife of a rich banker. She had eventually to leave Paris because of her friendships for those who could not reconcile themselves to the Bonapartist régime; taking refuge in Italy she returned to Paris only at the Restoration.

REUBELL (Jean François), 1747–1807. A lawyer of note in the Court of Colmar in Alsace before the Revolution, Reubell became a radical deputy in the Estates-General and an ardent Montagnard in the Convention. Rising to prominence after Thermidor, he became the strong man of the Directory from 1795 until he was eliminated by lot in May 1799 and retired from public life. The reputation he has for enriching himself at public expense would seem to be ill-founded, and it would rather seem that he had considerable stature as a realistic and practical statesman.

ROEDERER (Pierre Louis), b. 1754. A barrister at the *parlement* of Metz, he was elected to the Estates-General, in which he appeared as a moderate Jacobin, particularly interested in financial affairs. Elected *procureur-syndic* of the Department of the Seine in 1791, he was excluded from the Jacobins for his condemnation of the demonstration on 20 June 1792; but he nevertheless played an ambiguous part on 10 August 1792, when he was instrumental in persuading the Royal Family to abandon the Tuileries. Deprived of office, he narrowly escaped proscription for denying the competence of the Convention to try the King, and he remained in obscurity until Thermidor. Thereafter he re-emerged as a journalist, secured a seat in the Institut, supported the *coup d'état* of Brumaire and became one of Bonaparte's Councillors of State. Bonaparte liked him, respected his ability, and made extensive use of his services until 1815; but being a man of independent mind, he was long employed far from Paris. After living in retirement until 1830, he entered the Chamber of Peers, dying in 1835.

SIEYÈS (Emmanuel), 1748–1836, well known as the author of the pamphlet *Qu'est-ce que le Tiers Etat?* (1789), was a canon at Chartres until the

Revolution, when he became one of the most influential leaders of the Third Estate and the foremost exponent of the doctrine of the sovereignty of the nation. He was nevertheless partially responsible for the restriction of the franchise in 1789, and his dislike of his colleagues' treatment of the Church began his withdrawal from the centre of the stage. As a deputy to the Convention he voted for the death of the King, but thereafter he remained in obscurity until 1795. Returning to political life as a member of the Council of Five Hundred, he supported the *coup d'état* of Fructidor in 1797, became ambassador to Berlin in 1798, and, first as a Director and then as one of the Provisional Consuls, aided Bonaparte to acquire power in 1799. Being then discredited, he remained a shadowy opponent of Bonaparte throughout the Consulate and the Empire. After fifteen years of exile during the Restoration he returned in 1830 to end his days in Paris.

DE STAËL (Germaine, baroness of Staël-Holstein), 1766–1817. The daughter of Necker, the popular finance minister of Louis XVI, Germaine was married at the age of 19 to the Swedish ambassador, M. de Staël. Although best-known as one of the great figures of contemporary literature, she was also intimately associated with a succession of prominent statesmen, and she constantly sought through her writings and her receptions to influence the course of events in France. After returning to her home in Switzerland during the Terror, she came back to France in 1795 only to be banished again after the rising of Vendémiaire—which she had in fact sought to avert; similarly, her support of the Directors at the time of the *coup d'état* of Fructidor led to renewed exile as one suspected of aiding its victims; and her initial acceptance of Bonaparte's advent was soon followed by her emergence as his most consistent critic. Banished first from Paris and subsequently from France, she remained in exile until the Restoration. Though perpetually unsuccessful in political life, she constantly upheld liberal ideals.

TALLEYRAND-PÉRIGORD (Charles Maurice, prince de), 1754–1838. Prevented by a club-foot from becoming a soldier, Talleyrand entered the Church and was Bishop of Autun in 1798. Already notorious for his life of pleasure, he further scandalised contemporaries by initiating the Revolutionary seizure of ecclesiastical lands in 1789, by welcoming the Civil Constitution of the Clergy in 1790 and by consecrating many of the first elected bishops of the Constitutional Church. Thereafter he abandoned the priesthood and withdrew from France, first on diplomatic missions to England and then by going to America in 1794. Returning under the Directory, he became Minister of Foreign Relations in 1796 through the influence of Madame de Staël, and although he lost this post after two years, he was re-appointed to it soon after Brumaire. Realistic, cynical and outrageously corrupt, he was closely associated with Bonaparte until 1809, representing for him the support of the old aristocracy and all who favoured the re-establishment of a crown and a court. His character being redeemed by his brilliance as a diplomat and by his real concern for the welfare of France, he played a major part in the

Restoration of Louis XVIII and in the Congress of Vienna, and subsequently served both the Bourbons and the Orléanist Monarchy.

TALLIEN (Jean Lambert), b. 1767, was a lawyer's clerk who was active in the Revolution as a journalist. A member of the Commune of 10 August 1792 and deputy to the Convention for Seine-et-Oise, he was responsible for the repression of counter-revolution in the Gironde and was one of the principal conspirators against Robespierre at Thermidor. A leader of the Thermidorian reaction, he was accused of responsibility for the execution of the royalist prisoners taken at Quiberon in 1795. A member of the Council of 500, he was captured at sea by the British at the time of Bonaparte's Egyptian expedition; released in 1802, he was appointed consul at Alicante, contracted yellow fever, and eventually died in obscure poverty in Paris in 1820. *Thérésa Cabarrus*, whom he married after Thermidor, was a celebrated beauty of her day: known as 'Our Lady of Thermidor', she influenced Tallien against terrorism.

MADAME TALLIEN (*née* Thérésa Cabarrus, 1773–1835, was the daughter of a Spanish banker. Married to the marquis de Fontenay, she was imprisoned at Bordeaux during the Terror and saved from execution by Tallien (q.v.), a sequence of events which was later repeated in Paris. She is reputed to have used her influence with Tallien to save many from the guillotine; but after her marriage to him, she became associated with Barras, and eventually divorced Tallien and married the comte de Caraman-Chimay.

THIBAUDEAU (Antoine), b. Poitiers 1765. *Avocat* at 22, *procureur* and a founder member of the Jacobin Society at Poitiers, he was elected a deputy for Vienne to the Convention, in which he was initially a Montagnard and a regicide. Prominent after Thermidor and in the Legislative Body 1795–1797, he was a constant champion of constitutional republican government. Retiring after the *coup d'état* of Fructidor (1797) he became Councillor of State in 1800, but retired to become Prefect of the Bouches du Rhône 1803–1814. Refusing to accept the Restoration, he was in exile from 1815 to 1830, when he returned to France and lived to become in old age a Senator of the Second Empire. Died 1854. Much of the present volume is a commentary upon the earlier part of his life.

TREILHARD (Jean-Baptiste), 1742–1810. A successful lawyer from Corrèze who became famous as a jurisconsult, Treilhard was elected a deputy for Paris to the Estates-General in 1789, and as a member of the ecclesiastical committee was influential in establishing the Civil Constitution of the Clergy. Later, as a member of the Convention, he voted for the death of Louis XVI; but as he also favoured a reprieve, spoke critically of Paris, and proved ineffectual as an anti-'federalist' commissioner in south-western France, he had to remain inconspicuous during the Terror. More prominent after Thermidor, he emerged in the Council of Five Hundred as a stalwart supporter of the Law of 3 Brumaire. Compelled to retire from the Directory in June 1799, he supported the advent of Bonaparte, whom he subsequently served as a Councillor of State and one of the principal architects of the Civil Code.

VERGNIAUD (Pierre Victurnien), b. 1753. The son of a minor army contractor who became bankrupt, he was befriended by Turgot and educated at the Collège du Pléssis at Paris. Becoming a prominent member of the Bordeaux bar, he was elected both to the Legislative Assembly in 1792 and the Convention in 1793. A great orator who often rose above recrimination, he became one of the principal opponents of Robespierre and the Mountain, and was arrested on 2 June 1793. Disdaining flight, he was tried by the Revolutionary Tribunal and executed at Paris on 31 October 1793.

Further Reading

As any interested reader can easily discover, there are innumerable books on both the Revolutionary and the Napoleonic periods of French history. On the other hand, an inspection of any library or bibliography will soon show that comparatively little has been written about 1794–9, the central years of the first French Republic. Many of the best books about the Revolution end with the death of Robespierre in 1794, or (in recent years) with the defeat of the *sans-culottes* in 1795; and when the tale is resumed with the appearance of Bonaparte on the centre of the stage in 1799, it is of course told largely in terms of the life and achievements of that outstanding man. What is more, the days of the Directory and the endeavours of those who strove to sustain republicanism during the Consulate have generally received unsympathetic treatment both from the more-or-less revolutionary Left and from the more-or-less Bonapartist Right. It follows that many of the books given here are rather avenues of approach to the First Republic than straightforward histories of it, and that until there is a wider consensus of authoritiative opinion about the subject, few books can be recommended without some degree of reservation.

More positively, the fact that the field has yet to be thoroughly explored also means that it offers many opportunities for personal investigation, reflection and research. In this connection it may be remarked that the later stages of the Revolution are now attracting increasing attention amongst historians, and that several of the most valuable works which have appeared since 1965 (when my own earlier book in this series, *The French Revolution*, London, was published) have been concerned with aspects of the period 1795–9.

In these pages I have tried to avoid repeating the suggestions made in *The French Revolution* (pp. 246–50), to which the reader may be referred for an introduction to some of the works relating to the history of the Revolution before the fall of Robespierre in July 1794; and I have also tried to avoid becoming too entangled in the complexities of Napoleonic bibliography. For the whole of the wider field 1789–1815, see the *Bibliographical essays* in A. Cobban, *A Short History of Modern France*: Vol. 1, 1715–1799, and Vol. 2, 1799–1945 (Penguin Books, revised ed. 1961; Jonathan Cape, 1962); Crane Brinton, *A Decade of Revolution, 1789–1799* and Geoffrey Bruun, *Europe and the French Imperium, 1799–1815* ('The Rise of Modern Europe Series',

Harper Torchbooks, London and New York, 1965); Leo Gershoy, *The French Revolution and Napoleon* (New York, 1964); and John Hall Stewart, *The French Revolution: Some Trends in Historical Writing, 1945–65* (American Hist. Assn., Teachers' Service Centre, No. 67, Washington, 1967). Beyond these, the student should consult *A Select List of Works on Europe and Europe Overseas, 1715–1815* (ed. J. S. Bromley and A. Goodwin, Oxford, 1956); *Clio*: L. Villat, *La Révolution et l'Empire* (2 vols, Paris, 1936); the references cited in the successive chapters of Georges Lefebvre's *La Révolution française* and *Napoléon* (see below); and the reviews of recent writing which appear from time to time in the *Revue historique*—recently vols 236 (1966) and 237 (1967)—and the reports of new publications in each issue of *French Historical Studies*.

Those unfamiliar with the differences that have developed in the past about the interpretation of the Revolution and the Empire may discover this *historiography* in G. Rudé, *Interpretations of the French Revolution* (Historical Assn. booklet G.47, London, 1961); in J. McManners, 'The Historiography of the French Revolution, 1763–1793', *The New Cambridge Modern History*, Vol. VIII (Cambridge, 1965); and in P. Geyl, *Napoleon, For and Against* (London, 1949). Several of the papers in the late Alfred Cobban's *Aspects of the French Revolution* (London, 1968) are also indicative of the present state of Revolutionary studies and of the need for more—and more dispassionate—examination of the real structure of society in France between 1789 and 1815.

As these studies suggest, *the principal French historians* of the Revolution in the nineteenth century were, in general, creative thinkers and writers rather than scholars. Many of them, too, were active political figures who wrote their histories in order to promote a particular political creed which they were not free to express otherwise. Their views and their familiarity with the day-to-day development of the Revolution nevertheless remain important, particularly for the political historian, and the great works of L. A. Thiers—*L'Histoire de la Révolution française* and *L'Histoire du Consulat et de l'Empire*—may still be valued for their account of political events and administrative developments. The first general history to be based on the results of modern scholarship was, however, F. Aulard's *Histoire politique de la Révolution française, 1789–1804* (4 vols, Paris, 1901), which was translated by B. Miall as *The French Revolution, A Political History, 1789–1804* (4 vols, London, 1910). Although somewhat frustratingly arranged as a survey of successive aspects of the Revolution, this still remains the classical interpretation of it in terms of the rise and decline of republican democracy in the political sense.

Aulard's work, which may well be contrasted with the brilliantly written but far more generalised condemnation of the Directorial régime by A. Vandal, *L'Avènement de Bonaparte* (2 vols, Paris, 1907–1908), thus marks a new departure. His principal successors in scholarship have nevertheless replaced—rather than merely corrected—his political interpretation by one affording increasing primacy to economic forces and the conflict of social classes; and it should be said more firmly than is usually the case that this interpretation is generally advanced with a degree of fervour and finality more commonly thought characteristic of the great literary historians of the nineteenth century. Moreover, although a vast deal of intensive research has now been devoted to the background and to the early years of the Revolution, even the greatest historians have treated the period between 1795 and 1799 only as a subordinate subject of study. Thus Mathiez, both in his general history (A. Mathiez, *La Révolution française*, 3 vols, Paris, 1925–27; trans. C. A. Phillips, London, 1928) and in innumerable special studies, was primarily concerned to rehabilitate Robespierre as the champion of the common man and the prophet of social democracy; and although all his work reflects his intimate knowledge of original sources, his studies of the later period—*La Réaction thermidorienne* (Paris, 1929), which is available in the translation of C. A. Phillips as *After Robespierre: The Thermidorian Reaction* (New York, 1965), and *Le Directoire* (a posthumous edition of papers, ed. J. Godechot, Paris, 1934)—are almost as much marred as enlivened by the author's passionate determination to condemn the men who had destroyed Robespierre and the class which he believed to have halted a progressive social revolution.

Since the time of Mathiez the predominant figure has indisputably been that of Georges Lefebvre, whose masterly review of the whole period of both French and world history is contained in the two volumes *La Révolution française* (*Peuples et Civilisations* series, ed. L. Halphen and Ph. Sagnac, 2nd revised edn. Paris 1951, or 3rd edn., revised by A. Soboul, 1963) and *Napoléon* (*Peuples et Civilisations*, Paris, 1953, or 5th edn., revised by A. Soboul, Paris 1965), both of which are now available in translation in two parts each, particularly: *The French Revolution* (II): *From 1793 to 1799* (trans. J. H. Stewart and J. Friguglietti, London and New York, 1964); and *Napoleon* (I): *From 18 Brumaire to Tilsit* (trans. Henry H. Stockhold, London and New York, 1969). Beyond these, Lefebvre's more detailed studies of the years between 1794 and 1799, *Les Thermidoriens* (Paris, 1937, revised edn. 1960) and *Le Directoire* (Paris, 1946 and 1950) are also available in the translations of Robert Baldick as *The Thermidorians* (London, 1964) and *The Directory* (London, 1965). No reader of the present work need be reminded that all these are indispensable and invaluable: for much of the period of the First Republic, they are indeed the only general histories easily available in English. They are, nonetheless, books which presume that the reader is already reasonably well acquainted with the period, and they are fully as firm, if considerably less impassioned, than those of Mathiez in their adherence to a socialistic interpretation of it.

If we set aside the good general survey of M. Reinhard, *La France du Directoire* (2 vols, Paris, 1956) and the stimulating but exclamatory Bonapartist history of L. Madelin, *La Révolution* (Paris, 1912) and *Le Consulat et l'Empire* (2 vols, Paris, 1932–4), the outstanding names of today are those of Jacques Godechot and Albert Soboul. From the former, we have numerous special studies as well as important general works on the relationship between the French Revolution and revolutionary movements elsewhere, both of which may be more properly considered in a more appropriate context. More specific mention should, however, be made of A. Soboul's *La Première République, 1792–1894* (Paris, 1968) as being rare, if not unique, in its isolation of those 12 years for treatment as a unity. Succinct and stimulating, it is unfortunately not yet available in English. Soboul follows Mathiez and Lefebvre closely, differing from them not in his general interpretation of the period but in his conviction that it was the *sans-culottes* who provided the driving force of the Revolution and that it was their suppression which marked the real advent of the social reaction which ultimately and inevitably produced a Bonapartist dictatorship.

To turn to *the principal histories written in English* is to become still more aware of the dichotomy between the history of the Revolution and that of the Napoleonic period. There are sound and stimulating general introductory surveys of the years between 1789 and 1815, some of which are listed below; there are important biographies of Bonaparte; but it is striking that the chapter 'The Internal History of France during the wars, 1793–1814' in *The New Cambridge Modern History* (Vol. IX, *War and Peace in an Age of Upheaval*, Cambridge, 1965) is written by Jacques Godechot. As always, Professor R. R. Palmer has interesting things to say in *The Age of the Democratic Revolution* (Vol. II: *The Struggle*, Princeton, 1964), and so has Crane Brinton in *A Decade of Revolution, 1789–1799* (New York, 1934 and 1963); but the challenge of A. Goodwin's 'The French Executive Directory: A Revaluation', *History*, XXII (1937) still remains unanswered. To find a major work on the middle years of the Republic one must, indeed, return to the old *Cambridge Modern History* and to the chapter of G. K. Fortescue: 'The Directory' (Vol. VIII, *The French Revolution*, Cambridge, 1904). There is there a liberal view which is now unfashionable, but more unknown than superseded.

Among *other general histories* are G. Pariset: *La Révolution française, 1792–1799*, and *Le Consulat et l'Empire* (respectively vols II and III of *L'Histoire de la France contemporaine*, ed. E. Lavisse, Paris, 1921); and the following:

BRUUN, G., *Europe and the French Imperium, 1799–1814* (New York, 1963).
COLLINS, I., *The Age of Progress: A Survey of European History between 1789 and 1870* (London, 1964).
GERSHOY, L., *The French Revolution and Napoleon* (New York, 1933).
HAMPSON, N., *The First European Revolution, 1776–1815* (New York, 1969).
KNAPTON, E. J., *Revolutionary and Imperial France, 1750–1815* (New York, 1972).
RUDÉ, G., *Revolutionary Europe, 1785–1818* (New York, 1966).

Particular studies of the later republican period seem currently concentrated upon both the local and the international history of the time. Amongst numerous *local studies* are: R. Durand, *Le département des Côtes-du-Nord sous le Consulat et l'Empire, 1800–1815* (2 vols, Paris, 1926), which is particularly commended by G. Bruun (op. cit., p. 257); the well-known work of M. Reinhard, *Le département de la Sarthe sous le régime directorial* (St. Brieuc, 1936); and J. Surrateau, *Le département du Mont Terrible sous le régime du Directoire, 1795–1800* (Besançon and Paris, 1965). Very valuable perspective appears in T. F. Sheppard's *Lourmarin in the Eighteenth Century* (John Hopkins, Baltimore, 1971) and it may be hoped that Professor A. Cobban's call for a more open-minded approach to the social history of the Revolution (A. Cobban, *The Social Interpretation of the French Revolution*, Cambridge, 1964) will soon lead to the publication of further work like Olwyn Hufton's admirable *Bayeux in the Eighteenth Century* (Oxford, 1967). Since N. Hampson's *Social History of the French Revolution* (London, 1965) does not extend beyond 1795, general social history between 1795 and 1804 apparently remains the preserve of the popular writer. Reference may however be made to: E. and J. Goncourt, *Histoire de la société française pendant le Directoire* (Paris, 3rd edn., 1864); L. de Lanzac de Laborie, *Paris sous Napoléon* (8 vols., Paris, 1905–13); and to the fascinating but formidable collection of source material in A. Aulard's *Paris pendant la réaction thermidorienne et sous le Directoire* (5 vols., Paris, 1898–1902).

On *international affairs*, the major work remains that of A. Sorel, *L'Europe et la Révolution française* (8 vols., Paris, 1885–1904), the classic statement of the view that the enduring interests of states outweigh ideological changes. Considerable interest in the expansion of revolutionary France has nevertheless been stimulated of late by the work of Professors Palmer and Godechot, both of whom have separately suggested (with important differences of emphasis) that a democratic and egalitarian revolution was in process throughout the greater part of the western world in the late eighteenth century, and that France championed (rather than initiated or imposed) this movement. The introduction to this controversy by P. Amann, *The Eighteenth Century Revolution: French or Western?* ('Problems in European Civilisation' series: D. C. Heath, Lexington, Mass., 1963) may lead to:

PALMER, R. R., *The Age of the Democratic Revolution: A Political History of Europe and America, 1760–1800* (2 vols, Princeton and Oxford, 1959 and 1964).

GODECHOT, J., *France and the Atlantic Revolution of the Eighteenth Century, 1770–1799* (trans. H. H. Rowen, New York, 1956).

La Grande Nation: l'expansion révolutionnaire de la France dans le monde, 1789–1799 (Paris, 1956).

L'Europe et l'Amérique à l'époque Napoléonienne, 1800–1815 (Nouvelle Clio No. 37, Paris, 1967).

(with Beatrice F. Hyslop and David L. Dowd) *The Napoleonic Era in Europe* (New York, 1970).

Initial reference to the extensive literature on this subject may also be made to F. M. Markham, *Napoleon and the Awakening of Europe* (London, 1954);

R. Guyot, *Le Directoire et la paix de l'Europe* (Paris, 1911); and H. C. Deutsch, *The Genesis of Napoleonic Imperialism, 1800–1805* (Cambridge, Mass., 1938). Particularly interesting, too, is the appearance of several *important recent studies in English*. On the counter-revolution we already have both W. R. Fryer's *Republic or Restoration in France? 1794–97* (Manchester, 1965) and H. Mitchell's *The Underground War against Revolutionary France* (Oxford, 1965); and other works, particularly about western France, are in progress. On the other hand, there is the welcome pioneering work of I. Woloch, *Jacobin Legacy: The Democratic Movement under the Directory* (Princeton, 1970); and—happily beyond stereotyped classification—two works from Richard Cobb, *The Police and the People: French Popular Protest, 1789–1820* (Oxford, 1970) and *Reactions to the French Revolution* (Oxford, 1972). While the latter, like G. D. Homan's *Jean François Reubell: French Revolutionary, Patriot and Director* (The Hague, 1971), has unfortunately appeared too recently to have been used for the present work, all these studies can be strongly recommended.

Amongst *other works* in English*:

* BRINTON, C.,*The Jacobins* (New York, 1971).

·CAREY, R. G., *The Liberals of France and their relation to the development of Bonaparte's dictatorship* (thesis, Univ. of Chicago, 1947).

FAURIEL, C., *The Last Days of the Consulate* (trans. Lalanne, New York, 1886).

* GREER, D. M., *The Incidence of the Emigration during the French Revolution* (Glous., Mass., 1966).

HALES, E. E. Y., *Napoleon and the Pope* (London, 1962).

HARRIS, S. E., *The Assignats* (Cambridge, Mass. ,1930).

HEROLD, J. C., *Bonaparte in Egypt* (New York, 1962).

HOLTMAN, R. B., *The Napoleonic Revolution* (Philadelphia, 1967).

JONES, E. H. S., *An Invasion that failed: the French Expedition to Ireland, 1796* (Oxford, 1950).

* MCMANNERS, J., *The French Revolution and the Church* (S.P.C.K., London, 1969).

ROGER, A. B., *The War of the Second Coalition, 1798–1801: A Strategic Commentary* (New York, 1964).

* RUDÉ, G., *The Crowd in the French Revolution* (Oxford, 1960).

* SOBOUL, A., *The Parisian Sans-culottes in the French Revolution, 1793–94* (trans. G. Lewis, Oxford, 1964).

SYDENHAM, M. J., 'The Crime of 3 Nivôse', in *French Government and Society* (London, 1972).

TALMON, J. L., *The Origins of Totalitarian Democracy* (London, 1961).

---

* Neither this list nor those that follow should be thought of as being comprehensive. Similarly, it would be wrong to suppose that I am personally familiar with all the books mentioned: I have, however, placed an asterisk * beside some which I have found particularly useful in my own work.

THOMSON, D., *The Babeuf Plot* (London, 1947).

* WALSH, H. H., *The Concordat of 1801* (New York, 1933).

For *military history*, see:

CHANDLER, D., *The Campaigns of Napoleon* (New York, 1966).

* HUNTER, T. M., *Napoleon in Victory and Defeat* (Historical Section, Army H.Q., Ottawa, 1964).

MARSHALL-CORNWALL, SIR JAMES, *Napoleon as Military Commander* (London, 1967).

* WILKINSON, S., *The Rise of General Bonaparte* (Oxford, 1930).

ESPOSITO, V. and ETLING, J., *A Military History and Atlas of the Napoleonic Wars* (New York, 1964).

Studies in French (all published in Paris unless otherwise stated) include some *general works*, like:

BOUCHARY, J., *Les manieurs d'argent à la fin du xviiie siècle* (3 vols, 1939–43).

DUBREUIL, L., *Histoire des insurrections de l'ouest* (2 vols, 1929–30).

GABORY, E., *La Révolution et la Vendée* (3 vols, 1925–28).

* GODECHOT, J., *Les Institutions de la France sous la Révolution et l'Empire* (1951).

LATREILLE, A., *L'Église catholique et la Révolution française* (2 vols, 1946–50).

LEVASSEUR, E., *Histoire des classes ouvrières et de l'industrie en France depuis 1789 à 1870* (1903).

MARION, M., *Histoire financière de la France depuis 1715* (vols II–IV, 1919–21).

SAGNAC, P., *La Législation civile de la Révolution française* (1898).

VINGTRINIER, E., *Histoire de la contre-révolution* (2 vols, 1924–25).

More specifically related to the period 1795–1804 are:

AULARD, A., *Études et Leçons: iv: 'Le centaire de la Légion d'honneur'* (1904) and vii: *'La centralisation napoléonienne: les préfets* (1913). *Napoléon Ier et le monopole universitaire* (1911).

BESSAND-MASSENET, P., *La France après la terreur, 1795–99* (1946).

BOURDON, J., *La Constitution de l'an VIII* (1942). *La Réforme judiciaire de l'an VIII* (1942).

CHASSIN, C., *Études sur la Vendée, Sèr III: Les Pacifications de l'ouest, Vol. III: 1796–1815* (1899).

COBB, R., *Terreur et subsistances, 1793–1795* (1965).

DESTREM, J., *Les Déportations du Consulat et de l'Empire* (1885).

DURAND, C., *Études sur le Conseil d'État Napoléonienne* (1949).

DUTRUCH, M., *Le Tribunat sous le Consulat et l'Empire* (1921).

ESPITALIER, A., *Vers Brumaire: Bonaparte à Paris 5 déc. 1797 à 4 mai 1798* (1914).

* FUOC, R., *La Réaction thermidorienne à Lyon* (1957).

* GAUBERT, H., *Conspirateurs au temps de Napoléon Ier* (1962).

GOBERT, A., *L'Opposition des assemblées pendant le Consulat, 1800–1804* (1925).

* GODECHOT, J., *La Contre-Révolution: Doctrine et Action, 1789–1804* (1961 —also available in translation, New York, 1970).

*　*Les commissionaires aux armées sous le Directoire* (1937).

GUÉRIN, D., *La Lutte des classes sous la Première République, 1793–1797* (2 vols, 1968).

* HAUTERIVE, E. D', *Napoléon et sa police* (1943).

* MEYNIER, A., *Les coups d'état du Directoire:*
    (i) *Le dix-huit Fructidor An V* (1927).
    (ii) *Le vingt-deux Floréal An VI et le trente Prairial An VIII* (1928).
    (iii) *Le 18 Brumaire An VIII et la fin de la République* (1928).

* PONTEIL, F., *Napoléon Ier et l'organisation authoritaire de la France* (1956).

REGNIER, J., *Les Préfets du Consulat et de l'Empire* (1913).

SAVANT, J., *Les Préfets de Napoléon* (1958).

SCIOUT, L., *Le Directoire* (4 vols, 1895–97).

* SOBOUL, A., *Les Sans-culottes parisiens en l'an II* (1958).

TARLÉ, E., *Germinal et Prairial* (Moscow and Paris, 1958).

* THIRY, J., *Le Sénat de Napoléon* (1931).
    Le Coup d'état du 18 Brumaire (1947).
    L'Aube du Consulat (1948).
    La Machine Infernale (1952).
    Le Concordat et le Consulat à vie (1956).

* TONNESSON, K., *La Défaite des Sans-culottes* (1959).

VILLEFOSSE, L. DE and BOUISSOUNOUSE, J., *L'Opposition à Napoléon* (1969).

* ZIVY, H., *Le Treize Vendémiaire An IV* (1898).

Biographical studies of Napoleon are, of course, countless, dominating the period so far that it is difficult not to approach it through them. As a challenging introduction, M. Hutt's *Napoleon* (London, 1965) is admirable; and others of the same title are: Butterfield, H. (London, 1939); Calvet, H. (*Que sais-je?* series, Paris, 1966); Fisher, H. A. L. (London, 1912/67); Guérard, A. (London, 1957); Kircheisen, F. (trans. H. Lawrence, New York, 1932); Lucas Dubreto, J. (Paris, 1969); and Godechot, J. (Paris, 1969). While the work of Lefebvre (see *above*) remains the most authoritative, J. H. Rose's *The Life of Napoleon I* (6th ed., London, 1916) is a classic still of great value; J. M. Thompson's *Napoleon Bonaparte: His Rise and Fall* (Oxford, 1951/63) follows Napoleon's career closely from his letters, and F. Markham's *Napoleon* (London, 1964) is rightly recognised as both scholarly and readable. Contemporary views form the basis of J. Savant's *Napoleon in his time* (trans. K. John, New York, 1958), and of E. Knapton, 'A Contemporary Impression of Napoleon in 1797', *French Historical Studies*, I (1960), pp. 476–81. Both M. Hutt's *Napoleon* (*Great Lives Observed* series, New Jersey, 1972) and J. C. Herold, *The Mind of Napoleon* (New York, 1955/61) are useful anthologies of the sayings and writings of Napoleon and others, and the problems involved in the interpretation of his life are posed in: D. H. Pinkey, *Napoleon: Historical Enigma* (D. C. Heath's *Problems in European Civilisation* series, Lexington, Mass., 1969) and David L. Dowd, *Napoleon: Was he the heir of the Revolution?* (Holt, Rinehart and Winston, *Source Problems in World Civilisation*, New York, 1965).

Other biographies are:

Babeuf, G. Walter (Paris, 1937).
Barère, L. Gershoy (Princeton, 1962).
Barras, J. P. Garnier (Paris, 1970).
Bonaparte, Joseph, O. Connelly (New York, 1968).
Buonarroti, E. L. Eisenstein (Harvard U.P., 1959).
Cadoudal, J. F. Chiappe (Paris, 1970).
Cambacérès, P. Vialles (Paris, 1908).
* *Carnot*, M. Reinhard (2 vols, Paris, 1950–52).
Chaptal, J. Pigeire (Paris, 1931).
Cochon (*de Lapparent*), P. Boucher (Paris, 1969).
Constant, H. Nicolson (London, 1949); E. Schermerhorn (London, 1924).
David, D. L. Dowd (Lincoln, Neb., 1948).
Fouché, L. Madelin (2 vols, Paris 1900 and New York,, 1969).
Frotté, de La Sicotière (3 vols, Paris, 1888).
Grégoire, R. F. Necheles (Westport, Conn., 1971).
Josephine, the Empress, E. Knapton (Harvard U.P., 1963).
* *LaRevellière-Lépeaux*, G. Robison (Columbia, New York, 1938: entitled *Revellière-Lépeaux*).
Lindet, Rbt., A. Montier (Paris, 1889).
Merlin de Douai, L. Gruffy (Paris, 1934).
Moreau, Lapierre de Châteauneuf (Paris, 1814).
Pichegru (and his 'treason'), E. Daudet (Paris, 1901); G. Caudrillier (Paris, 1908); J. Hall (London, 1915).
Portalis (and the Civil Code), P. Bello (Nancy, 1949).
Reubell, G. D. Homan (The Hague, 1971; or see *French Historical Studies*, No. I (1960)).
Staël, Madame de, J. C. Herold (New York, 1958).
* *Sieyès*, P. Bastid (Paris, 1939).
Talleyrand, A. Duff-Cooper (London, 1932); G. Lacour-Gayet (6 vols, Paris, 1969); C. Brinton (New York, 1936/63).

(Very profitable reference may also be made to such *biographical dictionaries* as *A. Kuscinski, *Dictionnaire des Conventionnels* (Paris, 1917); A. Robert and others, *Dictionnaire des parlementaires français* (Paris, 1891); J. Robinet and others, *Dictionnaire historique et biographique de la Révolution et de l'Empire*,

1789–1815 (Paris, 1899); *M. Michaud, *Biographie Universelle* (Paris, 1843); or to the pocketbook *Dictionnaire de la Révolution et de l'Empire* (B. Melchior-Bonnet, for Larousse, Paris, 1965).

Printed primary material for the period is perhaps best described as plentiful but patchy. A, if not the, major source is the *Correspondence de Napoleon Ier* (32 vols, Paris, 1858–69), from which selections are: J. E. Howard, *Letters and Documents of Napoleon I: 1784–1802* (London, 1961), and J. M. Thompson, *Napoleon's Letters* (Everyman, London and New York, 1954/64), and there is also a pocket edition: *Napoléon Bonaparte: Proclamations, Ordres du Jour, Bulletins de la Grande Armée* published in the series *le monde en 10/18* (Paris, 1964). Neither these nor the St Helena material—notably Las Cases, E. A., *Mémorial de Ste.-Hélène* (Paris, many editions to 1968)—have been used extensively in the present work, since I have sought to see a developing rather than a remembered scene, and to avoid the danger of seeing it only as it appeared to Bonaparte. Somewhat inconsistently, however, I have placed a good deal of reliance upon some of the *memoirs* of the period, particularly those of *Caulincourt* (ed. J. Hanoteux, 2 vols, Paris, 1933, and published in New York as *With Napoleon in Russia* (1959) and *No Peace with Napoleon* (1936); of *LaRevellière-Lépeaux* (3 vols, Paris, 1895); of *Miot de Melito* (ed. Fleischmann, trans. C. Hoey and J. Lillie, New York, 1889); of *Pasquier* (*The Memoirs of Chancellor Pasquier*, ed. d'Audiffret-Pasquier and trans. C. E. Roche, New York, 1893, vol. I: 1789–1810); of *Roederer* (ed. O. Aubry, Paris, 1942); and of *Thibaudeau* (*Mémoires sur la Convention et le Directoire*, 2 vols, Paris, 1824, and *Mémoires sur le Consulat*, translated by G. K. Fortescue as *Bonaparte and the Consulate*, London, 1908). Some reference has also been made to the memoirs of *Barras* (4 vols, ed. Duruy, London, 1895), *Barthélemy* (ed. J. de Dampierre, Paris, 1914), *Dumas* (2 vols, London, 1929), *Durand de Maillane* (*Histoire de la Convention nationale*, Paris, 1825), *Fouché* (2 vols, ed. Knight, London, 1892), *Gohier* (see Lescure, *Bibliothèque des mémoires, nouv. sér.* xxx, no. 2, Paris, 1875), *Hyde de Neuville* (trans. Jackson, 2 vols, London, 1913), *Lacretelle, G.* (*Dix années d'épreuves*, Paris, 1842), *Marbot* (*The Adventures of General Marbot*, New York, 1935), *Molé* (*Life and Memoirs*, ed. de Noailles, London, 1923), *Réal* (*Indiscretions of a Prefect of Police*, ed. Hayward, London, 1929), *Madame de Staël* (*Dix années d'exil*, ed. de Broglie and de Staël, Paris, 1818/1861), *Thiébault* (trans. Butler, New York, 1896), and *Vaublanc* (ed. Barrière, Paris, 1857). There has also been some reference to the unreliable *Bourrienne* (*Memoirs of Napoleon Bonaparte*, Hutchinson edn., London, n.d.), but none to the doubtful *Talleyrand* (4 vols, The Hague, 1831) or *Constant* (London, 1896)—and, regrettably, none to the more valuable work of *Chaptal* (*Mes Souvenirs*, Paris, 1893), *Gaudin* (3 vols, Paris, 1826–34/1926) or *Méneval* (*Memoirs*, London, 1894). Generally, books such as these may be too much distrusted, for the prejudices of the writers are nothing if not obvious.

While it would be confusing to list here all the source material referred to in the footnotes, reference should be made to the invaluable work of J. Hall Stewart, *A Documentary Survey of the French Revolution* (New York, 1951), though this unfortunately ends in 1799, and to some books fairly easily available: A. Aulard, *L'État de France en l'an VIII et en l'an IX* (Paris, 1893); P. Mautouchet, *Le Gouvernement révolutionnaire* (Paris, 1912); V. Pierre, *18 Fructidor* (Paris, 1897); F. Rocquain, *L'État de France au 18 Brumaire* (Paris, 1874); and Madame de Staël: *Des circonstances actuelles qui peuvent terminer la Révolution* (ed. J. Viénot, Paris, 1906). In English, too, there is *The Defense of Gracchus Babeuf* (ed. and trans. J. A. Scott, Univ. of Mass. Press, 1967), and O'Brien's translation of P. Buonarroti, *Babeuf's Conspiracy for Equality* (London, 1886: cp. French ed. of the original, New York, 1966). More isolated material is gradually becoming available to students, e.g.: Leo Gershoy, *The Era of the French Revolution, 1789–1799* (Anvil Books, Princeton, 1957); J. Godechot, *La Pensée Révolutionnaire, 1780–1799* (Paris, 1964); and D. L. Dowd, *Napoleon* in the 'Source Problems in World Civilisation' series (New York, 1965).

As this somewhat miscellaneous list may imply, most of the iceberg is still below the surface, and so far as political history is concerned much more remains to be done both from archival material and from the greater printed collections in French. Amongst these may be specified: L. Duguit, H. Monnier and R. Bonnard, *Les Constitutions et les principales lois politiques de la France depuis 1789* (Paris, 1912); J. B. Duvergier, *Collection complète des lois . . . du conseil d'état . . . de 1788 à 1830* (2nd ed., Paris, 1834); P. J. B. Buchez and P. C. Roux, *Histoire parlementaire de la Révolution française* (43 vols, Paris, 1834-38); *L'Ancien Moniteur* (31 vols, Paris, 1850-54—becoming very brief and official in the later 1790s); and the *Archives Parlementaires* (Paris, 1868–1912). Students in Great Britain may also notice that in addition to the British Museum collections of pamphlets, much material on the Directory is held by the Goldsmith Library of London University.

Deliberately reserved for the conclusion of this guide to further reading is a note on the considerable importance of the journals in which both original articles and reviews of current scholarship are available. See, in general, *The English Historical Review*; *The Economic History Review*; *Past and Present*; *History* (the journal of the English Historical Association)—particularly for A. Goodwin, 'The French Executive Directory: A Revaluation', XXII (1937); *The American Historical Review*; *The Journal of Modern History*; *French Historical Studies* (particularly for G. D. Homan, 'Jean François Reubell, Director', I (1960); *History Today*; the *Annales historiques de la Révolution française*—particularly for the bicentennial of Babeuf's birth (CLX II, 1960), for the work of R. Cobb on the repression of the *sans-culottes* (XXVI, 1954) and that of J. Surrateau on the elections of 1795 and 1797 (XXIV, 1952 and XXX, 1958); the *Revue des Études Napoléoniennes*; the *Revue Historique*—particularly for R. Guyot's consideration of the transition from the Directory to the Consulate (CXI, 1912); and the *Revue d'histoire moderne et contemporaine*—particularly for the bicentennial of Napoleon's birth (XVII, 1970).

Index